ALL HELL FOR A BASEMENT

Ed Gould

Cataloguing in Publication Data
   All Hell For A Basement: The History of
   Medicine Hat, Alberta — 1883 to 1983
   ISBN 0-9691038-0-8
      1. All Hell For A Basement: The History
   Medicine Hat, Alberta — 1883 to 1983
         2. Alberta history. Gould, Ed, 1936-

Published in Medicine Hat, Alberta, Canada by the City of Medicine Hat on the occasion of their Centennial in 1983. Address all communication to The City of Medicine Hat, City Hall, Medicine Hat, Alberta, Canada, T1A 0C7.

Book design and cover by Nicholas Newbeck, 1112 Government Street, Victoria, British Columbia.

Printed by Friesen Printers

PROLOGUE

. . . In the words of the poet:

"This part of the country seems to have all hell for a basement, and the only trap door appears to be in Medicine Hat. And don't you ever think of changing the name of your town. It's all your own and the only hat of its kind on earth."

(Rudyard Kipling, as quoted in the *Medicine Hat News* of Thursday, October 17, 1907.)

For the Record

The City of Medicine Hat, Alberta, Canada is situated on the banks of the South Saskatchewan River on Trans-Canada Highway Number 1 in the southeast corner of Alberta. It is approximately 650 highway miles west of Winnipeg, 840 miles east of Vancouver and about 50 miles north of the border of the State of Montana.

Medicine Hat is a divisional point on the Canadian Pacific Railway's Trans-Continental line and Eastern terminal of the CPR Crow's Nest Pass branch. It has an altitude of 2,181 feet. The City is at Latitude 50/02 and Longitude of 110/40.

It can be said to have had several "births". Established as an unincorporated Town on May 31, 1894, it was incorporated as a Town on October 31, 1898 and received a City Charter on May 9, 1906. However, Medicine Hat was really "born" with the arrival of the CPR in 1883 and the town site survey later the same year. And it is for this reason that the City celebrated its Centennial in 1983.

Dedication

This story of Medicine Hat is dedicated to the people of Medicine Hat and District who have made the City and its environs one of the most attractive communities in which to live and raise a family in North America. To achieve such a goal in one hundred short years has not been an easy task. The struggle to move from tent town to metropolis has been intense at times. But it has been worth it.

The fact that so many of the original pioneering families still reside in Medicine Hat and area is testimony to their great love for and dedication to the community.

This history is also a salute to all those former Medicine Hat residents who have moved away, but who still think of "The Hat" as home.

It is the hope of the Mayor and City Council that Medicine Hat's next one hundred years will be as progressive and peaceful as were the first one hundred.

Happy Birthday, Medicine Hat!

Table of Contents

Introduction

When I was commissioned in February 1977 to write a history of Medicine Hat there was general agreement by the members of the Historical Committee that this be a popular history that would interest not only former and present Medicine Hat residents, but those outside the area. The Committee did not want a "family album" type of history; nor did it want an academic treatise. While there may be a place for both these approaches, it was felt that the history of Medicine Hat was an exciting one and the exciting, amusing and human touch should be given to it. It is the author's hope that at least part of that ideal has been achieved.

I am extremely grateful to several people who were of help in compiling information, checking facts and establishing contacts. First and foremost I must thank Jack Barrie, former Curator of the Medicine Hat Museum. While he was at the Museum, and after he retired, Jack was of inestimable value as a research assistant.

My dear friend Helen Beny Gibson former Alderman and original Chairman of the History Book Committee and well-known painter and tireless community worker, was a source of great inspiration, as well as contacts. Other members of the original Committee, Chief Librarian Bob Block, and the late former school Principal, Fred Millican, were helpful.

I would also like to express my gratitude to Mayor and Mrs. Ted Grimm; former Mayor Milt Reinhardt; Ian MacDonald, Peter Mossey, Ken Clements and Ernie Hall of the Medicine Hat News; former City Clerk and good friend, Alderman Bill Keith under whose Chairmanship this publication was finally prepared and published. City Clerk Larry Godin; Frank G. Millington; E. J. gave permission to quote from Archive tapes; Dr. Kenneth Glazier, former Director of the University of Calgary Library; Sheilagh Jameson and Georgeen Barrass Klassen of Glenbow-Alberta Institute in Calgary; Economic Development Manager, Dave Cormier; Carl and Merna Leviston of Edmonton; Ed McKenzie, who was very obliging while Acting Curator at the Museum; James T. Ward of Calgary; Barbara Gilmour, wife of native son Clyde Gilmour, of Toronto, who was very helpful in supplying contacts; all the present and past members of the staff at the Museum who were so kind and patient with me during my years of research; former Alderman, Lucille Moyer, and MLA for Calgary Millican constituency, David J. Carter, for information on the Prisoner of War Camp.

For acting as liaison between myself, the Committee and City Council, and for assistance in clearing human and legal hurdles, I particularly wish to thank City Solicitor Frank O'Connell. I sincerely believe that without Frank's calm understanding authority, this history would never have been completed. Thanks also to secretaries Linda Lamirade and Margaret Jesse. I would like to salute all those Medicine Hat residents and former residents who wrote to me or answered my queries and allowed themselves to be interviewed. This book is about you, and your assistance in helping produce it is much appreciated. All such letters, photographs and other materials dealing with the history of the City and area will (unless otherwise directed by the sender) be donated to the Museum. Included are several hours of taped conversations with oldtimers conducted by my friend Jan Fulton of Calgary. I am grateful for her interest and assistance. For photos, thanks to Grace Cousins, Jack Barrie, Mrs. Hartley Shannon, Bert Shannon.

Finally, I want to thank my wife Dolores who saw me through a major physical crisis that developed while I was halfway through the book. Without her, the whole thing would have been impossible. Thank you also for helping to type and proofread the manuscript.

Despite the ups and downs, writing and researching this book has been one of the most rewarding projects of my career.
Ed Gould

This painting by A. Bruce Stapleton shows Major A. G. Irvine (later Commissioner; the community of Irvine was named for him) standing at the left. In buckskins is interpreter Jean L'Heuveux. Seated: Colonel James F. Macleod (later Commissioner; the community of Fort Macleod was named for him) and Lt.-Gov. David Laird, the latter in civilian dress. At right is Chief Crowfoot, with an interpreter beside him. The occasion is the signing of the Blackfoot Treaty of 1877, without which there would have been much more difficult times for those who established in Medicine Hat in 1883. The Stapleton painting copied here is published by permission of the Calgary Brewery Horseman's Hall of Fame.

1.

What's In A Name Anyway?

The City of Medicine Hat, Alberta, has much of which to be proud. So do many other cities; however, with the possible exception of Moose Jaw, Saskatchewan, there is scarcely a city in Canada that has gained so much fame because of its unusual name. Although the name has fostered jokes, poems and ridicule, the natives of this burgeoning Western Canadian community would not change it to something more prosaic or mundane, although they have been tempted once or twice.

The origin of its odd-sounding designation is not precisely identified in myth, legend or fact, although oldtimers and amateur historians all claim divine right to the source. There have been many oldtimers and many stories, all "indisputable." The author of this history has no divine pipeline to the source and therefore will simply present the various versions and let the reader decide which is the most colorful and which is correct.

The simplest explanation given is that the city was built in a valley where the surrounding hills resemble the shape of a hat. This explanation is not only simple, it is also the least believable. No Indian or non-Indian headgear of early or later times can be said to look like the slopes of the South Saskatchewan River and surrounding hillsides.

The steel reaches the South Saskatchewan River and wooden trestle bridge is constructed in 1883 to carry CPR line across river and up the grade to the west. A tent town sprang up and was given the name of Medicine Hat.

We must go deeper than that to find the source of the name. One version is credited to Earl J. Gillett, who drew up in his so-called charter form the "correct" story. An early City Council accepted Gillett's account for use in a general history of the name. A few paragraphs contained in Gillett's scroll, which was sent to British education authorities who wanted to know the origin of the name, are printed here:

"To the north and south of the South Saskatchewan River, the Blackfoot claimed dominion, while the Cree proclaimed sovereignty over the hunting grounds to the south and east of the river. One day in 1870 a band of Cree resolved to examine the wooded parkland, an area on the north side of the river (now called Police Point, across from what was then an island, later to be named Strathcona Island). Having satisfied their curiosity, they turned their steeds up river to unravel the mystery of Hargrave's park (another wooded area on the hillside) which was fed by many springs.

"A band of Blackfoot had been spying and watching the Cree and shortly after they had quenched their thirst at the big spring, the Blackfoot made war whoops and surprised the intruders by coming down with driving battle force from the top of the hills to the north (later named Crescent Heights). The Cree frantically straddled their calico mustangs and stampeded for life against death back to the ford and splashed in for the southern shore.

In the early years, Medicine Hat's Flats areas were flooded almost every spring from the S. Saskatchewan River and Seven Persons and Ross Creeks. Large building is the Woollen Mill Building.

"The Blackfoot medicine man and his hideously painted war band in their eagerness for victory did not think and they followed right in on the tail of the Cree. The Cree, on reaching the north shore of Strathcona Island, about-faced. The Blackfoot could not land and while they were floundering in the water, with their medicine man in the lead, the Cree showered them with arrows.

"Naturally, the medicine man, being in the lead, received the first volley. One of the arrows apparently hit him in the heart. He raised upon his horse and he gasped for his last breath and fell into the water.

"As he sank beneath the surface his featherly war bonnet was blown off, or else the current pulled it off, or it might have been a last gesture of his to enable his braves to save their flag. However, it floated and the Cree grabbed the magic hat.

"The Blackfoot were overcome with awe on seeing their priest and physician disappear and the disaster to their leader and holy emblem. In the horror of the calamity, they imagined the Great Spirit had turned against them. Filled with superstition, they fled back to the north shore of the river.

"Afterwards, on the river's north bank appeared a mound to mark the spot. In later years the river in flood washed it away. In consequence of the stampede and battle, the hat being lost to the Cree and the mound to mark the location, it was by riders of the plains, named, The Place Of The Medicine Hat. In 1883, upon the advent of the Canadian Pacific Railway, the phrase was abridged to read Medicine Hat."

If the reader wishes to brush up on his purple prose, he has but to re-read portions of James Fenimore Cooper's *The Last Of The Mohicans* to recognize the style adopted by Mr. Gillett in his colorful account.

Although widely circulated, and not just by the English education authorities who asked for it, major doubt was cast upon the whole scenario by other city residents. A definite can of worms had been opened.

When Gillett's version of the origin of the City's name was reprinted in the *Medicine Hat News*, the editor of the day was besieged by requests from readers for the source of his information. In a letter to the editor, Gillette revealed that his information was based on unimpeachable documentation and thorough research. The "real stuff" was obtained from the late Sergeant Major J. H. G. Bray, Sergeant Robert McCutcheon, both formerly of the Northwest Mounted Police, and former NWMP scout, Michael Quesnelle.

Having gone to the three "fountainheads of information", Gillett met with interpreter T. Swain who corroborated the narrative with two local Cree: Sun Child and Little Corn. He took his results to Major Bray's son, Harry Bray, who also gave it his blessing. No one can say the Brays are not well-respected. For Mr. Gillett, that was that.

But it was not sufficient for another amateur historian and pioneer, William Henry McKay. McKay wrote the newspaper to give readers "the facts." McKay discounted Gillett's story on several points: first of all, "it is doubtful if war bonnets were carried around by war parties . . . the eagle feather headgear, named a 'war bonnet' by white people, was not considered either magical or medicinal by the Red Man, but was worn as an ornamental head-dress during celebrations."

McKay backed up his claim to superior knowledge of past events by revealing that he was "part Cree Indian and am well-informed on customs and superstitions of the Cree."

McKay said the Indian called Medicine Hat "Ka-As-It-Ah-Ta-Wah-Tik", which means "where it runs against." That is, "where the river runs against the Cypress Hills." (The location and importance of the Cypress Hills will be discussed in a later chapter.)

No, McKay argued, it was not the Indians who gave the city its name at all. It was Sir William Van Horne, the American-born chief engineer in the construction of the Canadian Pacific Railway. Van Horne, McKay said, applied the name after hearing a romantic story told to him by a Cree named Thunder Bear. The story was allegedly told to him at the McKay residence in the spring of 1883. Thunder Bear and Van Horne were enjoying a smoke together after dinner, prepared by McKay's mother. William Cornelius Van

3

View of the City of Medicine Hat 1894 taken from Crescent Heights area. CPR bridge to right.

Horne, a giant of a man and a huge eater, who boasted his coat of arms was "a dinner horn, pendant upon a kitchen door", undoubtedly had dined well.

Through an uncle, Alex McKay, Van Horne told the Indian that he planned to build an iron road through the district and asked his opinion of the flats on the river as a townsite. The town there would "float away", Thunder Bear told Van Horne. He then told a story about his experiences.

"Twenty-one summers ago I eloped with the youngest wife of an old chief from the Red Deer forks and came here. We camped on the island now known as Strathcona Island. After five days the water began to rise and we had to cross to the mainland on the sun (south) side of the river. We rode down to the first cutbank and pitched our teepee. In two days the whole flat, the island and the point across the river, were all under water.

"During the two moons we camped there, my wife had the same dream two nights in succession. She dreamt that her former husband, the old chief, spoke to her saying: 'If Thunder Bear will come back to my camp and give me an eagle feather head-dress made from the tails of seven eagles I will forgive him and let him keep you as his wife and live in peace in my camp.'

"So, I started right away to kill the eagles nesting in the cutbank. We made the head-dress out of the best-matched tails and then made our way back to the camp of the old chief. I presented the head-dress to him and, as my wife had dreamed, he was pleased with the gift and forgave us."

According to McKay, when Van Horne heard this conclusion to the story he exclaimed: "That was good medicine to appease the irate chief. I shall call this place Medicine Hat."

McKay further alleged that the battle between the Cree and the Blackfoot, as related by Gillett, was erroneous. The battle would have come in 1872 at a period when the two tribes had reportedly wintered side by side on the site of what is now the city of Medicine Hat. He said the two tribes had smoked the peace pipe at Wetaskiwin (Alberta) in 1867 and were "through warring by 1872."

4

He summed up his argument by saying, "I obtained a first-hand account of the naming of Medicine Hat from my uncle Alex and from Thunder Bear. Rest assured, the name was not given by the Indians."

Not content with debunking one "myth", McKay tore into another, this one ascribed to a Mr. Ashburner. According to Ashburner, another early resident of the district, a Cree named Kaskitawe Pwat was watering his horse at the river when a large serpent stuck his head out of an air hole in the ice and told him he knew of the hiding place of a powerful medicine hat and if he would sacrifice his beautiful young wife by throwing her into the air hole for him to devour, he would give him the secret and it would make him a great warrior.

After consulting with his wife, it was agreed that she would throw herself into the water to be eaten by the serpent so her husband could ride tall and proud over other members of his tribe. McKay said when he translated this story to some Cree friends they "all laughed at the absurdity."

He then listed the absurdities: "There aren't any snakes large enough to eat a human being and there weren't any in the days of Kaskitawe Pwat; a snake wouldn't feel much like eating or talking if he lived in ice cold water; there is no Indian cruel enough to feed his wife to a serpent, no matter how much he coveted a war bonnet; there's no woman living who would willingly be fed to a snake; snakes don't talk — and they don't speak Cree."

Mr. McKay might have had some difficulty explaining how an entire religion was built around the fact that a certain Serpent spoke understandably to a certain woman named Eve in the Garden of Eden, nevertheless he was on safer ground as he skipped from legend to local fact. Mr. Ashburner's hero, Kaskitawe Pwat was "a miserable little Cree Indian," McKay said. "I remember him well. He was no warrior; I doubt if he ever stole one horse. To be a good warrior he would have had to be a good horse thief and have a few scalps of his enemies as trophies. He was a lazy Indian; while all the other Indians went out working he was content to hang around the camp drinking whiskey. In fact, if his none-too-beautiful wife hadn't had so many friends among the Medicine Hat railroad men he would most likely have starved to death."

Despite the "evidence" that McKay compiled to shoot down Ashburner's theory of the derivation of the Medicine Hat name, the Industrial Development Branch of the Government of Alberta perpetuated the legend in its *Survey of Medicine Hat*, an early publication circulated widely and revised as late as 1959. In the "Accepted Source", the Survey went so far as to name the lovely daughter of the chief of the Cree: Wa-pa-soos. However, the Cree brave was not the hapless Kaskitawe Pwat, but Kaus-ke-ta-o-pot.

In this "official" version, Kaus-ke-ta-o-pot was watering his pony at the one spot where the river was not frozen over. It was believed that this was because the great Serpent dwelled there. While the pony drank, there was a great swirling of water and the serpent stuck out his head. He made his pitch about the medicine hat being available to the handsome Cree brave if he would throw his bride into the river for lunch.

"Sorely troubled, Kaus told the chief and his wife the experience with the Great Serpent." Apparently he needn't have worried. "Wa-pa-soos did not hesitate for an instant. 'Throw me to the Great Serpent,' she cried. 'So shall my husband become great.' Kaus resisted, but his own ambitions, and her entreaties, proved too much for him. That evening he hurled Wa-pa-soos into the water."

The serpent directed Kaus to the hidden medicine hat and that night the Blackfoot attacked the Cree who were driven back in surprise. However, with the aid of the charmed hat the Cree were eventually victorious. "And from that time on," the Survey story related, "the district has been known as Medicine Hat."

The charmed hat, incidentally, is described in various places as a "saamis", meaning the colorful head-dress of the Medicine Man. In a truncated version of the legend just related, *Maclean's Magazine* of November 1, 1953 described the hat as a "skull cap of dogskin hung with herbs, bear teeth and eagle feathers."

Whatever the real source of the name, the choice has led Medicine Hat to become known internationally, something that never would have happened if some of the later selections, such as Leopoldville or Smithville, had stuck. Neither would have caused poets to wax eloquently, as indeed they did, with Medicine Hat.

American poet Stephen Vincent Benet was enamored of the Medicine Hat sobriquet:

> *I have fallen in love with American names,*
> *The sharp names that never get fat.*
> *The snakeskin titles of mining claims,*
> *The plumed war bonnet of Medicine Hat.*
> *Tucson and Deadwood and Lost Mule Flat.*

Medicine Hat, you will note, stands out from even such as Deadwood. It also held its own with others in the poem, including Lundy's Lane, Wounded Knee, Painted Post and Skunktown Plain. All appear in Benet's famous "American Names."

South Railway Street, Medicine Hat, 1887. This shows the business area that was building up along the railway tracks. The CPR station, far right, was on the south side of the tracks, at the foot of Toronto Street (now Third St.).

Another American poet, perhaps even more notable than Stephen Vincent Benet, enshrined the city's name forever in "Prairie."

> The running water babbled to the deer,
> the cotton tail, the gopher;
> You came in wagons, making streets and
> schools;
> Kin of the axe and rifle, kin of the plow
> and horse;
> Singing Yankee Doodle, Old Dan Tucker,
> Turkey in the Straw;
> You in the coonskin cap at a log house
> door hearing a lone wolf howl;
> You at a sod house door reading the
> blizzards and chinooks let loose from
> Medicine Hat.

The passage from "Prairie" by Carl Sandburg might well have been written of the Canadian experience, even for the singing of Yankee Doodle, since many of the pioneers of Medicine Hat had come from the United States. But Sandburg touched a raw nerve when he placed this city as the source of bad weather on the continent. For many years the most northerly weather station in North America was indeed located here, and it became a sort of parlor entertainment to blame all the bad weather on the city. This criticism was usually accepted in good spirit: However, the editor of the *Medicine Hat News* decided on July 15, 1897 that the nonsense had gone far enough.

What aroused his wrath was not an earlier dispatch in the *Chicago Blade* "assigning to Medicine Hat the distinguished honor of being the weather pot of north America — the location from which you would trace the primary causes of the unusual atmospheric changes to the south of the boundary." No, the editor did not feel it was necessary to refute references to the city as the "weather pot" of North America because "to papers of the class referred to as yellow literature, it is never deemed worthy of framing a denial as it is for this imaginative, mendacious class of reading that the patrons of the paper look and are content to feast upon."

However, when "similar" statements creep into the columns of such a highly esteemed and valuable authority on scientific matter as the *Scientific American*, the gauntlet is down: "It occurs to the *News* that it is in the interests of the favored district of the Canadian Northwest that the assertion should find refutation."

The journal had had the effrontery to highlight a story in its July 10 issue of 1897 about "Fighting Snow On the Railroads Of The Northwest." In the article, the journal described a typical winter in the "far Northwest." It began in September with "no uncertain sound." The writer had seen "water pipes within the brick walls of a steam-heated building frozen solid on the 25th day of September." The railroader was unable to "lay up his snow plows until past the middle of next May."

The battle against cruel winter didn't end there either. "The latter end of summer in the shops and roundhouses at division points is devoted to putting in trim the snow fighting outfit. Engines are overhauled, plows buckled on flanges and 'white wings' got ready; the list of engineers and conductors are carefully scrutinized and those of most experience, or better fitted for service, told how to run plows and 'dragouts'.

The *Scientific American* article goes on to describe a situation (apocryphal, perhaps) at a railway site somewhere in the American west. The chief dispatcher looks into the superintendent's office and reports that "Medicine Hat says a blizzard is coming up." Later on, the watchful and worried dispatcher again opens the door and says: "Medicine Hat says the blizzard is getting worse."

Unmindful of the fact that the participants in this little drama are referring only to what the Medicine Hat weather station is reporting, rather than blaming the city as the very source of the problem, the editor swings into the defence of the city's honor, titling his editorial: 'A Libel On Our Banana Belt Winters."

He refers the author of the article to the records of the Dominion Meteorological Department to find out "that Medicine Hat has the evenest temperature, longest summers, shortest winters, lightest snowfall and fewest winter storms of any place in Canada east of the Rocky Mountains."

While not quite claiming that roses bloom in February (this was before the city's renowned greenhouses could claim such miracle), the editor, then a resident of Medicine Hat for 10 years, knew of "no winter storm which could be classed in the same category as the blizzards which sweep over the Dakotas, Minnesota and other parts of the United States."

Still he was not satisfied: "Canadians residing here do not know what a cyclone is, from experience. If one takes the country east of the Rocky Mountains for 1,000 miles and north or south, say 500 miles, one will find it next to impossible to discover a place where the weather-maker deals more

Medicine Hat's first residents were a motley sort, from Indians to Mounted Police and CPR crew and construction men and their wives and children, to NWMP scouts and the first businessmen. This gathering contains some of all of these. Also a few cowboys, Rocky Mountain Rangers and Highland Regiment men. Tom Ireland, owner of the first brewery, The Saskatchewan Brewery, is seen pouring a sample of his brew for the crowd. The photo was taken in 1885.

leniently. This summer at Medicine Hat there will be thousands of four-year-old steers marketed and during their life upon the ranges they have not known what it is to find the shelter of a stable in the winter and do not know what being hay-fed means.

"In this locality the railway finds use for snow plows in some winters. In New York State this is also the case. Last winter (1896) the small plows on the engine pilots were sufficient. Can this also be said of the railroad divisions within a few miles of where the *Scientific American* is published?"

Whether the magazine took any notice of the editor's tirade or not is not recorded. Whatever happened, the abuse heaped on Medicine Hat's good name continued. So much so that in 1909 a local resident named Harland E. Fitch took pen in hand and fought back. In an article headlined "A Dreadful Libel On Our Town", Fitch turned to poetry to protect his adopted city's reputation. The American-born Fitch retorted:

I have lived in Minnesota, North
Dakota and the West
(For across the Rocky Mountains is
the State I love the best),
But of all the winter weather
In the places I have been
Medicine Hat ranks high among
The finest I have seen.
'Tis a land of warmth and sunshine
Where the Chinook winds blow free.
Almost every week we have them,
Yes, and sometimes two or three.
'Tis a region slight in snowfall,
Hiding not the grass from sight,
Where the horses range all winter
with no shelter day or night.
'Tis the town that was born lucky,
As a noted writer says.
And the one who now derides her
Will some time sing her praise.
'Tis the place the weather howlers
Aim their fabrications at.
But the truth will some day conquer,
So, three cheers for Medicine Hat!

It is easy to see that outsiders who attacked the city's reputation could expect to get their knuckles rapped. Unfortunately, not all attacks on the name of the city came from outside. One of the most celebrated examples of treachery within the ranks came when some unimaginative individuals on the city council hinted that a plebiscite be held to have the name changed in order to appeal to investors who might have been offended by the city's unconventional name. After all, they said, how could one take a place named Medicine Hat seriously. This move to put the City on a different map, so to speak, came from real estate and industrial interests, several of whom got together to put out a short-lived newspaper.

A fine fury was built up in the community; almost a civil war resulted. No less a personage than Rudyard Kipling, the famous English poet, was brought into the fray. Kipling had visited the city in 1907 and enjoyed its amenities. He corresponded for years with civic officials and ordinary

9

residents, admitting that he had a soft spot in his heart for the city and district. He considered it had been "born lucky" considering its many natural resources, particularly its natural gas deposits. There is some controversy about whether he was referring to Medicine Hat or Redcliff when he said it had "all hell for a basement." It is believed that he was referring to Redcliff when he visited, but he was quoted in the *Medicine Hat News* of Thursday, October 17, 1907 as lumping both areas under the same warm umbrella: "This part of the country seems to have all hell for a basement, and the only trap door is Medicine Hat."

Now, three years after Kipling's visit, the council, at least some members on it, were considering changing the city's name. The subject of what to do about the plebiscite came up at a meeting of oldtimers at the city's famous Cypress Club. Bill Cousins, Walter Huckvale, Tony Day and others felt it was absurd to even consider changing the city's distinctive name. They sought ways and means to cut the culprits off at the pass. Someone in the club remarked: "I wish Rudyard Kipling knew of this; he would flay the hide off these blighters."

Francis F. Fatt, postmaster, was elected to write Kipling, telling him what was happening. Fatt recalled how Kipling had a "glorious" time in the city and remembered his time here with fondness. "You know how Kipling hated frills and public addresses," Fatt told J. M. Gilmour of the Canadian Pacific Railroad, in a letter recalling the event in May, 1936. "We just met him as man to man, in all our rustic habits, talked to him as if he was a beef buyer and really had a whale of a time."

When Kipling received Fatt's request to join the members of the Cypress Club and other public-spirited citizens in defeating any name change, the British author was delighted to do so. "I am aware — in fact all of us in Medicine Hat are aware — of the interest you took in our little city in your two trips across the continent," Fatt wrote on November 22, 1910.

The citizens and businessmen of Medicine Hat became very defensive about the reputation the city was getting as a result of its being the northernmost meteorological station and therefore the "source" of the worst weather. Here Mayor M. A. Brown is shown plowing on Riverside on January 23, 1919. As testified by the thermometer alongside, it was 70 degrees Fahrenheit and there was no frost in the ground. Photographs like this, with sworn testimonials as above, signed by the Mayor and a Notary Public, were sent to any Doubting Thomases who did not believe that Medicine Hat was a "Banana Belt" and not the "Weather Pot" of North America.

"Unfortunately, some newcomers have arisen and want to change the name of the city! It smacks too much of the Injin, smells fearfully of the teepee fire and kini-ki-nick — reminds outsiders of the whacking lies (may God forgive them) of the USA newspapermen in regard to our weather and so forth.

"In a moment of weakness our city fathers have agreed to submit the question to the vote of the ratepayers, instead of ordering the proposers to be cast into a den of fiery rattlesnakes. Can you help us with a few words of encouragement in combatting these heretics? Your influence here is great. If it is shown that you are against this proposition, it will help us materially."

Kipling was delighted to be able to do his bit for the city. He wrote from Bateman's Burwash in Sussex, England on December 9, 1910 "both as a citizen of the Empire and as a lover of Medicine Hat." Fatt had sent Kipling some clippings from the newspapers which led the famous author to deduce that the "chief arguments for the change are a) that some U.S. journalists have some sort of joke that Medicine Hat supplies all the bad weather of the U.S. and b) that another name would look better at the head of a prospectus."

Kipling noted that both arguments were developed at length by the *Calgary Herald*. "I always knew that Calgary called Medicine Hat names," he said, but I did not realize that Medicine Hat wanted to be Calgary's little god-child."

He then sat back and began to hit his stride: "As to the charge of brewing bad weather, I see no reason on earth why white men should be fluffed out of their city's birthright by an imported joke. Accept the charge joyously and proudly go forth as Medicine Hat, the only city officially recognized as capable of freezing out the United States and giving the Continent cold feet."

Kipling said the name echoed the "old Cree and Blackfoot tradition of red mystery and romance that once filled the prairies. Also, it hints at the magic that underlies the city in the shape of your natural gas. Believe me, the very name is an asset, and as years go on it will become more and more of an asset. It has no duplicate in the world: it makes men ask questions and, as I know, more than 20 years ago, draws the feet of the young towards it; it has the qualities of uniqueness, individuality, assertion and power.

"Above all, it is the lawful, original, sweat-and-dust-won name of the city, and to change it would be to risk the luck of the city, to disgust and dishearten oldtimers, not in the city alone, but the world over, and to advertise abroad the city's lack of faith in itself."

In concluding his rather long letter, Kipling said there appeared to be two arguments put forward for the name change and both were equally bad. "In the first case the town would change its name for fear of being laughed at. In the second it sells its name in the hope of making more money under an alias or, as the *Calgary Herald* writes, for the sake of the name that 'has a sound like the name of a man's best girl and looks like business at the head of a financial report.' But a man's city is a trifle more than a man's best girl. She is the living background of his life and love and toil and hope and sorrow. Her success is his success; her shame is his shame; her honor is his honor; and her good name is his good name."

Kipling summed up his scathing attack on those who would change the illustrious Medicine Hat name: "What then should a city be rechristened that has sold its name? Judasville."

When Fatt the postmaster received Kipling's reply he hastened to the Cypress Club and read it to the members. They were exultant. It was then published in its entirety in the *Medicine Hat News* and copied by newspapers around the world. The city garnered more publicity through the resulting coverage than it would have from any number of Chamber of Commerce pamphlets and brochures.

Needless to say, the plebiscite was roundly defeated by a margin of more than 10 to one. Medicine Hat, the "weather pot of the Continent" was here to stay.

When Rudyard Kipling, the famous English poet, visited Medicine Hat in October 1907, he fell in love with the city and its people, an association he continued until his death. It was probably as a result of his defence of the city's famous name that a plebiscite circulated to enlist support to change it to Smithville or Leopoldville was roundly defeated. This scene shows a parade along Second Street (then Main Street) in 1912. The automobiles were made by Oakland.

2.

Here Come the Redcoats!

The influence on Canadian history by the North West Mounted Police can hardly be over-estimated. The building of a ragtag group of shop clerks, school teachers, carriage builders, unemployed laborers and adventurers into one of the most respected police forces in the world has been well documented. However, some background has to be included here in order to stress the importance the Mounties had in the establishment of Medicine Hat as a city of peace and order.

For many years the Canadian West had been pictured as a vast arid land fit only for gophers and rattlesnakes, grasshoppers and some nomadic Indian tribes. This impression was mainly due to the reports filed by two men who had made scientific expeditions into the country: Canadian H. Y. Hind and British Captain John Palliser.

Hind, a professor of chemistry and geology at Trinity College in Toronto, was accompanied by Simon J. Dawson, a surveyor and engineer. In 1857 and 1858 they scouted the country from Lake Superior to the Saskatchewan River system. Palliser, an Imperial Army officer, had as his

The famous North West Mounted Police was made up of young men from all over Canada and Europe who wanted to make a career in the West. Sergeant J. H. G. Bray was an excellent example of the dedicated men who undertook the perilous journey and brought law and order to the country. Bray was the second man to join the NWMP in Toronto in 1873. He and the force marched west in 1874. He came to stay in 1892.

Captain John Palliser. It is difficult to understand in the light of time how Palliser could have been so wrong about the potential of the Medicine Hat area.

working companion, Dr. James Hector, a Scottish doctor and naturalist. They followed a route along the North Saskatchewan River to Fort Edmonton. In 1859 Palliser and his partner cut southward and reached the Cypress Hills where they made detailed observations. They did not, however, correct the impression made by the name, despite having a naturalist along. French-speaking Hudson's Bay men called them "Montaigne de Cypre", meaning "Mountains of Jack Pine." That was in 1825, and when the first English-speaking adventurers came along they turned the name Cypre to Cypress, although the closest cypress was several thousand miles away.

In addition to leaving a mistake in the "Cypress" Hills, Palliser described the vast territory he and Hind had covered as "worthless", "lonely", "uninhabitable". Articles and newspaper stories appeared that bolstered the image of "Palliser's Triangle" as dry and unfit for settlement. Of the region south and west of the Red Deer River, Palliser concluded: "The whole . . , is valueless, the grass being very scanty and timber very scarce." It seems almost cheeky that Captain Palliser should be immortalized by the naming of the landmark hotel in Calgary by the CPR.

His astonishingly inaccurate description certainly could not be applied to the Cypress Hills, a veritable oasis which had always been a magnet to travellers, Indian, Metis, trapper and trader. Neither true mountains nor true hills, this plateau straddles what is now the Alberta-Saskatchewan border, a haven for game. Set in the dry, short grass country, it was a haven for Palliser too, however his glowing description of that area seems to have had less impression than the balance of the "lonely land".

"The Cypress Mountains indeed form a great contrast to the level country through which we have been travelling," Palliser wrote. "They are covered with timber, much of which is very valuable for building purposes. The soil is rich and the supply of water abundant. These hills are a perfect oasis in the desert through which we have travelled."

The story would have been the same had he come upon them from any other direction because the Cypress Hills rise like an island, a thousand feet above the surrounding plains. At 4,400 feet, they are higher than the town of Banff, Alberta, several hundred miles to the west in the Rocky Mountains.

With "bench grass" four inches high, poplar bluffs and a solid background of stately pines, the Cypress Hills extend from Eagle Butte on the west end, not far southeast of Medicine Hat, to a line drawn from Piapot and Eastend, Saskatchewan. This "oasis" in the baldheaded prairie was also the setting for the infamous "Cypress Hills Massacre," an incident which had a most important effect on the formation of Canada as a nation.

In 1873 a group of American wolf trappers camped near Fort Benton, Montana had their horses stolen by a band of Indians. These were trailed to the Cypress Hills where an encampment of Assiniboine Indians was encountered near Abe Farwell's trading post. The band of stolen horses was not found but an altercation arose over the ownership of one particular horse belonging to wolfer George Hammond. The result was a shoot-out involving Indians and whites. Who fired the first shot has never been definitely determined and authorities disagree.

A full scale battle began and when the smoke cleared, 35 Indians and one white man lay dead. Farwell's trading post was burned to the ground.

Farwell, who was well-regarded by the local Indians, had tried to act as a mediator and soon found himself *persona non grata* on all sides. The wolfers, Thomas "Green River Renegade" Hardwick, John Evans, John Duval, Trevanian Hale, Jeff Devereaux, Jim Hughes, Jim Marshall, Charles Smith and Charlie Harper (Ed Grace was the white man killed in the mélée) decapitated the wounded Assiniboine Chief Little Soldier and eventually fled back to Montana.

Canadians everywhere were becoming increasingingly hostile, shocked and outraged at the impertinence of Americans invading Canadian territory. The news of the massacre was viewed as just another in a series of incidents of American interference. The story of Fort Whoop-Up and other whiskey forts was front page news for months and pressure was put on Prime Minister John A. Macdonald to take some positive action immediately. The whole west could slide into American hands by default.

The Cypress Hills Massacre has been descibed in detail so there is no necessity to go into it here. Suffice to say that a general increase in lawlessness in the North West Territories resulted in the formation of the North West Mounted Police in 1873. By 1875 a detachment of 102 men, led by Major James Morrow Walsh, was established at Cypress Hills. Fort Walsh was the headquarters of the NWMP from 1878 to 1882 when it was moved to Regina. Fort Walsh was abandoned by the NWMP in favor of Maple Creek, Saskatchewan in 1883.

On January 1st of that year the Force chose a barracks site in Medicine Hat at a spot on the open prairie one mile east of the town on the north side of the South Saskatchewan River. The adjacent wooded area became known, and is still known, as Police Point. The Mounties were immediately involved in policing the area while development was underway.

Commissioner (formerly Lt.-Colonel) A. G. Irvine readily understood that serious difficulties could be presented by the construction work involved in the crossing of the South Saskatchewan River by the CPR. Here are some extracts from Commissioner Irvine's reports dated at Regina on the 1st of June, 1883:

"During the month of April, work was resumed on the Canadian Pacific Railway and large numbers of men and horses pushed forward to the end of the track by that company. With this began what may be termed the commencement of our season's work. Order had to be maintained among the railway navvies, and every effort used for the prevention of whiskey smuggling. As the track-laying proceeded westward towards Medicine Hat, I found it necessary to place a strong detachment at that point. This detachment rendered excellent service. Owing to the heavy nature of engineering work, through the Seven Persons Coulee to Medicine Hat, this latter place was for a considerable time considered as a terminus, where large bodies of men were collected and where a settlement at once grew up. This being the case the services of our detachment were in constant demand in the suppression of liquor traffic, the prevention of horse stealing, quelling small strikes, and generally maintaining order."

The NWMP quarters on the north side of the river were quite extensive: an officers' quarters, barrack room, recreation and orderly room, guard room, Sergeant's mess, Quartermaster's store, two stables, blacksmith's shop, coal shed, wagon shed, bakery and latrine. The Commissioner was

A closeup shot of Sergeant Major J. H. G. Bray in his later years. The Bray family is still well-represented in the city.

pleased with the results: "These buildings are all in a good state of repair and it must be a matter of congratulations that their erection was completed at such comparatively small cost. I know of no such buildings, public or otherwise, having been built in an equally economical manner, more particularly bearing in mind that efficiency was never lost sight of."

The Commissioner reported in 1885 that there was one officer and a total of 47 other ranks stationed at Medicine Hat. He had asked for at least that many men with an equal number of horses because of the vast territory the force would be expected to protect. "From (this) point west is a large tract of country," Irvine pointed out, "uninhabited, and easily traversed. South of the boundary lies the Territory of Montana. From Medicine Hat west to Fort Macleod is about 130 miles. The railway construction will no doubt offer great inducements to the whiskey traders of Montana to run cargo of liquor in. The difficulty in preventing this will be great."

Commissioner Irvine was right. And devious were the methods employed in getting the liquor over the border and into the bellies of the CPR workmen and other residents. One shipment came in barrels marked flour. But the most ingenious was a shipment of Bibles, which when opened displayed containers of an amber liquid not considered to be sacramental wine.

As well as the whiskey trade, Irvine was concerned about the possibility of an Indian uprising. "I do not wish to produce any unnecessary disquiet," he reported, "but I would call to your attention the fact that the railway will next summer enter the Indian country proper, passing close to the Blackfoot Reserve. The large number of horses employed will be a great temptation to horse stealing, both by white men and Indians from south of the line, where they can be readily run across — as well as by our own Indians."

Although the feared Indian attack on the railway construction crew did not materialize, the first members of the force stationed at Medicine Hat faced many problems. Those who served during that challenging period included Inspector Macdonnell, Inspector Norman, Inspector Moodie, Sergeant Duchesnay and Sergeant Spicer. Many of the young men who came west with the police did not return home. A number of small marble slabs in an ancient cemetery by the side of the trail just north of Fort Walsh pay solemn tribute to those who met their death in the service of their country.

The most famous example of that service was new recruit Constable Marmaduke Graburn who was ambushed near the Mounties' horse camp northwest of Fort Walsh. A Blood Indian named Starchild was charged but acquitted of the crime. Graburn's Coulee, named for the murdered police officer, is marked by a commemorative cairn in Cypress Hills Provincial Park. Graburn was 19 years old when he was shot.

The flat area the police chose for their first barracks in Medicine Hat was ideal at the time. It was bordered on three sides by the South Saskatchewan River and was served by a scow ferry operated by the Force from Police Point. Located about 300 yards west of Strathcona Island, it was built by George Martin, a ships' carpenter who arrived in Medicine Hat in 1885. The ferry was moved further west to the foot of Third Avenue (behind the present library) in 1889. It operated from this area until the Finlay Bridge was opened on May 14, 1908. Ferry operators were a Mr. McQueen, Vincent Minneszewsky, Dave Williamson and Captain W. J. Johnston.

Commissioner A. G. Irvine of the North West Mounted Police. His detachment was in demand in the suppression of liquor traffic, the prevention of horse stealing, quelling small strikes and generally maintaining order.

The Mounties protecting the CPR crew and their families and the other settlers and merchants who were making the tent and boxcar community of Medicine Hat into a law abiding city were led by Inspector John MacDonald. The men called him "Paper Collar Johnny" because of his absolute insistence upon spit and polish. The citizenry respected MacDonald and his men, and the mood in the area was relatively calm.

Robert McCutcheon was one of the originals in the NWMP station at Fort Walsh in 1874 or 1875. He was employed as a farrier. He moved to Medicine Hat in 1882 to establish the first homestead on Riverside. Sheriff for 22 years, McCutcheon lived in the city for 53 years. He shot the last buffalo seen in the Medicine Hat area and died in 1945 at the age of 92.

In 1891 the Mounted Police left the original site and moved into new headquarters on the south side, establishing on what is now the site of the Royal Canadian Legion. The old police barracks buildings sat empty for many years. The wooded area beyond and to the east of the buildings is a silent, haunted-looking place. It was once distinguished by dense stands of yellow willows which lined the river banks. Old cottonwoods, twisted by wind and flood, sheltered deer which were drawn to the area because of generous undergrowth.

Gooseberries, raspberries, loving sage, prairie buttercup, brown-eyed susans, bald cactus and wild asparagus thrived on the "Point". The lush vegetation provided good habitat for a variety of wildlife, ducks, meadowlarks, ring-necked pheasants, red fox, bobcats, beaver, muskrats and mule deer.

For many years Police Point was left to picnickers, nature lovers, tourists, Boy Scouts and vandals. It was designated a park and playground by the city in 1920 but little was done until early fall of 1980 to make it the attraction it could become, aside from the installation of an attractive, hand-carved sign by local historian Jack Barrie. By spring of 1981 the River Valley Authority made plans to make this area a beautiful nature hiking spot, excluding motor traffic entirely. The area was fenced to exclude unauthorized vehicles.

Police Point, silent, hauntingly beautiful. The site was given new life in 1980 when the City unveiled a plan to turn it into "an environmental education and interpretive area" as part of the development of the river valley park system. (Photo courtesy of Medicine Hat City)

17

Grace Cousins, whose father came to Medicine Hat in a covered wagon and a 10-horse team from London, Ontario in 1883, recalled that the Point has another romantic history. "It was a place that the young and foolish would drive out to sit and look at the moon." In that, at least, little has changed.

Grace Cousins (on the left in the front) as she appeared in 1926 on a cruise back from England on the SS Montcalm. Above her is George Galloway. The couple next to her are unidentified. On the right are Mrs. William Cousins and William Cousins.

One of the area's many noted Mounties was James Crockett, better known as Barney. Crockett came to Canada from Scotland and went to work for Thomas Hargrave at his Fort Walsh ranch in 1903. He joined the NWMP as a special constable employed in stock work. In one memorable case he investigated some big steers in a shipment from the Cypress Hills to Moose Jaw. Crockett felt something was wrong and took it solely upon himself to find out what it was. The other RCMP (The "Royal" was added to North West Mounted in 1900 and the name changed to Royal Canadian Mounted Police in 1920) officers were not so sure and warned Crockett he had better be right if he were to hold up the shipment of the herd on a "hunch".

On his word, the cattle were held and, with dubious officials helping, the brands inspected. Crockett began clipping hair and two or three cattle passed his scrutiny. Then the special constable found what he had been expecting: Mack Higdon's Bar N Bar brand had been changed by a running iron. Only a detective with Crockett's experience could have had the "sixth sense" necessary to foil some rustler's bid to an easy fortune.

In an article in *Canadian Cattlemen* of January 1960, the editor quoted fellow Mountie Denny Ashby as saying that Crockett was "strong but gentle, a pillar of strength to every N.C.O. who ever served with him in Medicine Hat."

As can be expected, the Mounties then as now were confronted with unusual cases that broke the monotony of routine police work. For example, there was the case of J. B. Casey of St. Paul, Minnesota. Some laborers who were hauling gravel from the river bank were startled when a man came running out of the bushes with no coat, vest, shirt or boots on. He claimed that he had been stabbed. One of the laborers ran to get the police.

Corporal Humby arrived on the scene with a team and wagon and took the wounded man off to the hospital. The man had a large cut on his thigh, inflicted he said, by two men who had set upon him, gagged him, and removed part of his clothing. They burned the clothing along with his satchel. At first Casey said he was knocked unconscious and woke up in a pool of blood but later changed his story: he was stabbed in the leg by one of the assailants.

Front: Barney Crockett, Rancher, Brand Inspector for RCMP. Back: Harry Minor, Cattleman, Rancher, in the Medicine Hat area for years.

Upon investigating the police found a small fire in which smoldering remains of the man's clothing and satchel were found. Casey, who said he was a telegraph operator who had come to Medicine Hat to seek work on the CPR, stuck by his story but the police considered that he alone was responsible for whatever happened to him.

As the reporter for the *Medicine Hat News* summed it up: "Whatever his actions are attributable to, a too-liberal indulgence in intoxicants or some other source, is a question. He is still very weak from loss of blood but seems to be recovering his courage as he has already threatened to murder his attending physician."

Although the Mounted Police are still a force to be reckoned with in the city, in actual fact the day to day policing has been done by a regular police force. Protection within the city has been under the jurisdiction of such a body since Medicine Hat was incorporated as a town on December 12, 1898.

The first town policeman filled three or four positions: Health Officer, Licence and Building Inspector — and Policeman. A bylaw passed in January 1899 enabled the Town Council to hire a man for this position. He was John R. Clark who filled these duties until June 1899 when John G. Calder was appointed Health Officer, leaving Clark with duties of Inspector and Policeman.

On October 15, 1900 George Marwick was appointed local Police Constable and Licence Inspector. He was followed by Vincent Minneszewsky as Police Chief. Mr. Minneszewsky had led an interesting life. An exiled Polish Count, he had at one time served in the American Civil War, with the NWMP at Fort Walsh, and in 1889 operated the ferry for the Mounties at Medicine Hat. He ran a dairy farm after resigning as Chief of Police.

Adam Mayberry served as Chief for a short time after Minneszewsky resigned. John Meiklejohn from Calgary, formerly with the Glasgow Police Force, acted as Chief until 1910 when James Bruce succeeded him in office. Bruce resigned in 1916 in order to join the army where he attained the rank of Major.

The Mayor and Council in 1889. Left to right in the back row are T. Blachford, N. Adsit, A. C. Hawthorne, George Marwick (Police Constable and Licence Inspector in 1900) and J. Spencer. Seated in the front row are (left to right) T. Penhale, W. B. Marshall, G. Noble and Harry Yuill.

Bruce was replaced by Archie Johnston who left a year later to join the Alberta Provincial Police. Johnston lived for several years in Vancouver before meeting a tragic end, being shot down in his office by an unknown murderer. The mystery was never solved. The next Chief was Jonas Lait who also served a short term. He quit to join the Saskatchewan Provincial Police in 1919 and died in their service several years later.

On September 17, 1919 Captain James M. Taylor became Police Chief. Born in Scotland, he served on the Calgary force from 1910 to 1915, the year he enlisted in the army and attained the rank of Captain. Joseph B. McQueen who served under Chief Taylor was appointed Acting Chief in 1940 when Taylor retired. McQueen retired five years later and was replaced by Arthur R. Bull, formerly with the RCMP. Bull retired in 1967 and died in the city in 1974.

Another former Mountie, Sam Drader, was appointed Chief of Police until 1974 when his assistant, Jack Judge, took over until Judge's untimely death in 1975. Eric M. Lloyd was appointed Chief in 1975, having served the Medicine Hat Police Force since 1951. He had been employed as plainsclothesman and Inspector before taking on the job as Chief of Police.

Medicine Hat could never be described as a one horse town, although it did have one policeman who patrolled by horse for many years. The first to be provided with a trusty steed was Chief Vincent Minneszewsky and later Sergeant James Cairney took to the saddle. It was while Cairney was employed that the City dispensed with horses and motorcycles entered the scene.

Magistrates serving over the years were James Rae. Rev. W. H. Ellis, S. G. Main, A. J. Raiment and E. W. N. MacDonald. In 1982 Phil Wambolt and Dietrich Brand were the Provincial Court Judges.

The police force in Medicine Hat has always held an enviable record in the eyes of less fortunate communities. Newspapers in other Western cities have repeatedly pointed out the low percentage of crime compared with the city's population and development. Not the least of Medicine Hat's good points is that it is a law-abiding community.

Above all, it was a peaceful town where women and children were safe on its streets, even in the early days. This photo, taken in 1903, shows the William Cousins Furnishings and Dry Goods Store and the Klondyke Restaurant on South Railway Street.

20

The Coming Of The Steel

Delegates from the newly-formed colony of British Columbia got more than they expected when they went to Ottawa to propose that a wagon road be built to the West Coast as part of their agreement to become a Canadian province. They also wanted a railroad survey to be undertaken immediately. The Dominion Government was more than generous: it committed itself to start the railroad within two years and to finish it within ten. The year was 1871.

What an undertaking! This was a country that had only 3.5 million people living in it — and only 23,000 of them lived west of Lake Superior. It was a pipe dream surely, to contemplate building such a railroad over a route that no one knew, at a cost that no one could estimate, and one that the "experts" said couldn't be done at all.

It was the Englishman, Captain John Palliser, who said no transcontinental railroad could be built across North America. He made his report in 1863. Luckily for Canada, the Dominion Government decided to assign its own engineer and survey crew to study the terrain. It was a positive step because work began on the railroad in 1881, a bit behind schedule, but nevertheless a beginning was made on the ribbon of steel that would eventually bind the whole country together.

The route finally chosen by the Canadian Pacific Railway Company was far to the south of the original survey (Winnipeg instead of Selkirk; Calgary instead of Edmonton; Vancouver instead of Prince Rupert), making the distance shorter. It was also closer to the American border so no rival company could slip their steel in to reap whatever benefits came from the south. It also neatly dovetailed with Sir John A. Macdonald's plans for expansion and colonization of the west and to ward off any American plans for the same property.

By 1881 the steel stretched as far as Brandon, Manitoba. Bridge builders labored along with grading crews to prepare the way for the steel-laying gangs. For weeks at a time the track crept along at a rate of three and one-half miles a day. Gangs completed their stretch of road and leaped ahead to the next allotment. A number of Ontario farmers came west with outfits to help build the grade, getting three dollars a day and board and feed for their horses. Laborers received 30 dollars a month. Despite the enormous distances over which all the supplies had to be moved, work went quickly on the prairie section. In one three day period, 20 miles were built.

In a final burst of speed, track-laying during June of 1883 totalled 67

First train across the South Saskatchewan CPR. Trestle Bridge at Medicine Hat, 1883.

miles but the record month for the whole project was July when the track advanced 92.3 miles over the plains between Medicine Hat and Calgary. That same month the rails were laid across the Blackfoot Indian reserve east of Gleichen, arousing the wrath of Chief Crowfoot. He threatened to annihilate the CPR crew but was averted from doing so by the Oblate missionary, Father Albert Lacombe. Father Lacombe was rushed from the east on the first available train and talked the Chief out of any precipitous action.

The crossing of the prairies had been accomplished with little disturbance by the Indians, although construction began at a time when trouble could have been expected: the great buffalo herds upon which the Indians and Métis depended for food, clothing, fuel and shelter were fast disappearing; the government was trying to get the Indians to move on to reserves and take up agriculture; and to many Indians the steel rails and telegraph lines were just more indications that the white man was out to limit their freedom of movement.

The Surveyors for the CPR arrived in Medicine Hat before the track. Housed in a log cabin, the first house in the townsite, they posed for the camera in 1883.

At times they became angry and exasperated and took action against the intruders. Lines of surveyors' stakes were pulled up and on one occasion teepees were set up on the track. In the forested areas of the east, logs were piled on the right-of-way and other efforts were made to derail the trains.

Workmen who were unfamiliar with the Indians were fearful of them and upset by their habit of squatting in rows near the line and stolidly observing everything that took place.

If there was any hesitation on the part of the Dominion Government to continue building the route, the Riel Rebellion added incentive. Prime Minister Macdonald dispatched a military unit via the new railway to quash the violence. To put this important event into perspective, a brief background may be useful: When Rupert's Land was sold to the Government of Canada the fate of the Red River settlement was left in abeyance. French-speaking Métis were fearful that their culture and religion would be encroached upon by Eastern homesteaders. Louis Riel, leader of the Comité National de Métis, proclaimed a provisional government before the territory transfer and, taking over Fort Garry (Winnipeg), appointed himself President of the Republic of Red River on December 27, 1869. In the following year Garnet Wolseley arrived with a police detachment to enforce order in the new province of Manitoba, forcing Riel to flee to the United States.

Riel was elected to the House of Commons four years later (for helping repel American Fenian raiders) but was shortly expelled after advocating radical policies. At the request of Red River residents, Riel returned to his homeland in 1884 to protect Western Canada's interests; this time his movement erupted into violence, culminating in the North West Rebellion. It was at that time that Macdonald sent the troops out on the CPR.

After surrendering, Riel was tried for treason and executed at Regina. French-Canadians claimed that the Métis leader was used as a scapegoat against the political aspirations of French-speaking settlers. During the days when the Rebellion was on, many Medicine Hat residents went to bed with their guns nearby and others made plans to be ready to move quickly if the violence spread in their direction. It didn't. (See Chapter 13 on the Rocky Mountain Rangers.) The Rebellion had its positive side since the Cabinet in

Part of the Halifax Highland Regiment camped at Medicine Hat during the Riel Rebellion. The site was the top of the Sixth Avenue Hill in 1885. Commanding Officer is Alfred Whiteman, standing just to the right of centre with beard and forage cap. No others were identified in this picture which was sent to the Lethbridge Museum in 1915. Notice the straw hats on some of the soldiers.

Medicine Hat from North Hill. Notice white tents on top of hill above town. This was the camp of the Highland Regiment from Halifax, sent to guard the town during the Riel Rebellion. They saw no action.

Ottawa was now convinced that the CPR was worth the high financial and political price it was costing.

To cross the South Saskatchewan River at Medicine Hat the work crews and horses forded the shallows near Police Point. The railway bridge was ready for rail traffic by 1883 but there was no foot bridge and consequently a ferry was put into operation, as described in the previous chapter.

Medicine Hat became a divisional point of the Canadian Pacific Railway and the terminus of the Crow's Nest Branch. The company had first given consideration to a site at Seven Persons Creek, further east. The present location was found more suitable and the district was established that extended from Swift Current to the east to Calgary in the northwest, and from Medicine Hat west 100 miles to Lethbridge. Extensive shops, a huge roundhouse, stock and freight yards were built and bridges constructed.

In 1885 four freight engines were working out of Medicine Hat, along with four passenger locomotives, plus a spare. Each engineer had his own locomotive. The first passenger engineers were Pete Grace, Billy Walker, Jim Fisher and John Spencer with Jim McLeod as spare. Freight engineers were Pete Robertson, Tom Fleming, Karen Kelly and Charlie Calkins. By 1886 there was a through passenger train daily each way, but since no trains left Montreal or Vancouver on Sundays each week saw one blank day at Medicine Hat. The first passenger train with J. H. Fisher engineer, arrived July 2, 1886.

Walter Leveque, who came to Medicine Hat in 1902, told interviewer Martha Jussila that the Lord's Day Alliance decreed that no trains, except stock trains, should move on Sunday. But the population was equally ingenious at devising ways and means of getting around government regulations, he said. It was quite evident that there was more profit in running trains seven days a week than six, so the one that ran on the Sabbath had to be a stock train. The CPR bought old animals cheaply and put a few head on each train. This made it a stock train and automatically released the whole train.

24

CPR passenger train at Medicine Hat in 1889. Engine Number 98. The boy in the centre front is young Thomas Hargrave. As early as 1886 there was a through passenger train daily each way out of the city. The first passenger train to arrive in Medicine Hat was on July 2, 1886 with J. H. Fisher the engineer.

Mr. Leveque recalled an old grey horse and an old roan bull who became familiar to train crews. One Sunday they would go to Swift Current. They were fed there all week by the section men and returned to Medicine Hat the following Sunday where they were put in the stockyards and fed until it was time to take the train ride back to Swift Current.

The first divisional superintendent was C. S. Shields who came from the United States with the "Father of the CPR", Sir William Van Horne. When Shields returned to the U.S., J. N. Niblock took over. Niblock was an outstanding citizen who was a major force in establishing the first hospital here. He had a great aversion to the use of strong language. To illustrate his point, he posted a verse in all train cabooses:

It chills my blood to hear the blest Supreme
Appealed to lightly on each trifling theme.
Maintain your manhood; profanity despise.
To swear is neither brave, polite, nor wise.

The first railway station in the city was situated at the foot of what is now Third Street. It was a red, two-storey frame building on the south side of the tracks. There were living quarters for the stationmaster in the second storey which were reached by outside stairs. A large archway connected this part of the bulding with the express office and was used later as a storage place for trucks.

The construction of the roundhouse began in 1903. There was no fence on the CPR property at that time; anyone could walk across the tracks at any time, anywhere. Joe Day, a well-known local rancher, walked across one day and ducked past some moving stock, catching his arm on one of the switching trains. He lost the arm in the operation that followed and sued the CPR for negligence. After that a fence was erected.

The contract for the present brick station on the north side of the tracks was let to MacDiarmid's of Winnipeg in 1905 and was officially opened on July 12, 1906. The freight sheds stayed on the south side. Trees, lawn and

25

flowers were planted and a gardener detailed to look after them. They were on the west side of the station and were much admired by the residents and passengers who watched them bloom.

As an experiment, an apple tree was planted in the garden and in July 1891 it bore fruit for the first time. The blooming tree was carefully protected with wire netting and was the pride and joy of Superintendent Niblock. He was boasting about the fruit on the tree while travelling west with Van Horne. Sir William would not believe him. Apples in Alberta? Such nonsense. It was an illusion, surely. Niblock insisted. He was adamant. If there were apples on the tree as Niblock claimed, then Sir William would lose his bet and would put up enough cash to furnish a ward in the proposed hospital at Medicine Hat. The bet was on.

Curious necks craned from the train as it steamed into Medicine Hat. "Hah!" Van Horne gloated. "There are no apples on that tree!" He was right. Niblock was stunned. There was not a single apple to be seen. He thought of all the work and pride that was invested in that tree and its armload of apples. To make matters worse, Van Horne did not have to donate money to Niblock's favorite cause, the new hospital.

Showing his generous nature, Sir William eventually did make a donation. But not before the word got around that he had rigged his bet with Niblock by sending a telegram in advance of their arrival at Medicine Hat ordering that all the apples on the tree be removed. It is not recorded whether Niblock was amused or not, but he was a very public-spirited individual and the Van Horne donation was gratefully received. With George Noble, Niblock was mainly responsible for having the hospital completed in 1889.

Incidentally, the hospital was the site of the community's first telephone, while CPR train dispatcher R. E. Starks had the second one installed in his home. It ran from the station to his house and was useful in routing out crews and keeping tabs on train movements.

The famous CPR gardens by the railway station as it appeared in 1889. The pride and joy of Superintendent Niblock was the blooming apple tree which became a source of fun to President of the CPR, William Van Horne.

In the early construction days, while other residents were living in shacks and tents, CPR crewmen lived in comparative comfort in boxcars which had been assigned for that use. An immigration shed was situated where the present Canadian Legion now stands (it was also used by the Mounted Police when they left Police Point to move to the city) and for years served as a halfway home to immigrants waiting to get on to their homesteads. The shed also served as a dance hall on Saturday nights and as church and meeting house on Sundays. It was a scene of weddings as well.

Charles Wagstaff is believed to be the first man to walk the wedded path in Medicine Hat. His romance with Sarah Cotton actually began in 1882. Wagstaff and Miss Cotton came across from England on the same ship that year, blissfully unaware of the fact at that time. They were still unaware of each other as they travelled across the United States by train on their way to Winnipeg. In the immigration office in the Manitoba city, Wagstaff, then a seasoned youth of 18, saw a comely lass of 14 attempting to draw some water from a pump to make tea. He offered to assist, but she was an independent sort and demurred.

In 1886, Wagstaff was working for the CPR in Medicine Hat. Word came from the sister of Albert Cotton that she was coming to keep house for him. Cotton was the CPR storekeeper. There weren't many young, eligible women in the community at that time so the young lady's arrival was a significant event to the young blades of the town. Wagstaff was among them when Sarah Cotton stepped off the train. He recognized her as the young lady who refused help at the pump.

History does not record what happened the time of their second meeting but something significant must have occurred. They were married in 1889. Mrs. Roy Keating, daughter of Charles Wagstaff, wrote that the young couple exchanged vows at the Cotton's boxcar house near the CPR roundhouse.

It seems that the railway crew felt that this occasion should be marked for all the color and sound of the historic event that it was. Every whistle that could toot and every horn that could blast did so. The sound was deafening and the preacher, the Reverend Mr. Teetor, was deaf. Consequently, he continued the service throughout the din, despite the fact that no one could hear a word of it. Nevertheless, the happy couple walked from the house through a torchlit procession of brooms dipped in oil and lit, up to their new home on Third Street, near the land upon which the T. Eaton store now stands.

In addition to bringing young couples to the blessed state, the CPR brought other benefits to the burgeoning community. The decision to make Medicine Hat the division point meant employment of shop workers, track maintenance crews and train crews. Fifty men worked in the shops and almost that number again were employed in keeping the tracks open and in good condition year-round. Sixty-six trainmen were based at the depot.

The railway served the needs of the community by maintaining a demand for fuel and by its transportation of coal and ceramic clay to and from local centres. It also provided the only effective means of long distance traffic into and out of the area. Additionally, it heralded the end of another era: stage coach travel.

Frank Pollinger, known far and wide as "Polly", was one of the most

Sarah Cotton, later Mrs. Charles Wagstaff. Although she and Mr. Wagstaff's meeting was unceremonious, much ceremony attended their historic wedding in 1889.

View of City of Medicine Hat about 1889. CPR bridge.

colorful of the stage drivers in the Medicine Hat, Lethbridge, Macleod area. He was born in Oklahoma and grew up on a ranch. He was said to know all the trails in the Old West; he knew the bad holes, how to cross the streams and how to get out of sloughs, if he were unfortunate enough to get in one. It was also said that he knew how to charm rattlesnakes. He would lay his rawhide lariat on the grass around his camp and swore that no snake would ever wriggle over it. (Don't count on this to work for you, Mr. Tenderfoot!)

After many years of branding stock and following roundups, Polly took up stage coach driving. He arrived in Fort Benton, Montana and drove stage between there and Fort Macleod when that trail was established. He would leave Fort Macleod on a Monday morning and return in three weeks. Carrying mail at that time was voluntary; Polly charged 10 cents a letter to carry it to Fort Benton where he bought stamps and mailed the letters.

As the country opened up, Pollinger drove the Calgary-Edmonton trail and it was on one of these trips that he was held up by three men who demanded the mail bag. He threw it down to them and yelled at the horses so they took off at a gallop. By the time the holdup men discovered that the locked bag contained nothing but waste paper, Polly and the stage coach were well out of range. The wily old driver always carried a dummy bag for just such an occasion.

When the CPR reached Medicine Hat and mail carrying by stage was no longer feasible, Polly went to work on one of the local ranches. He continued at this occupation until rheumatism forced friends to place him in the Medicine Hat hospital. There he spent the remainder of his days as he said, "among strangers."

A. F. Grady of Fort Macleod was on a business trip to Medicine Hat one day. While chatting with the chairman of the hospital board, mention was made of a man who was in hospital, a former resident of Fort Macleod. The old man had no visitors. "Perhaps you would like to see him," the chairman said. "His name is Polly." Grady knew him right away. He had often wondered what had happened to Polly, the old stage driver.

Grady stood at the bedside and said, "How are you, Polly?" The old man, recognizing the voice, revived enough to say, "I'm lonely, why didn't you come sooner?" Just then he stuck a foot out from under the sheets and hung it over the side of the bed. He put his hands up as though hauling on reins. Grady was alarmed. "What is it, Polly?" he asked. "We are going down the hill and the brakes won't hold," the old driver yelled.

Grady called a nurse, but it was too late. Frank Pollinger had taken his last drive down the long hill, he was buried in Medicine Hat. The grave is simply marked, "Polly".

When the possibility of Medicine Hat developing into a focal point for transportation was realized, the more optimistic members of the community contracted regular attacks of railway fever. In 1912, for example, it was seriously considered that the local station could accommodate no less than seven different railway companies operating in Alberta, Saskatchewan and Montana. For 30 years this optimism resulted in spasmodic buying and selling of land considered potentially useful for track development.

The construction of the *Minnow* on the South Saskatchewan River in 1884. The vessel was 73 feet long, 10 feet wide and was propelled by a six horsepower engine.

Building steamboat, *Baroness*, at Medicine Hat 1884. South Saskatchewan River. Note CPR trestle bridge in background.

According to an early copy of the *Geographical Bulletin,* early ties with Lethbridge were due largely to the initiative of the Galt family who first sought a CPR contract for the coal from their mines. For supply and transportation purposes, sternwheel river steamers and barges were built. The North Western Coal & Navigation Company engaged in an attempt to

29

haul coal, passengers and freight between Medicine Hat and the Galt family mines at Coal Banks (which became the City of Lethbridge). The capricious flow of water in the South Saskatchewan River proved to be the undoing of this navigation route.

Nothing conquers the pioneer spirit, however, and the mine owners then constructed a narrow gauge railway — The Turkey Track — from Lethbridge to the CPR line at Dunmore. The CPR locomotive superintendents were convinced that the coal from Coal Banks had excellent qualities for their steam engines. They offered the infant North West Coal & Navigation Company a contract. After some swift negotiating over land prices and corporate moves that saw the emergence of the Alberta Railway and Coal Company in 1891, the Coal Banks to Dunmore Siding of 109 miles in length was officially opened.

It was the first railway, other than the Canadian Pacific Railway, to be built in Canada west of Winnipeg, and the first railway to cross the International border west of Regina. This narrow gauge railway was in revenue operation two months before the last spike of the CPR was driven at Craigellachie, B.C. As Jack Barrie wrote in a 1968 edition of *Saamis Review,* "in August 1885 a little Mogul engine with 20 loaded gondolas of coal labored eastward from Coal Banks over the three foot gauge line to Dunmore Junction. It passed points along the line eastward — Fourteen Mile Tank, Woodpecker, 77 Tank, Grassy Lake, Winnifred, Seven Persons — and for a seven year period delivered a large number of trainloads of coal to the standard gauge CPR. It was aptly named the 'Turkey Trail' for it re-

Engine #21 from the Alberta Railway and Coal Co. Loaned to CPR. This was probably one of the narrow gauge line engines.

sembled the path made by wild turkeys as they hunted for seeds and insects among the thickets and grassy patches on the prairie."

With 400,000 acres of disposable land at the Lethbridge end, this rail line offered more than an outlet for coal. Within 10 years the narrow gauge was replaced and the company purchased by the CPR in 1893. William Van Horne had his eye on the Alberta Railway and Coal Company line hoping this would be the first stage of a railway to the Crowsnest. By 1912 the CPR had control of all narrow gauge lines in Canada and they were all converted to standard gauge.

For the most part the present CPR line from Dunmore to Lethbridge still follows the original road bed of the old Turkey Trail line. Of local interest was the official opening of the Coal Banks to Dunmore line on September 24, 1885: A free excursion was offered to Medicine Hat citizens and some dignitaries were also along for the ride, including Governor General, the Marquis of Lansdowne, Sir Alexander Galt, Saskatchewan's Jack McLean, the Anglican Bishop of Saskatchewan, and the CPR's General Superintendent, J. M. Eagan.

Despite the success of the narrow gauges, the possibility of using the South Saskatchewan River as a means of transporting goods and passengers lingered in the minds of some entrepreneurs for years. Surely such a resource could be developed for fun and profit. The time was ripe for the right man to come along and do something about it.

Capt. Ross' first launch in which he arrived at Medicine Hat The Assiniboia I from Calgary, in 1898.

The man of the hour turned out to be Captain Horatio Hamilton Ross. Ross convinced a group of Medicine Hat citizens that they should have a steam boat in the river to be used for excursions and pleasure trips — as well as for hauling coal from Lethbridge and other freighting work. Jack Barrie wrote about Ross in an article published in the July 2, 1975 issue of *The Rattler.*

Ross told his Medicine Hat backers that such a boat could be built for less than $20,000. Several citizens agreed to take a chance on the venture. William Cousins was elected president and J. W. McLean, CPR agent, was secretary of the newly-formed company. Money was borrowed from the Medicine Hat Bank to start construction of the boat.

31

Capt. Ross had this boat built at the shipyard located below the old hospital, Medicine Hat in 1903. This boat was known as the "Assiniboia Two" and being a small paddle wheeler, low draft, it was able to travel up creeks when they were in flood in the spring, as well as up and down the river.

It should be added that Captain Horatio Hamilton Ross was no fly-by-night operator. He was the son of Sir Charles and Lady Ross of Rossie Castle in Scotland and had been in Canada since the late 1800s. When he fell heir to some money back home, he left, but returned because he felt this part of the world had more to offer in the area of business and excitement. He built a small inboard launch and sailed it from Calgary to Medicine Hat with a companion he referred to as his valet. (The valet called him captain and he was known forevermore as "Captain Ross".) In June 1898 friends in Medicine Hat convinced him that the town needed a good hotel and that he was the one to build it.

The result was the Alberta Hotel, built by contractor H. C. Yuill. (Enlarged and under different ownership, the Alberta Hotel became the Assiniboia, a landmark in the city for many years. It originally contained 63

The Assiniboia Hotel, originally the Alberta Hotel. Built by Mr. Harry Yuill for Capt. Ross in 1898. Remodelled in this view, added to, and known for years as Assiniboia. Burned down Dec. 2, 1944.

rooms of which no fewer than 45 had bathrooms *en suite*, an innovation at the time. A tourist brochure of the time remarked that "bedrooms with baths *en suite* are fully occupied, whilst the less expensive rooms, fitted merely with basin and hot and cold running water, are vacant." The diningroom accommodation provided for 60 persons, the drawingroom, lounge, writing-room and billiard-room "are fitted in the most modern style, and a barber's shop may be found upon the premises." The brochure indicated that the Assiniboia was conducted "upon the European plan, by which meals are paid for as an addition to the charge made for the bedroom. The rates for the latter run from $1 a day upwards." In an interesting little racist note, the brochure indicated that the Assiniboia "unlike many hotels in Western Canada, does not find employment in the kitchen for Oriental labor.")

When Captain Ross built a second boat in 1903, he named the small sternwheeler, Assiniboia Two. It served for several years, taking the Captain's many friends for cruises up and down the river until it was wrecked on a trip to Prince Albert, Saskatchewan in July 1903.

His final and most enterprising craft, *The City of Medicine Hat*, was made from special long timbers ordered from Vancouver with machinery from Eastern Canada. The material was assembled at the "New Edinburgh" boat yards where a Scottish boat builder named McQueen went to work on the 130 foot long, 32 foot wide steamer.

SS City of Medicine Hat paddle wheeler loaded for a picnic excursion, 1907, on the South Saskatchewan River.

The Southern Alberta Navigation Company then negotiated with the government for a long term lease of Galt Island (four miles upstream, near Redcliff) for the sum of one dollar. Concession booths, cookhouse, dance pavillion and other buildings were built on the island in readiness for picnic excursions on the *City of Medicine Hat* paddle steamer.

The boat was launched on July 1, 1907 with Captain Ross, dressed like a British admiral, first on board. Grace Cousins, daughter of the president, broke a bottle of champagne across the bow of the boat and at 3 o'clock the *City of Medicine Hat*, heavily loaded with gaily dressed passengers, sailed off for Galt Island. It was a familiar scene, repeated from

33

Another view of the SS City of Medicine Hat. Captain Ross is identified as the man standing at the rail in the light suit, beside the lifesaver. An inglorious end was in sight for the intrepid river craft.

then until the spring of 1908 when it was decided that coal as a cargo might help make up for the deficit the boat was losing as an excursion vessel. To launch the experiment, company officials and their families started off up the South Saskatchewan for Lethbridge; everything went swimmingly until they reached some rapids near what is now known as Bow Island. After struggling for two hours to get through the rough water, the captain decided to turn back. So much for carrying coal to Medicine Hat by paddle steamer.

In June of the same year, a trip was planned down river to Saskatoon with a load of flour and other freight for ranchers along the route, and for the Saskatchewan city. Near the bridge at Saskatoon, the boat ran into a steel cable that was stretched across the river and which could not be seen by the pilot. The steering mechanism was destroyed and control was lost of the boat. It crashed into one of the bridge piers and quickly turned on its side in the swift current. No lives were lost and some of the freight was recovered, but — as Jack Barrie wrote — "this was the inglorious end of the *City of Medicine Hat*."

SS City of Medicine Hat in mid-stream, South Saskatchewan River, 1907.

SS City of Medicine Hat. Wrecked at bridge in Saskatoon, 1908. Farewell to an era.

While the paddlewheeler was coming to her "inglorious" end, many newcomers to the Medicine Hat area were making a glorious beginning, although it may not have seemed so at the time. Early travellers, especially women alone or with small children, found the rail trip from Eastern Canada lonesome, and even frightening. Mrs. Charlotte Hawthorne recalled in a Provincial Archives interview in August 1957 that she was lonely and scared, and she didn't like the lay of the land either. "The prairies were too rough," she said. She had been accompanied to Winnipeg by another woman, but from there on she was the sole woman passenger. However, when the 20-year-old Peterboro, Ontario bride-to-be reached Medicine Hat she was impressed by the hills and rivers. She was met by her future husband and the Cousins family. Her fiancé was working in the Cousins store.

Mrs. Hawthorne, who went on to bear 10 children, was also frightened by the Indians. "They would just walk right into the house without knocking and sit there," she said. "I would serve them afternoon tea. They never said much as they sat drinking it. I didn't know how to talk to them. I learned later that this was their custom and I got to know and like them. They were very well behaved and sometimes brought little gifts of handcrafts to me."

Mrs. Lucinda Florence Stewart (born Bassett, in Toronto on October 13, 1869) was train-sick all the way West. When the train stopped at Winnipeg on her trip out in 1896 she was asked what she ate: "I didn't eat!"

The Brunswick Hotel, first hotel built in Medicine Hat, in 1883. It was situated on the south corner of what is now Third Street and South Railway Street.

35

she moaned. It was Frank Oliver who advised her father, Richard Thomas Bassett, to come West. Oliver who founded the *Edmonton Bulletin* went on to become Minister of the Interior for Canada, had many glowing words to say about Medicine Hat and surrounding country. Mr. Bassett took up a farm near the town, worked as a section foreman on the CPR and then managed the Cosmopolitan Hotel, the original, which was burned and rebuilt.

Mrs. Stewart also found the manner of the Indians alarming at first. "The stores stayed open until 11 p.m.," she recalled in an Archives interview. "We never pulled our blinds down at night until the Indians started to peek in to see how the white people lived. They weren't unfriendly, but it was unnerving seeing them doing that. I used to feel sorry for some of the children and once when I was invited to visit their camp I saw a child dying. The teepee was filled with smoke and there was no fresh air. Many of them died from tuberculosis. Even after the government moved them to reservations they used to come back and visit the 'white man's squaw', which is what they called me."

Some of the women who moved here in the early years were adaptable, others were not, and more just took their time getting used to the vastly different environment. John and Ida Chamberlin came from Ottawa in 1897 and lived in a boarding house run by a woman who catered to CPR employees. They stayed there until they found a small shack to live in where Mrs. Chamberlin learned to cook. Her first attempt at baking bread was a disaster because she forgot to stoke the stove with wood. Mr. Chamberlin consoled his tearful bride by taking the results to the Blackfoot Indians who relished the gift.

After being coached in baking by some older women in the town, she tried again. She was preoccupied with her efforts until she pulled the bread from the oven. She turned around and was terrified to find 10 Indians had come silently into the kitchen and had seated themselves along the wall behind her. She gave them all a loaf of bread and they left just as silently as they had arrived. It was another bread-less night for the Chamberlins, but at least the cook felt she had learned how to bake it right.

Orlis Chamberlin McCandless, daughter of the pioneer couple, recalled that her sister was born in the shack in January 1899 with only the assistance of a midwife. Her mother often spoke of "social gatherings" which consisted of travelling by bicycle to the "rattle snake pits" outside of town, and by travelling by handcar along the railway tracks to picnic spots.

Once, while visiting a neighbor who had been in the area for a long time and was used to snakes, she met one curled up outside the front door. She ran around to the back and informed the woman, who calmly picked up a rock, walked through the house, opened the front door and squashed the snake flat.

Mrs. McCandless also recalled when her father brought his youngest brother, Phil Chamberlin, to the city to work for the CPR. He lived in the same boarding house the young couple had lived in. A fire somewhere in the town was being fought with a horse-drawn wagon equipped with a bell and casks of water. It had sped past the boarding house, making a din that would wake the dead. Phil, realizing that Mrs. McCandless was alone in her shack at the time, ran over to the structure and began to knock vigorously on the bedroom window. She sprang out of bed, nearly scared to death. "Don't worry," Phil soothed. "There's nothing to be afraid of. The fire is quite a distance from here." Mrs. McCandless couldn't have cared less. "I was sound asleep and still would be if you hadn't started banging on the window!"

As Medicine Hat grew with the arrival of the railway, its fame spread in other ways. For at least two years the central attraction down by the railway station was a live black bear locked inside an eight foot enclosure. The shenanigans of the bear and its spectator-tormentors reached the eyes and ears of people as far away as Detroit, Michigan. The *Detroit Free Press* reported in October 1898 that the bear was "an object of interest and curiosity to the townspeople but more particularly to passengers of trains which stop at Medicine Hat to change engines."

Senator F. W. Gershaw said in his book *Saamis* that the bear was given by Indians to James Hargrave who donated it to the Hospital Board; they moved it to the CPR yard. The bear, called "Nancy," had been around since early in 1892, having outlasted several brushes with two-footed heroes who wished to show off their courage. It made one attempt to escape. The escape attempt came on a Sunday when, as a *Medicine Hat News* reporter explained, "Non-churchgoers had an entertainment all to themselves." According to the reporter, Medicine Hat "seems to have its quota of these degenerate sons of worthier sires." It was a few minutes after the bell on St. Barnabas Church had tolled its last call when the bear broke loose. The newspaper reporter takes up the story from there: "In less than five minutes a motley group of men of all professions and no religions crowded the CPR platform to witness the roping of the wild animal. A tall, slim, but otherwise unidentified merchant acquired a rope and made some ineffectual swings at the bear's head. The rope was then passed to a cowboy who secured the bruin on the first throw."

This photograph shows the famous bear "Nancy" in her pen near the CPR station. It was then located at the end of Toronto Street (now Third Street). Also shown is part of the Medicine Hat business section as it looked in 1889.

Strong hands were lent to drag the bear unceremoniously back to its corral where the "merchant" resumed his role as director of the scenario. He climbed over the top log and played hide and seek with the bear until he managed to get close enough to get him back into his familiar chain. The bear made several savage attacks on the post to which he was attached.

The Detroit newspaper account deals mainly with a rash young man who belonged to "the class known as Smart Alecks" who began grunting at the bear and then throwing sticks and small stones at it. When this failed to elicit the bear's attention, the man resorted to fixing a handkerchief on a stick and flaunting it in the bear's face. He tickled him on the nose, poked him in the ribs, but still he did not get the response he wanted.

Ignoring warnings from others in the audience, the tormentor came close to the pen and thrust his arm between the logs. The bear reared up on her hind legs, towering above the log enclosure. The man was so frightened that he lost his sense of motion. With one deft swipe the bear shredded the man's coat sleeve and made several ugly wounds on his arm.

As the reporter put it: "The bear's revenge was complete. Swift and sudden justice had been meted out and, with shaken nerves and ruined clothing, the smart man made his way to the train, while some unfeeling men in the crowd laughed outright and the grizzly lay down with what resembled a sigh of relief."

Perhaps the young man learned a lesson from that encounter with the bear. The story has been told many times in many places, embellishments increasing with the years. During its entrapment, the bear — Nancy — earned a considerable sum for the hospital fund. She came to an ignominious end when she fell seriously ill and had to be destroyed. The old bruin was variously described as "a black bear" and as a "grizzly". Whichever it was, Medicine Hatters and visitors seem to have enjoyed their captive bruin for several years.

The wreck on the CPR Bridge, Feb. 2, 1889, in which three lives were lost and engine plunged through the river ice.

There were more serious events to keep residents' attention on the workings around the CPR. There were, over the years, several serious train wrecks, the earliest being one that took place on February 2, 1899. An eastbound freight descending a hill slid on icy rails and plowed into another freight which was stopped on the South Saskatchewan River bridge. Engineer William Muir and fireman Robert Long were killed while conductor Benjamin French died later in hospital from injuries he received in the collision. In the caboose with French were Superintendent Niblock and conductor McDonald, who escaped by scrambling out of the caboose on the bridge side before the crash came.

Minor accidents were fairly common. Men lost limbs, were crushed between cars and were scalded by escaping steam and broken pipes. John Cunliffe was coupling cars at Dunmore on December 24, 1891 when he slipped and had his shoulder badly smashed. He was taken to hospital where his right arm was amputated. Fred Fisher, fireman and later engineer on the CPR from 1907 to the time of his retirement in 1947, was originally hired as a "steam man". He was scalded in the face and received an ear injury when a steam pipe exploded in his engine cab. He recovered very well but the accident left him slightly deaf in one ear and with a throat injury that affected him in later years.

Fisher told Jack Barrie in May 1980 of a trainload of 40 cars of cattle from the Crane Lake branch of the old '76 Ranch. He recalled that cattle herded to the track area were terrified of the unfamiliar sound of a train and steam engine up close. Many times cowboys had to pursue the stampeding cattle back to the prairie pasture to round them up again and return them to the holding pens for loading.

Signals between the engineer and brakeman were not as effective as they are on today's modern trains, with the result that many minor accidents occurred. On one occasion the engineer of a freight was warned to stop as he approached a bridge. He tooted the whistle to no avail, the conductor and brakeman at that time being busy frying meat and onions in the caboose. The train kept on going. A bridge crew was at work and had part of the crossing track up on jacks. (This was the reason for the engineer wanting to stop before crossing the bridge.) The crew foreman urged his men to get clear and then yelled to the engineer and fireman to jump, expecting to see the locomotive go cascading into the river. He was amazed to see the train go gaily ahead across the bridge, start up the incline, slow down, stop, then start to back down for another try at it.

The brakeman, his mouth full of freshly-fried onions, sensed something was wrong and rushed to the back platform. Before the train got much reverse momentum he applied the brakes. The only casualty in this comedy of errors was endured by the engineer. He had jumped into a clump of rose bushes and was badly scratched.

On another occasion a car of fresh fish was put behind the engine of a passenger train headed for the East. Going around a bend the car jumped the track and took the train with it. Injuries, except to the fish, were slight. For some days afterwards fish was the staple item on neighboring farmers' tables.

One cold February day a member of a wrecking crew sent to Goose Lake to recover a snow plow lost his life. The wrecking train's engine went out of commission and the crewman, a man named Ward, started to walk into Swift Current but failed to reach his destination, dying from exposure.

Another snowplow incident was more humorous. Engineer Pete Robertson and his fireman Bill Veal were having difficulty getting through heavy drifts. Robertson got angry when he was told he did not come up against the drifts hard enough. Next time he hit it with such force the plow went off the track and the engineer disappeared from sight. Fireman Veal ran up and down yelling, "my mate is killed, my mate is killed." Suddenly Robertson appeared from beneath a mound of snow. "Quit yer yellin'," he told Veal, "I ain't dead *yet!*"

A certain Doctor C. F. Smith, a CPR medical doctor, based in Medicine Hat, adapted what is believed to have been the first automobile to run on CPR rails in Canada. Accommodation for the doctor in his territory was very limited. Roads and trails were primitive, and undependable. Train service for the good doctor was not always convenient or opportune and he had to make trips to outlying points, sometimes in a hurry. So he converted a Model T Ford for use on the track.

This is how the CPR railyards looked from the air in 1981. A far cry from the days when the first ribbon of steel reached the city — in 1883. The photograph was taken for the City of Medicine Hat by Thomas Willock.

A. E. Price, the general superintendent at Calgary — later general manager in Montreal — was so impressed with Dr. Smith's contraption he obtained one for his own use. Eventually the idea snowballed and there were soon at least 21 "track motors" running on CPR rails for the use of operating and maintenance-of-way officers.

One of the duties of the maintenance officers and construction crew foremen was to make sure that fences on both sides of the track were in good order and to protect wherever possible the CPR from any lawsuits over horses and cattle killed by oncoming trains. Range stock sometimes picked inopportune moments to graze in the middle of the track. When an expensive bull or fat steer was run down by a locomotive, lengthy settlement litigation resulted.

One Medicine Hat oldtimer recalled how he was compensated on the spot by Sir William Whyte at the CPR office in Winnipeg. He accepted the $400 for the loss of two horses and damage to several others. The oldtimer considered that fair and Sir William told him something of how the value of stock usually rose after collision with a locomotive. That was not to say that stockmen overpriced their departed animals. Perish the thought. But "nothing improves stock like crossing them with a CPR engine!" Sir William said.

The last steam engine to head out of the Medicine Hat terminal was No. 2372, towing freight to the East at 5:15 p.m. on May 14, 1958. The engineer was S. Herb Wilson and the fireman E. A. Wohlgemuth. It signalled the end of an era, an era that meant a great deal to the development of Medicine Hat as a city. The railway still plays a large part in the daily life of the community but for many, the age of the modern freight train and truck will never quite compensate for the loss of the Days of Steam.

Settlers who travelled west in the CPR Colonist Cars were given a picture of relative comfort aboard. They cooked their own meals, cleaned their own quarters and provided their own entertainment. The contented looks on the faces of the passengers depicted in this poster may have been deceiving. After several thousand miles on hard wooden benches and beds of blankets on slats, the "colonists" were ready for whatever the rigors of the new land offered them.

FOR the comfort and convenience of settlers going to the CANADIAN NORTH-WEST, the

CANADIAN PACIFIC RAILWAY

PROVIDES A SPECIAL FORM OF PASSENGER EQUIPMENT, KNOWN AS

COLONIST CARS

Which are run through to MANITOBA and BRITISH COLUMBIA on the regular Express Train leaving MONTREAL each week day. They are really "SLEEPING CARS," modelled after the style of the first-class "PULLMAN," with upper and lower berths, closets, lavatories, &c., &c., the only difference being that the seats and berths are not upholstered. Occupants may supply their own bedding, or can purchase of the Company's Agents at QUEBEC, MONTREAL, or TORONTO, a mattress, pillow and blanket for $2.50 (10 shillings), which they can retain at the end of their journey.

The accompanying cut shows the interior of a Colonist Car, with a portion of the berths made up for sleeping purposes.

Holders of COLONIST or SECOND-CLASS TICKETS are allowed FREE USE OF THESE CARS FROM THE BEGINNING TO THE END OF THEIR JOURNEY OVER THE CANADIAN PACIFIC RAILWAY.

The Phantom Train of Medicine Hat

The year is 1908, a pretty good year, as years go. Certainly the men working for the Canadian Pacific Railway had little to grumble about, although the winter had been pretty rough: lots of snow; lots of snow to plow. But it was June and the spring was good and summer looked even better. Then came the Phantom Train.

Bob Twohey was engineer and Gus Day the fireman on an engine travelling from Medicine Hat to Dunmore. It was about 11 o'clock when the strangest thing happened. As the engine proceeded towards Dunmore, where they were to couple up to the Spokane Flyer, a train appeared before them, approaching on the single line that wound around the cutbanks before climbing a steep grade from the valley to the tableland of prairie.

Twohey and Day were not expecting any trains coming toward them and commonsense dictated that this was not happening. Their job was to take the engine to Dunmore and pick up the Flyer. The Flyer did not enter Medicine Hat and there were no other scheduled trains at that time.

"The headlight of the approaching train seemed to be about the size of a wagon wheel," engineer Day told Andrew Staysko later. Staysko retired in 1955 after 48 years in the service of the CPR. "The reflection ahead was as though the firebox was open on the locomotive," Day said.

He shouted to fireman Twohey and made for the gangplank to jump. Twohey reached instinctively for the brake valve, but his hand stopped in mid-air. The approaching train whistled a warning signal for the curve around which Twohey and Day's engine had just come.

Day was stunned; he stood at the doorway of the cab. Twohey was similarly immobile. His hand remained suspended over the brake valve. As they stood there in silence, their engine still moving, a string of phantom coaches sped past them on non-existent tracks!

"The coach windows were lighted and crew members waved a greeting from places where crew members would be expected to be found waving greetings as trains pass one another," Staysko recounted.

Then the phantom train disappeared.

Twohey and Day looked at each other in silence, and went about their jobs of getting into Dunmore and coupling up to the Spokane Flyer. Each was fearful of what the other may have thought, had they expressed their feelings. They reached Dunmore, coupled to the Flyer and the night ended without any further incidents.

Two weeks went by before the engineer and fireman met on a street in Medicine Hat. Feeling safer with the passage of time since the incident, they found the courage to talk about what had happened on that strange night. They admitted that they were thankful to learn that what had happened had at least been shared by both. But it certainly left them with an eerie feeling.

It worried Twohey in an additional way: he told Day that he had been to a fortune teller in the city. The seer told him he would die within a month. Since he was in good health, this bit of candid news was disconcerting, to say the least.

"I'm going to lay off for a couple of trips," Twohey told Day. There was no sense in tempting fate. Day agreed, although he decided to stay on the job.

A few nights passed. Nothing untoward happened. Then one night Day was on the same engine, going about his duties. He was jolted to rigid attention when he heard a gasp from J. Nicholson, the engineer who replaced Twohey when he booked off sick. "What the hell's *that*?" Nicholson yelled.

They were at exactly the same spot where the phantom train had appeared a few weeks before. The train came straight at them, whistle blowing and headlight gleaming like a beacon in the pitch blackness. At a crucial moment, the train seemed to veer onto a separate track and pass them. Again, crew members waved greetings from their respective positions in its engine and cars. The two men were stunned to silence as they headed into Dunmore to complete their shift. The phantom train again had vanished into the dark toward Medicine Hat.

On the morning of July 8, 1908, Gus Day reported for duty. He was assigned to yard duty. Fireman H. Thompson took Day's place on the engine that was to make a morning trip to Dunmore to pick up the Spokane Flyer. This time the job was to take the Flyer east to Swift Current. The engineer was J. Nicholson. The train pulled out of Medicine Hat and headed into the hills.

Up until two miles out of Medicine Hat, the trip was uneventful. But as they approached the spot where the phantom train had been seen on two separate occasions, another train appeared. This time it was broad daylight — and the train was real!

Passenger train number 514 was barrelling in from Lethbridge. With brakes screeching on the in-bound passenger train and the single engine heading for Dunmore, the inevitable resulted: a terrible, grinding collision.

When the smoke had cleared and rescue teams had reached the scene, the tragic toll was taken. Both engineers were killed. A fireman named Gray and a conductor named Mallet, both on the Lethbridge train were killed, as were seven passengers on that fateful journey.

Thompson, the fireman on the outbound engine, escaped by jumping at the last moment. He recalled later that just before the crash he had seen a farmer standing on a hill, waving his arms. The gesture was misinterpreted as a friendly salute. Apparently the farmer could see both the engine and the passenger train as they headed towards each other on the single track and realized that a crash was coming.

44

The warning given by the farmer was the third to be given — two "phantom" warnings, and one that was extremely real. Tragically, all were ignored. Fireman Day was the luckiest man alive that morning. He was firing up an engine in the yard back at Medicine Hat when the news arrived about the wreck. Engineer Nicholson was not so lucky. He was in charge of that engine on its way to Dunmore. He had seen the phantom.

Even stranger is the fact that the engineer on the oncoming passenger train had also seen the phantom. He was Bob Twohey, who had overcome his fear of the phantom train and had come back to work. Unfortunately for him he had been picked to drive the engine of the train that followed the Phantom Train route to Medicine Hat!

The so-called Phantom Train, the #514 Passenger Train from Lethbridge, collided with an engine out of Medicine Hat on July 8, 1908 on the line from Medicine Hat to Dunmore. Four CPR employees on the engine and train were killed; seven passengers were killed.

The settlers came from everywhere, from Europe, the United Kingdom, and in growing numbers from the United States. This trainload came from Colorado in March 1914.

"An Unmixed Blessing"

"In the mad rush to secure settlers, the North West, like other countries, has thrown its gates wide open to all nationalities and creeds. While the settlement of our broad prairies is certainly a thing to be desired, yet when the attempt is made to blend these various nationalities with their inherited prejudices against each other into one nation, our liberal immigration policy may be looked upon as an unmixed blessing."

The editor of the *Medicine Hat Times* was taking issue with the policies of the Prime Minister of the time, Sir Mackenzie Bowell (1894-96). Bowell had been Minister of Customs in the Macdonald government, Minister of Militia in the John Abbott government and Minister of Trade and Commerce in the John Thompson government. He became Prime Minister upon the death of Sir John Thompson in 1894. He had put his "benedictions" (according to the *Times* editor) on such disparate groups as Mormons, Mennonites, Icelanders and Skye Crofters.

"These peoples," the editor puffed, "are hardly the stuff out of which a strong, sound patriotic community is made."

Of the "motley" collection, the Icelanders were "materially the most prosperous" but when they vote "they are said to be generally weak." He did not elaborate on what constitutes a "weak voter" but went on to defame the Icelanders further by declaring they were the type to "decline the duties of citizenship."

The North West does not want "shreds of outlandish nationalities and equivocal sects," the Times editor wrote in reference to the large numbers of Mormons, Icelanders and Scots fishermen from the Hebrides who were flocking into the area. Despite the dire warning of the Times editor, the "motley" collection of immigrants turned into solid citizens. This group posed in front of the Hewitt Hardware. Joe Hewitt is holding his son Robert Leigh by the hand.

Rev. Jas. Herald

Mrs. Jas. Herald

Rev. Chas. Stephens

Group of
Early Day Medicine Hat
DISTINGUISHED
CITIZENS

Mr. Henry Stewart

Dr. Calder
Mr. St. George   Mr. Wm. Cousins

Rev. Tudor

Mr. J. K. Drinnan

Mr. & Mrs. Shaw

Mr. & Mrs. Jas. Hargrave

The Mormons, on the other hand, were fine enough folk, particularly since they had eschewed polygamy, but Mr. Bowell "is hardly to be congratulated on having to appear at once as the champion of Jesuitism in the East and Mormonism in the West." The editor thought it was outrageous to "transport the herdsmen and fishermen of Skye from the mild air of the Hebrides and set them farming in the North West." (The Skye referred to is one of the Inner Hebrides islands off northwest Scotland; with its hilly terrain and many lochs, sheep and cattle raising and fishing are its main occupations. The weather there can scarcely be termed "mild.")

"What the North West wants," the editor continued in his front page editorial, is "not shreds of outlandish nationalities and equivocal sects" but "the Canadian immigration which is now peopling Dakota, Minnesota, Montana and Washington Territory."

A few decades were to pass before the tide of Canadians (many born elsewhere) into those American territories would end and the flow would reverse, bringing settlers of Scandinavian, German and British origin into Medicine Hat and other Western Canadian communities. The impetus was to be the terrible Dust Bowl that the American mid-West would become. Although, on July 26, 1911 the district passenger agent for Canadian Pacific Railway said "from the number of inquiries about western rail rates and about western lands, it looks as if the Canadian prairies will shortly have a strong tincture of settlers from New York State." Thompson said travel westward from the Eastern States was unusually heavy.

Ontarians were also investing heavily in the West. Ontario land offices sold about 425,000 acres between February and June in 1911. "These have been intending settlers and speculators, but the speculators are in the minority," Thompson said.

Time and a more enlightened attitude has shown that the "outlandish nationalities and equivocal sects" have become good citizens indeed. The reluctance, on the other hand, of the more timid and "acceptable" nationalities to rush to populate the prairies, particularly before the railroad was completed and the Mounted Police had driven out the lawless elements, was understandable. But one can hardly condemn the government for allowing in all those Europeans and hardier types who would gamble on their chances for a good life in a new and untested land.

The CPR, according to a Government of Alberta publication of the day, said that the Railway "in disposing of the large acreage of farm land which it still holds, is endeavoring to act not only as a land selling agency but as a colonization agency. That is to say, the speculative element is eliminated, and the land is now being sold to those who will develop and reside upon it."

Then the prejudice creeps in: "This principle is designed to appeal to the best class of land worker in North America, the British Isles and Northern Europe. Special terms are offered likely to encourage the immigration of skilled agriculturists who may possess only moderate means."

The terms included: the period over which the purchase of land was spread has been extended from 10 to 20 years, unpaid instalments bearing interest at the rate of 6 per cent per annum; to approved married men with agricultural experience, the CPR offered a loan of the value of $2,000 (also repayable in 20 years) to be expended under the supervision of the company in the erection of a house, barn and other necessary buildings, the

This is a very important photo for the historical record of Medicine Hat. It was taken on the steps of the old Court House. A group of gentlemen all wearing ribbons with carnations, "Old Timers of 1883." A group of Medicine Hat pioneers in one photo is quite rare. All are identified. *Front Row:* (Left to Right) Stan Hay, Bert Bassett, C. Coulter, ? Porter. *Second Row:* (Left to Right) Capt. Johnson, Jim MacDonald, R. D. Porter, Michael Leonard, Thos. Tweed, J. H. G. Bray, Harry Ireland, ? Moorehouse, Bob McCutcheon, Harry Tweed, L. C. Brown, Vincent Minneszewsky, Tom Bassett. *Third Row:* (Left to Right) W. Huckvale, W. Cousins, J. Hay. *Fourth Row:* (Left to Right) L. Hay, R. Rutherford, J. Clark, J. C. Coulter. *Fifth Row:* H. Bray (top left), W. T. Finlay, Joe Leonard, (centre doorway) J. Reid, J. McCutcheon (top right).

construction of fences and a well and the breaking of a certain area of land; the company also was willing to provide approved settlers with high-grade cattle, sheep and hogs on a loan basis to the value of $1,000.

According to the government publication, this in effect was equivalent to "hand-picking" the immigrant, "the man who declares his intention of taking up residence and placing his land under cultivation, thereby becoming an important factor in the development of the West."

For some years after immigration began in earnest, Medicine Hat was not considered a prime location, particularly that part of the city which is now the most populated. Until the arrival of the railway construction workers, the river side of the area did not appear to have any permanent attractions for either native or white people. Although a river terrace site was used by the Cree during the hunting season, the only resident was the part-Indian trader Roderick Ross who, in 1875, settled nearby at the creek that now bears his name.

Explorers like Captain John Palliser had passed the site by. The North West Company and the Hudson's Bay Company trading posts were established in the Saskatchewan basin at what they considered more advantageous locations: the confluence of the Red Deer and South Saskatchewan Rivers and the junction of the Oldman and Belly Rivers.

Even those fur traders and wolfers from the United States, described in a previous chapter, preferred seclusion for some of their nefarious activities and shunned this locality. The only native encampments, described by Palliser, lay well to the north. Because the more favorable physical conditions on the higher ground to the south offered a timber supply to the Indians and a strategically placed control point to the North West Mounted Police, the early overland trails also bypassed Medicine Hat, crossing the South Saskatchewan only at easily forded points to converge upon the Cypress Hills.

The naturally graded, flat floor of the Ross Creek area must have seemed a solution to the railway men's problems of which way to turn once

View City of Medicine Hat from Crescent Heights area, year 1915.

they had left the glacial spillway that had brought them as far as Dunmore. There was an assured supply of river water, timber in the Cypress Hills 40 miles south that could be used for construction purposes, and outcrops of workable coal seams. Beyond the local, low terraced banks of the river, the regional gradient of the area increased westward toward the Rocky Mountain and the suitability of this easy bridging point must have been apparent to the railway men. Local historian J. W. Morrow contends, however, that the railway bridge site was fixed further upstream than originally intended because of questions of title.

The dozen or so people who were anticipating the arrival of the railway track were joined before the end of 1883 by about 200 more. The establishment of a railway bridge, ferry and railway depot was the first phase of settlement on the south bank of the river. The Mounties came, as already mentioned, in 1883. They were followed in 1885 by some troops from Nova Scotia, and Rocky Mountain Rangers, organized out of Fort Macleod, who arrived at the time of the North West Rebellion scare. The troops and Rangers stayed for about four months.

The early settlers were chiefly occupied with the railway, coal and the land. They lived in railway boxcars, in log cabins made from local cottonwood and in tents on land that was not yet officially conveyed. Squatters began sod-breaking for cereal and root crops. They also grazed about 100 head of cattle. In the same year, two Experimental farms were established at Dunmore and Stair by the CPR. Maize (corn) and garden vegetables were also introduced and successfully ripened on both farms. In 1885 and 1887 the Canadian Agriculture, Coal and Colonization Company acquired land in the same vicinities for the settlers but by 1888 both these colonies had become primarily turned over to the raising of stock.

Credit is given to James Sanderson for bringing cattle and horses down to Medicine Hat from Fort Walsh. He was born in 1848 in Fort Garry, the son of a Hudson's Bay Company officer. In 1869 he joined with other English-speaking residents to oppose Louis Riel's attempt to form a provisional government. In February 1870 he was one of 48 men taken prisoner by Riel's forces and was in prison when the rebels executed Thomas Scott.

In 1872 Sanderson married Maria McKay, daughter of Edward McKay,

51

a leading trader. In the following year Sanderson went west as an Indian trader and settled at Fort Walsh when the North West Mounted Police built the post in 1875. During the next few years he was a scout and interpreter for the Police, as well as carrying on freighting and ranching activities.

In 1882, learning where the CPR would cross the South Saskatchewan River, he moved to the future site of Medicine Hat. After the town was established he became a prosperous rancher and operated a livery stable and contracting business. In 1896, when taking a shipment of cattle to England, the *Montreal Herald* described him as a "stalwart Scotsman with the frame of a Hercules, and the suspicion of a strain of the Cree chieftain's blood in his bearing." He died in Medicine Hat on December 6, 1902.

It wasn't long before there was a good market for beef. Nevertheless, there were those small ranchers who complained that the big ranchers would eventually drive them out.

To help dispell such thoughts, Sir John Lister-Kaye, General Manager of the Canadian Agriculture, Coal and Colonization Company, wrote to the *Medicine Hat News* on January 1, 1890: "I hear with regret that the impression has been made that in consequence of our having so large a supply of beef, mutton and pork always ready, we shall destroy the small ranchers who have from time to time a few head of cattle, sheep or pigs to sell. . . I wish most earnestly to assure you and Medicine Hat and its surroundings that the above-mentioned impression is an entirely erroneous one. We shall at all times be happy to constitute ourselves the market for those ranchers who have stock to sell and I hope that it will be clearly understood that we are anxious to provide markets and thus do good to the ranchers and the country generally."

By 1885 Medicine Hat had become a village in which church and school were represented and the services of a doctor, a carpenter and a

The Federal Government and the CPR encouraged immigration and population of the West. As well as filling up the land with settlers, there was a very real need for skilled craftsmen and laborers to create the towns and cities to hold the country together. This photo shows construction (left) of the Royal Bank building in 1913, at the corner of Toronto Street (now Third Street) and Sixth Avenue. The Royal Bank still operated from this site in 1982.

lawyer were available. The first store was established in 1883 to serve the railway crews and by 1884 South Railway Street boasted a modest frontage of two hotels, four stores, two bakeries, a drugstore, a dressmaker and a brewery. Dr. Walter R. Hawke, son of John Hawke who operated a ranch on the Gros Ventre Creek south of Dunmore, was the first white male born in Medicine Hat.

The first "store" has an interesting background and beginning. William Cousins arrived on May 10, 1883 with a 10 horse team and wagon loaded with saleable supplies. Originally bound for Calgary, he and a partner decided to stay in Medicine Hat for a while. They arrived at dusk; the river was in flood. After pitching a tent, the two men tossed a coin to see who would have a meal with the dollar they had between them. The partner won; he ate.

Next morning, with the materials they had brought with them, they went into the drygoods business, right on the spot. The goods were displayed in and around the wagon and tent. Miss Grace Cousins, daughter, recalled the story her father told of his first customer:

"The man asked to be outfitted from outside in. From underwear to boots and overalls. Dad didn't have a mirror so the customer didn't know that what he was putting on didn't fit very well. No matter. He wasn't in a mood to be fussy. 'How much?' he asked. Dad told him. He was amazed. 'Boy, are you a tenderfoot. In Fort Macleod this would have cost twice as much.'

"He unrolled some money from a large wad and handed both to Dad. 'Keep this for me,' he said. 'Hell,' Dad said, 'I don't have a safe.' 'Keep it in the flour barrel,' the stranger directed. The man came and went for some time, taking some money from his roll in the barrel. He trusted Dad and never counted it. One day he took it all.

"Shortly afterwards, Dad found out the man was an outlaw from Montana. The Mounties arrested him for stealing horses. They were taking him to Prince Albert to the penitentiary when he suggested a game of poker. 'But I can't play shackled," he explained. The Mounties let him loose and he got away. Another patrol spotted him on a Mountie's horse and carrying a Mountie's gun. They shot him on the spot. And that was my father's first customer in the first store in Medicine Hat." (The *Medicine Hat News* states that Donald Archibald of Halifax, Nova Scotia was the first merchant in Medicine Hat. He had a store on the North Side of the river.)

While the prosperity of Medicine Hat is usually associated with the fortuitous discovery by accident of a cheap supply of natural gas by a CPR water well crew at Alderson in 1883, the growth and development of the city have been determined by a number of physical and human factors. These factors have changed in importance over the years.

To live successfully in this distinctive part of the Prairies, people have had to adjust their perspectives, values and habits to a spacious and fickle physical environment as well as to changing economic and social conditions. To illustrate, here are accounts of some of the experiences of early settlers:

Miss Margaret Ireland had been a resident of Medicine Hat for 84 years when she was interviewed for the *Medicine Hat News* on June 29, 1967. Her father, Thomas W. Ireland, travelled to the end of the steel,

53

Miss Margaret Ireland

Dr. C. E. Smyth

Medicine Hat, in 1883. His wife made the journey by train with six children. It took three days just to cover the distance between Regina and Medicine Hat.

The Irelands' first home was a CPR work car which the Indians peered into at night. Later the family moved to a house on what is now South Railway Street and in September 1903 they moved again to Second Street (which was known at that time as Main Street).

During the early years water was delivered to homes in a barrel and milk in a jug. Both often arrived in the form of frozen blocks in winter months. Mr. Ireland opened and operated the first brewery in the city. The Saskatchewan Brewery was situated on the present site of the Central Block and was opened in 1884.

Miss Ireland worked in the post office for seven years and later served as receptionist to Charles E. Smythe, physician and surgeon. When the Medical Arts Clinic opened in October 1927 she became keeper of records, serving in that capacity until her retirement in 1965.

Mrs. A. S. Bomford, who came to the city in 1886 as an infant, recalled what the community was like when white residents totalled no more than 250. There were few homes, she recalled. It was a solid "tent city", those that were not set up by new arrivals were occupied by Indians, the difference being that "one was referred to as a tent, the other as a teepee."

For many pioneers the best of both worlds was to be found by commuting between farm and town homes, summer and winter. Mrs. Olla Mildred Barnes was born at Dunmore on August 12, 1893. Her parents homesteaded there but moved in 1897 across the South Saskatchewan River because grazing on the 1,289 deeded acres and 640 leased acres of land was better. The family owned a home in the town and divided their time between both places. "Father stayed alone on the ranch in winter," Mrs. Barnes said. Her sister Ina was born on August 2, 1899 and brother George on December 13, 1903.

"Our nearest neighbor on the ranch was William Winterburn, who lived six miles up the river," Mrs. Barnes said. "It was a seven hour drive to the town from the ranch. We would stop and make a meal from a fire made from cow chips. During the winter Dad would get into town every three weeks, but from Christmas to Easter we never saw him at all. It was a very lonely life."

Mrs. Barnes said cattle were kept in open corrals, except for the bulls and stallions which were under a roof shelter. They were led out for food and water. "Dad grew corn for sileage, which was stored in underground silos. He always kept one team and some saddle horses in the barn in the winter. After a storm, he and other ranchers would saddle up and hit for the coulees where the cattle, sensing a storm was coming, would bunch up. Sometimes the cowboys had to get off their horses and coax the cattle to get to their feet to keep them from freezing to death. It took a lot of nerve. Those Galloway cattle were wild and hard to handle. As long as you stayed in the saddle they recognized you as boss. They wouldn't charge a horse. Dad would never allow dogs on the ranch. The cows thought they were wolves or coyotes and would charge them. The dogs would run to you for protection, and then where were you?"

Mrs. Barnes said her mother would keep a quarter of beef in the barn in the winter. "She or us kids would cut a piece of the frozen carcass off as

L. B. Cochrane Home formerly on the corner of Sixth Ave., and Fourth Street, S.E.

we needed it. Winters were colder then. The diet was supplemented in the summer with cured hams. Two or three of them always hung in the cellar. The chickens we kept in town were always useful and everyone in the family knew how to cook. Mom kept gardens at both places and Dad baked the bread.

"Rattlesnakes and bull snakes were common, even in town in the stable. But I don't remember having any fear walking through the grass at the ranch.

The bride of William A. Woolfrey Sr. did not have such confidence in the new country she had come to with her soldier husband in 1918. Mr. Woolfrey, who was born in Dorset, England in 1884, had had time to become acclimatized to Medicine Hat where he had worked at the power plant until his enlistment in 1915. "You call this God's country?" Mrs. Woolfrey asked him after she had had her face frozen in a ride by horse and sleigh into town from their homestead on the present site of the airport. "If this is God's country, well give it back to Him — and a pound of tea for takin' it!"

Mrs. Woolfrey said, "People used to say to me when I came over that there were lots of English and Scots and they thought they had got to Heaven and shut the gate after them. But it didn't seem that way for me." She'd had a good job in England and the loneliness of living on a homestead with infrequent trips to town depressed her. The three hour ride by sleigh or buggy to their only friends was not a pleasant journey for her either.

"We got lost in the snow once but we had been told 'give the horse her head and she'll get you home.' She got us home all right — but not at the right end of the property." Mrs. Woolfrey said she had a "natural affinity" for cats and dogs and bulls, but horses were different. "They somehow sensed I didn't like them. The only way I could get the horse to go for me was to put blinders on him. When he couldn't turn around and see me at the reins he would pull, but not before that." The Woolfreys lived in a two story log house — one of the first homes built in the Medicine Hat area, situated 1/8 mile east of the airport. They, with a son William, ran a dairy herd of registered Ayrshire cattle. Bill married and built a new home on the property. His parents lived in the old house in retirement.

55

When they died, Bill and his wife closed the doors of the old family home leaving everything intact, just as his parents had left it. The house remains today as a complete unit, full of beautiful old furniture and memorabilia of an early pioneer couple.

The weather played a big part in the economic and social life of the residents in and around Medicine Hat. The weather seemed different then. Herb Smith, who was born in the town in 1911 and whose father came here in 1890, recalled that the chinook winds were more frequent and lasting in the "old days." "They swept all the snow away," he said. "The winters were not as mild as they are today but the summers were warmer. We used to get extreme heat and extreme cold."

The Smiths, who once ran a small store across from the hospital, also drilled one of the early gas wells in the area. "In 1917 Dad and I drilled a well in the Milk River sands. We used rods with a solid bit and made ground by pounding it. It took us three days to get through a boulder we struck at the 500 foot level. Dad didn't know anything much about handling gas but he learned by experience.

"The gas came out of the ground at about 250 to 300 pounds of pressure and had to be reduced to about six or eight ounces pressure before it was legal to have it in the house. There must have been a leak in the gas house where the regulator was because Dad was knocked over when he walked in there. Luckily, he didn't catch fire because the gas house was blown all over the place. He was lying in the snow for half an hour before he revived. Very painfully, he walked all the way back to the hospital. The first we saw of him was when he came into the house all covered with bandages."

Mr. Smith's mother had met a fortune-teller who had predicted an accident would occur to someone close to her. "She came into the store and told Mother that someone she knew was in pain about the hands and face, someone who spent a great deal of time in the store. Dad was subject to arthritis attacks and Mother worried about him. She was really surprised that the fortune-teller was right. She figured later that the woman was telling her about Dad at about the same time the explosion was taking place."

Like many others of British origin, the Smiths had to adapt to a country with customs which were not entirely compatible with what they had been accustomed to in their former homeland. For some time there was mistrust or wariness about fully accepting immigrants from Europe and other parts of the world. A good experience went a long way to dispelling such prejudice.

"One day Dad was trying to get a big pipe off an old flatdeck truck. He was using a pry block and when the block tipped he was sent sailing through the air. It knocked him out. A husky hobo came along who was working his way across the country on the rods. He pitched in and helped Dad. Dad offered to pay him but he refused but stayed on as a hired man for three months. He was Hungarian. Very clean. 'Must be from a good family,' my Mother said. Dad offered him a dollar a day but he would only take 75 cents a day. Dad gave him a dollar anyway. He was a very good worker and we really missed him when he left."

Mr. Smith enjoyed the early social life in Medicine Hat. The United Farmers of Alberta hall was the scene of Saturday dances. It had beautiful hardwood on the floor, that was 20 feet wide and 50 feet long. "Grandparents, parents and kids, all went to the dance," he said. "A six year old kid danced just like a grown-up." Mrs. Ralph Hargrave agreed, adding that drinking on the premises was frowned upon, especially by youngsters. "A good-looking boy who came to one dance drunk was ostracized by everybody," she said. There were other prejudices. "This was a very social town," Mrs. Hargrave said. "No Chinese or Indians came to the dance. They were very fine people but they had their own friends."

Violet Pearl Sykes was born in Helena, Montana, in 1892 and went to business college in Seattle, a course which did not outfit her for the life she was to lead with one of Canada's top rodeo performers and champions, Emery LeGrandeur. "I met Emery when I was at the Spencer Ranch in the Milk River area in 1907," Mrs. LeGrandeur said. "I always loved horseback riding, which is why I was staying with this relative at the ranch. The cook had the day off once and my cousin asked me to get a meal for this cowboy who showed up late.

"One of those strong-backed, weak-headed fellows who have come over to see the new girl at the ranch?" she asked. Cowboys would ride many a mile to have a look at the all-too-few females who showed up in the ranch country. "I'll give him a good dose of strychnine," she said. "I didn't know that he was standing right outside the door and heard every word I said. He wouldn't speak to me even after I made a good meal for him. He was so mad. I used to go down to see him break horses at the corral but he still wouldn't forgive me, or even let on that he knew I was there.

"However, one day I was put to hazing the horses and he had to yell at me about something. I smiled and he smiled and pretty soon we started talking. We eventually became friends and got married in 1911. I rode on roundups and drove cattle in the wintertime. When Emery became a professional cowboy and won the world championship bronc riding, we lived just like gypsies. That went on for a long time, but I enjoyed it. Wherever his interests were, mine were too."

Medicine Hat women had to be adaptable. Their men were away a lot of the time. It was necessary to develop talents useful in times of loneliness. Children were an asset and a blessing. Families tended to be large and close-knit. There were seven girls and six boys in the Bray family, well-known Medicine Hat area pioneers. They were the children of John Henry Gresham Bray and Jemima McKay. Mr. Bray served in India with the 10th Royal Hussars and in Ireland during the "Fenian troubles". He was credited with being the second volunteer to join the North West Mounted Police in Toronto in 1873. Certainly a pioneer, ironically J. H. G. Bray was not considered an "oldtimer" by W. Henry McKay in an article about the early history of Medicine Hat in Canadian Cattlemen in July, 1951. McKay said Bray (his uncle) could not be classed an oldtimer since he had not come to Medicine Hat until June 1892! Mrs. Bray's father, Edward McKay, was the man who reported the Cypress Hills Massacre to the authorities and was later made a Justice of the Peace.

One son, Colin Bray, born at Pincher Creek, Alberta in 1888, told an interviewer about his youth working on Walker Brothers Ranch in 1906, the most severe of all winters. He had two brothers, Harry and Reg, who became well-known rodeo cowboys. Their specialty was the relay race. In this competition, each participant had two horses. The rider would ride off half a mile, change the saddle and harness onto the second horse, remount

J. H. G. Bray, Mrs. Bray, and nine of their 10 children. It was families such as the Brays, originally from England, who settled in Medicine Hat area and brought prosperity to the city. Standing, left to right, are Mrs. Johnson, Mrs. Mike Crockford (Nellie), Harry Bray, Reg Bray, Mrs. Billy Crockford (Clara), Collin Bray. Mrs. Bill Feeney (Lillian), Mrs. Erickson (Etta) and Bertha (one of twins, who died in 1926. Her sister died in 1918). Seated in front are Colonel Bray and his wife. The family posed in front of the original family home on Steel Street which was later torn down and the site became a ball field.

and keep changing horse and equipment every half mile throughout the two mile race. "The man who could change a saddle fast had a big advantage," Colin Bray said. "When they introduced racing stock into the stampede it reduced the popularity of the relay race."

The famous Medicine Hat Stampede was the social event of the year and will be described later in the book.

In the September 1974 issue of the Bulletin of the Medicine Hat and District Historical Society, John M. McLaren talked about some of the problems faced by pioneers in preserving food. "The care of meat was a problem," he said. "I came across a couple once with a small sod smoke-house using dried cow chips to smoke their meat. They had raised the pig and now had to save the meat for winter. They merited my pity and admiration. Some people cut up the meat after it had cooled overnight and put the hams and shoulders in brine. The bacon was rubbed with dry salt and smoked with green willow or other wood if available. All the rest was made into sausage, fried and covered with lard in a crock and kept in a cool place.

"Every bit of fat was rendered and saved. A beef animal could be killed after freeze-up, cut up and wrapped and stored in a deep snow bank. In later years 'Beef Rings' were organized — a dozen neighbors each agreeing to supply an animal. It was killed and cut up by a capable person and distributed among members, each getting a different portion each time until he had received practically the equivalent of the whole animal. Ice was cut on sloughs or dams and stored in sawdust or straw. An 'ice well' frozen gradually during the winter and kept covered would serve as a refrigerator well into the next summer.

"It was difficult to keep the bread dough warm overnight when the fires went out and houses were cold. The bread pan was covered with robes, fur coats, anything that would protect its warmth. One woman I know confessed she took it to bed with her! But that worked too well and the dough overflowed onto her feet!

"Sourdough was saved from time to time and used to start bread or

58

make biscuits or pancakes. In wooded areas settlers made lye from wood ashes and by adding it to melted tallow made their own soap. In many places the water for drinking and cleaning was difficult to obtain. People hauled water from sloughs or established wells, others had dugouts which caught the spring runoff. In winter they gathered snow and melted it in barrels or in metal tanks over a straw fire for the stock. After shingle roofs came along, rain water was gathered into a cistern and even filtered through a brick box which gave reasonably good drinking water."

Mr. McLaren's ancestors came from Ontario in 1876 by rail to St. Paul, Minnesota and then by barge down the Red River to Emerson, Manitoba. They followed straight west along the International Boundary to Clearwater and Crystal City — 100 miles — crossing the Pembina River enroute. They used a wagon box for a boat to carry their chattels. The stock swam.

"This country, in comparison to much of the open country in Saskatchewan and Alberta, had many advantages," McLaren said. "Along the streams there was much wild fruit, firewood and logs for building. Game and fish were plentiful. Fruit was dried rather than canned. Although these people improvised a lot, their struggle for existence was not so severe as those on the open prairie."

McLaren said that prairie fires were an ever-present danger to early settlers, particularly those living on bald plains. "There were no roads or fire guards to stop them," he said. "Thousands of acres were sometimes burned over. To protect their buildings, homesteaders plowed furrows around the outside and burned the grass between the furrows or burned a backfire strip to combat the oncoming flames. Cowboys would kill an animal and drag the carcass or hide on two ropes between their saddle horses along the line of fire. If water was available, wet gunnysacks were used to smother and beat out the flames."

Mrs. Lucinda Florence Stewart was 13 when she came to Medicine Hat on August 24, 1883. She recalled Indian tom-toms keeping her awake at night and the local residents' dances held at the old Immigration Hall. At that time, church was being held outdoors with a Calgary minister presiding. At 15 years old she attended her first dance. "It was very exciting," she said. "Most of the young Mounties came and there were far more men than women so we all got lots of dances. After a box social at midnight, we danced until 5 a.m."

On the subject of the Indians scaring people by staring in windows, Mrs. Gail Holt Klasky told the author in August 1979 about a prank played on her relatives by her great-grandfather. "He came out with his three sons from England," she said. "He did not care for the West. Rather uncivilized, he called it. In order to discourage the boys from staying, he tried to scarce them with tales of the wild Indians.

"One Saturday night as the boys were heading out for a night on the town, a group of terrible looking Indians appeared from nowhere. The boys ran for home. It was my grandfather and some of his friends dressed up to look like the real thing."

Two of the boys were not deterred, however, and stayed to become prosperous residents. Mrs. Klasky's grandfather homesteaded in what is now the Crescent Heights area in the city. William Klasky's grandmother, Mrs. Ellen Lynch, celebrated her 104th birthday in 1981.

Main Street (now Second St.) Medicine Hat looking east about 1912, 1913.

The city's natural resources, the services offered by the CPR, and effective propaganda by the railway, the City and the Chamber of Commerce led to an influx of comparatively young immigrants. The distribution of homesteads was generally related to the distance from the railway, as was true right across the West. The ethnic mix was typical of that in the American West, with perhaps a larger number of British coming to this part of the world than to the U.S. In addition, so many Americans also arrived during the boom days that their national holiday, July 4th, was celebrated here almost as much as July 1st.

The Americans melded in very well; others took longer to become part of the Canadian mosaic. Discrimination was shown toward Orientals, but there were few of them; most were working in cafes and restaurants and hand laundries where they remained "out of sight and out of mind", abandoned to their own devices after the CPR no longer required them for "coolie" labor. The Germans came in such numbers that discrimination against them during the two World Wars was not extreme, although there were instances, as related in other parts of this book.

In the Canadian census of 1961, over one-fifth of the population of Medicine Hat gave German as their native tongue, giving a startling indication of the influences these industrious nationals had on the community. The figure shown is that 5,707 out of a total population of 24,484 spoke German first, English second.

The largest group of these speakers of German originated in Bessarabia, a region in Russia. They either emigrated from there or were first generation Canadians of Bessarabian parents. Doctor Elvire Eberhardt, writing in *Saamis Review,* noted that emigration from Bessarabia can be traced back to 1857, but Canada did not benefit from it until the beginning of this century. It was after the CPR reached Calgary in 1883 and provisions made for homesteads that they came in large numbers. Those coming prior to 1927 were, almost without exception, farmers, although some of the men worked at other jobs until their farms could sustain them and their families. They spoke a dialect which persists to this day, but mostly among the older residents who moved to the city to retire.

Fairly typical of the early Bessarabians to arrive in the district was Andrew Klaiber who settled in Josephburg after being nine weeks in transit from Russia. Klaiber's father and mother unloaded their supplies at Dun-

60

more on May 10, 1898 after being met at the CPR station by another Bessarabian who had arrived there three years earlier.

The family built a sod house with walls four feet high and a floor that was two feet beneath the lay of the land, making the hut walls six feet in height. They cut trees in the Cypress Hills for logs and purchased slabs from a Cypress Hills mill to make the roof. Beds and furniture were homemade from lumber from the same mill. Utensils were those they brought with them, plus some purchased in Medicine Hat.

Life was simple but harsh in the one room "soddie", six miles from the Cypress Hills. No one in the family spoke English and in 1900, when Andrew Klaiber was six years old, he went to a school built in the Cypress Hills. All the students spoke German of one dialect or another; only the teacher spoke English. "Some of the kids were 14 years old in grade one," Klaiber told Karl Kaesekamp in a Provincial Archives interview on November 11, 1972.

Farming went so badly Klaiber's father sold his homestead as soon as it was "proved up". With the $1,000 he got for his 160 acres, 30 of it "broken", he bought two quarters of CPR land near Dunmore for three dollars an acre. It was a good investment: one dollar an acre down and the rest in payments. With the balance of his $1,000 he built a new house and acquired 18 yearling heifers and a team of horses. Young Andrew was given an Indian pony so "we were well-equipped."

In 1908, Andrew Klaiber went to Longfellow School, South of Dunmore, and at 14 years old got a job in Medicine Hat working for a bricklayer. For every 10 hour day he was paid $2.50 which enabled him to take up his own homestead at Little Plume at the tender age of 16. He continued to help his father on his homestead until he married in 1914.

"It was a tough life," Klaiber recalled. "But we were almost self-sufficient. We had lots of meat of our own, and lots of wild game. We made do with what was available, even making our own coffee from roasted wheat. It was a much better life than in Russia." Andrew Klaiber passed away at age 86 in 1980.

Among the avalanche of immigrants to the Medicine Hat district early in the 20th Century came the Dutch. Fairly typical of these was Luite Visscher who left the Netherlands with many other young men in March 1910. He obtained a homestead in the Alderson-Suffield area (now and since 1942 popularly known as The British Block). A community of about 20 families settled there, all from Holland. The focal point was the Dutch Reformed Church and the New Holland School, which the residents built. A post office known as Brutus was located on the Visscher homestead which was centrally located and Mr. and Mrs. Visscher acted as postmaster and postmistress.

These early settlers found life difficult as most had no experience in farming and the very dry climate produced only a few good crops. Visscher was experienced as a carpenter so he spent several months off the land each year working in Medicine Hat. Three daughters were born to the young couple: Mrs. Minnie Plomp, Mrs. Ida De Jong and Mrs. Johanna Alexander. Mrs. Alexander, who gave an account of her father's experience to the author, recalled that Dr. F. W. Gershaw travelled many miles by horse and buggy to tend to the physical requirements of these people.

61

Original Court House at Medicine Hat, 1899. Now site of Canadian Legion Building.

Court House at Medicine Hat, as of 1981. Built 1919.

Senator Fred W. Gershaw (1883-1968) practised medicine in Medicine Hat for many years. He was Liberal Member of Parliament from 1925 to 1935 and from 1940 to 1945, when he was called to the Senate. Dr. Gershaw was author of a number of privately-printed booklets, including *Short Grass Area, History of Fort Walsh, Ranching in Southern Alberta,* and a history of Medicine Hat and District called *Saamis.*)

After more crop failures the Dutch decided to leave for greener pastures. Some went to Oak Harbor, Washington, some settled at Crossfield, Alberta and still others went to farm on irrigated land in the Monarch-Nobleford district. It was a sad day for the Visscher family in February 1925 when they loaded all their worldly goods on wagons and shipped them from Alderson by CPR to Nobleford.

All that remains of where these energetic people gave about 15 years of the best of their lives are some crumbling rock foundations where their small homes had been. On what was the Visscher homestead, one can also see a few scraggly remains of what was once a row of caraganas, carefully nurtured in the early years by well water. On this same property is a small graveyard which was situated next to the church and which has been preserved by personnel from the Canadian Forces who now have this land as a training centre (The British Block).

Just as tenacious as the Dutch and the Germans were the Icelanders who were making their contribution to the building of the Canadian West around the end of the 1880s. One such immigrant was Jon Tryggvi Bergman who arrived in Winnipeg in 1900. He soon established a reputation as a builder, after making a stake in the Yukon. He expanded his business in Vancouver and Seattle, Washington. On a stopover at Medicine Hat in 1911, he was attracted to the opportunities available here and bought several lots. (Two of them are the sites of the present View Court and Diana Court apartments.)

The family continued to live in Seattle until 1921 when Bergman grew restless and dissatisfied with the way his property was being managed in Medicine Hat. He decided to try life in a small town and moved here in 1921. Of her father, Mrs. Helga Thomson of Redcliff told the author: "He was a true pioneer who, with little formal education, came to a country where he had to learn a new language and a new culture — and he prospered."

While the people of Nordic extraction prospered and avoided discrimination, the Chinese, as noted, were not so fortunate. Lloyd Stepanic, writing in the September 26, 1973 issue of the *Medicine Hat News* noted that "no ethnic group suffered more in regard to discrimination, especially at the hands of the rougher elements of the land."

It may be recalled that in the days of the Manchu Dynasty in China, all males were compelled to wear a pigtail to acknowledge their allegiance to the Emperor. This pigtail, also worn in North America by Chinese immigrants until the Manchu Dynasty fell in 1912, brought much abuse to the wearers from pranksters and drunks. Pigtail-pulling and other harrassments were fairly common occurences in Medicine Hat in the early days. Some discriminators went so far as to snip off the pigtail, which led to much yelling and occasional bloodshed.

While Chinese in Canada today are to be found in the highest professions, particularly law and medicine, in the early days they were lucky to find jobs even at the most menial tasks, which accounts for the fact that so many went into business for themselves, especially as tailors, launderers or cafe owners. Chinese residents in Medicine Hat and District have distinquished themselves in all of the above fields.

*   *   *

Sam Goldie, certainly one of the city's most colorful residents, and an excellent story teller, has two anecdotes which help illustrate the type of individualism and the mood of the time when "men were men and women were glad of it." In a taped interview with Jan Fulton, Mr. Goldie described the pioneer humor and spirit which prevailed in early Medicine Hat:

"Before the coming of the railway, the community received its mail and supplies from Eastern Canada via the Missouri River to Fort Benton, Montana. From there it came across by ox team along the trail to the Cypress Hills. When steel was laid as far as Maple Creek, this Montana route was abandoned. Until the CPR reached here in 1883, the ox team made a weekly journey to Maple Creek for supplies.

Senator Gershaw, a pioneer doctor and author of an earlier work on the Medicine Hat area.

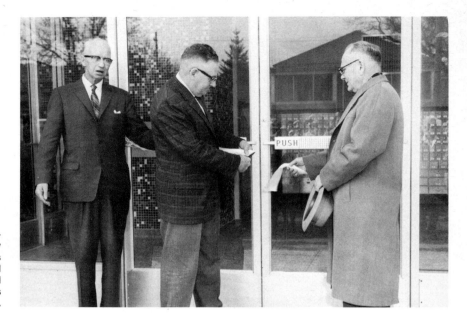

Storyteller Sam Goldie is shown here snipping the ribbon to officially open the new Post Office on April 28, 1961. On Goldie's left is Member of Parliament for Brooks, Ted Brunsden and on the right is retired Postmaster Warden J. Johnson. Goldie was Postmaster at the time the photo was taken.

"Since there were few white women in Medicine Hat, the unattached males tended to spend their leisure hours drinking and raising hell. While not altogether lawless (on account of the Mounted Police), the town was by no means a model of virtue. One day the ox team was making its way slowly towards Maple Creek when it was stopped by a solemn-looking person in a clerical garb. He was an intinerant evangelist of the kind that roamed the West at that time.

"These individuals never passed up an opportunity to try to convert sinners, and everyone they met was grist for glory. From atop of his mule the evangelist called to the teamster: 'Mister, do you know how to get to heaven?' The bearded teamster surveyed him for a long time, spat out a huge mouthful of chewing tobacco and said, 'If that's where you want to git

Original Cosmopolitan Hotel, Medicine Hat.

64

to, mister, you're headed for Medicine Hat, and you can take it from me, you sure as hell are headed the *wrong* way!'"

Sam Goldie told the following story to highlight the primitive and inadequate heating facilities in early Medicine Hat hotels. It is believed to be the old Cosmopolitan he was referring to in this yarn:

"The comforts of modern heating we take for granted. The heating system of this hotel consisted of a huge, pot-bellied stove in the centre of the lobby. Heating for the rooms was obtained by leaving the doors open. On really cold nights the rooms became unbearable and guests would carry their mattresses and blankets down to the lobby and sleep around the stove. One night, after a blizzard had raged all day, the rooms seemed as cold as the frigid outside. The guests, mostly travellers or farmers and ranchers caught in town by the blizzard, were all huddled in blankets around the stove in the lobby.

"John Dempster was still on his way there after everyone else had fallen asleep. He had fought his way through the blizzard to carry the mail and supplies to the small community of Eagle Butte, in the Cypress Hills area. It was after midnight when he got back to Medicine Hat. His beard and moustache were like his clothes: completely encrusted with ice and snow. After putting up his horse at the livery stable, Dempster headed for the hotel. He came into the lobby stomping his feet and beating his garments. Awakened by all this racket, the guests around the stove sat up and stared at the apparition in white that had entered their midst. At last, one of them recognized the figure of John Dempster under all the snow and ice. 'Good grief, John,' he said, 'what room are *you* sleeping in?' "

Fort Walsh as it appeared in 1878. Photo courtesy Saskatchewan Archives Board.

Fort Whoop-Up as it appeared — American flag flying — when the North West Mounted Police arrived in 1874. The fort was built by American whiskey smugglers who found ready customers for their "rotgut" among the Indians who traded valuable furs for it. Photo courtesy Public Archives of Canada.

66

Home On The Range

There was a period in the building of the Canadian West when the two main bodies of settlers, the ranchers and the "sodbusters", came to blows. Confrontations between the cattlemen and the farmers were not as serious as those that led to the range wars in the United States; however, they did occur.

The ranchers came first, many of them from the Eastern Townships of Ontario and from Quebec. Others came as members of the Northwest Mounted Police and stayed on. Some arrived as English "Gentlemen" who preferred to spell ranch with an "e" and pronounced it "rawnch". (The Prince of Wales, who owned a ranch in the foothills west of High River, Alberta, called the E. P. Ranch, was asked what was the difference between a ranch and a ranche. The Prince — who later became the Duke of Windsor — quipped: "The one without the 'e' makes money!")

And there were two other contributors to the Canadian Ranching

The Prince of Wales, on extreme right leaning forward, watches cutting operations on steer on his E. P. Ranch. Asked what was the difference between a ranch and a ranche, the Duke quipped, "The one without the 'e' makes money!"

Fraternity: "Remittance Men" and seasoned American cowboys. Let's deal with the "Remittance Men" first. These worthies were the "second sons" of wealthy English parents who were sent off to the "colonies" because there wasn't enough in the family purse to launch them on a career at home. There was enough, however, to keep them away from home — a "remittance", usually sent monthly, sometimes less frequently. Although some of these men were also the "Black Sheep" of the family, most were upstanding, trustworthy and — above all — intelligent. Which is not to say they were industrious. Or even tidy. Let's say that the shacks they inhabited on tiny homesteads across the land were not always clean, but they probably contained more *interesting* items in the form of books objets d'art and such than would be found in the average home of the time.

The Remittance Men quickly gained a reputation for being inept at anything that required manual dexterity. After all, they hadn't been trained in anything "practical" like fencing, pitching hay, shovelling manure, cutting and branding calves. They could, however, ride — some even on a western saddle, as opposed to the English side saddle. They were good at polo and they could be counted upon to win, place or show at the races at fair or stampede. They were less successful on the end of a lariat, but they were willing to learn.

They were frequently seen at the local watering holes buying a round or two for other hangers-on and drifters, until they had spent the remittance cheque. Then they would cadge a few dollars, buy some supplies (including a bottle of scotch or so) and head back to their shack to catch up on their reading material (which had arrived with the cheque) from Britain.

The Remittance Men are not to be confused with the hardworking English immigrant who adapted as quickly as he could to the Canadian way. Nor is it fair to say all Remittance Men were dismal failures; some made good ranchers and farmers. What they did do is to add a new and interesting dimension to the overall Canadian scene.

The Canadian West was more peaceful than the American, mainly because of the presence of the Mounties. These stalwarts and their scouts patrolled the Medicine Hat area in the early days from Fort Macleod. Left to right are Cecil Denny, Black Eagle and Elk Facing The Wind, Blood Indians, Staff Sergeant Chris Hilliard, Sergeant George S. Cotter and Scout Hunbury. Photo courtesy RCMP Museum, Regina.

The final group of individuals who moved restlessly across the Canadian West in the early days were the American cowboys. They came in two main varieties: serious stockraisers who were fed up with the loss of open range in the United States and attracted to Western Canada because barbed wire hadn't conquered all the plains here yet; and the footloose and often lawless gunslinger who either settled down — as some did — or caused trouble and either ended up in jail or was driven back over the line. Canadian history books and popular magazines have alluded to many of these desperados, enough of them to make their existence believable. In this chapter we will discuss a few of their exploits.

Although incidents of shootouts between gun-totin' cowpokes in Southern Alberta and Saskatchewan were relatively few — mainly because of the stern presence of the Mounted Police — there *were* incidents. Acts of violence on a large scale were rare in the Medicine Hat area after the arrival of the Mounties, but the first murder committed in the district was in the tradition of the Old West.

The setting was the Culley Ranch, now in the city limits west of the airport on Number Three Highway. The time was about 9 p.m. on July 8, 1885. Corporal W. B. Dobbin wrote about the incident in a back issue of the *RCMP Quarterly*. It seems a cowboy named Ben Hales stopped at the Culley place for a meal and soon became embroiled in a violent argument with Robert Casey, proprietor of one of the early hotels in Medicine Hat.

Casey heaped abuse on Hales who drew his gun and ordered the hotelman to put his hands up. Moving toward the door, Casey shouted, "If you're going to shoot me, wait until I get outside." He then walked outside and mounted his horse. Casey, who was a bit the worse for liquor, then defied the gunman to shoot him. Hardly had this dare been uttered than Hales fired twice and Casey fell to the ground. Several bystanders carried the wounded man back into the house. Hales followed. With a sixgun in each hand, he put on a dazzling display of shooting, knocking the lid off the kettle and striking the pivot in the centre of the clock. He then placed a saddle on the fastest horse available, ordered George Culley, the ranch owner, to take no action until he was out of sight, and rode off toward the American border.

Casey, bleeding profusely from a wound above the heart, was taken to Medicine Hat where he died about 5 a.m. the next morning.

Word of the incident reached the Northwest Mounted Police detachment at Maple Creek at 10:30 p.m. and a party of men was dispatched to the Culley ranch. Told that the fugitive had headed for the border, notice was sent by telegraph of his flight to several posts along the way. A Sergeant Jones of the NWMP was sent to Fort Benton in Montana Territory to arrange for the arrest of Hales by U.S. officials. However, a sheriff there named Healey refused to divulge Hales' whereabouts unless a reward was offered. Jones wired Superintendent McIllree. No reward was forthcoming and consequently no action was taken against Hales. An American gunman had shot and killed an unarmed Canadian on Canadian soil and got away scot-free.

Although police action in this case was ineffective, the fact that the Mounties were ready at any time to establish that law was available (and breaking it was a punishable offence), kept such occurrences to a minimum.

Although the wearing of guns was never very popular in the Canadian West, some cowboys did it anyway, as long as it was away from the prying eyes of the Mounted Police. Ostensibly the weapons were for killing snakes and disposing of dying cattle and horses. Gordon Forster shows the garb of the well-dressed cowboy of the late 1800's.

69

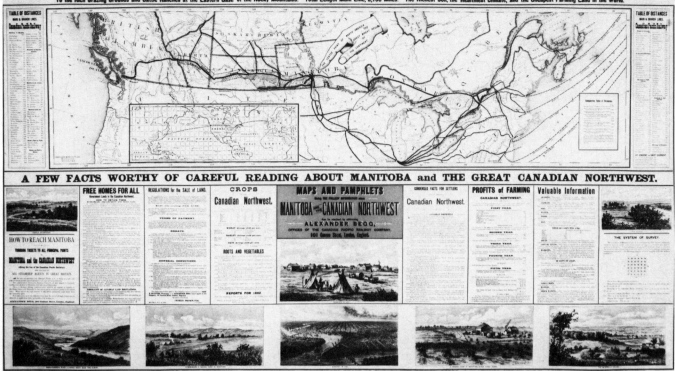

Canadian Pacific Railway poster urging settlers to come to Western Canada in 1882.

Nevertheless, the environment for violence was certainly present as the decade passed and more and more people moved into the district.

Year by year, down to 1888, the amount of land leased to ranchers increased. Immense spreads were populated with cattle and horses including, in 1886, the first big ranch in the Medicine Hat area, the Medicine Hat Ranching Company. In a very few years the country that Captain Palliser had regarded as useless desert came into its own. Medicine Hat herds were as flourishing and the ranchers as progressive as any in the whole country.

Among those who came to this area before or around the turn of the century were: Walter Huckvale, L. C. Brown, Syd Hooper, Jim English, James Robinson, Jim Hassard, R. E. Starks, W. A. Burton, R. Marjisson, Louis Pruitt, John H. Spencer, Simon Peppen, P. Cross, Mack Higdon, Billy Taylor, the famous Days: Tony, Ad, Billy and Ford, Joseph John Hewitt, Dick Porter, Henry Cavan, A. C. Crate, Frank Sissons and many others.

According to the census returns of 1881 there were in the North West Territories (Alberta and Saskatchewan) 5,690 "horned" cattle (not counting milk cows), and during the next five years cattle poured in by the thousands. Most of these came from Montana, but some also came from British Columbia, Manitoba, Ontario — and a few from the Eastern States and Great Britain.

One industrious rancher had his herd taken to Winnipeg by rail and then drove it over 800 miles across the prairie to its new home west of Calgary, where it formed the nucleus of the Mount Royal herd. It was reported that it took the owner from April to late autumn to cover the distance with his four-legged charges.

In the year that the Medicine Hat Ranching Company was formed, 34,000 cattle, 3,500 horses and 7,000 sheep, mostly from the United States, came into the country. The Mounted Police estimated that there were in southern Alberta in 1892 about 200,000 head of livestock of all kinds south of the main line of the CPR.

Credited with bringing in the first cattle and horses to the district in the early 1880s was James Francis Sanderson, mentioned in a previous chapter. Sanderson and his fellow ranchers pretty well had the range to themselves in those early days, but when the "sodbusters" arrived on the scene with their barbed wire, the days of the big leased rangeland was ending. For it was really barbed wire than won the West — for the farmers and small ranchers. It became the enemy of the men who had no regard for boundaries, not even the 49th Parallel.

Cattle roamed across from the United States in the thousands. The grass was better in Southern Alberta than it was in Montana Territory, and it was free. The Canadian cattlemen complained about the invasion by American cattle, some of them suffering from mange, others inferior breeds which watered down the quality of the northerners' stock.

Walter Huckvale became president of the Stock Growers' Association, an organization that did much to stop cattle rustling, destroy predatory animals and improve conditions for the industry. Rustling was a popular pastime, right from the time when horses and cattle were first seen on the plains. Nelson Adsit and his brother Earl operated a sawmill when horse-stealing was popular in the Cypress Hills. Earl was sleeping in the barn guarding the horses one night when he heard a noise. He pulled his gun and lit a match. The prowler fired at the light and ran away. Earl dug the bullet out of a log next morning and wore it as a good luck charm for years.

It was through the efforts of the Stock Association that better terms for leases were secured and transportation for the products of the ranch were improved. As time went on, farmers and ranchers aired their complaints over the meeting table rather than over the cursed fence that kept them at each others' throats.

In some celebrated cases the settlers would string their wire around choice watering areas favored by the ranchers' cattle. In retaliation the ranchers would cut the fences or herd their cattle through a settler's farm and devastate the growing crops. There were instances where fire — that most fearful of prairie scourges — would be deliberately set to drive off the settler who was squatting on land he did not own. The sodbusters lost their possessions and, in some cases, their lives.

The grass that both factors were after varied from area to area, mile to mile, depending on the soil. The short grass country, as it became known and is still known today, grew a high-nutrient variety that was highly favorable for cattle destined for beef production. The short grass plains of southeastern Alberta and the Medicine Hat area merged into the mixed grass prairie in the slightly moister climate of the Lethbridge region. Blue grama spear grass and sand grass, typical of the short grass region, dominated the drier slopes while the wheat grasses and other taller grasses mixed with them on the plains above.

Emery LaGrandeur who won the World Champion Bronco Rider title at the Winnipeg Stampede in 1913. Rode for Spencer Brothers outfit from 1907-1912.

71

Western Stock Growers' Association meeting at Medicine Hat. Some of those identified include William Playfair, Charles Kettles, Charles Mitchell, William Stewart, Gilbert E. Goddard, Richard Porter, Duncan McEachren, Walter Huckvale, Sid Hooper, James "Dublin" Rodgers, Robert Porter, Andy Gordon, Monty Leeds, Howell Harris, A. R. Springett, S. W. March, H. M. Hatfield, A. B. Macdonald, L. B. Cochrane, William Roper Hull, W. Findlay, Patrick Burns, James Hargrave, Adam Sturn, Archie McLean, George Emerson, Billy Metcalfe, A. E. Cross.

Slight depressions supported shrubs, such as chokecherry and saskatoon, and Western cottonwood trees were found along the river banks. Several species of prairie sage thrived on these semi-arid dark brown soils; their leaves and stems were covered with fine hairs which added to their drought resistance.

The settlers attempted to put the plow to the land with the hope that wheat and other cereal crops would grow as well as the hardy grasses. In many cases they were wrong and reaped only weeds and Russian thistle. Giant "dustbowls" were created when the wind whipped up the soil; — but the grass never again grew in such abundance.

It was the drought and the cruel winters, combined with the farmers' wire, that finally defeated the ranchers and their domination of the Great Plains. Some winters were so cold that they still chill the memories of survivors. They ended the hopes of many courageous cattlemen to create and maintain their vast spreads. With land for lease in amounts as much as 100,000 acres for one cent per acre per year, it is no wonder that the area was attractive to them.

When the killing winds and heavy snow arrived, cattle drifted south. As long as they could move they had a slim chance of survival in coulees and near river banks. However, thousands were cut off by barbed wire before they could find shelter. Their bodies were piled up 15 deep in some places.

HALT!

Although the cattlemen complained of cattle rustling they were not prepared to take the law into their own hands but left it to the Mounties in most cases to make the arrests. This painting from the Ernest Brown Collection in the Provincial Archives of Alberta shows two rustlers being stopped by a Mountie as they attempt to run off a steer.

73

The photo shows the first load of merchandise shipped to Lethbridge (a distance of 120 miles) from Medicine Hat on June 23, 1885. Shipped by Tweed & Ewart (see store on left). The wagon boss was Ezra Pearsons. Load weighed 12,400 pounds.

The *Calgary Herald* of February 7, 1907 carried an item about the desperate situation facing Medicine Hat ranchers the terrible winter of 1906-07. "A public meeting of the citizens was held in the city hall last night with the mayor presiding for the purpose of discussing the cattle situation which affects the city directly insomuch as the cattle are following the trails into town, and the weaker ones are perishing on the streets, it was decided that the cattle which fell within the city limits should be shot as soon as they are down in order to put them out of their misery.

"Those which show signs of being weak will be corralled in the CPR stockyards and fed at the city's expense and the stronger beasts will be allowed to roam about the city and rustle around the stables and manure piles for fodder. It would be impossible to handle all the cattle as hay and straw are very scarce at present.

"Ranchers will be asked to reimburse the City for the outlay involved in carrying the cattle through the cold spell. A committee, composed of Walter Huckvale, Eugene Starks, David Milne, A. C. Hawthorne and Captain H. H. Ross, with the members of the city council, was appointed immediately after the public meeting and were given authority by that body to incur the necessary expense."

Medicine Hat's Business Section, about 1902. View shows corner of Main St., and South Railway St. (now Second St.), and South Railway St.

74

Incidentally, one of the most tragic events that ever occurred in Medicine Hat District was when two teenaged youths died in a blizzard on November 20, 1892. Moran Cochrane, 15, and Harold Walton, 10, were caught in the sudden storm while riding along Bullhead Creek about two o'clock in the afternoon. The sky suddenly turned black around four o'clock and a sixty mile wind sprang up accompanied by snow so that visibility was reduced to a few feet. The youths' horses drifted before the wind until Walton, the youngest, too cold to continue, fell from his horse, about 10 miles southeast of the city.

His body was found under six inches of snow, covered with the saddle and horse blankets. The body of Moran Cochrane was discovered about a half mile away, face down, beside a haystack. His pony was quietly feeding, the picket rope still held in the youth's lifeless hand. Police speculated that the older boy had covered the Walton lad with saddle and blankets before striking off to find help. A Mr. Miller of the Payton Ranch found the Cochrane youth's body and a Sergeant Matheson of the NWMP found the other lad. The mountie camped out overnight with the lifeless youth and was still there when a search party of ranchers reached the scene the next morning.

The relentless fencing of the huge ranges went on as the Federal Government, through legislation, showed its favoritism to the CPR and to mass settlement. The CPR sold land and encouraged immigration. Fence posts went in and more and more wire was strung. It was a diabolical business, this fencing. Barbed wire cuts and tears, trips and slips, tangles and knots and breaks with a savage backlash. Settlers and squatters often had to wire a fence alone. The trick was to unroll a length of about 50 yards. One end was tied around a solid corner post and the other to the end of the wagon. By driving the horse until the wire was taut — but not so as to strain or break it — the sodbuster would leap out and secure it by stapling it to the posts. He kept his head carefully turned away in case the wire snapped and lacerated him.

However the farmer fenced the land, it stayed fenced in the end. Although the size of the ranches diminished, many ranchers thrived on smaller portions of the plains. The Medicine Hat Ranching Company, already referred to, prospered at Seven Persons Creek, west of the town of Seven Persons. It had been developed by a group of local businessmen led by Thomas Tweed, William T. Finlay and John Ewart. Tweed, postmaster and politician, left many descendants. A famous one, namesake Tommy Tweed, an actor, was heard for many years on CBC radio. William T. Finlay represented Medicine Hat in the Territorial Assembly in Regina and also served as the city's first representative in the Legislature at Edmonton after Alberta became a province in 1905. A Liberal, Finlay won the seat by only 37 votes over his Conservative opponent, Frank Sissons. He became the province's first Minister of Agriculture. In the general election of March 22, 1909 William Finlay was re-elected by a landslide, polling 1,139 votes to 494 for Major Sissons. In June, 1910 Attorney General Charles Mitchell succeeded Finlay as the Member for Medicine Hat as he defeated Conservative Walter Huckvale by 1,124 votes to 655.

It was his ranching friends who supported Finlay and rallied around him as he took his seat in the Legislature. As the three owners of the Medicine Hat Ranching Company were too busy elsewhere to operate the ranch themselves, they hired Ezra Pearson, who had served as a bull train driver freighting supplies from Fort Benton to Fort Macleod.

The grave of the Cochrane boy and the Walton boy marked by a bedstead and frame for many years in the old cemetery near Kin Coulee.

75

(Left to Right) Isaac Bullivant, R. B. Davidson, C. S. Pingle, E. G. Ellerton, Mr. Egbert, Walter Huckvale, William Parker, Horace Whiffin, William Cousins. All Old Timers of Medicine Hat.

In the Cypress Hills, where ranching was the most concentrated in the district, the Mitchell brothers set up a ranch. More on them later. Jim, Dick and Bob Porter took up land for that purpose at Gros Ventre Creek, south of Dunmore. The R. P. brand was still in Porter hands in the 1980s. An ex-minister named William Biddle was another of the pioneer ranchers in the Cypress Hills. He was such a kindly, humane individual that he couldn't bear to brand his cattle, tying strips of red blanket around their necks instead!

There were others who had imagination: James Sanderson, according to an account in the *Medicine Hat News* of June 29, 1967, collected the bulls of other ranchers and herded them on to rangeland 45 miles northeast of the city. The area became known as "Bull Springs". Sanderson charged the owners two dollars a head per month and often herded together as many as 700 bulls at a time.

In 1885 an English capitalist named Sir John Lister-Kaye arrived in Medicine Hat with a grand vision of the ranching potential. With seemingly unlimited financial backing from Britain, he obtained 10 large tracts of land from the Dominion Government. One of these, the '76, so-called because of its brand, was located partly at Dunmore, with another section at Stair (now Redcliff).

The agreement provided that the company would cultivate all arable areas on the land received and demonstrate the feasibility of growing crops in those areas. The government in Ottawa would supply a subsidy of 35 cents per acre per year for all land in crop. As it happened, the region was undergoing a severe drought cycle and from 1887 to 1894 the Dunmore venture never saw one cash crop raised. The Lister-Kaye interests even attempted to irrigate the land with a fleet of horse-drawn tank sprinklers but these efforts failed to coax more than a few shrivelled shoots from the parched ground.

Sir John was of stern stuff, however, and continued to try out his innovations. In 1889 he decided to ship frozen beef to England. Refrigeration was still unknown but he intended to make use of the intense cold of the Alberta winter. About 300 cattle were brought to the Dunmore ranch and fattened on the good forage crop produced that year. An impressive slaughter house was erected and during a suitable cold spell the animals were butchered.

Unfortunately for Lister-Kaye and company, Alberta's famous but capricious chinook wind blew across the land just as the cattle carcasses were frozen enough to be loaded in rail cars. The temperature went from minus 30 degrees Fahrenheit to 60 degrees above zero. Although the meat was loaded, more and more had to be thrown away as the train rolled east. As it turned out, not one single beef carcass reached shipboard.

The collapse of the Lister-Kaye empire affected the Medicine Hat area for many years. The venture had pumped money into the city; the success of the dry land irrigation scheme would have been welcomed; the experiment was carefully monitored by ranchers and farmers everywhere who were in the same predicament. Some sold their ranches and farms during the droughts and severe winter years and moved away. Others moved into the town where they carried on in commerce or took up employment with the greenhouses, brick plants, mills and other industries that were beginning to spring up.

Avery steam tractor on Wheatlands farmland at Suffield in 1915. Property was controlled by Ginther-Finlay group. Finlay (cap) and Ginther in rear of Studebaker car.

For many years residents of the city kept at least a milk cow, several chickens, a pig and a horse or two in the back yard. A. G. Wallace, now a resident of Lethbridge, was born in Medicine Hat in 1909 and recalls that the pony he kept in his back yard was easily pastured until spring:

"In October I'd pull his shoes off, ride him to the outskirts of town — about a half a mile — then slap him on the flank and say, 'See you next spring.' He'd work his way back to the ranch country he was raised in about 25 miles away. Then each spring we'd inquire of the ranchers and squatters if they had seen a horse of his description and then go out and bring him in again."

Nearly every kid in the town had a horse of some sort. Horse-trading was a brisk, even among youngsters, and it required sharp eyes to sort out the "baddies", the spavined, the otherwise useless "cayuses". There was an old saying current at the time that may or may not have had some truth in it when it came to the selection of a good horse:

One white foot, buy me.
Two white feet, try me.
Three white feet, deny me.
Four white feet and white on my nose,
Knock me on the head
And feed me to the crows!

Among those ranchers who had a home in the city were the Tinneys. While living part of the year on the IV Ranch, 42 miles northeast of the city, across the river, they moved into town where three of their children went to school in the fall and winter. The IV Ranch became well-known for its fine herd of Galloway cattle and Clydesdale horses.

Thomas H. Tinney was born in Oakwood, Ontario in 1865 and first unloaded his settler's effects at Dunmore on March 17, 1893. His wife joined him at his homestead on the shores of Feldman Lake in April. (The property was later sold to Caleb Goldsmith.) A second year graduate of Guelph Agriculture College, Tinney was an expert on all lines of livestock and for years was in demand as a judge of cattle, sheep and swine at smaller fairs and exhibitions in Alberta.

Ima Tinney and Peter Bromberg wedding. Rev. Morrow and Mrs. Morrow in centre of photo.

"Medicine Hat became a sort of mecca for those who would become judges with the first 'school' run here in the winter of 1906," according to daughter Mrs. Olla Barnes. "Farmers and ranchers took the courses and wrote exams here. Two top achievers went to Calgary and wrote again for the province. The winner was given a trophy to bring home for a year. Dad won it so many times he was finally given the trophy to keep."

The romance of the early ranching days stays fresh in the memories of many oldtimers. It was this romantic attraction that stayed long in the recollections of James Owen Gresham Sanderson. James' grandfather, James Francis Sanderson, mentioned in this and earlier chapters, was a famous stockman. Following in that tradition, this James Sanderson spent his early life on his father's ranch north of Medicine Hat. The ranch is now part of the Hargrave Mitchell Ranch. "It was a happy place to be, "Mr. Sanderson recalled. He told E. S. Bryant in an interview recorded for the Provincial Archives in 1957: "grandfather built the first livery barn business in Medicine Hat."

He only dimly remembers his father because he died tragically when young Sanderson was only five. "Dad was only 27 years old," he said. "He had a habit of riding out to look over his stock on a horse that had been broken, then catching a 'green' one to ride home. One day he went out into a blizzard without a coat on and was too cold and tired to catch any kind of horse — after letting the first one go. He walked home to the ranch and died there five days later from bronchial pneumonia."

Dr. Sanderson lived with his grandparents quite happily in the city but the upset caused by his father's death intensified his desire to become a success. "I wanted it for my mother's sake," he said. His mother was Mae F. Bray Sanderson. The grandparents had homesteaded within the east quarter of town where Dr. Sanderson continued to visit and look after cows, calves and saddle horses.

At 14 years old he had his first visit away from the Medicine Hat area. "I went to the first Calgary Stampede in 1912 under my own stampede," he told Bryant. "Although I was young and far from home, I felt safe because I knew so many of the contestants. We had roping, bucking contests and our own Medicine Hat stampede long before that. My uncle, Harry Bray, taught me to ride at 10 and by 14 I thought I was pretty good. I learned later that my confidence was more than a little misplaced."

Dr. Sanderson became acquainted with the Texas family of Days who came from near Austin. The name of "Uncle Tony" Day is famous still in the Medicine Hat area. A prominent Texas rancher for many years prior to coming here, A. J. Day "followed the grass" through the new western States and finally settled on a 65,000 acre lease south of Medicine Hat. He and his relatives brought some 22,000 head of cattle and 700 horses with them. Day paid the Dominion Government $40,000 duty when he brought his huge herd into the country.

In 1913, after the success of the first Calgary Stampede, Tony Day agreed to supply all the livestock for the Stampede — this time to be held in Winnipeg. Again led by Guy Weadick, the Winnipeg event was even more successful than the first Calgary Stampede. On September 1, 1913, 55,000 people crowded into a makeshift grandstand that entrepreneur Weadick had built around a racetrack to see the largest sporting event in Canadian history. The two sons of Anthony Jay Day — Addison P. Day Jr. and Horace Day — teamed up with Dr. James Sanderson.

"Ad Day and I had the job of sorting out 24 horses for the trick riders," Dr. Sanderson said. "We decided then to develop our own trick riding stunt. We rode on one horse, at full gallop, for 15 minutes, performing the Russian Drag and the Drunken Stand — two routines we worked out. We were paid $10 a day and expenses to get there. It took us two months to develop the horses for the show."

His saddle was a present from Emery LeGrandeur, the world champion Canadian rodeo rider. Dr. Sanderson wished he had kept it but, "I sold it for $35 or $40 with my other equipment when I went to University in 1917."

To earn money to continue his education, Dr. Sanderson went in 1915 to a branch of the '76 Ranch near Shaunavan, Saskatchewan where he rode Mexican ponies from the Don Louis Terasses Ranch in Chihuahua, Mexico. "They were like small Arabians," he said. "On the '76 there were no corrals

79

for the horses, just a single rope corral. The pay was $20 a month 'and found'" (room and board).

Earlier, the author referred to gunfights that occasionally occurred in the Canadian West, often involving cowboys from the States. In 1915, Dr. Sanderson helped break up one between a Montana cowboy who got jealous because a Texan was given the job as foreman on the ranch he was working on. "Three of us jumped on the cowboy and two tackled the foreman after they had gone to their bedrolls for their sixguns," Dr. Sanderson said.

Dr. Sanderson said the Americans' "built up the story of their exploits in actions of this sort" while similar activities in Canada have been downplayed. "The cowboys carried six shooters in our West too," he said. "But they usually kept them out of sight, not in plain view, like in American movies."

Dr. James Sanderson graduated from the University of Alberta in 1922 and went on to become a well-known geologist involved in oil exploration for Imperial Oil.

There was no denying that Medicine Hat was as rough and tough as any Western Canadian town. Cowboys were known to play pranks and get involved in highjinks. Note the horse and rider poking out of the building in this early photo. This view of revellers was taken in front of the Saskatchewan Brewery office in Medicine Hat in 1884. T. W. Ireland, owner, is on the harnessed horse on the left. The horses are from the brewery wagon on the left. The brewery was located on what is now Second Street where Tamblyn Drug was, across the street from Beveridges. Boy in long trousers and white shirt (on sidewalk) is Tom Ireland Jr. One of children in wagon may be Maggie Ireland. Others unidentified.

One of the most colorful personalities of the era was David James "Joe" Wylie, a two-fisted cowboy who became a cattle baron and an elected member of the Saskatchewan Legislative Assembly. Gabe Lavallie recounted in an early edition of *Canadian Cattlemen* magazine that he first met Wylie in the summer of 1884: "It was a Sunday afternoon. About the only thing to do in Medicine Hat in those days was to get drunk, fight, or go horse racing. And horse racing was forbidden on Sundays. This particular Sunday the Blue Law was overlooked and a large crowd gathered at the race track which was a flat place up on the river bank about a mile or so south of town, between the river and Seven Persons Creek."

Lavallie recorded that a man named Ed Rowe was selling whiskey at the track for 50 cents a cup out of a keg that had "the head knocked in." "You just paid your 50 cents and stuck the dipper in and drank it straight down," he said. "Needless to say, there were quite a few men lying around too drunk to get up and go back to the 'Hat at the end of the race."

Lavallie himself of French extraction, described a "big guy named Jack Boudoin who was riding a large horse with a heavy Mexican saddle. The horse was the favorite of a bunch of Frenchmen — lumberjacks from the East — who had just come from Calgary." The visitors suggested Lavallie race against Boudoin for stakes of $25, which Wylie would hold. They then asked Lavallie if he spoke French and he said, "no, just a little Spanish."

"They were talking away to themselves in French — which of course I understood — and saying that if they won they would get the money, and if they lost they would take the stakes away from Wylie anyway. I told Joe and he gave a short laugh and said, "All right. Let them try it out."

"I won the race and the Frenchmen came running towards Wylie to collect the stakes, saying it had been a foul start. Wylie was waiting for them and began to peel off his coat. He gave it to me and told me to start for town on his horse with the money. I told him he would be killed.

"I did not exactly see what happened next, but the biggest of the Frenchmen went flying, thanks to the foot of a six-foot-four-inch Englishman who was watching the proceedings. Joe, who had been a professional football player, seemed to know just how to trip and hit his assailants. Three or four caught up with him but he just turned around and faced them all and you could see flying legs and arms and all you could hear was cuss words in English and French.

"Wylie downed them all and then jogged on into town on foot. I never saw such a man to fight. The next day I saw him in the bar and he bought me a couple of drinks. Although he had black and blue arms, the Frenchman who showed up in the bar later had closed eyes and cut cheeks."

Joe Wylie and his flying fists went on to operate the Lister-Kaye farm out of Kincorth, the first station east of Piapot, Saskatchewan. He took over the Michael Oxarat Ranch in the Cypress Hills in 1897. He was elected to the first Saskatchewan Legislature in 1905.

On July 4, 1953 a large crowd lined the streets of Medicine Hat to pay their final respects to Barney Simpson, one of the most beloved ranchers in the south country. The *Medicine Hat News* described the event as one of the largest parades in the city. The mile-long procession included 21 mounted cattlemen. Simpson's large ranch was in the Wildhorse district (about 50 miles south of Medicine Hat) and was a frequent meeting place for cattlemen.

In 1966 the city lost another prominent rancher when George Murray died. Murray and his sons ranched on a large scale. The Murray Ranching Company was the largest of its kind in Southern Alberta, comprising some 250,280 acres, owned and leased land, of which two sections were used to raise feed for stock.

The Murrays came to Alberta in 1895. George Murray eventually bought the Medicine Hat Ranch which adjoined his father's spread. Termed the home ranch, the MHR was originally owned by two English brothers

Bert Hargrave, Member of Parliament for Medicine Hat, seen here at the stock pens at Walsh after driving some cattle from his ranch in the summer of 1979. Photo taken by Ed Gould.

named Jenkinson. Mr. and Mrs. Murray raised two daughters and two sons who continued in the ranching enterprise.

A number of pioneer ranchers in the Medicine Hat district achieved fame. Rancher Frank Sissons won acclaim of stockmen in 1898 by successfully delivering 100 cattle to the Klondike during the Yukon gold rush. The cattle went by train to Vancouver, by boat to Skagway, Alaska, overland to the Yukon River and downstream to Dawson City.

Much of the romance associated with the open range centres on the roundups. The cattle were herded together twice a year: in the spring for cutting and branding and in the fall for the shipping to market of the saleable cattle. J. C. Hargrave organized the first roundup in the Medicine Hat area, according to the *Medicine Hat News* of June 29, 1967. More than 30 riders gathered up to 15,000 head of cattle during the fall roundup, which lasted two months.

Bert Hargrave, Member of Parliament for Medicine Hat, still ranches on land owned by his famous ancestors. His father came to Medicine Hat in 1886 from Ontario as a clerk for the Hudson's Bay Company. Hargrave ran a store where he sometimes took cattle in trade for goods. This way he built up a herd which he placed on land bought from the Territorial Government. Bert Hargrave took over the ranch properties built up by his grandfather and his father, Thomas Hargrave. "I operate on 43,000 privately owned acres and leases in two provinces," Hargrave told the author. "This means I get to pay taxes in both Saskatchewan and Alberta."

A longtime champion of the farmers and ranchers in Southern Alberta, Bert Hargrave was being assisted on the ranch by sons Colby and Harry, and wife Amy. Bert's brother Harry, eight years his senior, was for many years Superintendent at Manyberries Experimental Farm before going to the Prairie Farm Rehabilitation Administration, then to Harry Strom's provincial government as Marketing Commissioner.

Thos. A. Hargrave

Grandfather James Hargrave was born in Beech Ridge, Quebec and arrived in Manitoba in July, 1867. He entered the service of the Governor and Company of Gentlemen Adventurers Trading into Hudson's Bay and left Fort Garry the same year for York Factory where he remained in the Company service until 1871 when he was transferred to Portage La Prairie. In 1873 he married Alexandra Helen Sissons, sister of Mrs. Thomas Sissons of Portage La Prairie. The couple had four sons, four daughters and about 20 grandchildren.

Continuing in the service of the Hudson's Bay Company, Hargrave was transferred in 1876 to Fort Francis and from that post was moved in 1878 to Cumberland House, west of The Pas, where he remained until 1882. He farmed for a short time until moving to Medicine Hat in 1883.

Alexandra Sissons' family was of French Huguenot background, having left the district of Soissons, France at the time of the French Revolution, to settle in England. From there her father, Thomas Sissons, born in Nottingham, emigrated with three brothers to Canada in 1835.

In 1884, James Hargrave entered into partnership with Daniel Sissons, father of Colonel F. O. Sissons. Their general store handled merchandise and traded in furs with the Indians until 1896 when they sold out to J. K. Drinnan, one of the first school masters in Medicine Hat. Drinnan was also a colorful publisher of the early *Medicine Hat News*.

82

No history of this region would be complete without some mention of the Mitchell family of pioneers and ranchers. William Mitchell, when he died in July 1946 was one of the few pioneer cattlemen left in the district. As man and boy he had ridden the range from the White Mud to Pincher Creek. But it was in the unsurveyed territory between the Cypress Hills and the International Border that is especially associated with his activities. Here at the age of 17 he secured his "squatters' rights" on Willow Creek, establishing the first ranch in the area.

Jim Patterson, well-known Alberta cattleman, advised him to "play safe on that place, kid, or someone will move in on you. Them springs will be worth $1,500 some day." Located in the heart of the best winter range in the country, Bill Mitchell's ranch became the rendezvous of cowpunchers for hundreds of miles around. Thousands of cattle graced the hills and coulees, drifting in from ranches as far north as the Bow. Montana cattlemen, who had had their ranches "sheeped out", poached it in a big way year-round.

Maverick (stray or unbranded) cattle were considered the property of the first man to run his brand on them and during round-up, still unbranded, they were slaughtered for the chuck wagon or sold to help defray operating expenses. The American stock that had fattened on Canadian grass were considered legal tender because they had poached on the Canadian side of the border. The attitude of some ranchers was, "After all, ain't we feedin' the critters — thousands of them, for free?"

The NWMP took a dim view of this sort of trade but in so vast a territory it was difficult to obtain proof.

The Mitchell brothers, James and Robert, came with their wives and families from Sterling, Scotland to the Regina area in 1885. In 1887 they brought in cattle from the Regina district to a newly-acquired homestead in the Cypress Hills. This was the start of the LA Ranch. At first they used the main logging camp buildings of the defunct Sands Lumber Company at Elkwater Lake, but soon built a log house and buildings of their own. The Sands buildings were in good shape because they had been used for two years to house a detachment of the NWMP who were waiting until their Medicine Lodge post, further west, was constructed.

Because of climatic conditions and a heavy snowfall, the Mitchell cattle mostly ranged on the bench and in Medicine Lodge Coulee. During the winter of 1892-3 the cattle drifted south of the hills and the losses were great. Thirty-two head of an original 200 were all that were recovered. Rather than bring the remnants back, it was decided to camp where the herd was. In 1893 this site became the LA Ranch headquarters.

James Mitchell looked elsewhere for ranching and eventually established in South America with sons Robert and Alex. Leaving the sons to operate a sheep ranch he purchased in South America, he returned to Canada. His intention was to bring out his family, but he died on board ship and was buried at sea. Robert died in South America. Alex returned to Canada in 1937.

Jas. Mitchell

He left the LA Ranch in an estate to be operated by his sons. James and John became owners, and later John sold his interest to James. The ranch was in the southeast corner of the province, on Lodge Creek, about four miles east of the highway, 25 miles from the popular Alberta Cypress Hills Park.

83

James Mitchell for years carried on the tradition of ranching that was the trademark of his father. He married Izzette Foster of Medicine Hat in 1932. The year that Izzette arrived at the ranch as a bride, the Depression was on. The ranch was a good place to be. The LA had 50,000 acres in deed and lease. That year the ranch sold 1,200 steers. The Mitchells were happy and Izzette learned to love ranch life. A family of two boys and two girls were raised on the LA Ranch, so it wasn't all luxury. Some things, especially in the early days, she had to learn the hard way.

"James was not always on time for dinner," Mrs. Mitchell told the author in 1979. "He was a man who felt it was best to teach by example and instead of just telling me that he had been kept late trying to get some steers out of a slough or something, he asked me to come with him one day and see how the operation worked. After seeing the difficulties a cowboy can run into in the course of a day's work, I never again asked him why he was late."

J. L. Peacock was one of the first livestock dealers to enter Western Canada from the United States. He entered by way of Canada Crossing in 1900. Driving 5,000 sheep over the Milk River, bound for the stockyards at Maple Creek, he met Will Mitchell, his first contact with a Canadian rancher. It was to become a lifelong friendship.

Peacock liked what he saw of the country so he joined up with Bill Babb, a wealthy horse rancher and race track enthusiast, who operated the Cold Springs Ranch south of the Cypress Hills. Together they acquired the Billy Penland ranch near the border, trailing in horses in large numbers to be broken for the market. The ranch became known as the JDot, their trail brand. Following the disastrous winter of 1906-07, the JDot was sold to Ray Knight. Cold Springs was sold to T. B. Jenkinson.

Peacock dealt in sheep, horses and land, often at the same time. He bought cheap in the U.S. and sold at much higher prices on this side of the border. Born near Buffalo, New York in 1871, Peacock bought the Kenneth Meek outfit on the South Saskatchewan River after the First World War. With yearlings from the McIntyre Ranch near Lethbridge and registered stock from Britain, he was credited with improving the stock in the area. After he was killed in the U.S. in a car accident, members of the Cypress Club recorded: "His advice though seldom given was always sound and good. His humor was keen and his personality lovable. A great sadness weighs down our hearts that this man who meant so much has been taken away."

It was another sad day for members of the Cypress Club when "Uncle Tony" Day sold his Turkey Track Ranch to J. J. Bowlen in June 1917. Bowlen later became Lieutenant-Governor of Alberta. On January 1, 1914 the Cypress Club presented Day with a "Proclamation". Here it is in its entirety:

WHEREAS the insidious charms of California's allegedly balmy climate have lured from our fireside one for whom our regard is only equalled by the fear in which he was held by the wild and untamed Apaches in the warlike days of his youth.
AND WHEREAS at the festive season, when not engaged in dodging our bankers and other creditors, we want to turn our thoughts to those who in the past year have departed from our midst and must seek fields and pastures new
WHEREAS those who have departed from us have, in departing, taken with them most of the available loose change which

formerly grew in abundance in the vicinity of Medicine Hat and we are therefore unable to extend to you a more substantial token of our esteem than this little testimonial

NOW THEREFORE we, the undersigned members of the Cypress Club, send greetings and our best wishes for a happy, prosperous and more or less sober New Year, with the added hope that the easy chair which has been kept warm for you during the months in which you have been absent may before many moons be once more dented by your recumbent form, and the bar receipts be swelled in consequence thereof.

Sixty four signatures of ranchers and businessmen were listed below.

If we were to name all the ranchers and farmers who pioneered the Medicine Hat area, this book would read like a telephone book rather than a history of the district. The list of ranchers would include Sam Andahl, Elmer Sommers, Walter Hutchinson, A. D. Grant & Son, Thompson & Taylor, Frank Reesor & Sons, Emerson Porter, Myrl Smith, Ted Slack, Harvey Hassard, Lance Brown, Clark Brothers, McKinley Brothers, Eugene Burton, Letellier O'Connor, Ray Dubeau, Frank McLeary, Jacob Good, Jim Mac-Arthur, John Fulton, James English, the Frandrichs, the Rutherfords, Paul Helliwell, Tansley & Hassett, Dan Hamilton, Fred McLean, Billy Penland, Harry Minor, Alf DesBrisay and J. Alcock. There are many others; some have appeared already, others will appear in other parts of the book since their activities may not be concerned specifically with ranching in this particular reminiscence.

Time and the plodding of progress have made big changes to the Medicine Hat ranch scene. Memories may be all that remain of old ranchers and their ranches. Henry Cavan, born in his father's boarding house at Dunmore in 1887, owned a 10,000 acre ranch that straddled the Trans-Canada Highway east of Dunmore. Cavan pioneered a large private irrigation scheme which utilized the runoff waters from Ross Creek to irrigate 600 acres of grain and forage crop land. Lionel Cavan still operates the ranch land.

Lord Delaval Beresford as a young man. Owner of ranches in Mexico, the United States and Canada, he was killed in a train wreck. Photo courtesy of University of Texas.

Medicine Hat was pretty wild and woolly when A. G. Crate arrived from Montana in 1903. Crate, writing in the Medicine Hat Historical newsletter some years ago, said the cowboys would give the "town folks" lots of excitement in those days by staging bucking horse contests and other competitions. "When the Salvation Army used to hold their street prayers in front of the old American Hotel, our boss, Lord Beresford, would be feeling good after a few drinks and would heave a handful of American silver half dollars down on the big bass drum for their collection. These would bounce off and the kids would scramble for them while the oldtimers standing on the hotel veranda would laugh their heads off."

One local cowboy, Saul Boyer, was renowned for two things: his outstanding ability as a rider and roper; and his sense of humor. A sense of humor was an absolute necessity if a man was to remain sane in those tough days. Boyer recalled for Tommy Primrose of *Canadian Cattlemen* magazine how he once walked 70 miles after his horse got away from him. The walking was only part of the endurance trial. A good portion of the way he herded nine trail-broken steers on foot.

The Longhorns belonged to James Mitchell who had lent Boyer the horse to take the steers to market. His feet swelled twice their normal size after the experience but for Saul Boyer, a Métis born in Eastend, Saskatchewan in 1882, it was all in a day's work. With 70 miles on foot and nearly 300 miles in the saddle to get the cattle to market, Saul Boyer's days were grueling even to the tough cowboys of that era.

Gone, but not forgotten, are the many pioneers like George and Horace Jenkins, who settled on Ross Creek in 1888, where the Drowning Ford Ranching Company was established. Hundreds of men and women like them made farming and ranching dominant industries in the Medicine Hat economy. All residents can look with pride at their accomplishments.

Dipping vat at Drowning Ford Ranch, north of Medicine Hat. The photo was taken in the early 1900s. Identified are E. Hicker, W. Hawke and J. H. Spencer.

7.

From Tent Town To Metropolis

Part One

By 1885 Medicine Hat had begun to look more like a regular village than a squatter's nest of tents, boxcar homes and shacks, all hastily thrown together for accommodation for the hundreds of bright-eyed new residents. Prior to 1885, while the land was still unsurveyed, these industrious souls camped wherever their fancy directed them. Even a few Cree families drifted into the vicinity, but they camped apart and to the east of the railway tracks in the area now known as "The Flats".

Construction workers were in demand and began to be attracted to the area. Harry Yuill, who was born in Nova Scotia in 1863, arrived in the community in 1884 and began a construction business which was responsible for the building of most of the first houses.

He was instrumental in establishing a number of local industries, including Medicine Hat Flour Mills, the Alberta Linseed Oil Company, the Medicine Hat Brewery and the Monarch Theatre Company. Under his leadership Alberta Clay Products was established in the city in 1920 and Yuill started the Medicine Hat Potteries, a division of ACP with son Harlan Yuill as president of both plants. These two companies were to develop into two of the most outstanding industries in Southeastern Alberta.

Sir Wilfred Laurier was in Medicine Hat in 1894 and spoke from the band stand in Riverside Park. He predicted a wonderful future for anyone who came here. It wasn't always easy.

Photo taken c. 1920. An old view of the Alberta Linseed Oil Co. Ltd. plant still operating under the same name in same location in 1982.

Yuill did not restrict his activities to industry. He owned at one time about 1,000 acres of land within a half mile of City Hall and in 1915 had some 10,000 acres under cultivation; the land was rented from the Wheat Lands Limited. Married to Elizabeth Marjorie Price, Harry Yuill was preceded in his move to Medicine Hat by his brother, Silas B. Yuill, a jewellery store owner. Sister Elta J. Yuill was also well known in the community where she taught school for a number of years.

In his booklet *Early History of the Medicine Hat Country,* J. W. Morrow stated that W. T. Finlay established the first lumber yard in 1884 while Fred Pope ran the first water cart. Later on, Jack Clark, R. Watson and James Porter delivered water to early residents at 25 cents a barrel. Clark also ran the first mail between Medicine Hat and Dunmore; the mail was picked up at the Tweed and Ewart store.

The first hotel, according to Morrow, was run by Casey Brothers (one of whom was killed by an American gunslinger, as detailed in a previous chapter) on the river bank near the site of the present grandstand in the park. George Cully built the Brunswick Hotel on what was the site of the Maple Leaf Milling Company's office.

The Cosmopolitan Hotel, Medicine Hat, after enlargements and alterations, c. 1918.

The American Hotel was erected in 1883, as well as the Landsdown, where the Cosmopolitan stood until torn down in 1978. It was to the Cosmopolitan that proprietor T. Bassett invited residents to celebrate Christmas in 1913. The dinner menu had a wine list and a program of "Selections to be rendered by the Dreamland Theatre Orchestra." Below that, before the food, was the Daily Motto: "Let Christmas be a bright and happy day, but let its brightness come from the radiance of the star of Bethlehem."

The menu was loaded with delicious suggestions such as, "Lake Superior salmon with Genoise Sauce and Potato Duchesse; Dale Prairie Chicken a la Demi Devil; Pauplette of Jackrabbit, French Mushrooms; Westphalia Sweet Ham, Shirley Sauce; Island Young Fowl, Maitre d'Hotel

Sauce; Pickled Sheep Tongue au Gelee." To tempt the sweet tooth, the menu offered "Queen Fruit Floating a la Meringue; Strawberry French Roll, St. Louis Style; Green Apple Pie and Panama Ice Cream with Lady's Finger."

Today's hoteliers would be hard-pressed to come up with a better Christmas menu than that of 1913!

Within 15 years, the population of Medicine Hat had reached 1,000 and, now incorporated, took on the character of permanency. It had churches, schools, a hospital and two, and sometimes three, newspapers. (The *Medicine Hat News* was begun in 1885, moving from weekly to daily status on January 1, 1911. The *Medicine Hat Times,* which delivered its first edition in 1905, went daily for a while, slipped back to a weekly on April 22, 1916 and ceased publication later the same year.)

The most colorful period in the history of the paper was the boom era shortly before World War I when Medicine Hat boasted three dailies: *The News,* Liberal; *The Times,* Conservative and *The Call,* a paper put out by a group of real estate men who felt the other papers were too modest in their assessment of.the city's future potential, especially concerning its natural gas assets.

On one occasion the *News* opposed the granting of a franchise for a street railway. The real estate agents who sponsored the franchise proposal won their campaign, however, and celebrated the victory with a torchlight parade through the city and a ceremony during which an effigy of the editor of the *News* was hurled into the river.

Items culled from copies of the early *Medicine Hat News* and from the minutes of early council meetings at City Hall make interesting reading. The *News* reported on January 12, 1898 that the council moved "that the salary of a police officer be $40 per month and two uniforms per year be supplied."

The ferry operating on the South Saskatchewan River became a topic of heated controversy. In 1899 the Territorial Government in Regina allowed a grant of $125 to operate the ferry while the City was to pay the ferryman. In 1900 the City was charging 20 cents a trip which was raised a year later to 48 trips for $10. The ferryman was paid $40 a month to operate the ferry, plus expenses for putting the ferry in the water ($25) and for taking the ferry out of the water ($35).

The CPR bridge across the South Saskatchewan River at Medicine Hat, probably about 1907-08 when it was single tracked. Particularly interesting in this view is the sign which reads: "CPR Co. Danger. The people are forbidden to walk across this bridge. Trespassers will be prosecuted according to law. By Order." "The people" paid no attention to this sign and used the bridge continually even when the ferry was available, and particularly on Sunday when the ferry was not running.

The ranchers in the area complained about having to pay *any* fee. T. H. Tinney wrote a letter to the newspaper on April 10, 1902 contending that the connection between opposite sides of the river should not be a cost on the rancher and his products. The ferry was in operation for about six months of the year, every day except Sunday. Meanwhile, work had been held up on the new Finlay Bridge. The *News* reported that severe winter weather had delayed the completion of the bridge. On Sundays the CPR bridge was the only means of river crossing for pedestrians. It was used extensively but illegally, warning signs being ignored. During winter months crossing the river on the ice was a common but dangerous practice.

The new bridge was an impressive structure for the day. Engineer J. A. Carbert announced that the bridge piers 40 feet above the bed of the river would go down 25 feet below the river bed — four piers and abutments on each side with steel arches 31 feet high and 180 feet in length. The bridge would be 900 feet long and 16 feet wide.

Construction commences on Finlay Bridge across the South Saskatchewan River in 1907.

There was an amusing incident involving Henry Cook (father of Thora Barrie) who operated the donkey engine used in driving pilings for the bridge. One day he fell into the river — twice. Since he could not swim, Cook decided that a third time might be fatal. So he took the rest of the day off!

An item in the *News* of March 19, 1908 was of a nature one does not encounter in classified advertisements today: "For Sale — The Crockford Coal Mines consists of 84 acres of coal land with one seven foot seam and one four foot seam of coal. Mine in good shape and can deliver 100 tons of coal per day at the mouth. Easy terms for quick sale. Apply D. Milne or M. J. Crockford."

From the minutes of the village dated May 29, 1899: ". . . that the rate of taxation for 1899 be 18 mills on the dollar." At the same meeting the Mayor, W. B. Marshall, reported that a Mrs. Wheatley had made a verbal complaint to him respecting the cow stable belonging to a Mr. Winterburn. Alderman Harry Yuill said Winterburn had sold out his business and the stables would soon be moved from town. A motion was passed that all persons having buildings on the Esplanade (now First Street) would be asked to move them

William Cousins Home in Medicine Hat, year 1900. In buggy, Mr. W. Cousins, Isabel Cousins. On verandah, left to right: Miss Thornton, Grace Cousins, Mrs. Cousins. Behind fence: Gerald Cousins, Jessie Cousins.

off "at their earliest convenience." On Monday, January 15, 1900 it was moved by Aldermen Spencer and Ross that a public meeting be called to discuss the matter of organizing a fire brigade. Two hundred handbills were to be circulated announcing the meeting.

Mrs. Jean Bryan recalled for the author some of the early days, such as, "Buying suckers for one cent at Hemeon and Newell's grocery store on Columbia Avenue; looking down from our house at the flood when Seven Persons Creek was jammed with ice and overflowed; gas wells being blown off just to honor the visit of some duke or some celebrity who visited the city; the city gas lamps on the street lit day and night; seeing large herds of cattle and sheep from the country being herded right down Columbia Avenue; the doctors arriving by horse and buggy to make house calls on the family; Dr. MacDonald performing a tonsillectomy on me on the kitchen table of our house."

L. B. Cochrane Store on South Railway Street in Medicine Hat.

The Canadian Tractor, made in Medicine Hat by Canadian Farm Implement Co., formerly Alberta Foundry and Machine Co. Probably only 20 of these were produced before World War I.

91

Mrs. Bryan is the daughter of Mr. and Mrs. John G. Munro who came to Medicine Hat in 1909 at the invitation of Mr. Munro's cousin, J. E. Davies. (Munro helped with the beginning of the Alberta Foundry and Machine Shop as a pattern maker who went on to design "The Canadian Tractor". A restored original of about 20 which were manufactured is now on display in the Provincial Museum in Edmonton.)

As in many other parts of the continent, land developers, nicknamed "Boomers", whose interests were primarily to sell lots at greatly inflated prices, arrived on the scene. Through misleading advertisements placed in Eastern newspapers, the boomers managed to sell lots ranging in price from $50 to $350 a lot. By today's prices these are cheap, however such bargains were not bargains at the time since many were located on bald prairie. At Suffield, for example, $24,500 worth of lots measuring 25 by 130 feet were sold in the price range quoted.

Mr. Haystead's Barbershop, Medicine Hat. Notice natural gas mantle type lamps in use. The year, probably 1900.

Suffield did not flourish despite such brisk sales of property. It wasn't until the Second World War that this neighboring community underwent a rapid and almost magical transformation. The Commonwealth Air Training Plan turned the bald and barren plains into a series of busy airfields that dotted the entire area from Winnipeg to the foot of the Rockies. Service colonies like Suffield became temporary homes for armed service personnel.

The war years marked the second time in Suffield's history that this quiet, desolate area experienced an invasion from the United Kingdom. Shortly after the turn of the century Canadian Wheatlands Limited, a speculative land development corporation with its roots in Britain, moved out to the prairie site and established its headquarters there. About 64,000 acres were put to the plow and steps taken to establish a large-scale wheat-growing development.

The venture was plagued with a variety of problems and after a series of very dry years and the advent of the First World War, it collapsed. The once thriving village, which boasted five grain elevators and three hotels,

swiftly deteriorated into almost a ghost town. One of those hotels, incidentally, has a romantic history.

The Alamo was built by two transplanted Americans and an Englishman; two other hotels — the Temperance and the Albion — were already established. The Americans, A. P. "Tiny" Phillips and W. R. "Frosty" Martin, gained fame when their Medicine Hat-based Martin & Phillips drilling firm brought in "Old Glory" gas well at Bow Island in 1909. A. M. Grace, the other partner in the Alamo venture, raised $30,000 on his personal credit rating. He was chief engineer of the land company.

The name Alamo was decided upon by Martin who had drilled wells in Texas. The battle that glorified Jim Bowie, despite his defeat by the Mexicans, was soon a Mecca for other hard-drinking, hard-driving transplants from the Lone Star State. The *Medicine Hat News* waxed fairly poetic as it described the hotel when it was opened on October 20, 1910: "The most

Eighteen binders and teams taking off bumper wheat crop in 1915 on what was formerly 5,000 acre Wheatlands Farm, west of Medicine hat (Suffield District). A syndicate of Ginther-Findlay-Yuill took over the land from Wheatlands.

The Stinson Detroiter Tractors manufactured by "Frosty" Martin and "Tiny" Philips of Medicine Hat, 1919-1920. The tractor was manufactured in Medicine Hat, the motor was brought in from Detroit. Very limited production. Maybe only 20 or less were manufactured.

93

"The most beautiful hotel alongside the CPR from Winnipeg to Calgary stands on the prairie within a stone's throw of one of the biggest gas wells in the Medicine Hat district, in what promises to be in the near future the City of Suffield. Seen from the train, the big hotel with lights blazing, is not un-promising of the renown about to come . . . This jewel box of a hotel has every conceivable modern attachment for the safety and comfort of the guests, and the interior is particularly beautiful."

It was, indeed, a sight to behold: "Rough-finished walls are colored in soft brown tints to set off weathered oak furniture. Hard maple floors lead to a bar at the rear, suggestive of Eastern forests, with rich deep green walls and dull mission oak furnishings. A front bar of solid mahogany is mounted on a base of utterly plain lines. The back bar is buffet style, filled with rare cut glass of beautiful patterns. Above unobtrusive but elegant mirrors, small windows of art glass admit subdued light. The bar itself, a stand-up affair, is 40 feet long and considered one of the finest in the country."

Alamo Hotel, Suffield, Alberta. For a hotel on the Prairies in the early days it was one of the best.

We are indebted to Hilda Wharton for preserving the description of this beautiful hotel in *The Miller,* Spring issue 1958. The hotel had a gorgeous dining room decorated in deep Turkish red and featured its own silverware with a distinctive Alamo stamp. There were 17 apartments, two suites and a drawingroom on the second floor. More rooms were on the third floor. There were fire alarms, hot and cold running water (the hot water heated by gas from the City's wells). Sunday dinner was a highlight and people from Medicine Hat drove out to sample it. Leo Hughes was the manager.

When the capital for the money-losing Southern Alberta Land Company was cut off during the First World War, and Prohibition was enacted in 1915, the hotel foundered. It stood empty for years until it was bought by the Calgary Brewing and Malting Company who needed a hotel at Sylvan Lake (11 miles west of Red Deer) when the hotel in that resort town burned down in 1926. The brewery acquired the Alamo and moved it there where it was drastically altered. Missing when it was reopened was an old-fashioned square flush toilet which a Chicago visitor liberated from the structure, possibly to Remember the Alamo!

In the spring of 1941 a small nucleus of British scientists came to Canada to form the core of the Suffield Experimental Station, a group dedicated to research into chemical warfare. The site chosen was preferred over several studied in the Maritimes and Manitoba. Basil Campbell of the Department of National Defence arranged the purchase of the former Canadian Wheatlands property, most of which was then in the hands of the CPR and the Hudson's Bay Company. The price was a nominal one dollar an acre, with substantially more paid to farmers who had to be evacuated from the area.

The scientists made their headquarters in the armories in Medicine Hat until their buildings were ready at Suffield. The first shipment of toxic stores, consisting of several railway carloads of mustard gas, phosgene and base-ejection artillery shells, arrived from the United Kingdom. They had to be stored in trenches which had been dug for that purpose — a makeshift method of storage, to say the least.

Mustard gas and phosgene, another dangerous and poisonous gas, were later manufactured in this country and the Canadian Army established an operational reserve of these chemical agents at Suffield, except that this time the toxic materials were stored in lead-lined tanks acquired from the United States Army Chemical Corps.

Although Suffield was originally established as a chemical warfare station, it was equipped to carry out research in many other fields as well. With the longest artillery range in the Commonwealth, the base possesses good facilities for high-level bombing trials. Laboratory facilities were ultimately available for research into all of the basic sciences and organic insecticides.

In 1946 the Suffield Experimental Station was taken over from the British and is now an all-Canadian operation. The community of Ralston, about two miles from the main laboratory, was built to accommodate married personnel. The old wartime accommodation was demolished. The RCAF detachment at the base was withdrawn at the end of 1957 with the Station receiving the necessary air support for its trials from several of the Canadian Armed Forces units in Western Canada.

The history of Suffield turned out to have a happy ending, if by that we consider having a chemical warfare plant in our backyard a "happy ending". However, the "City of Suffield" as envisioned by the *Medicine Hat News* writer, never materialized.

Returning briefly to the "boosting" of land through incentives and extravagant promises, the practice worked well in some instances. An example can be found in what happened to the Stair Farm, six miles west of Medicine Hat, when it was bought by Doctor R. R. Stoner in 1906. Clay deposits in the riverside gullies proved suitable for brick-making and, with an available local supply of good coal, Stoner quickly organized the Redcliff Brick and Coal Company. A year later the brick plant burned to the ground but was reconstructed and later became the Perry Brick Company.

The abundance of high-grade shale and the seemingly inexhaustible supply of natural gas prompted certain Medicine Hat businessmen to take advantage of Redcliff's possibilities. Herbert J. Sissons, James Hargrave and James Mitchell formed Redcliff Pressed Brick Company Limited in 1912 with Hargrave as president, Sissons as manager and Arthur W. Woodcock as superintendent. A fine quality of brick of excellent color and durability was the result.

At the beginning the clay was mined underground, the material being hauled to the surface up a ramp by a powered cable. Later the earth was stripped off the clay deposit, in the open pit fashion. An immense hole some 30 to 40 feet deep was dug near the plant.

Woodcock retired in 1925, turning management over to Harry G. Sheasby who acted as superintendent until his death in 1958 when Harry M. Sangster carried on. The company acquired Premier Brick Company in 1945. During the Second World War the Pressed Brick Company operated only sporadically, a skeleton crew coming in to work whenever orders were available. Demand for quality bricks increased after the war and the plant was in peak production until 1960 when a fire destroyed the building and much of the machinery.

In a short time a new plant was designed and built and brick again was being shipped to points as far east as Ontario, west to British Columbia and south to the United States.

The land that Doctor Stoner had acquired was developed through Redcliff Realty Company and sold as industrial sites. A cigar factory, an ornamental iron manufacturer and the Dominion Glass Company settled on the land. Specializing in a wide assortment of pop bottles, medicine bottles, lamp globes, beer bottles and fruit jars, Dominion Glass branched into fancy glass with the importation of expert glass workers from New Jersey. This ambitious project was nearly destroyed on June 25, 1915 when disaster struck Redcliff.

The day began like any other fine Southern Alberta summer day, but Friday, June 25th was different. The heat at midmorning was exceptional. The blazing sun and a southwest wind combined to send the temperature up over 100 degrees Fahrenheit. Residents were welcoming the freshening wind, hoping it marked a cooling off. However, the wind continued to increase and by mid-afternoon it was becoming difficult to walk comfortably outside.

Strange clouds began to form along the southern horizon and the sky took on a purplish, Armageddon look. Residents looked fearfully at it as they tugged children indoors and stock owners watched their uneasy animals heading to gulleys and shelter points. By dinner time the wind had become a howling gale, the black clouds scudding across the sky. Dust and debris flew through the air and Redcliff residents turned on their gas lamps. The flurry of activity in the streets suddenly ended. A dead calm fell over the town. Then — crash!

The steel roof of the water tower was torn off like a sheet of brown paper in the hands of a giant. The roof of the Laurel Hotel was rolled up like a carpet and flew through the air to crash to earth far away. The Ornamental Iron Works also lost its roof. A cigar factory located near the CPR station was blown over on its side, the lower part reduced to kindling, the top storey practically untouched. The frame home of George Gibson was tipped over on its side. The family was all inside but, miraculously, no one was badly injured. It took several teams of horses to pull the house back onto its foundation when the cyclone was over.

Redcliff Tornado of 1915

Rupert Cann told Angela Stubbs of the *News* the wind lifted one of the bleachers from the soccer grounds and blew it away. It was never found. Nor were the chickens belonging to a family on First Street. The wind whipped up the coop and its occupants. "They just disappeared," Cann said. A Mr. Rossini escaped injury when the cigar factory collapsed.

About the same time, the staff at the post office were called in to sort mail, in an unexpected way. The tremendous wind had carried away a portion of the new post office roof and the heavy rain that followed the wind poured into the building. The staff scurried around salvaging letters and parcels from the deluge. Next day was spent drying out the mail.

Some firms had their premises demolished and didn't bother to re-build. They simply packed up what was packable and either sold it or took it with them when they left. The Redcliff Knitting Mill had been building a factory about a half mile east of the community's water tower. It was on bald prairie and the fearsome wind demolished it. The company never rebuilt it.

When morning dawned, citizens of Redcliff were stunned by the devastation wrought by the big wind.

Completely wrecked steel water tower. Men standing are (left) George Esmonde-White and Dr. Milton Moore, both of Medicine Hat. (These photos were provided to the Museum by George Esmond-White's daughter, Frances.)

Views of Tornado damage in 1915 at Redcliff, Alberta, six miles west of Medicine Hat. Frame building next door to brick building, Alberta Cafe, completely wrecked.

For many it was the end. It was just not worth starting over. But with a tenacity born of adversity, the community bounced back from Mother Nature's rampage and continued its bumpy road to maturity. As if it needed any reminder, Redcliff was hit by another cyclone in 1923. Anna Plews recalled in 1980 that the cyclone went right through her family's farm, wrecking all the buildings except the house. "It took out the granaries, chicken coops, cowsheds, fences and the barn. Everything was gone."

Frame building (Rosen's) blown over.

It was in 1890 that Sampson Dutton dug a farm well on his Redcliff property and came up with a good source of natural gas, thus setting Redcliff's future as a "smokeless Pittsburgh." The town in 1912 had 1,000 citizens who called it home and a mayor who was a graduate of West Point, son of a wealthy Minneapolis mill owner: Edward Danelz was only 30 years old, wore a Van Dyck beard and drove a White steamer car. Danelz went overseas with the Canadian Army in the First World War. He served with distinction but did not return to the community with the red cliffs. In time, the flour mill he had established burned down and the basement was turned into a swimming pool.

Three models of trucks manufactured in Redcliff, Alberta in 1913. They carried the name "Redcliff" across the radiator and were built by Redcliff Motors Company Ltd. Seventy-five men were reported to be engaged in the plant, a pioneer commercial car factory in Western Canada. Redcliff is six miles west of Medicine Hat.

The town's future remained rocky through several decades, the population bouncing along with it, up to 3,000, down to 1,500, as the boom and bust economy dictated. At one time three hotels did land office business, and one enterprising chap set up a 75 foot long tent, renting out cots at a dollar a night. Water was piped through 14 miles of mains along 12 miles of streets and — as Ken Liddell recounted in his book *Alberta Revisited* — "dogs frolicked around 39 fire hydrants, some of them far out on the prairie."

Redcliffe's problem was that it was optimistically ahead of itself. And the 1915 and 1923 cyclones did not help matters. When the Depression came along, the City Fathers decided to tear down some of the derelict buildings left after economic and natural disaster and make sidewalks from them, indicating again the practical nature of the Redcliff citizens. History is the only record of some of the businesses and factories that were begun with such enthusiasm. Gone are the cap and shoe factories, the motor factory and the furniture plant. No more is the Redcliff Motors Co. Ltd., the factory that turned out 10 trucks and three buses, chain-driven and with hard rubber tires, that were said to have ridden "like lumber wagons."

Through it all, Redcliff was a free-wheeling community. The first Chief of Police was dismissed for taking bribes from gamblers. Another official of the law was convinced that Redcliff was a nest of spies during the First World War. He had every street and back alley patrolled. He sat on the roof of his hotel office and watched the community through binoculars. Assured that it was safe from spies, he joined the army, went to France, and was killed in active service.

Up and down though its economy may have been, Redcliff prospered in many ways, partly due to its proximity to booming Medicine Hat, and partly because of the diversity of its natural resources. At one time in 1915 there was a short-lived oil boom. E. H. Sellhorn, manager of one of the brick and coal companies, persuaded an American oil drilling outfit to try for a gusher in the community. A well was put down near the present water tower. After drilling 3,000 feet, only gas was encountered. The gas that had come in at 1,200 feet was ignored and the hole was plugged with a telephone pole and tons of bricks and coal.

In addition to natural gas, the community was the source of other commodities. There is gold in the river and during the Depression, unemployed men coaxed a dollar a day's worth of the elusive metal from the sand and gravel. Some used a sluice box; others a cradle or pan. Another form of income was from a fairly large deposit of silica sand located about a mile west of the town. It was the combination of silica sand and natural gas that led to the manufacture of glass at Redcliff. It was not suitable for fine glass, but use was made of it in the molding shops of the Ornamental Iron Company Ltd., and at the rolling mills.

Another interesting item was the seismotite or volcanic ash which was used in making hand-cleaner. For a short time it was manufactured and marketed but lack of advertising and competition forced the company to withdraw from business. Still another resource was limestone rock. Farmers gathered the limestone and brought it by wagon to be burned in natural gas limestone kilns. It was used by the local building trade for mortar and plastering and the rolling mills consumed vast amounts in processing steel in their open hearth furnaces.

Other communities around Medicine Hat did not fare as well as Redcliff. A prime example of complete failure to live up to its developers' promises was the hamlet of Dauntless, five miles south of Medicine Hat. It was built around a Canada Cement Company factory which never produced one bag of cement. The houses of the community that began around 1910 were nowhere to be seen by 1920, although the concrete building for the factory remains and is used for other purposes today.

According to the bulletin of The Historical Society of Medicine Hat and District of November 1916, the first settler at Dunmore was Dan Cavan, an Irishman who farmed and ranched on Bullhead Creek, west of what was to become the community of Dunmore. Dunmore was named for Lord Dunmore, one of the shareholders in Sir John Lister-Kaye's ill-fated Canadian Agricultural, Coal and Colonization Company. Henry Cavan, Dan Cavan's son, is believed to be the first male white child to be born in the area. He became active in Dunmore community affairs, was a member of the Medicine Hat Stampede committee. "Cavan Place" in Medicine Hat was named in honor of his participation in community affairs.

Tweed and Ewart operated a store at Dunmore which was managed by Henry Stewart. Supplies were brought to Dunmore from Medicine Hat by horse and wagon. R. C. Porter built a hotel in the town which stood unpainted for many years before finally being torn down. Miss Madge Walker was the community's first teacher, followed by James Sallows, who tried homesteading for a while before returning to his original profession. He finally retired to his farm after many years as a highly-respected teacher. The old school house became a restaurant, run by a couple from the United States, Mr. and Mrs. John McCarrol; the new brick school house that replaced it was eventually dismantled when children from Dunmore were bussed to Irvine for schooling.

Hotel at Dunmore when it was a thriving centre competing with Medicine Hat.

There was considerable rivalry between Dunmore and Medicine Hat in the early days. Dunmore was quite a busy spot when coal was king and shipments totalling 300 to 500 tons a day were transhipped from Lethbridge east. The Dunmore CPR station, originally at a site two miles west of the community before being moved into town, required an agent, three telegraph operators, a car checker and other office staff, a yard engine and two crews for it, and a full complement of car personnel.

A second hotel was built and operated by a French-speaking family named Lecieux. This hotel was painted white and had the town's first telephone which the Lecieuxs graciously let everyone in the community use.

The community began to grow considerably when "Tiny" Phillips and "Frosty" Martin had several test wells for oil pushed through the willing clay and sand. No oil was found, although the community had natural gas for cooking and light. A pool hall, a barber shop and several stores were established in Dunmore and a taxi service between there and Medicine Hat was available for 75 cents single fare, one-way trip. A large, modern brick hotel was erected but it burned to the ground in a short time. Buildings in Dunmore had a habit of burning to the ground fairly frequently, as one old resident remarked to the author.

As mentioned, there was rivalry between Dunmore and Medicine Hat, but with its prime location and its access to water, the city that was "born lucky" was a thriving community while Dunmore quickly faded to become a tiny place, peopled mainly with memories.

Medicine Hat's progress was not, apparently, due to any assistance from the city of Calgary. An early edition of the *Medicine Hat News* carried an item that reported a censure by the city council of the Calgary press for "suppression of all reports of Medicine Hat's municipal and industrial development and the publishing of distorted and incorrect reports of the City Council, tending to convey the impression that there is bad feeling between the Council and its citizens."

Be that as it may, there may have been some truth in the statement: carried in the very same paper was an item that there was bad feeling between the Council and the City Solicitor. The Solicitor complained that he had heard nothing of his long-standing request for a pay hike. He also objected to a resolution that he attend every Council meeting. He had been absent (for business reasons, he said) on the night the resolution was passed.

If the Calgary press did not give good coverage to Medicine Hat's progress in the fields of industry and culture, it did carry stories of a humorous vein. In the *Calgary Herald* of July 27, 1906 it was reported that a certain Ben Buller, working on a mine a few miles up the railroad tracks from Medicine Hat, had gone into town, full of "bad whiskey". In these early days there was prohibition in the Territories and any whiskey to be found was in the "blind pigs" or "speak-easies."

The *Herald* reported that Buller was even worse for wear as he made his way home across the CPR bridge. "He did not get very far before he had to lie down to sleep off some of the effects of his potations." The next morning a couple of Medicine Hat citizens walking along the tracks came upon him. They shook him and got him to his feet, only to discover that the miner had been sleeping alongside a rattlesnake. As the newpaper noted, the two Good Samaritans looked around for rocks to kill the rattler but on closer examination found that the snake was already dead.

They then examined Buller and found that he had been bitten in several places by the reptile. It was assumed that a combination of the bad whiskey, Buller's tough disposition, and some Medicine Hat "luck" proved to be an effective antidote for snake bite.

Medicine Hat continued to be the brunt of snide remarks and newspaper items that tended to make fun of the city. The haughty matrons of Calgary and Winnipeg could laugh behind their fans at the foolish goings-on in the little cowtown with the strange name.

The *Winnipeg Times* of October 22, 1883, for example, carried an item noting that since strong liquor was prohibited in the "Territories:, Florida water mixed with Worcester (sic) sauce is the popular drink in Medicine Hat. Bay rum also finds a ready sale and fruit syrup finds a ready market." What "Florida water" is, is not explained. Bay rum is a fragrant liquid used in medicine and cosmetics, often favored by "rummys" on skidroads everywhere.

The Winnipeg paper recounted a story where a local merchant purchased a case of fruit syrup which turned out to be brandy. Customers bought the "syrup" at $1.50 a bottle, discovered the mistake, and sold it for $5 a bottle. "The Winnipeg shipper has since been informed of what occurred and one of the Commandments has been broken at a frightful rate ever since," the reporter concluded. In that instance, at least, the lowly Medicine Hatters had the last laugh.

More serious than the chuckles that easterners got at Medicine Hat's expense were the stories about its boom and bust economy. Thomas Gordon Allan, who came to the city in 1910, is a fairly typical example of the type of pioneer who took advantage of the boom periods and lost when the bust arrived. But he stayed on to become one of the city's most beloved citizens. Allan was originally hired to run the Alberta Government Experimental Farm, on Crescent Heights above the city, by Agriculture Minister Duncan Marshall. He resigned as manager after disagreeing with government officials over farming procedures.

Thomas Gordon Allan as he looked in 1912.

101

F. M. Ginther was a progressive real estate agent in the boom years in Medicine Hat and always welcomed an opportunity to advertise.

He sold his own land and moved to Castor, Alberta, but returned to Medicine Hat when he learned of the great bumper crops of 1915 and 1916. With the Ginther Brothers, he formed Gas City Farming Company and put 2,000 acres into wheat, one of the largest acreages in one crop at that time.

Ginther, in the form of F. M. Ginther, established the F. M. Ginther Land Company, Ltd. in 1907. He was instrumental in placing a great number of homesteaders in the district. In addition to real estate, the firm also dealt in the sale of first mortgages on city and farm properties and represented British Crown Assurance Corporation, Credit Foncier and several Canadian investment firms.

There was no rain to speak of in 1917 and the crop Allan and Ginther planted was so poor it was not even harvested. In 1918, the same acreage was seeded to wheat and again there was a drought. Lesson learned, Allan farmed on a reduced scale for two more years and then gave it up to follow a different career. In 1924 he bought Mac's Newstand from Mac MacDorman, renamed it Tom's Newstand and gave the business his inimitable stamp. He brought in "old country mail", magazines and newspapers from Abroad. Regular customers had their copies placed in special boxes at the back of the store each week.

Tom Allan in his famous garden, the secrets to which he broadcast over CHAT radio for five years. Allan on left. Man on right unidentified.

He also dedicated himself to his love of gardening and his garden on 200 feet of road frontage at his home on Ninth Street South East was well-known locally for the quality of its fruit and vegetables. He was encouraged at the age of 70 to share his knowledge with fellow residents. The gardening broadcasts that resulted were heard over radio station CHAT for five years.

Thomas Allan's newsstand was a mecca for everyone. Ranchers and farmers down on their luck during the Dirty Thirties knew they could count on him for a ten or twenty dollar loan. Allan had shared in bad luck and knew its humiliating sting. Beneficiaries of his largesse seldom let him down and some went on to become wealthy men. Mothers of newborn babies would bring them in to the newstand to receive Thomas Allan's chuck under the chin and blessing.

Almost synonymous with Medicine Hat are flour mills and brick plants. Names such as Five Roses, Ogilvie and Cream of the West have contributed much to the area's economy since the time that John McNeely built a large mill in the city in 1902. After managing Medicine Hat Milling Company with his son for a number of years, McNeely sold out to Lake of the Woods Milling Company which produced Five Roses flour.

The Medicine Hat Milling Co. which John McNeely built in 1902 and sold to Lake of the Woods, manufacturers of Five Roses products.

George Preston was the first manager of the Lake of the Woods plant and he was succeeded by Colin Moir who played an active role in community affairs. George Armstrong was the first manager of Ogilvie Flour, followed by Ashton Fletcher Andrews, H. Norman Davis and Art Atkins. Both Davis and Atkins rose to the position of president of the firm.

Two other flour mills established in the area: the Maple Leaf Milling Company managed by W. J. Smallacombe, and a plant operated by Alberta Wheat Pool and managed by Thomas Montgomery.

When the Duke of Devonshire was Governor General of Canada he stopped off in Medicine Hat for a visit and to inspect the Ogilvie Flour Mills

103

plant. Joe Tyas was asked by foreman Ernie Riley if he would operate the elevator in the plant that day. Tyas agreed but about 10 minutes prior to the Duke's arrival an emergency arose: a workman was trapped in another part of the mill and Tyas was required to help get him free; he came back all covered with flour.

"He had no time to change and had to get back to the elevator in time to bring the Duke and his family, the Mayor, aldermen and the manager of the mill up for the inspection," David Tyas told the author in 1979. "The Duke took one look at my father and said: 'Well! Joe! Come and meet my family.' He also asked dad if he would come down to the royal railway car that evening for a chat about old times in England.

Lake of the Woods Milling Co., c. 1925, later sold to Ogilvie Milling Co. The brick mill section only was converted to a restaurant and hotel in 1980.

"The other members of the royal party were stunned that the Duke would single out a common worker covered in flour and then invite him to his personal railway car. It was because when dad lived in England he used to play cricket in Yorkshire near the Duke's father's estate, and at that time the young duke would come over and umpire the games. This was how they knew each other."

Another company employee, Joe Pennington, was known to the Duke through his father, who had been a gatekeeper at the Duke's father's estate. Both men kept their appointment with royalty that night.

In 1888 Ben McCord began manufacturing brick in the east end of the city. Shortly afterward Charles and Jacob Purmal took over this plant and greatly expanded the operation. L. H. Pruitt, a retired rancher who was a shareholder with the Purmals, became president in 1909. In September of 1911 the Birnie Brothers took control of the plant. Two years later Warren Overpack entered the scene but in 1914 the operation returned to the control of the Purmal Brick Company.

Charles Purmal's daughter-in-law, Mrs. Freda Purmal, widow of Wilfred G. Purmal, told the author in 1978 that the Purmal brothers cut hay on the open prairie that is now part of the city to feed the horses they used at the brickyard. Charles Purmal built and owned several homes in the city but sold them during the Depression because he could not collect the rentals.

104

Charles Purmal contracted to construct buildings for the Sarnia Ranching Company when it expanded to the district from Lethbridge. The Purmals were made of stern stock. Mrs. Purmal noted that Charles Purmal had almost all of his own teeth at the age of 90 and would not go to a dentist if he needed dental care. "When a tooth needed pulling," she said, "he did it with an ordinary nail."

The CPR built a spur track into the Purmal property and more gas was developed for use in the plant operations. After a slow recovery following the First World War, the company began to manufacture hollow building tile in 1923. Six years later the firm was purchased by the Redcliff Pressed Brick Company and became known as Medicine Hat Brick and Tile with H. J. Sissons serving as manager of both plants.

When Mr. Sissons died in 1949 his sons Gordon, Jack and Tom assumed control of the company. In later years the addition of a research department greatly added to the success of the company.

For many years Medalta Pottery Company was a name closely associated with Medicine Hat. It began when John A. McIntyre of Spokane, Washington opened a pottery called Medicine Hat Pottery Company in 1913. Using clay imported from Washington state, the plant was economically unsound and went into liquidation a year after opening. When it closed it was in the hands of rancher John Read, who also owned the Royal Hotel, John Bending, a farmer and manufacturer, and Addison P. Day who owned a 6,000 acre plot of clay land at Eastend, Saskatchewan. Bending was the principal shareholder.

In May 1916 Bending, Read and Day reopened the plant under the name of Medalta Stoneware Limited with W. Clark as superintendent and using clay from Eastend, which cost one-sixth of the price of the Washington clay. In November of that year Clark incorporated with Read to set up a small pottery in a building near Medalta known as Gas City Pottery Ltd. Often called the Clark Pottery, it was renamed Canada Pottery.

In 1918 a trio of businessmen acquired control of Medalta Stoneware: Charles Pratt, W. A. Greer and Ulysses Sherman Grant. By 1924 the name had been changed to Medalta Potteries Ltd. Jessie William Wyatt, an English potter from Ontario, took over as superintendent of manufacturing. Meanwhile, Canada Pottery closed its doors and Clark returned to the States.

The **Medalta Potteries, Medicine Hat.** A view of the plant and stock yard in the earlier days of their operation.

The next few years in the turbulent Twenties, Medalta tried new ideas to stimulate growth. The manufacture of electrical insulators was begun and discontinued in short order. The company then made Stone Gingerbeer bottles but there was a problem with leakage and the emergence of glass led to its economic demise. Tom Hulme was brought out from England to head the firm's art department and stayed on for 27 years.

On March 15, 1929, the year of the stock market crash, Charles Pratt sold the assets of Medalta Potteries to Reginald C. Carlisle and O. Clair Arnott of Calgary for $250,000. Pratt and W. A. Greer returned to the United States. Walter Armstrong became general manager and Karl Baumler was brought out from Germany as superintendent.

A year later Jessie Wyatt left the firm to start a small pottery with his two sons in Redcliff. The venture failed because of lack of funds but within six months Wyatt formed a new company with shareholders. The company became Alberta Potteries Ltd. and sprang to life in an old automobile factory which was purchased for one dollar. In 1935 Alberta Potteries was liquidated. The building and kiln were left intact in Redcliff.

In 1937, Karl Baumler and Walter Armstrong left Medalta to work for Yuill's new plant named Medicine Hat Potteries division of Alberta Clay Products Ltd. Armstrong became sales manager. Ed Phillipson took over as superintendent from Baumler. The year was an exciting one for pottery in the city. Medalta got a quarter million dollar injection to update plant equipment to compete with Yuill's Medicine Hat Potteries. Phillipson developed a line of hotel ware and other products to put Medalta back on its feet. The competition between the two potteries was keen for the next few years.

In 1941, Harlan "Hop" Yuill took over the former Alberta Potteries plant in Redcliff and hired Luke Lindoe to run it as a private venture separate from Medicine Hat Potteries. Lindoe left Yuill six months later.

At war's end Medicine Hat had two potteries still in operation and Redcliff had one. In 1947 Medalta expanded its operations while many other incidents occurred to keep the industrial pot boiling. Phillipson and others started National Porcelain Company, manufacturing insulators. The firm was sold to Motor Coach Industries of Winnipeg, then to Greyhound Lines and eventually to IXL Industries.

Karl Baumler, Superintendent and Jack Barrie, Sales Manager, both resigned from Medicine Hat Potteries and Malcolm McArthur, office clerk, took over, with "Hop" Yuill, to keep the plant operating.

At the end of 1947 Medalta had a new board of directors. A Mr. March of Montreal became the new owner and Phillipson was later named director. In 1952 there was another change in ownership for Medalta. A Hamilton, Ontario group took over and six months later Phillipson left to go to work for Yuill at Medicine Hat Potteries. Unknown to Yuill, his family and shareholders arranged to sell ACP and Medicine Hat Potteries to Marwell Construction of Vancouver. Harlan Yuill was out of the pottery business. Malcolm McArthur stayed on to help run the Medicine Hat Potteries but 18 months later the new owners wanted to sell and in 1957, renamed Hycroft Potteries, the Vancouver company sold to Harry Veiner. Six months later McArthur quit Hycroft and with six or seven employees from Hycroft endeavored to run the Alberta Potteries at Redcliff for Hop Yuill. The venture failed after six months.

In 1958 Medalta was $585,000 in debt. It declared bankruptcy and closed its doors. McArthur and his small group returned to Medicine Hat to re-open the Medalta Pottery building at a very low rate of rent from the City of Medicine Hat, which had the largest claim on the building because of unpaid utilities bills. The company was just rejuvenating when a fire on Christmas Eve 1958 wiped out the business.

The next year McArthur convinced the Thralls family of Lethbridge to put up $110,000 to buy the old Medalta plant and install him to run it under the name of Sunburst Ceramics Ltd.

A group of British manufacturers visited Medicine Hat July 1912. Shown here is the group visiting the plant of the Alberta Clay Products Co. This plant was destroyed by fire in 1961 and was never rebuilt.

In 1961 the Thralls decided to buy McArthur out; they established their Sunburst Ceramics operation in Lethbridge but soon they were out of the pottery business, as was McArthur. The old Alberta Clay Products building, owned by IXL, burned down that year and it was never rebuilt.

Like Medalta and the other major potteries, the City of Medicine Hat had its ups and downs, but the ups were in the majority. In a November 1973 edition of *The Roughneck,* the City of Medicine Hat placed an advertisement, quoting Kipling's famous statement about having "all hell for a basement", then went on to add that there had never been such a surge of activity in exploring the area for gas reserves. "Drillers, services and industry are working very hard to get the "Hell" out of our basement. You could have a stake in this 'Boom'."

Kipling also said the city was "born lucky", while others had good things to say too: Edward, the Prince of Wales, said it was "a lovely spot." Governor-General Vincent Massey said it was a "friendly, busy place." John Fisher, well-known broadcaster and commentator, called it "Canada's Prairie Pittsburgh" and Lady Baden-Powell, founder of the Girl Guides movement, said it was a "fine place to raise children."

With so many positive statements and opinions of the City, residents were well advised to turn a deaf ear to all insults. Where were the early critics? And where will today's critics be tomorrow?

107

G. W. Elliott

W. H. Turpin

G. A. Cochran

C. S. Pingle

H. S. Ireland, Vice-President

A. P. Burns

Dr. O. Boyd

J. C. Beveridge

Wm. Cousins

MEMBERS OF THE BOARD OF TRADE COUNCIL, 1910

From Tent Town To Metropolis

Part Two

"Every unprejudiced person must heartily agree with your remarks regarding incorporation of this town," a resident wrote to the editor of the *Medicine Hat Times* on April 2, 1896. "We want an unselfish spirit manifested in the matter."

Incorporation would have definite advantages: "We might have some sanitary laws enforced, in the removing of festering heaps of disease-breeding matter which is at present, and generally always is, adorning some of our back lanes. We might even rise to the height of having a drain or two."

As the writer pointed out, "The place has splendid advantages. Water supply and lighting arrangements would obtain some attention as to their possible development."

The author of the letter signed himself or herself, "For An Enlightened Policy" and suggested that the town council urge "the government to aid in getting some small system of irrigation for the town and neighborhood instead of letting a half dozen companies in Alberta tap the river and perhaps during some periods of the year finding ourselves able to play baseball in its bed. This idea of irrigation is a serious consideration."

At the time the southeast area of the province was awash with various agricultural schemes to turn it into a veritable oasis. The land that had been opened up for wholesale homesteading, regardless of its potential for farming, was now being looked at again: irrigaton was the salvation; the prairie would bloom with water from its many rivers.

Pure water, it must be admitted, is an absolute necessity for any· community and almost from the beginning the City Fathers were aware of this need. Luckily, in Medicine Hat the good and pure water was close at hand. Jim McCombs, who came to the area in 1902, recalled that water at that time was hauled straight from the river and sold at 25 cents a barrel. It was not always of the finest quality. "I was appalled at the debris that floated down the river in the spring," he said in an interview with Jan Fulton in 1979. He installed his own filtering system and his water supply became popular with his neighbors who did not have such "modern" conveniences. Water, in the form of ice, was cut in deep sections of the South Saskatchewan River and hauled by teams and sleighs to ice houses located on both sides of the river. Ice was delivered by team and wagon to city homes in the summer time.

As well as drinking water, the river was early used for fire fighting.

109

(Left to Right) Chief Bill Hatcher in buggy with rein on "Old Barney." Behind team "Tom and Jerry", "Dunk" Sanderson and ? Collier. Motorized Webb chain drive pumper manned by Dan McLeod at wheel and Bill "Buck" Buchanan, c. 1912.

Medicine Hat Fire Engine in front of Fire Hall section of City Hall building. Standing, Chief Bill Hatcher. At the wheel, Bill Buchanan, Dan McLeod. Tail enders, . . . Collier, Dunk Sanderson. About 1912.

110

McCombs, who worked for the CPR for more than 40 years, noted that the town's "fire brigade" was nothing more than a "two-wheeled thing with a hose wrapped around it that was pulled by a horse. When a fire broke out there was a great rush to get there first with a horse as the successful one would receive a dollar for his efforts."

At that time two of the best known fire fighters were not of the human variety: Tom and Jerry were fire horses. According to oldtimers, the horses started prancing whenever the fire gong sounded (it wasn't until 1912 that a fire siren was installed). When they were put into their harness, they raced eagerly to the scene of the blaze.

Deputy Fire Chief Bev Bray said in 1978 the fire horses seemed to love the fast-paced, dangerous life they sometimes led. "The story goes that the men had to set fire to the horses' hay to get them to eat it," he said. Bray said the city kept only one team of horses on hand and, beginning in 1905 when the old fire building was completed and the gong sounded, the horses were pulled from their stall and a harness, suspended on pulleys over their heads, was dropped on them.

The fire brigade soon proved inadequate and in 1901 W. T. Finlay undertook the task of reorganizing the department. Dougall McNab was appointed fire chief and W. C. Cavanaugh was his assistant. H. L. Tweed served as secretary-treasurer. (The function of a secretary-treasurer in a fire department was not spelled out.) The equipment available consisted of a chemical engine which weighed several tons and required 30 men to haul it with its attendant 500 feet of hose. Some of the earliest volunteer firemen included Isaac Bullivant, William Barrie, Ed Middleton, Dave Williamson, Mort Fulton, Percy Yeo, Sam and Abe Taylor, Hume Pingle, and later Ron McAffer, Cliff Wright, Claude Daniels, Reg Stone, Jim Rae, Bill and Bruce Buchanan and Jim Connors.

In 1911 the City purchased its first fire truck and in 1913 two more trucks were bought by the department. It was at that time the horses were put out to pasture, much to the dismay of the city's residents. The stalls in the old fire station were used for office space until the Fire Department moved to its new Maple Avenue quarters in 1975. For three years Fire Hall Theatre used the old hall until the thespians were forced to move out to make room for the City's land assessment office employees.

During the early years the fire department was called upon to fight a number of serious blazes, including those that broke out in the Pump and

Isaac Bullivant

Mr. J. H. Preston operated an extensive planing Mill near the Medicine Hat Feeding Company's present location. Being situated close to Seven Persons Creek they had problems with spring flooding. His losses from floods forced him to discontinue the operation.

Brass Manufacturing Company, the Preston Planing Mill and the Lake of the Woods Flour Mill. The most tragic fire of the early period occurred on March 19, 1913 at an abandoned cannery building on Main Street. A gas explosion killed five persons and injured nine others. Killed were Reginald Rimmer, William Green, Charles Behannon, William Stewart and Johnston Blair. The sturdy brick building which once housed Malcolm Canneries was reduced to a heap of broken bricks and twisted beams.

Medicine Hat Fire Department, now one of the most efficient and modern in Alberta (as early as 1910 the Medicine Hat Fire Brigade carried off the championship at the Sports of the Union of Alberta Fire Brigades at Red Deer), more than once saved the city from a conflagration that would have wiped it out. On December 2, 1945 the landmark Assiniboia Hotel burned to the ground. Approximately 100 guests escaped without serious injury as smoke and sparks drifted as far as the railroad tracks, forcing the moving of the CPR passenger train, which had just stopped in front of the station prior to the fire. Firemen worked for 24 hours to keep the blaze from spreading to adjacent buildings.

Medicine Hat Fire Department with trophies won in inter-city sports.

Medicine Hat has since had other spectacular fires, including the January 14, 1965 fire when Moore's Furniture store was destroyed, involving a loss of nearly half a million dollars worth of property and stock. Two firemen narrowly escaped death or serious injury when they found themselves in the basement of the burning building.

Moore's Furniture literally grew up with Medicine Hat. J. J. Moore arrived from Toronto in the early 1900s, opening a shop in the former Methodist Church building on Sixth Avenue, adjacent to the present Royal Bank site. In 1910 larger premises were opened on South Railway Street. In 1918 a still larger store was occupied on Sixth Avenue and eight years later another move was made to a location on Second Street. In 1933 Moore's was established in a large three-and-one-half storey structure formerly known as the LePage Building, which originally housed the LePage Broth-

112

ers Department Store. It was this building that was demolished in a fire in 1965. For some years Moore's was located in the lower floor of OK Economy Supermarket. In 1980 they took over and remodelled the Beny Motors Building on South Railway Street as a modern furniture store.

In their aim to have the best of everything, Medicine Hat residents pressed for a filtration system that would make their water as pure as it could be. A deputation of city council went to Brandon, Manitoba around the turn of the century to investigate a highly-regarded filtration system in use there. Brandon also took its water supply from a river: the Assiniboine. In 1906 a contract was let to the Roberts Company of Philadelphia to construct a filtration plant consisting of two one million gallon units. Also let was a contract for the erection of a one-half million gallon steel standpipe. One of the largest in Canada, it was located at the highest point in the city at the corner of Third Avenue South East and Fourth Street South East. It cost $15,000 and had a capacity of 500,000 gallons. Height was 70 feet, diameter 35 feet.

An editorial writer boasted: "The citizens of the city take a great deal of interest in the public-owned utilities . . ." The satisfaction of the ratepayers with the steps taken by the council for improvement showed itself when the bylaw for waterworks, to provide additional money for extension, was voted upon and unanimously approved." That was in 1907, a very good year for Medicine Hat.

The filter plant, located at the foot of Third Avenue, South East, necessitated the digging of a hole 80 feet square and 30 feet deep, a formidable task for that time. Concrete was used in the construction, the filter beds and basins being ponderous affairs of solid cement and masonry, portions of which were reinforced with steel. The water source, from a well alongside the river, was elevated to the receiving basin by a centrifugal pump operated by a 25 horsepower Columbus gas engine.

(In April 1980 the City announced that it had the highest per capita water use in Canada and a $2 million expansion of the City's water treatment facilities was necessary. Lorne Thompson, Public Works Director, said: "Our philosophy of maintaining an oasis in the midst of a desert, and the arid climate, account for the high consumption." Equipment added increased capacity from 109 million litres a day to 150 million litres. A new water clarifier removed dirt particles from an additional 41 million litres of water a day and an additional interceptor pump system was installed to divert more water from the power plant into the treatment facilities.)

So . . . Medicine Hat had pure, drinkable water. But there were still those muddy streets to contend with. The good citizens had slogged their way through Alberta gumbo and dust for years, cursing the sticky mess that impeded each step along street or lane. In that same go-ahead year, 1907, at a cost of $40,000, Navin Brothers contractors installed 16,316 lineal feet of concrete sidewalks. At an average of six and one-half feet wide, the total covered area was 106,054 square feet, a fair accomplishment for the time.

For transportation the City had the Bluebell Bus, owned by Slim Blair, and it covered the whole city. The driver was George Matheson.

The constant striving to become better and better, coupled with municipal ownership of the waterworks and gasworks, resulted in Medicine Hat leading all Canadian cities in building permits in 1912. The nine month

Cement crosswalks and cement sidewalks were now installed but if Madam forced you off the crosswalk you were in the mud. This is a scene on Sixth Ave. crossing from what is now Black's Hardware to what is now Toronto Dominion Bank.

"Slim" Blair, who owned Blair Bus and Taxi Service.

113

The City's primary sewage treatment lagoon as it looked from the air in 1981. In April 1980 the City announced it had the highest per capita water use in Canada. Public Works Director Lorne Thompson said the philosophy of maintaining an oasis in the midst of a desert, and the arid climate, account for the high consumption.

increase over the same nine months of 1911 was a whopping 340 per cent. (The figures were supplied in a comparison chart with other Canadian centres by the *Financial Post*.)

As if to celebrate her new-found prosperity, Medicine Hat imported "Professor" T. W. Hand of Hamilton, Ontario to provide a $2000 display of fireworks for July 1st, 1912. A. F. Binning, chairman of the Dominion Day celebration committee, described the display as consisting of "beautiful large set pieces, a full display of aerial fireworks of all the very latest effects such as you see only at such places as the Toronto and Winnipeg fairs and other large cities."

Binning, understandably proud, remarked that trains just "hesitate" at most western towns, while at Medicine Hat "all trains stay 25 minutes so we must be doing things in a big way." The "monster" celebration on July 1 went off on schedule and as the newspaper reported, "a good time was had by all."

A visitor to the city that year was Cyril B. Browne. As he recalled in an interview with Diana Howe, "Medicine Hat had a population of 10,000, there were a few houses in Riverside and on Crestwood, and the streets were lighted by gaslights day and night because it was cheaper to leave them on than it was to hire someone to turn them off and then light them again in the

114

evening." This practice was duly noted in a "Believe It Or Not" column by Ripley much later on.

Educated at London University as a chemist, Browne served two years as an alderman, following his election in 1923. In 1935 he began the Canada Extract and Manufacturing Company and during its 40 years of operation Browne patented 10 medicines. He retired in 1975, but only because he broke his hip. He was 96 years old. He could not see what all the fuss was about as he celebrated his 100th birthday at the River View Nursing Home. "If you have a clear mind, good eyesight and good health, it doesn't matter what the count is," he said.

Cyril B. Browne was an entrepreneur, and Medicine Hat was blessed with many of his type. Two others were the Littlefords, Thomas and Marthina

The Littleford's Grocery Store on South Railway Street. Photo shows the senior Littlefords and their five daughters.

Interior of the Littleford store. At the back are Mrs. Littleford and youngest daughters.

115

(née Thompson) who arrived in Elkwater in 1889. Thomas helped Harry, Bill and Jim Smybert operate their farm and sawmill. After obtaining his own homestead at Dauntless, seven miles from Medicine Hat, he delivered milk to the city for a number of years.

The Littlefords raised eight children, but that was not enough of a career for Marthina. She ran her own store on South Railway Street for a time, selling it and opening another on Ash Avenue, which had a boarding house attached. Granddaughter Mabel Jordahl recalled in correspondence with the author that the house had many closets, a prime attraction to her and her sisters and brothers. "We nearly drove grannie crazy with our screaming hide-and-seek games."

While Marthina ran the store and boarding house, husband Thomas operated a pool hall in Redcliff and during the First World War ran a stage to Dunmore, and enroute taking men to and from work at the Dominion Radiator Plant, located west of where the Furniture Barn now stands. They were manufacturing shells there for a short time.

Mrs. Jordahl's mother, Mable Baldwin Littleford, was born on April 1, 1890 and lived in Medicine Hat all her life. The maternal grandmother, Mary Reeves, lived in a house right across the street from Toronto Street School, now the site of OK Economy Store. "Mother hated that fact," Mrs. Jordahl told the author, "because she had to do dishes and make the beds before she was allowed to leave for school. She was one student who was happy to hear the school bell go."

As the daughter recalled: "Mother was so happy when the second school was built because she didn't have to do morning chores because she had so much further to walk."

Mable Baldwin Littleford married James Hole in June 1906. He worked as a stationary engineer at Alberta Clay Products and, later, for Medicine Hat Greenhouses. Hard work was the order of the day. Mr. Hole, who was a city alderman for 13 years, was not one to complain. He had only one day a year off — Christmas. It is ironic that he died on that particular day in 1946. Daughter Mable Jordahl recalled that her father worked for Harry Yuill at the clay products plant and as a child she looked forward to going through her father's pockets when he came home to see what he had created for his offspring out of little bits of waste clay. "Sometimes it would be a little clay frog, a dog, a cat, or even an image of Mutt and Jeff," she said.

The Littlefords and the Holes were representative of the calibre of men and women who settled in the Medicine Hat district prior to the First World War. Another was Hector Lang, one of the city's most beloved mayors from 1939 to 1946. The city was his home from February 1913 until his death in March 1952. He was born on a farm in Elgin County, Ontario in 1871, graduated from the University of Toronto in Honors Mathematics and in 1905 was appointed principal of Regina Collegiate. However, he decided to pursue a new career in the booming community of Medicine Hat.

With his wife Ethel (Craig), whom he married in 1907, he moved to the city in 1913. Daughters Margaret and Helen, who were born in Regina, came with their parents; Hector Junior was born in the city. In partnership with his brother, Wilson Lang, Hector established Lang Brothers Insurance Agency. He served on the School Board as well as City Council and in a Provincial byelection in 1928 he went to Edmonton as Liberal Member of the Legisla-

Hector Lang, beloved alderman, Mayor and MLA. A Liberal, he lost the Medicine Hat riding during the Social Credit sweep of 1935.

116

ture. He won again in 1930 but was defeated in the Social Credit sweep of August 1935.

Hector Lang was active in church affairs and played leading roles in establishing the Medicine Hat Historical and John Howard Societies. As his daughter Margaret Lang O'Byrne remarked in January 1980, "During his years in Medicine Hat the population was fairly static; how happy he would be now to see so many of his dreams for the city come true."

As will be noted, many of the pioneers reached ages far beyond that considered possible by actuarial compilation. The Board of Trade in 1910 laconically recorded in a promotional bulletin that the health of the city was so good and business at the cemetery so bad that the Presbyterian Church had offered to hand over the land to the City to keep it as public cemetery for all denominations. "This makes one wonder what the climate may be like. It is no exaggeration to say that at no place on the whole American continent is the climate so ideal as that of Medicine Hat."

There was just no stopping the flow of superlatives by the Board of Trade promoters: "Situated as it is at an altitude of 2,161 feet above sea level, the climate conditions compare favorably with those of the South of France and Italy. With the spring coming at the beginning of March, the summers last from May to the end of September, then comes the fall or 'Indian Summer' during which it feels good to be alive, for right up to the end of the year there is one long spell of bright, sunshiney weather when it is a delight to be out of doors."

Medicine Hat residents will be happy to know that winters here are "very short and are broken by Chinook spells and on this account a change of 80 degrees has been known for six hours. The cold weather is just keen enough to render outdoor skating and curling a delightful pastime. Small wonder that the health statistics show an abnormally low death rate."

Despite its salubrious climate outdoors, the smart business people of Medicine Hat decided early on to put their vegetable and flower production under glass. The city gained fame as the greenhouse centre of Western Canada with the largest area under glass of any city in the country, with the exception of St. Catherines, Ontario.

Early days in the Rosery Flower Company industry, Medicine Hat. This photo was taken probably about 1916.

117

The most famous was the Rosery Flower Company which was established in the city in 1907. The "Rosery" as it was familiarly referred to, went from very humble beginnings to a firm that supplied not only local but export trade. Located on Woodman Avenue between Third and Fifth Streets, the business operated from 1909 to 1928. It was founded by Ed Ueberrhein, who read about opportunities for gardeners in Canada while living in his native Berlin, Germany. Prior to establishing his incredibly successful business in Medicine Hat he gained experience in both Newfoundland and Winnipeg.

After many years of dedication, Ueberrhein at 58 years of age was paying in income taxes as much as the Prime Minister of Canada was receiving in salary. The young man who came to Canada in 1892 was unable to converse in English when he arrived, but he soon learned and success was only a lot of hard work away. "I never had any false ambitions," he said. "I always tilled the soil, watched things grow to fruition and looked to the soil for my living. I never wanted to be a lawyer, a doctor, a teacher or a white-collared businessman. I knew I was destined to be a gardener."

He did, however, have ambitions beyond that at one period in his life, a period when all around him it seemed people were making money in real estate. "I flew off on a tangent and lost a lot of money," he admitted of his lapse into land speculation. "But I swallowed my losses and took my experience as proof that I was not a real estate dealer but a grower of flowers."

Mrs. Clara Baird, daughter of Ed Ueberrhein, told Jack Barrie in May 1980 that her mother was the real business head of the firm while her father was the greenhouse operator — a winning combination. When the first Mrs. Ueberrhein died, Mr. Ueberrhein remarried and, following a short visit to Germany, the entire family joined in the operation of the "Rosery". It was not a happy time, however. Trouble came in May, 1916:

At that time the Fair Grounds was being used to house and train World War One units at Medicine Hat prior to departure for Overseas. A group of men from the Crow's Nest area were assembled as 13th Mounted Rifles, a cavalry unit under Col. Whittaker. They had just received word that they were to be dismounted and made an infantry unit, to be shipped overseas without their horses.

Evidently they were very annoyed at this and took their vengeance out on the persons they knew to be German, namely, Mr. Ueberrhein and his Greenhouse operation. They appeared equipped to do damage and they attacked the glass greenhouses, breaking 2,000 panes of glass. From there they marched uptown to City Hall, threatening to tear the building down.

Mayor Archie Hawthorne would have none of this. He appeared on the steps of City Hall and read the Riot Act to these men. This appeared to bring them to their senses and they soon dispersed.

In 1924 William Lyon Mackenzie King visited Medicine Hat and was presented with a bouquet of the Ueberrheins' finest roses by daughter Clara. Clara recalled the beautiful floats the family entered in local parades and her father's hobby of growing orchids. The business was sold in 1928 to a syndicate from Calgary and Ueberrhein retired to Vancouver, where he died in 1927. At publication, two daughters survived, still living in Medicine Hat: Mrs. Clara Baird and Mrs. Beth Ford.

118

As well as the "Rosery", Medicine Hat boasted several other well-established greenhouse businesses including Mill's (1035 Yuill St.) which sold out to Fraser's Florists; River View Greenhouses, established in June 26, 1940 by Eric Ziehran, specializing in cut flowers and hothouse tomatoes at 902-1st Street S.W.; Power House Greenhouses Ltd. (First Street S.W. along the river), was established in 1940 as a market garden by Hop Sun Co. It was sold in 1946 to the Knodels with John S. Knodel and son Herb operating it as a commercial vegetable farm. It once comprised about five city blocks of land with Highway 1 dividing the property which is located near the Trans-Canada Highway bridge. John Knodel's share was sold to son Edward who operated the property on the east side of the highway while Herb Knodel ran greenhouses on the west side. Ed Knodel, a former school vice-principal in Lethbridge, operated his business under the name of Greenwood Gardens while Herb continued his side under the original name of Power House Greenhouses Ltd.; Canadian Greenhouses was established around 1926 and continued to expand at the corner of Elm Street and London Avenue under the management of G. S. Rabb.

As elsewhere in Canada and the world, the advent of the "horseless carriage" changed "one horse towns" into fast-moving communities. Along with the automobile came the repair shop (often a sideline for the local blacksmith) and, later, the agency. The pioneer firm in Medicine Hat, Beny Motors, had its birth in Irvine, a sister community east of Medicine Hat. In the year 1917 Carl Beny was selling general merchandise in his large well-stocked store in Irvine — everything from fresh produce to drygoods, and Chevrolet cars. Previously he had sold Fords and International Harvesters. The latter firm made a brief foray into the auto trade, the success of which may be exemplified in the following story:

Carl Beny was interested in showing one of the International Harvester automobiles to a rancher who lived several miles away. He entrusted the huge cumbersome vehicle to a relative of the former owner of his store. The man left in high spirits and low gear and was not seen for several days. When he finally returned, Beny wanted to know how he had made out. "Oh, I never got there," the man said. "I got only so far and she wouldn't go no further." "Well, how did you get back?" Beny asked, pointing to the mud-spattered vehicle. "Oh," the man replied, "when I turned her around she come right on home."

Which may be one reason why International Harvester went into the manufacture of trucks: they performed well and didn't have "homing instincts." At any rate, Carl Beny switched to Chevrolet and General Motors products and the association lasted a long time.

In 1913 Beny built a large family home on Walsh Street in Irvine. Son Charlie was sent to New York for schooling while his mother's sisters, Elizabeth and Louise Hefner, came to assist in the store. Everything seemed to be coming up roses in the new land. Then tragedy struck. A fire, believed to have been deliberately started in an adjacent building, completely wiped out the store and its stock, which had only just been put on the shelves. Insurance on store and goods had not been renewed.

Standing in the ruins of an earlier fire at a hotel about 30 feet away, daughter Helen recalled the horror of the moment. "We were practically scorched with the heat from the fire," she said. But there was no time to feel regrets. Beny immediately set about to have a new store built, this time with bricks. While it was being constructed, the senior Benys took a short trip back to Germany, returning about a month before the First World War began.

People of German origin, even in a community with a large German population, were regarded with suspicion by some, and they became the target of discrimination. Nevertheless, the Benys prospered.

Young Charlie Beny and his father opened an automobile business in Medicine Hat which developed into a substantial operation and was a City landmark until recently. (In 1980 Beny Motors moved their operations to the Trans-Canada Highway in the southeast area of the city.)

Roy Beny worked at his father's garage for several years before opening his own in Brooks, Alberta. Charlie did the same in Lethbridge while father sold the store in Irvine to Phil Silver.

Helen, meantime, obtained her education at Mount Royal College in Calgary. After marrying Dr. Ross Gibson and raising a family, she entered politics and became one of the best-known and hardest-working aldermen in Medicine Hat. Among her many accomplishments was the declaration of the Prairie cactus as the official floral emblem for the city. But her crowning achievement came on August 2, 1973 when she became the first person in the city to be given the Order of Canada for her contributions to the community. She is also an accomplished artist.

(Another pioneer, Mrs. May Laidlaw, received the award a year later. A Griswold, Manitoba native, Mrs. Laidlaw was a graduate of the New England Conservatory of Music in Boston who came to Medicine Hat with her husband, Lorne N. Laidlaw, in 1910. She helped establish the Historical Society and was instrumental in the growth of music, drama and the Operatic Society.)

Another famous Beny is Roloff, internationally famous photographer whose collection of photographs stirred up a controversy in 1979 when the Alberta Government wanted to purchase them. Roloff Beny resides in Rome. A grandson of Carl, he established a worldwide reputation for his huge "coffee table" book of photographs of India and Iran and particularly for *For Everything There Is A Season* to commemorate the Canadian Centennial in 1967. Mrs. Gibson's daughter Elan, a well-known Canadian stage and television actress, also achieved considerable success.

Bread, according to the old adage, is the staff of life. That being so, Medicine Hat with its adjacent wheat fields, its flour mills and pioneer bakeries has had plenty of "staff". Richardson Bakery has been in the hands of one family for four generations, dating back to the time when John Bryden Richardson (known far and wide as "J.B.") emigrated from Glasgow, Scotland to Toronto. After marrying, he moved to Winnipeg where he started a bakery that used nine delivery wagons to deliver his products.

Alberta beckoned, so Richardson sold his bakery to Canada Bread and moved to Medicine Hat in 1912 and bought the Michael Leonard Bakery, the first bakery in the community. It had been founded in 1884. After several moves within the city (a fire destroyed one located on Seventh Avenue S.E., now Kingsway), Richardson built large premises in the vicinity of the present Gershaw Terrace.

With no large companies to compete with, business was excellent.

"I've seen them take drays loaded with great slatted wooden cartons lined with newspapers, filled with bread that was unwrapped and unsliced and ship them all over the country," grandson Harold Richardson told Ann Crowley in an interview in May 1980. "Golden Prairie, Thompkins, and even Bowell were thriving little towns then that kept two or three stores going," Richardson said.

In 1929 "J.B." got an offer he couldn't refuse from Five Roses Flour Mill. Five Roses enlarged the bakery, renaming it The Medicine Hat Baking Company. The firm became part of a chain that operated from Winnipeg to Vancouver. Five Roses later sold out to Weston's.

Baking was in the Richardson's blood, however, and in 1934 "J.B." and his son Bert bought the former Ideal Bakery and began Richardson's Bakery all over again. Bert had experience with his own bakery in Redcliff. When the cyclone of 1915 destroyed much of the town, Bert, his wife and son Harold went into business with "J.B."

The Depression was on and Bert Richardson was selling bread to the stores at 28 loaves for a dollar. Harold Richardson was amazed at how his father could do it and survive. "Hail, sunshine, rain or sleet — you'll see our wagons on the street." That was "J.B.'s" slogan in 1924 and the tradition was maintained right up to 1962. Customers in 1980 were being served bread made from local flour with no chemicals or additives used, but house-to-house deliveries were no longer made, except to stores as far away as Maple Creek, Empress, Hilda and Bow Island.

Along with bread, milk is important to human beings and the establishing of dairies in and around the city of Medicine Hat began early. Milk cows were at first kept by almost anyone who had a piece of property and a shed. Up until comparatively recent times this practice was continued. When health regulations were imposed and pasteurization of milk was demanded, the city family cow disappeared into history. Dairies sprang up and farmers carted their milk and cream to the distributors, like Crystal Dairy, established in 1914.

Archie Toole was following the tradition set down by his father Edward when he began his dairy farm on 15th Avenue S.E. A family business, the property took in what is now the golf course and College property and one section which contained the Stampede grounds and armories. It was taken over for the internment camp in the Second World War. A carpenter by trade, and a fearless one at that (he shingled the spire on St. John's church), Archie and wife Ruby delivered milk to Crystal Dairy with a Clydesdale horse and single dray.

That must have seemed utter luxury to Frank Toole who had a city herd when he was just a boy. Father Edward Toole had a dairy farm south of the present Furniture Barn and a milk route for more than 15 years. Frank meantime walked into town early in the morning and collected cows that residents kept in their backyards and herded them out onto the prairie. He watched over them all day and then trotted them back to their owners at night to be milked.

Frank Millington started as a herdsman at the Golden Valley Farm, having lived in the district since 1926. He was 18 at the time and recalled that one day in the middle of June in 1927 he was taking a load of milk in a wagon to Crystal Dairy. The road to Golden Valley at that time went through the

Canadian Fertilizers Limited expansion as seen from the air in 1981. "Money attracted by natural gas led Medicine Hat into the land of the big time, with all the pleasures and pain it promises."

brick and tile yard, along the river and up the hill. When Millington got to the hill he looked down. It had been the wettest summer on record and rain was teeming down at the time.

"I couldn't see any road," he said. "It had sunk about 35 feet down. It was impossible to get into town that way so I went back to the barn, hooked on two more horses, and took off across the prairie and up over the cliffs." Milk was delivered like that all winter. But the road down the hill became almost an obsession with the owner of the dairy, Ed Ueberrhein, who also owned the greenhouses already mentioned.

"When I told him about the hill, he blew his top," Millington said. "He blamed Bill Weir, his former partner, who started Golden Valley around 1920. He got the city engineer who told him it couldn't be fixed and the Alberta Government engineer who said it would be a waste of time. So Mr. Ueberrhein figured the valley was doomed and sold out to Bob Black and Harry Minor for $17,000." The new owners wanted Millington to take over the entire operation but he declined and suggested they bring Bill Weir back from the States. "There's as much dirt there now as there was when Bill built that road the first time," he said. "I figured it could be fixed again."

122

Weir did come back and shortly after that he and Millington went to look at the hill. "We took two shovels and dug a path up on the slope of the hill so one horse could walk down without sliding down the side. Then we took a walking plow and went down; and then we widened it with a Martin ditcher. On the second morning I was back on the hill road again with my wagon load of milk."

The road lasted for another 20 years before it slipped away again. In the meantime, Frank Millington had started his own dairy farm, Echo Dale, with a herd of Red Rock Holsteins. While he was delivering milk around town just a few days before Christmas 1930, he looked up from Sixth Avenue towards Golden Valley. "There was no barn in sight," he said. "I thought that was kind of strange. So when I finished delivering I drove over there. The barn had burned and 54 cows and four horses lay dead. That was quite a shock after I had built that herd up from 10 cows."

The dairy industry in Medicine Hat has come a long way since Frank Millington and the Tooles delivered it by wagon door to door. In the Thirties there were 84 licensed producer/distributors in the city and area. Milk was selling from five to seven cents a quart. When a bylaw was introduced during the Second World War that kicked the cows and the chickens out of the backyards, most milk was shipped to Crystal Dairy in eight gallon cans. Cows were in stanchion barns being milked by machines. In the mid-Fifties loose housing, milking parlors and bulk tanks completely altered the dairy industry. No more the sound of the milkman's horse clopping along the street and straining up the hills.

The City of Medicine Hat, which complained that it couldn't get a line of positive reporting out of the Calgary press at the turn of the century, was reaping its reward 80 years later. The *Edmonton Journal* on June 13, 1977 called it "the action city of the province." Reporter Jerry Brown said big money attracted by natural gas led Medicine Hat "into the land of the big time, with all the pleasures and pain it promises."

With a population topping 40,000 in 1982, the city boasted the lowest municipal taxes and utility rates in Alberta, and probably Canada. Expanding at a rate of five per cent per annum, a population of 50,000 is expected by 1987. Starting in 1976, the district was subjected to another boom and faced the results: inevitable slump. Alberta Gas and Chemical Ltd. and Canadian Fertilizers Limited projects were completed and more than 2,000 construction workers left town. However, to counteract the problems of the lull, a five-year capital works program was put into effect which kept the economy moving so that it was possible to cool it down without dramatic and negative results.

Business Life In Western Canada, a bimonthly business journal, declared that "Medicine Hat is looking more and more like Success City, Alberta. There's a row of petrochemical plants on the skyline and at night, from a distance, the city is a blaze of lights strung far across the horizon . . . But at heart, Medicine Hat still has the warmth and intimacy of a smaller community."

Those must have been comforting words for those who have lived here for a long time, through good times and bad. There was no chance of the City "getting too big for its britches."

Top: Old City Hall, Medicine Hat, Alberta. Bottom: New City Hall, Medicine Hat, Alberta, completion date 1983.

Hatfield, The Rainmaker

Like most parts of the Prairies, Medicine Hat district has been subjected to serious droughts. Droughts that have lasted for years, wiping out crops, wiping out farmers and ranchers, wiping out dreams. But such is the resourcefulness of the average citizen of the 'Hat, no mere disaster can keep him down forever. So, when the drought in 1921 threatened to become longer, drier and more disheartening than all its predecessors, the good burghers of Medicine Hat decided on drastic action. They called upon the services of a professional "rainmaker."

Charles M. Hatfield had already established a reputation in the United States and Australia as a man who could make rain fall on a specified area at a specified time. His reputation for wetness had preceded him to Medicine Hat, where he arrived in early April. Everybody who was anybody was at the Corona Hotel to welcome the Californian.

Mayor Walter Huckvale was there, as were the Honorable C. S. Pingle, Speaker in the Legislative Assembly of the Government of Alberta, Reverend J. W. Morrow, representing the Agricultural Society, G. F. Herbert of Canada Land and Irrigation Company, Father Fitzpatrick, A. J. N. Terrill of the *Medicine Hat News*, lawyer Lorne Laidlaw and Colonel Nelson Spencer, to name just a few.

Altogether, there were some 60 representatives of town and farm on hand to give a rousing welcome to Hatfield and his brother Paul A. Hatfield, the rainmaker's assistant. F. S. Ratcliff, a dealer in farm land and loans, was master of ceremonies. A. W. Lang declared that the credit for bringing Hatfield to Medicine Hat was largely due to Ratcliff.

"Most of us here are not from Missouri," the Mayor said, indicating that all were not as doubtful about things as people in that State are supposed to be. "But some of us are probably tainted by the same spirit." If Hatfield was to be believed, he had to perform.

"We are honored to have you here, Mr. Hatfield," the Mayor added. "And we will be happy to give you whatever assistance and cooperation you want." The presence of so many people from the country was an indication of the trust put forth. "We in Medicine Hat have great faith and as the hub of this district, our neighbors look to us for aid in building up their prosperity."

R. S. Stevens, who had also assisted in acquiring the services of the rainmaker, noted that Alberta and Saskatchewan farmers were looking on the coming of the rainmaker with great interest. "The guest of the day is welcomed as a gentleman and a scientist, and as a respected citizen of the great republic to the south," he said. "Given the moisture, no district can produce better crops than that around the 'Hat. Many places in the States and Canada, and even in Africa and Australia, are after Mr. Hatfield's services. It is gratifying that he has come to our district."

While the speeches went on, a telegram arrived: it was from Superintendent Cameron of the Canadian Pacific Railway in Calgary. Cameron apologized for not being at the reception. He wanted so much to meet the rainmaker and wish him the best. However, he was sure that he would do well without his presence. As a postscript he said that the arrival of Hatfield augered well. "It is already starting to sprinkle in Calgary!"

It was time for Hatfield to take the floor. He was greeted with tumultuous applause. It was as though he had already wrought his miracle.

"I have never seen a country with more potential for production than this," Hatfield told the crowd as the applause died down. "I propose to prove beyond all doubt that rain will follow my operations on your behalf. For 20 years my operations in making rain have been successful in many parts of the States. There are always knockers, of course, but these doubting Thomases will fade away as the results occur."

Sitting down to even more applause than before, Hatfield was prepared to take and answer questions. More than questions, there were affirmations. There was more faith in him than shown in the workings of the Lord at a southern revival.

"I'm with him," A. W. Lang said. "There are no bigger or broader class of citizens in the world than in Medicine Hat," the Reverend Father Fitzpatrick said, with a nod at 300-pound F. S. Ratcliff, chairman, who filled the chair adequately and beyond question. Publisher Terrill said that Hatfield's arrival meant lots of news for the paper and "I hope it is all good news." He added that what Hatfield proposed to do "looks feasible."

Colonel Spencer rose to speak. "Among the many things that have happened to make Medicine Hat known all over the continent," he said, "none is greater than the coming of the rainmaker. If he is successful, it will mean not only great prosperity for this district but also for the lifting of a great burden from the Governments of Alberta and Saskatchewan. The soil here is as good as lies out of doors."

Colonel Spencer concluded his remarks with the promise that Hatfield, if sucessful, "can have a steady job here."

H. H. Brown then proposed a toast to the farmers of Southern Alberta, saying that it was a great pleasure to be a businessman in a city where such a representative gathering could be got together to welcome a man of Hatfield's reputation and calling. "It is to everyone's interest to cooperate with the rainmaker," he said. "No part of Canada is peopled by go-getters to a greater extent that this district. A bigger acreage in crop will result from Mr. Hatfield's coming. I like the way Mr. Hatfield speaks and I feel that he is confident he can deliver the goods."

"The greatest thing in the world is to have an idea," G. L. Fraser said. "The proof of the pudding is in the eating," shouted N. A. M. McLarty. Lorne Laidlaw smilingly accused several other lawyers present for being on hand to bring damage suits if too much rain came. "I will undertake the defence of the rainmaker," he said. "I wish him every success — let there be rain."

126

C. S. Blanchard said the sincere trust of the people in Hatfield would be rewarded with results. "People are bound to be skeptical because the accomplishments credited to the rainmaker are not fully capable of proof." The "would-have-rained-anyway" type of person made his job a thankless one.

Mayor Huckvale expressed the thanks of the guests for the splendid luncheon arranged by the United Agicultural Association and — with a final thunderous ovation — the rainmaker and the others left the hotel. Outside, it had begun to sprinkle.

Later, with a contract in his pocket, Hatfield prepared to go to work. He was to produce up to four inches of rain within a specified period and within a 100 mile radius of Medicine Hat. To that end, he journeyed to Chappice Lake, about 20 miles north of the city, with two wagon-loads of equipment.

With great industry, Hatfield and brother Paul built a tower, 14 feet square at the top and 18 feet square at the bottom. Secret chemicals set in trays in the tower were to send fumes up in the air to condense the moisture in the clouds and to cause rain to fall in abundance.

For the first few weeks in May, rain did fall; more than usual for that time of year. The skeptical now became worried. He began to get telegrams: "Rain enough. Stop for three days and take a holiday." "Bring a shower every three days, preferably at night."

In June, the rain stopped and the skeptics were back. Some even travelled out to Chappice Lake (more of a slough than a lake at that time) to heckle the Hatfields at work. One thing they had to admit: Hatfield was optimistic. The shack that had been built to house the brothers at the site had been provided with eavestroughs!

The end of June came and with it came hot winds, and there was no sign of rain. July was worse. Although there were a few sprinklings, more of a tease than a torrent, the district began to dry up. Crops withered where they had sprouted. It was time to take drastic action.

Members of the United Agricultural Association began to mutter to themselves and to fellow farmers. They called a meeting in Medicine Hat, to which rainmaker Hatfield was summoned. "Produce or else," the Californian was told. Hatfield defended himself:

"Conditions are unusually poor for this time of year and I am having problems with making contact with the clouds. Be patient."

The farmers said if Hatfield didn't make a better showing there would be no $8,000 fee.

Meanwhile, as Colonel Spencer predicted, Medicine Hat was the focus of worldwide attention again. But it was not the sort of good news the residents of the district wanted to hear.

After four fruitless months of rainmaking operations, Hatfield had to admit that he was beaten. By then it was too late anyway. The crops were ruined and tempers were frayed. "I'm sorry I couldn't bring you all the rain you needed," Hatfield told the Association prior to leaving town. Some of the members were sympathetic; others were plain disgusted. What was the reason for the failure, they wanted to know.

"I guess I set the tower up in the wrong place," Hatfield said. The

Praying for rain at the Rainmaker's Tower, Chapice Lake. (Left to Right) Grace Cousins, Ann Wagstaff, Dorothy Niblock, of Medicine Hat.

127

Group seated beside the tower constructed by Charles Hatfield, "The Rainmaker," in 1921 at Chapice Lake, about 18 miles north east of Medicine Hat. (Left to Right) Douglas Kelly, Dorothy Niblock, Elliott Macdonald, Ann Wagstaff (later Mrs. Keating), Roy Keating.

applause at the end of his speech this time was less than enthusiastic, although it is variously reported that he was told "never return," and "come back soon." At any rate, he pocketed $5,000 of the promised $8,000 and rode off into history, never to be seen in Medicine Hat again.

One thing that can be said for Charles M. Hatfield: he stayed to the bitter and parched end. Earlier in Medicine Hat history another rainmaker did not hang around. He had been called in from Regina to keep the rain *away* from the Stampede and Fair. His prop was a "magic magnet" which he was to point at the sky and draw the clouds away to a safe distance.

History does not recall what happened to this rain dispeller. It rained on Stampede day!

10.

"The Pittsburgh Of The West"

An early publication of the Chamber of Commerce paid generous tribute to the natural gas of the city that had "all hell for a basement". Medicine Hat truly was "born lucky" where "smokeless, dustless, ashless fuel is sold for both domestic and industrial purposes cheaper than any other city on earth."

The domestic price was 25 cents per thousand cubic feet, six and one-half cents to three cents for industrial users. "Those who have never used it cannot realize the comfort of using natural gas for both heating and cooking, to say nothing of the cheapness and the amount of work it saves, and which makes Medicine Hat the cheapest place of residence in Western Canada."

Such glowing phrases should have brought settlers bustling into the new settlement. And they did. From the census of 1901: 1,570 people had taken up residence; the population leaped to more than 3,000 five years later, to 5,606 in 1911 and then doubled again by 1921. Alfred W. Tyas came in 1911 "when the town was booming." He told the author that houses at that time were virtually unattainable. "When enquiries were made to a real estate agent he replied: 'Ask me for something reasonable, like hen's teeth. But not a house in Medicine Hat'."

Mr. Tyas recalled that the local political scene was lively. James (Jimmy) Hole was running for mayor. "He advocated buying up what he called good Medicine Hat dirt by the municipality. Looking back today, he was farsighted."

The Medicine Hat Chamber of Commerce, which had recovered from its earlier gaff of trying to change the city's name, now spent much of its energies in trying to attract industry to the city of "smokeless, dustless, ashless" fuel. Neighboring Redcliff benefitted as well from the propaganda mailed out to prospective investors, for this was where many of the area's industries located, as shown in Chapter Seven. Almost all were dependent upon natural gas for heat or power.

These early years excited the residents of the city, who were led to believe that Medicine Hat and district would soon become "the Pittsburg of the West." Homage was paid to the CPR crew who were drilling for water and discovered natural gas at a place called Langevin (now Alderson), about 30 miles west of the present city.

Following the gas discovery at Langevin in 1892, the town council decided to drill a well in Medicine Hat. The rig punched through the earth to 1,000 feet without striking the dustless, ashless fuel. By then, the money authorized for the drilling had evaporated, so Mayor Thomas Hutchison took

These two photographs were taken at widely separated times but from approximately the same location. Top photo shows Toronto Street (now Third Street) looking east, the way it appeared about 1900. Notice fire hydrant on corner. BOTTOM PHOTO: This photo was taken about 30 years later when the age of the automoble was quite apparent.

View showing A. C. Hawthorne's Clothing Store and Furniture Store in one building, with Opera House above the stores. James Rae Hardware Store building on the right, year 1901. Mr. Hawthorne is the tall person in straw hat in centre of photo. The location almost exactly where Hawthorne's Clothing Store operated in 1981.

Oil and gas development in Medicine Hat. This well was probably in the city about 1925, judging by the power poles and age of the cars.

it upon himself to direct the driller to go a little deeper. The site of the well was at the back of W. A. Begg's residence. In charge of the drilling was J. A. Grant, a sheep rancher from Walsh who had gained drilling experience at Petroleum, Ontario, home of some of the first oil wells in North America.

At 1,010 feet an enormous flow of gas was struck, gas under 550 pounds per square inch of pressure. Dry, with a chemical composition of methane 99.47 per cent, hydrogen .51 per cent and a slight trace of oxygen, it was a tremendous way to launch the city's entry into the world of energy. The council turned down an offer from a private company to operate the well, establishing a precedent in the Province to own and operate its light, heat and power services.

Much credit has given to Charles Colter, a stonemason, who first used the natural gas to burn limestone for his building operations. His friend, Dr. C. E. Smyth, who came to Medicine Hat to practice in 1895, recalled that gas soon flowed from two sources: through a two-inch pipe situated along the CPR track a short distance north of what was then the Second Street

131

Medicine Hat City Hall and Fire Hall shortly after completion of the building in 1905. The building was faced with material to make it appear more "modern" much later and in 1981 plans were made for the City Hall to be located in a new building on the site of the Medicine Hat News building which was demolished.

crossing, where the gas burned continuously with "a flame from six to 10 inches high." The second well was more productive at its location along the river just below where the old hospital stood. Colter decided to get his own supply, so he drilled a well in his backyard. At 700 feet he brought in a well that was a good source of natural gas.

Dr. Smyth benefitted from this well, as did residents near the Colter site. Colter bored a hole from his cellar across Second Street beneath the road and into Dr. Smyth's cellar. From the pipe inserted, Dr. Smyth's house was heated, his food cooked and home lit.

Like many other outstanding citizens and pioneers, John Charles Colter came to the city to work on the construction of the first CPR bridge. He was extremely adaptable to the place and times. When the town baker left to cook for the soldiers putting down the Riel Rebellion, Colter took up the baking business. When another baker moved to town, he resumed his trade of contractor and plasterer. The buildings erected by this industrious settler are too numerous to mention here but they included the old hospital and nurses' home, and a building on Toronto Street (now Third Street) which later housed the community opera house. Before the turn of the century, Colter built a frame structure on the corner of Ash Avenue and Second Street which became Medicine Hat's first indoor skating rink.

Dorothy Linfield recalled in the *Medicine Hat News* that Colter obtained his limestone in a pit located near the present ball park. As mentioned, he later moved his operation to his backyard when he found that water mixed with the natural gas and frequently his power source was cut off by it. Incidentally, the CPR had two "experts" check the flow from the well near the tracks. They decided there was nothing commercially feasible in the resource and had the well capped.

Miss Linfield credits Colter with having the initiative, courage and perseverance that started natural gas development, not only in the Medi-

Wm. Cousins   W. G. Niblock   Thos. Tweed

cine Hat area, but in all of Alberta. But, as Medicine Hatters were to learn later, it was mixed blessing to have "all hell for a basement."

Geologist L. G. Huntley recalled that the gas used by Colter to burn lime rose from a "colonade of ice" in the winter, giving skaters on the river the impression of a giant candle set in the snow.

Other entrepreneurs wanted in on the act and without even a written contract, William Cousins, Thomas Tweed, Henry Stewart, W. T. Finlay, J. G. Niblock and a few others formed a company and began to drill on the river bank below where the general hospital stood. They got a strong flow of gas with a pressure of 250 pounds to the square inch at a depth of 650 feet.

Records of what other wells were drilled, when and where and by whom were not kept in those days and the failure to keep such records became embarrassing and dangerous because of the frequent leaks in the distribution system. It is known that between 1890 and 1904 a number of wells were drilled to the shallow gas horizon at 650 to 750 feet below the river flat. And not one of them had cemented casing.

Percolation of ground water containing dissolved air so corroded some of the loose casing that pieces of it looked like lace work. When gas well casings leak, the gas escapes, not only up the drilled hole but through porous beds to the surface. The loss of gas that could be used was not as serious as the fire hazard it created. For a considerable distance around some of these old wells a person could shove a stick into the ground and pull it out, then light the gas that came out of the hole.

Naural gas explosion wrecks houses on the Hill Area, Medicine Hat.

Under such conditions, gas would enter cellars and basements, and fires and explosions would occur. Dr. Smyth recorded some incidents: "The roof of one house was blown a half a block away but no one was injured. One householder installed a homemade furnace in his cellar in which to burn gas but forgot to build a chimney to carry off fumes. He thought that since no smoke could be seen, a chimney would not be needed. There were two or three dead the next morning after the furnace was started."

Dr. Smyth said a man came into his office complaining of various symptoms. "I couldn't find much wrong with him on examination, so I gave

133

him a simple tonic. He came back a few times, no better. Getting worse, he sent for me. On entering his room I knew at once what his trouble was. He was heating his room with a stove but the damper was shut off, filling the room with poisonous fumes. All I had to do to effect a cure was to turn the stove damper. The man promptly recovered."

The incidents related by Dr. Smyth seem minor compared with others involving gas that followed. Gas was piped through the town in 1902 and into residences. The line in the basement of R. Nicoll was corked with a wooden plug, which the pressure soon blew out. Next morning, Mrs. Nicoll went into the basement with a lantern and was greeted with an explosion. Both she and her husband were taken to hospital while the fire brigade went to work. With lantern in hand, the fire chief dashed into the house, which promptly went "boom" again, tossing firemen through the windows, according to the *News* reports.

On March 19, 1913 Malcolm Canneries was the scene of a gas explosion (mentioned in Chapter 8) which killed five people and seriously injured nine or 10 more. In zero weather, firemen and rescuers dug through the debris to get the bodies and injured out. Joseph McQueen, the caretaker of the building, recalled later that he struck a match to light his pipe and gas began to burn along one side of the room. An explosion followed when firemen cut into the floor to get at the source of the blaze. One theory was that the gas came from an old well beneath the building.

Ed Middleton at the wheel, Ford Day seated beside Ed. Hector Ross, mechanic. Joe Day's Cadillac, about 1912, in front of Ford Garage (Medicine Hat Garage) which later became Gas City Planing Mill building, which was demolished in 1980.

Within a year or two of the time that dependable gas supplies were discovered at Medicine Hat, gas lights were installed on standards on the railway station platform and on street corners in the central part of town. Mounted on three-inch diameter pipe standards and suspended about 10 feet off the ground, the gas could be turned off and on by a long-handled key. But it was found to be more economical to let them burn day and night, a circumstance that brought Medicine Hat to the attention of Robert Ripley who drew a cartoon of a lamp standard in his *Believe It Or Not*, published on

134

May 5, 1931: "The gas street lights are never turned out in Medicine Hat, Alberta — Natural Gas is so plentiful that it is cheaper to let them burn."

The presence of gas was used to attract industries — as has been made abundantly clear — and about 1912 the City issued a number of permits to drill wells for their own use. No thought was give to the number of wells that could be successfully operated on a given area without all of them suffering by rapid depletion of the supply. As a result there were quarter sections of land with four wells on them. At one place there were a dozen wells within a space of 500 acres.

By 1926 the gas system in Medicine Hat was giving trouble. Some of the wells were leaking gas and some of the pipelines as well. The utility owned by the City carried a large part of the City budget and received little of the money for maintenance. The Dominion Government was invited to report on the situation and the recommendations that came out of the Calder Report met resistance from those who had to appropriate the money; but eventually they were acted upon and Medicine Hat ended up with a steady, safe supply of natural fuel.

CITY COUNCIL 1926

City Council 1926. Centre, Mayor Isaac Bullivant. Top Left: Jack King. Top Right: Joe Marsh. Centre Left: James Hole, Centre Right: R. B. Davidson. Botton Left to Right: Peter M. Simpson, Dr. Oliver Boyd, Hector Duggan, Jim Robertson.

As everywhere in the pioneer west, Medicine Hat had its share of illicit businesses, including brothels, "blind pigs" or speakeasies where forbidden liquor was available, and other imaginative ventures. *The Medicine Hat News* is a fine source of court news that indicates the temper of the time: "Corporal Johnston, assisted by two constables, raided a house of ill fame on Toronto Street on Tuesday night and arrested Alice Smith for having whiskey in her possession without a permit." Miss Smith was not chastised for operating a "house of ill fame". The sin was not having a permit to sell liquor. She was tried before Inspector Davidson next morning and acquitted. J. P. Mitchell appeared in her defence.

135

An attempt to impose a measure of Prohibition on the early settlers proved to be less than a resounding success. It was the North West Mounted Police who, in 1874, introduced a "permit system" to preserve order in the construction camps and among the Indians. Colonel Sam Steele of the Force reported that the measure had some useful effect but noted in a letter to his superiors in Ottawa that "public opinion is strongly against it, with the result that the law cannot be properly enforced."

City of Medicine Hat had a fleet of Model T's, 1912, 1913 vintage. Here are a few in front of City Hall. Police Chief James Bruce is identified as uniformed person behind Model T. Roadster with 1914 licence plate.

That was putting it mildly. Liquor in Medicine Hat was made not only in illegal stills, but was brought into the community by every device available to the ingenuity of man: eggshells were emptied of their contents and filled with Scotch Whisky while canned goods were also emptied and filled with Irish. Also shipped into the area were "books" made of tin and bound in Morocco leather. These were in the exact shape of a copy of the Holy Scriptures and contained flasks of whiskey. Reverend J. W. Morrow, who has written pamphlets about Medicine Hat district, noted that everyone in the area "seemed to manifest a great hunger and thirst for these Bibles, in fact, nothing less than a big family Bible would suit most."

Mince meat was also very popular with the populace, particularly if it was soaked in brandy. Peaches similarly flavored were also found in most households. A cache of this forbidden fruit was reportedly found underneath a church, the minister of which was an outspoken prohibitionist. When the discovery of the contraband was reported in the newspaper, one of the community's most colorful characters, "Dublin Dan", called on the minister and suggested a Thanksgiving service be held; he offered some appropriate hymns for the occasion: "There Shall Be Showers Of Blessing", "I've Reached The Land Of Corn And Wine" and "Riches Freely Mine." The pastor was apparently unamused.

The use of too many spirits on the one hand and too little of the right kind of spirit on the other led to many debates between those in favor of looser liquor law and those who wanted more respect for church and state. Medicine Hat has always been a city of churches and the churchmen truly felt they spoke for the people (or for the peoples' good) when they harangued against the evils of booze. Meanwhile, the newspaper editors felt the system of licensing was discriminating and unconstitutional. The two factions met in print.

The *Calgary Herald* ran a front page editorial on the inequities of the law which affected all those who lived in the North West Territories. Getting a permit was too difficult by far, the editor moaned. He wrote that an application for a permit was sent "nearly a month ago to the Lieutenant Governor at Regina for a permit for a small quantity of whiskey for medicinal purposes for an invalid in the doctors' hands." According to the account, the licence had been recommended not only by the medical attendants but by a "leading justice in the town."

The Lieutenant-Governor was absent and the application and fee were returned. The editor was enraged. "What is a patient who wishes to respect the law to do?" he railed. "As the law does not permit a person to have liquor in his possession without a permit, and as the government refuses to issue a permit in this case where the doctors have ordered the whiskey as a remedy, it is an outrage. Certainly we are living under a regime which, if it prevailed in Siberia, would lead us liberty-loving people to renounce Russian law as barbarous and tyrannical to the last degree."

For once, the editor of the *Medicine Hat News* agreed wholeheartedly with "our able contemporary." He told of a similar incident in Medicine Hat where another patient "must take a dram a day to maintain his health." He also was refused a permit and as a consequence "his life hangs in the balance." "It is," he concluded, "about time this barbarous liquor law was abolished."

One resident, writing to the local newspaper, found the law not only demoralizing, but demoralized. "It is the North West Mounted Police who have to enforce the law who help to break it." He said that seized liquor was taken to the Police Point barracks across the river where the kegs were "ceremoniously broken and emptied into a selected part of the grounds." According to this gentleman, the onlookers did not know that underneath a clean "stratum of gravel" was another keg, waiting to receive the whiskey.

Model T Ford on Finlay Bridge, Medicine Hat, 1912.

To add insult to injury, "I have known a judge who had just sentenced a man for smuggling whiskey go right to the American Hotel and join lawyers and counsel in a round of drinks — probably from the same seized whiskey!"

The cudgel against the uses and abuses of the amber fluid was taken up by the men of the cloth who decried the condition of some of the populace who could be seen reeling about the streets and in and out of the saloons in disgraceful fashion. A certain Reverend Doctor Douglas, a "worthy divine of the Methodist Church," according to the *News*, toured the West lambasting evil everywhere. Although Medicine Hat boasted a "commodious and up to date theatre for the speaking drama at which numerous theatrical troupes play from time to time" and was noted for its "amateur musical and dramatic talent and performances that are staged during the season that are well worth the nominal fee charged," there was evil afoot.

Dr. Douglas fearlessly impeached a society which not only tolerated but courted impurity and vice in its theatres, "its literature and its public men." He vigorously denounced the theatres because of the "sensuousness of the language of modern plays and the vileness of the characters too often impersonated in them."

He then attacked the sensational literature of the day, showing that the chief danger lay in its penetration "into the bosom of the family," thus poisoning the minds of innocent youths and ruining their prospects of becoming "noble men and women." In a final fling at the sin assailing the land, Dr. Douglas passed to an eloquent barrage of those legislators whose private characters were "impure", thus censuring in the course of his remarks the constituents which elected such men.

Among those constituents were two women who made regular appearances in court for disturbing the peace and related activities, including bootlegging: Anna May "Slippery Annie" Barclay and "Nigger Molly". Molly had come from the United States following the end of the Civil War and slave emancipation. She worked as a cook on a bull train that freighted between Fort Benson, Montana and Fort Walsh. She used to boast that she was "the first white woman that ever came to Fort Walsh", probably referring to the fact that all women before her were either full or part Indian. Molly moved to Medicine Hat about 1883 where she reportedly operated the first bootleg joint.

Henry McKay, writing in the July 1951 issue of *Canadian Cattlemen*, said Molly started her bootleg business in a tent but had a shack built when she found a couple of rattlesnakes under her bed. "She was also an itinerant bootlegger," McKay said. "She would drive around to a construction camp carrying an enormous cane made of chokecherry wood. The authorities wondered where she carried her liquor since her wagon did not contain any. I heard in years later that her method was this: she wore a bustle — which was the style of the day — but it was not an ordinary one. It was made to order out of well-tanned buffalo hide. It had six compartments, each large enough to hold a short quart bottle. She also had a brassiere made of the same material, capable of holding two quart bottles."

Molly and Annie used to hide their whiskey, brought from across the border, in bushes and sage brush which grew in profusion in the area. At an arranged time, Molly would go forth and load up her bustle and brassiere and, with her trusty cane, head for the camps. The cane was not so much for steadying her gait as for knocking down any man who tried to challenge her right to bargain and dispense her goods. Annie must have been equally good at concealing the goods to earn her name "Slippery". McKay said she was so named because "although she was arrested a dozen times for stealing money, she always got clear because they could never find the stolen money on her."

Annie and Molly were fated to become rivals in another branch of business as the community settled down: both opened laundries. On one occasion Molly chased Annie with a butcher knife until Annie stood her off with a pail of boiling water. The newspapers loved the antics of the two and carried items frequently mentioning the rivalry. But love entered the picture and settled everything out of court and in church — at least for Annie.

She eventually became engaged to a French-Canadian, a man who is nameless but who was known to have shared her love of the bottle. Standing room in the church was at a premium when Annie suffering mightily from the ravages of the evening before, weaved into the hallowed hall with her fiancé on her arm. The groom was decked out in a frock coat, white vest and silk hat while Annie was at her bride's best in purple and fine white Irish linen, befitting her ancestry.

There was a hesitation before the organist, F. F. Fatt, made his appearance. Annie, no mean organist herself, sat down and began to hammer out "Comin Through The Rye" and "Pop Goes The Weasel" to the merriment of the crowd. Mr. Fatt rushed in from the vestry and commanded her to stop at once, crying, "Don't you know you are in the house of God?" Annie replied: "Yiz. It was the house of God, but yez have made it a den of thieves."

F F Fatt

The Reverend Tudor, who was to perform the ceremony, arrived on the scene and advised Annie that she and her groom were too drunk to get married. "Go home and come back when you are sober," he said. "The trouble, yer Riverence is, he won't come back when he's sober," Annie wailed, indicating with a waggling finger her blushing groom.

The story has a happy ending. Annie May Barclay and her French-speaking groom did get married and took a honeymoon in Quebec.

To conclude this chapter, we turn again to the inimitable Sam Goldie who delighted in entertaining Medicine Hatters with stories of the old days, when men were men and women were glad of it — and sermons were full of hell and damnation.

"One Bible thumper in the 'Hat was just coming to the height of his tirade when a blue-bottle fly landed on his lectern," Goldie told Jan Fulton in 1979. "As sure as I am about to smash this fly, you are going to . . ." Before he could deliver whatever judgment was to befall his congregation, the fly flew tantalizingly about his head, across the church, and out the window.

With the expression of a man who has just had his sentencing overruled by a higher authority, the preacher looked at the silent parishioners and said sourly: "Folks, I've got news for you. You're all going to have a second chance!"

ROMAN CATHOLIC CHURCH.
MEDICINE HAT. N.W.T

11.

Fire And Brimstone Come To The Bible Belt

If the "Bible Belt" truly exists, Medicine Hat must lie smack dab in the middle of the New Testament. Populated by hardy individualists who carved out a place for themselves in the barren short grass country of sourtheastern Alberta, the city "with all hell for a basement" is well represented by religious institutions.

According to the story, the "Bible Belt" is a region that extends west from the head of the Great Lakes to the Rocky Mountains, and south from the Canadian Prairies to the Gulf of Mexico. The residents of this vast swath of land are believed to be more fundamentalist in their religious outlook than are their more liberal-minded neighbors living closer to the Atlantic or Pacific coasts.

What would make this so? Why are there so many churches, so many blood and thunder preachers and traditionalist sects on the Prairies? The theory is that when the pioneers headed out across the nearly empty plains, they needed more than just lots of provisions, a rifle and a good compass to guide them. In addition to extremes in weather, there was also the threat of hostile Indians — to say nothing of hostile whites. A well-worn Bible and a belief in something beyond this world were as much a part of a settler's effects as were his rifle and water canteen. The physical hardships and the loneliness of the land were difficult to face at times. Men and women who endured long winters in sod shacks and log houses on the plains sought refuge and solace in their Bibles. And when the churches were built, the faithful flocked to them. They flocked to services no matter where they were held — in the railway station, in tents, in the open air. Until there was a church and bell steeple, their God was worshipped wherever there was a preacher in good voice.

And if it took "fire and brimstone" to drive home the message, that was all right too. A preacher who could deliver the Word with emphasis was more welcome than those who couldn't. No simpering, sweet-talking parlor parsons wanted here. The plain word that is in the Bible needed no gussying up. The preacher who could spit tobacco and shoot a rattlesnake gained respect from ranchers, railway crews and settlers. It was simple, down-home religion delivered straight from the shoulder that got the people to come back every Sunday, God willing.

According to the records of missionary travels among the Indians, the

Roman Catholics were in the Medicine Hat area first. A Father Thibault travelled by canoe up the South Saskatchewan to where the Bow and Oldman Rivers unite near Ronolane, west of Medicine Hat. That was prior to 1845, when Father Bourassa made a similar trip. The famous Oblate, Father Albert Lacombe, who had been in the West since 1852, served for a time as a chaplain to the construction crews of the Canadian Pacific Railway. He ceased these duties by the time the steel reached Medicine Hat in 1883.

Composite photo showing the *proposed* building program for Roman Catholic Church, Medicine Hat. Some of the proposals did not mature. Pictures: Rev. Father Cadoux, top centre. School, top left. Interior of Cathedral (St. Patrick's) top right. Proposed Hospital Left centre. Proposed Academy Right Centre. Convent, Centre, Left. St. Patrick's Church and Priests' home Centre. Lower: Plan of interior of cathedral (St. Pat's).

142

Prior to the building of the old St. Patrick's at the corner of Third Street and Fifth Avenue in 1887, services were held every second Sunday in the home of Superintendent Shields of the CPR. The priest in charge when the church was built was Father Therien, who was assisted by Fathers Gratton, Doucet and Claude. The first actual records show that on May 12, 1901 Emile J. Legal, the Bishop of St. Albert, was here for the blessing of the bell for St. Patrick's Church. Father Edward LaPointe is shown as the Pastor. The records at St. Patrick's archives show that Father LaPointe's first entry was a baptism on June 7, 1899.

On November 30, 1912, the diocese of Calgary was separated from St. Albert, and on July 27, 1913, the first Bishop, the Most Rev. John T. McNally, D. D., assumed charge of Southern Alberta. Meanwhile the first church at Medicine Hat proved too small and shortly before the parish passed from the jurisdiction of Bishop Legal, Father Cadieux obtained permission to sell the property (where MacLeod's Store now stands) for $67,000 and erect a new church, the present church in Medicine Hat at its riverside site. Only the basement was finished and opened for use in 1914, although the whole structure (constructed entirely of cement) had been completed exteriorly.

The Missionaries of the Sacred Heart withdrew from the Parish and the Diocese in 1916; and the Rev. M. F. Fitzpatrick, a priest from the Diocese of Peterborough, Ontario, was placed in charge in 1916. He labored long and hard, reducing the debt on this magnificent church until in the late summer of 1927, Father Fitzpatrick died and was buried from St. Patrick's church. Rev. M. J. Fitzpatrick, nephew of the deceased Father Fitzpatrick ordained in Medicine Hat, January 16, 1921, by Bishop McNally, succeeded his uncle as parish priest till April, 1937. During his pastorate the interior of the upper church was completed and opened for use in 1932. With the completion of the church, St. Patrick's Church became one of the finest examples of Gothic architecture, and one of the largest churches in Southern Alberta.

On June 3, 1883, when the population of Medicine Hat had reached about 260, most of them still in tents or boxcars, Reverend James Robertson, Superintendent of Missions for the North West, held a Presbyterian service in the tent store of G. F. Tupper. Subsequent services were held in a special tent that was erected to serve as a church later in the summer. The still incomplete railway station and the new Brunswick Hotel were also used for Presbyterian services.

There is a certain amount of controversy about which of the various denominations came first to Medicine Hat. It is generally accepted however that the Presbyterians held the first congregational service while the Methodists were the first to put up a church building. As mentioned, the Roman Catholics claim the distinction of having pioneered missionary services in the district. Anglicans arrived on the scene in 1883 when Reverend W. H. Cooper commuted between here and Saskatchewan.

The Methodist congregation established their new church with the arrival in July 1883 of Reverend Wellington Bridgman. That meant the end of services in the CPR depot, where planks placed on nail kegs served as pews. With no loss of time, an official church board was elected and the frame building at the corner of Third Street and Sixth Avenue (present site of the Royal Bank) was packing them in. The church was dedicated by Reverend George Young.

Reverend Bridgman — called Captain Bridgman out of deference to his military rank — remained as minister until 1885. He returned briefly in June 1912 to lay the cornerstone for the Fifth Avenue Methodist Church. At a cost of about $100,000, the congregation built the new church at the intersection of Fifth Avenue and Fourth Street. On the opposite corner they erected a manse, also of red brick. In 1925 the Fifth Avenue Methodist Church became the Fifth Avenue United Church, marking the Canadian union of Methodist, Presbyterian and Congregational churches.

The road to union locally was not easy, but despite Depression and the aftermath of the First World War, the finance committee managed in June 1931 to stage the traditional burning of the mortgage. The jubilation was short-lived: one month later the building was gutted by fire with only the walls and iron framework that supported the roof remaining.

The spirit that carried the pioneers across the lonely prairie was still evident because five months later the church was rebuilt. The congregation had worshipped in the water-damaged basement during the interim.

The Presbyterians held their first service on June 29, 1884 when the shingles were still being put on the roof. David Anderson, a missionary student from Manitoba, organized the first service. The Church Board consisted of George McCuaig, James Hargrave, William Cousins, Thomas Tweed, Samuel Porter, C. F. Tupper and Samuel Archibald, who met in McCuaig's store on May 1.

The Baptist Church in Medicine Hat was begun in either 1889 or 1890, depending on which account you read. The *Medicine Hat News* published an article during the Jubilee Year of the City's churches that declares that the church was founded by Christopher Lean in 1889 when he found that there were six other citizens of the Baptist persuasion in the village. He organized prayer meetings which were held in the immigration building which later became the court house (now the site of the Canadian Legion building).

A submission to the Medicine Hat Museum by an unidentified parishioner states that the Baptist Church in the City was organized in 1890 with eight charter members: Mr. and Mrs. J. Waldock, Miss Edith Waldock (later the wife of D. L. McGibbon), Mr. and Mrs. Chrisopher Lean, Mr. J. Dark, a Mrs. Gerow and a Mr. Matley. The newspaper account contends the first minister was Pastor S. C. Everton while the parishioner says it was Reverend H. E. Wise.

The accounts also vary regarding the origin of the first and present-day churches. The Museum version has it that the present church was built in 1904 with Reverend Everton as pastor while the *Times* reported that the present church was built in 1903, the older one being moved to an adjoining lot in 1922 as part of the church parsonage. It is still part of the house there.

However they began, the Baptists prospered in the City. A second Baptist church, Grace Baptist, was built on Yuill Street, with Temple Baptist Church establishing later in the southwest district of the City. Grace Baptist was in favor of such a work and shortly after that decision in January 1955, Grace Baptist became the mother church of this new venture. On February 2, 1955 property in an undeveloped area of the city was purchased at the corner of 7th Street and 6th Avenue South West for the prospective church building. Cornerstone laying was on July 31, 1955 with Rev. Rudolph Mill-

First St. Barnabas Church, Medicine Hat. Photo taken 1886.

brandt as interim Pastor and Leader. Temple Baptist was received into the fellowship of the North American Baptist General Conference on October 12, 1955. A parsonage was dedicated on March 27, 1960.

St. Barnabas Parish was inaugarated with a service held in the Presbyterian Church. The Anglican church was named St. Barnabas because it was dedicated on the festival of St. Barnabas. A rectory was built in 1886 on the river bank. In 1894 a lot was purchased adjoining the church property and the rectory was moved there. It was replaced in 1925.

In 1894 the Anglican parish exercised the right to obtain a grant of Crown land, taking up 40 acres on the north side of the river. In 1910 this property was sold, the net proceeds going into a fund for a new church. In 1912 the present St. Barnabas Church was erected and the first service held on December 12 of that year.

On February 9, 1910 a small group of German-speaking people met at a local home to discuss forming a congregation. The name was to be, The First German Evangelical Lutheran St. Paul's Congregation. The Congregation was served by Rev. Rehban, Rev. John Sillac, Rev. L. Walper, and Rev. H. Arndt, all known as "Circuit Riders". By November 22, 1911 the Congregation, under the guidance of Pastor G. Griesse, set up and signed a constitution with signators Friedrich Weiss, George Hehr, Bernard Bueschel, Johann Bross and Friedrich Quast. A cornerstone was laid for the church on December 31, 1911.

By January 1939 the church minutes were being written in English instead of German, although the Walther League (St. Paul's Lutheran Youth since 1966) aimed to "keep the German language in practice". At a council

145

meeting the matter of whether to continue to conduct services in German was discussed at length. It was decided that German would be the language used "until the law forbids us." No such law was passed.

In 1955 plans were made to build a new church. It was dedicated October 28, 1956. The church loan was paid off on May 25, 1970. Rev. Gerhardt E. Knoernschild of Winnipeg was installed as Pastor on Sunday, July 29, 1979,

The 1911 census indicated that approximately 6,000 people lived in the valley on both sides of the river. After the turn of the century many German-speaking people settled here, coming from Russia, Romania, Hungary, Germany and the United States. The August Wirsh family opened up their home on Clay Avenue and Bridge Street so the Lutheran services in the German language could be given. The house proved to be too small within a few months. Gottlieb Butgereit, who had moved with his wife and family from North Dakota, became the first pastor.

Elm Street School was home to the worshipers for a time until farmers with horses, plows, scrapers, picks and shovels came to build a place of worship at 1166 Queen Street. Meantime, services were held in a tent. The small, three-storey building that was erected there was referred to affectionately as Das Heim, The Home.

The Lutherans purchased the Methodist Church on Washington Avenue in 1929 for $3,000, all of which was raised at one Sunday service. Early in the 1950s an English-speaking service was started and in October 1954, Central Park Church of God was dedicated.

Dedication services were held on September 4, 1977 for the Southview Church of God at 2366 Southview Drive, South East.

And still the churches came. With the tremendous influx of Germans and Scandinavians, there was soon a need for another Lutheran church. St. Peter Evangelical Lutheran Church was organized on November 10, 1910 by Reverend John Oberhammer. Founders were Frederick Sailer, Gottlieb Hehr, Michael Entzminger, Samuel Zarbock and Christian Lentz. For two years the congregation worshipped in private homes and in 1912, with a loan of $500 from the Mission Department of the Ohio Synod, the faithful undertook to build a church. On May 19, 1912 the chapel was finished and dedicated. Pastor Oberhammer performed the rites, assisted by Pastors Spohr, Volk and Grant.

Ernest Hertz of Lutheran Seminary in St. Paul, Minnesota was called to become the first resident pastor. The church had undergone several facelifts and additions over the years until it was decided it was too small and must be replaced. The wooden structure was torn down and a church made of concrete blocks rose on the same site. During the building of the new church the Lutherans rented a hall belonging to the United Church. The cornerstone was laid on May 31, 1953 with Pastor G. H. Senft, assisted by R. Busch of Lethbridge, performing the sacred rites.

As well as serving as a place of worship, the church in Medicine Hat was a focal point for social events. Scarcely a week went by that the church or church hall was not used for some gathering. Church was not just a Sunday happening, it was a continuing celebration of life. In those early days the churches were involved in education as well. The board of St.

First school held in Medicine Hat was in this Presbyterian Church. J. K. Drinnan was first teacher.

John's Presbyterian, for example, opened the church as a school. The first indication that school was held in the church was recorded in the minutes of October 10, 1884 when the School Board offered to pay one-half of the expenses to build a shed at the back of the church to hold firewood and seats.

There were no funds in the church coffers to pay for this expense. But something had to be done to keep the building warm for the 75 pupils who had turned up for their Readin', 'Ritin', and 'Rithmetic. Sam Porter was paid five dollars to bank up the church with earth outside to keep out some of the draft. The building at that time was only a shell with rafters and studs still exposed. On November 17, when the first snow began to fall, the interior was "ceiled with good dry lumber." The students were sent home for two days so the work could be completed.

The School Board and The Church Board did not always agree on how details should be managed, particularly when it came to financial matters. The Medicine Hat School District had become sufficiently organized to start construction of the Toronto Street School, which was completed by the end of 1888. The Church Board was not sorry to see the departure of the students. Rent from the School Board was $190 in arrears in February 1888. Arbitration was required to settle the account.

A history of St. John's makes reference to the fact that the church had sustained "abuse" by the students and in April 1885 the Church Board sent a notice to the School Trustees that "unless they engage a responsible person to put the church in perfect order on Saturday, for Sabbath services, the Board will refuse them the use of the building."

When the Toronto Street School was finally opened, "this closed the record of a difficult but important service rendered to the entire community by the Presbyterian Congregation."

Incidentally, the Methodists claim they operated the first school in the

147

St. Barnabas Church under construction.
Lussier Construction Co. Medicine Hat.

community. In his *Breaking Prairie Sod,* Captain Wellington Bridgman said that two dollars a month was collected from every family, "a teacher was employed, and the first public school was held in the Methodist Church."

The students were undoubtedly happy to be in their new surroundings, at least as happy as students can be to be in school at all. Meantime, things warmed up at St. John's as well. In the fall of 1890 a cellar was dug under the church and a furnace installed and in 1897 storm windows were purchased at a cost of $40. Mrs. A. C. Hawthorne recalled a story about Reverend James William Morrow who came to call on a hot July day. He was wearing a coonskin cap with the earflaps down, apparently oblivious to the blistering heat.

"Why are you wearing that hat in this hot weather?" Mrs. Hawthorne asked him. "I am going to wear this until the managers of the church take those storm windows down for the summer!" the good Reverend fumed.

For the record, the name St. John's was first used in a Session minute book on September 10, 1891 in copying a Presbytery report. The title was not used again until August 7, 1894 when the Board of Managers' minutes first used the name in recording the annual meeting of January 1893. St. John's Historical Committee concluded that the name came into use in 1890, but how it was chosen is not known.

Reverend Morrow, already alluded to in various parts of this book, became minister to the Presbyterians in June 1896 and for 22 years continued in that capacity. A graduate of Dublin and Princeton Universities, Reverend Morrow was one of the most colorful individuals to stand before a congregation in Medicine Hat. He was bluff, outspoken, careless in manner and dress, but he had a great understanding of human nature and was generous with his own meagre pay.

It was Morrow's style to give to the poor, but in an unobtrusive way. Gladys McDougall Bannan recalled that one day Reverend Morrow dropped in to see her mother. A tea party was in progress but the minister walked in

148

and sat down anyway. He did not bother to remove his coonskin coat, but as he joined the ladies for a cup of tea, he suddenly gave a loud exclamation and jumped to his feet. It seems he had filled his pockets with eggs for delivery to a poor family, not wishing to be seen by the neighbors carrying them into the house in a paper bag.

"My mother was obliged to come to his aid to clean the sticky mess out of his coat pockets," Mrs. Bannan said.

Reverend Morrow earned the respect of ranchers and farmers in the district when he visited them. If the men were busy working, he took off his coat, rolled up his sleeves and helped out. He had a great interest in horses, including race horses and was an eager visitor to the stampedes and at races held at Medicine Hat, Walsh and Irvine.

After his resignation in 1918, Mr. Morrow continued to reside in Medicine Hat, and in 1925 entered the United Church of Canada. From 1927 to 1930 he ministered to United Church Congregations at Walsh and Dunmore. He died on February 4, 1932.

Various churches in the city commemorate the pioneers of the faith in their own way. When the Jubilee Year was being celebrated, the early Methodists who sat on planks on nail kegs were remembered. A display of these rustic seats was placed in front of the altar at the Fifth Avenue United Church (the former Fifth Avenue Methodist).

A lasting memorial to a pioneer family is to be seen in St. Barnabas Church which salutes members of the Charles Taylor family, who came to Medicine Hat in the early 1900s. The lovely stained-glass window is dedicated to the original settler and his descendants. Charles Taylor was born in County Limerick on the River Shannon in Ireland. He learned his trade as a carpenter in Kincardine, Ontario and later became a contractor. In 1880 he married Martha Jane Copeland; the couple had seven children. One died in infancy. Two of the sons, Samuel and Abram, were well-known businessmen in Medicine Hat, having operated Taylor Brothers Grocery from 1911 to 1962. After their retirement the store continued for several years under Charles (Chick) Taylor, Abram's son, and Frank W. Butler, Samuel's son-in-law.

Ada Taylor, the eldest daughter, served as a nursing sister in the First World War and afterwards married Charles Anderson, who established the Anderson Insurance Agency. It was continued by their son, Frank.

Mary Taylor became a teacher and was married to William McIntosh. Lillian Taylor married H. Norman Davis who was associated for many years with Ogilvie Flour Mills in Medicine Hat and in Montreal. The youngest son, Edward (Ted), also worked for Ogilvies for some years.

The Taylor boys were all good athletes, especially in field sports, baseball and lacrosse. Sam and Abe Taylor were on the Medicine Hat professional lacrosse team which made a name for itself across Canada in 1910 and again in 1912.

As time went by, more and more churches established in Medicine Hat. Knox Church, for example, was founded in 1907. It is now known as Memorial-Salem, a union of Knox Presbyterian and Washington Avenue Methodist.

Reverend J. W. Morrow earned the respect of ranchers and farmers among his parishoners because he was always willing to roll up his sleeves and lend a hand at chores. He was the author of an early history of Medicine Hat and District.

When Salem United amalgamated with Memorial it was a Congregational unit. The founders of the new church considered it a sort of Trinity: the uniting of three faiths — Presbyterian, Methodist and Congregational — making it the only Trinity Church in South Alberta presbytery. Rev. Sidney Vincent was the Minister in 1981.

Westminster United Church came into existence when the "hill people" living around Central Park decided they wanted their own church separate from St. John's. First services were held in Alexandra High school on August 31, 1913 with Rev. J. O. Watts of Oakwood, Ontario as first minister.

The name Westminster does not refer to the famous abbey in London, England. "West" describes the location, and "minister" is old English for monastery.

Under the supervision of James Rae, the new church was completed in just two months at a cost of $4,781. Dedication of Westminster Church took place on June 21, 1914. The Westminster Memorial Hall is the former church building. The name was changed from Westminster Presbyterian Church to Westminster United Church in 1925. A new church and a new site were chosen to keep up with the increasing number of churchgoers. The first service was on Sunday, September 22, 1957 under the auspices of Reverend Len Harbour.

On April 25th, 1979, at 1:10 a.m. the incumbent minister was awakened by three young people reporting a fire in the Westminster Memorial Hall. The fire destroyed the Hall, did extensive smoke and water damage to the sanctuary, including the new Regent Hammond organ which had been recently purchased.

A young man was charged with deliberately setting the fire. An item used to set the fire was the minister's pulpit robe. The young man went to trial and was acquitted.

Westminster Church was closed for three Sundays; weddings were held in homes and at Fifth Avenue Church. Sunday Services were held in Fifth Avenue United Church. One of those Sundays was Mother's Day and the Westminster crowd was lined up along Fourth Street for half a block waiting to get into the church. The insurance claim which was finally paid amounted to $404,000.

In May 1980 the ground was broken for the new Church Hall building. This new building was made 20 feet longer than the old building. The new building was completed and occupied early in 1981.

Reverend William Bell, who was the minister at the time the original discussions about the need for a larger church began, told a story that challenged the excuse that there was a lack of money available for such a venture: "There was a man who complained that ever since he made his vows at the altar his wife was always begging for money, money, money. When asked what she did with all the money he gave her, the man replied, "Oh, she don't do nothing. I ain't give her none yet!"

In 1934, Rev. D. A. Gunn established the "Church of the Open Door" on Fourth Avenue. The congregation met first in a house across the avenue from the present O.K. Economy Store. This original building was purchased near the IOOF hall. A City parking lot is now located there. Later on, the congregation moved to a plumbing shop on Fourth Street, just a little east and across the street from Fifth Avenue United Church. Still later, there was a second move to Macleod Trail. A lot was obtained alongside Purity Dairy.

In 1944 the "Church of the Open Door" joined the Christian & Missionary Alliance, and thus, Medicine Hat Alliance Church came into existence. A church building was begun in 1946. The basement was dedicated in 1947. It was here that the congregation met for two years. The main sanctuary was completed and dedicated in 1949. An educational unit was added and dedicated in 1960. This building served the need of the growing congregation until 1973.

In 1972, 1.8 acres of new property was purchased for $18,500 at the intersection of 13th Avenue and 22nd Street. A sod-turning ceremony was held in May of 1972. Rev. Edward Carlson led the congregation in a new church building program. This new building provided more than 11,000 square feet of space. It was erected at a cost of $146,000 and is capable of housing approximately 900 people when the folding partitions are all opened up. This building was dedicated on December 2, 1973. It was built largely through the voluntary labor of its members and adherents.

Rev. and Mrs. J. C. O'Brien came to Medicine Hat on September 8, 1946 to establish a Pentecostal Assembly. The first service was held in the Moose Hall on October 1, 1946. In January of 1947 services were begun in the Eagles Hall and continued until May, 1948, at which time a meeting place was acquired on North Railway Street.

The first Sunday School Bus service was begun February 10, 1947.

Rev. and Mrs. Keith Running became pastors of First Assembly in April, 1979 and were continuing to pastor the Church. The Assembly was experiencing a steady growth and the congregation was looking forward to the completion of a Senior Citizens Home in 1981.

Christ the King Parish came into existence in 1954. It is centered in "the Flats", the oldest section of Medicine Hat. A Chapel of Ease was established on January 25, 1942 as St. Edmund's, administered by St. Patrick's Parish. The building, located at 975 Elm Street was built in 1925 and was turned over to the City in 1941. Monsignor McCoy, then Pastor of St. Patrick's, purchased it for use as a mission church. It wasn't until 1945 that regular weekly masses were celebrated there.

By 1954 the city's population had increased to 18,285 from 10,571 in 1942 and the decision was to establish St. Edmund's as a district parish. Rev. Paul J. O'Byrne was named pastor with Father J. Kelly as assistant. Andrew Thomas and Amelia Vollman were the first couple to be married in the new parish; Marie E. Nikiel, daughter of Oliver and Edna Nikeil, the first child baptised and Egidis Conte the first parishioner to be laid to rest from St. Edmund's.

In 1958 the present site, 1101 Queen Street South East, was purchased and by November 12, 1960, construction began. On November 15 of the same year Francis P. Carroll, Bishop of Calgary, blessed the church under the title of Christ the King. With the official opening of the new church, St. Edmund's was converted for use as a parish hall.

For some time in the early 50s, a community Sunday school had been operating on Riverside so that Presbyterian youngsters would not have to take the long trip across the river to church. When it grew difficult to find staff, the classes were adopted by the Presbyterian Training School in Hargrave House with Miss Marguerite Quickfall as the Superintendent. From the ensuing services of worship, attended by parents and friends of the pupils, a new congregation was formally organized in February of 1955 with Rev. David Crawford as minister. Two years later the growing congregation began laying plans for their own sanctuary. Mrs. Charlie Ross, a charter member, turned the first sod in the fall. The first service, in a still-unfinished building, was held on Christmas Sunday, 1957 and the dedication took place the following Easter.

Riverside Presbyterian Church was to have many ups and downs in the intervening years, led by half a dozen ministers after Rev. Crawford's departure in 1960. One was Rev. Gordon Williams (1969-1972), the first Cree Indian to be ordained by the Presbyterian Church in Canada. By 1975 the mortgage on the sanctuary on Third Street North West was paid off and the congregation has been growing since. Riverside's minister in 1981 was Rev. Noel Kinnon.

St. Mary's is a relatively young parish. Construction of the church building, located at 1240 Division Avenue South, was begun in 1962 and completed in the fall of the same year, only two years after the idea of a church in the Southwest part of the city was first conceived.

The speed with which this project proceeded from conception to fruition was in a large measure due to the efforts of a group of enterprising would-be parishioners. Their efforts ensured that a good deal of the necessary funding had been raised locally before construction was started.

For the first five years, St. Mary's was administered as a mission church by St. Patrick's Parish. Then on April 15, 1967 a letter requesting that St. Mary's be made a Parish was sent to the Most Reverend Francis Klein, Bishop of the Diocese of Calgary. On September 1, 1967, St. Mary's officially became a parish with Father Phillip Tessier as first Pastor.

The first baptism in the new church was recorded on September 17, 1967 and was that of George Alan Yuhas. The first funeral was that of Mrs. Pauline Dirk on September 9, 1967 and the first marriage brought together Richard Ebry and Sharon Rose Miller on September 2, 1967.

A rectory has been built. St. Mary's mission in Redcliff came under the charge of the church in Medicine Hat.

Victory Lutheran Church at 2793 Southview Drive South East came into being in 1974, mainly as an outgrowth of St. Peter Lutheran. Also, it was deemed necessary by the congregation to open a mission in the Crestwood area due to a large number of homes built there, and in the suburb of Ross Glen. The Mission Board of the Evangelical Lutheran Church of Canada accepted and endorsed the project and Pastor Walter Lexvold was commissioned pastor of the mission.

For the first three years the new congregation held services in the Seventh Day Adventist Church. On Sunday, June 4, 1978 a ground breaking ceremony took place at the church site and construction began the following week. The total cost of land, construction, furniture, landscaping and parking lot paving amounted to $295,000, of which $40,000 was donated by members and friends of Victory Lutheran.

As the reader will have noted, there was friendly cooperation among the various religions, early Ecumenism that continues to the present day. To emphasize different attitudes of earlier times, two stories are told:

Reverend Hugh A. Tudor was an Anglican who was well-known throughout his huge parish, although not liked by everyone. Stocky of build and "manly" of nature, he would not stand for any irreverence and, if required to do so, he would use his fists. It seems that Reverend Tudor held a service at the North West Mounted Police barracks in Medicine Hat, the officer in charge being a certain Inspector McIllrae. McIllrae, and his wife, both Irish, made no bones about their dislike of Reverend Tudor. Mrs. McIllrae told a new officer's wife, "Yes, my dear, I can assure you that he looks just like a Catholic priest." The newcomer went to see Tudor and when she returned, Mrs. McIllrae asked her if the description was apt. "Why no," the woman replied, "if you meant that he looked like a Roman Catholic priest, he does not — for he had on a clean surplice and was clean-shaven!"

Whatever slight damage was done to church union and interfaith cooperation was quickly mended by the action of Reverend Wellington Bridgman, of the old Methodist Church in Medicine Hat. Reverend Bridgman had to take over duties of doctor and his wife as nurse when the community was without the services of either.

"Often our cabin home would be deserted at night, my faithful wife looking after the women and I doing my best to take care of the men," Bridgman wrote. The first year Reverend Bridgman visited 77 victims of fever and attended 11 funerals. He also found himself in the role of "priest", according to an account in his diary book *Breaking The Sod*.

"One time that summer a gunfight had taken place on the prairie and Bob Casey had been brought in to his hotel mortally wounded. Casey was a good-hearted Roman Catholic. But, in the absence of his priest, was not I his pastor and had he not given me a ten dollar bill for my church? So, I went and found him very ill. I said to him, 'Mr. Casey, we have always been good friends. We belong to different churches, but the same God is our Father. When I found out I was a Prodigal I went to Him and confessed my sin and asked Him to make me His child. And He did. I am sure if you would ask Him he would do that for you.'

"He thanked me, and when I left I am sure that the grip of his hand meant more than a mere farewell."

Although all churches and members of other faiths were asked to submit brief histories to the author for inclusion in this chapter, not all did so, despite repeated requests. A history of churches in Medicine Hat would be incomplete without at least some mention of the Salvation Army, which has been here from earliest times and which continues to minister to the poor and heavy-laden.

The only history of the Sally Ann in the City available is a rather irreverent account in a back issue of the *Canadian Cattlemen*, which is repeated here verbatim:

"When the Salvation Army started up in the fall of 1899 at Medicine Hat there were only two Salvationists. Both were beautiful girls. One came from MacDowel, about 20 miles west of Prince Albert. She was the eldest

daughter of Mr. William Little and her name was Isabell, but we all called her Bella for short.

"I believe the other girl came from Edmonton. I don't know what her name was but anyway, Walter Cooper fell in love with her after hearing her sing hymns a few times. He soon joined the Salvation Army as he was a real sinner, and by doing so he killed two birds with one stone. He was saved and the girl fell in love with him and married him the same winter. But Walter didn't remain a Salvationist after he married the beautiful girl. He quit the Army and went to ranching a few miles west of Walsh. He may still be leading a Christian life as there's nothing to prevent it."

St. Peter Lutheran Church. Many changes have taken place in the churches in Medicine Hat.

154

12.

The Little Red School House . . . And Beyond

Before Alberta became a province of Canada in 1905, the government of the West was controlled by a Lieutenant-Governor and Council of the North West Territories, with headquarters in Regina. In 1884, Territorial legislation permitted the organization of tax-supported schools under the direction of a Territorial Board of Education. In September, 1886, the ratepayers in Medicine Hat voted for the establishment of a public school system.

The ratepayers also authorized the collection of an educational fee of two dollars from each citizen in town. L. B. Cochrane, E. Walton and James Hargrave were elected trustees, with Walton as chairman. Hargrave was the first secretary.

J. K. Drinnan of the noted "Canadian Voyageurs" who transported Imperial troops up the Nile in a daring attempt to rescue Charles "Chinese" Gordon, besieged in Khartoum in 1898, was the first teacher engaged by the new Board of Education. He held forth in the Presbyterian Church, a small frame building on the corner of what is now Fifth Avenue and Second Street.

L. B. Cochran

Toronto St. School. Original building, 1889, situated where O.K. Economy Store now stands.

155

From Monday to Friday, school was held in the church, but on Friday the pupils had to move the desks out and put the pews in place for Sunday service. On Sunday the desks were put back ready for school the next morning. No doubt some children of the Presbyterian faith were convinced that five days of school, then Sunday school and church in the same building, was special treatment for them from the Deity.

By 1887 it became apparent that a permanent school building was required and in 1889 Toronto Street School was erected where the present O.K. Economy Store now stands at Third Street and Fourth Avenue. Two classrooms were built with others added in succeeding years. In 1902 the community had expanded to such an extent that additional space was required and the School Board purchased the original frame building of St. John's Presbyterian Church and located it on the site of what was to become Montreal Street School. It served the educational needs of the community for many more years than it had the spiritual needs.

Between 1889 and 1896 Toronto Street School acquired two more classrooms, a basement, and connection with the town water supply, together with a principal, W. H. Gee, whose salary was $1,000 a year. In 1902, high school education was added to the curriculum and the end-of-year report showed a school population of 528 pupils. In 1904 Montreal Street School was completed and all City pupils attended there while the original Toronto Street School was razed to make room for a new brick building on the same site.

Toronto St. School, showing addition made in 1907 to original building 1889. This school building was demolished and O.K. Economy Store now stands on the site.

Between 1900 and 1914 the City was caught up in another period of growth and prosperity. In 1909 Alexandra High School was built, followed closely by Elm Street in 1911, the Bridge Street wing of Elm Street in 1912, Connaught School in the same year, and Elizabeth Street School in 1913.

In addition to these permanent structures, six "cottage" schools were built in 1915: two were located on the 400 block of Seventh Street South East, one each on the Elizabeth and Elm Street School sites, and two located on the site of the Riverside School. These structures served for periods far exceeding the years for which they were constructed, particularly the last one, at Elm Street School: as a home for the school custodian.

156

The first section of Alexandra High School opened in 1909 with the following staff: M. E. Lazerte (Grade 12), Miss Jessie Frazer (Grade 11), Miss M. L. Rorke (Grade 10), J. T. Cuyler (Grade 9) and E. E. Oliver (Grade 8).

In January 1912, W. E. Hay was appointed Superintendent of Schools, a position he held until June 30, 1923 when the position was discontinued along with all supervisory and consultative positions. The school system was without the services of a superintendent until 1938, at which time P. L. F. Riches was appointed.

The period from 1910 to 1920 was a decade of progress in the early years of the Medicine Hat school system. It was characterized by a progressive building program which resulted in the construction of Earl Kitchener and Elizabeth Street Schools, specialized for primary education; Elm Street, Montreal Street, Riverside, Connaught and Toronto Street, as middle grade schools; and the new Alexandra High School providing special facilities in manual arts, commercial education and household economics for high school students.

Classroom, Toronto St. School, 1902.

During this same decade ambitious plans were made for a technical school to be built on the Northwest corner of Aberdeen Street and Fifth Avenue. This school was to be one of the most up-to-date in the West, providing a full range of technical and vocational trade courses. Unfortunately, an economic recession immediately prior to the First World War forced the School Trustees to abandon their plans. The results of this decision were to occupy the Trustees in litigation suits for several years because the contractor had completed the foundation for the school and had ordered boilers, lumber and a variety of other equipment items for the construction. The building was never completed and some two decades later the Medicine Hat Rotary Club investigated the possibility of building a swimming pool on the site; another location was used. Ultimately, the City took advantage of the area and completed a swimming pool which was used for many years.

The same recession which had sunk the new technical school forced the School Trustees to retrench in many of the educational programs. The high school commercial program, the manual arts and household economics courses were discontinued; in addition, all the supervisory staff was released from the school system. Pupil loads in classes were increased and teachers were asked to work at salary reductions of up to 20 per cent.

George Henry Davison told the author in 1979 that he was happy to have a job teaching, even at reduced scale. "I was lucky to get work," he said. "Even though I had to work most of first session with no pay." Davison, now a City of Medicine Hat alderman, began his teaching career at Valley View School, a rural school about 14 miles south of Seven Persons. It was attended by mainly Scandinavians and Germans. "The English language was sometimes the only common denominator among the diverse settlers," he said. "There were very few Anglo-Saxons among the children, but the kids picked up English by Grade 2. I didn't notice any social problems, or ethnic problems."

Davison boarded three miles from where he taught in the one-room school house, making the round trip daily on horseback. He would ride in early, start a fire in the stove, haul water, sweep the floor and get things prepared for the classes. In severe weather, the students abandoned their desks and took their lessons sitting around the stove in the centre of the room.

Like many other teachers during this period, Davison had to supplement his teaching income with off-season jobs working on threshing crews or accepting other ranch and farm employment. But, there were compensations. "There were always social events and a bachelor teacher was always welcome. The parents were very hospitable. They invited me for dinner and there were always dances and picnics and other good times. I doubt if teachers today have such fun. Although the pay was only $90 a month, the fellowship was great."

As the years passed the economic situation gradually improved and the school system reinstated the programs and services which had been removed. The decade of the Twenties marked the emergence of the Alberta Teachers' Alliance as the fledgling teachers' professional association. C. E. Peasley, a local teacher and later school principal, became a charter member, an early president, and an articulate advocate of the new association. Along with others, Peasley prevailed upon Trustees to provide a uniform salary schedule based upon equitable standards.

Peasley, who arrived in Medicine Hat in 1911, had been principal of Elm Street School for some 40 years when he retired in 1955. For several years he had been Senior Principal of the Public Schools of Medicine Hat. A founder of the Alberta Teachers' Association, he served eight years on the ATA executive, one term as president and two as vice-president. He was also president of the Alberta Educational Association, which later merged with the ATA. He was honored frequently for his long, devoted service to his community in education and sport. He was a strong advocate of sports as part of the school curriculum.

From the minutes of the school system the following items were culled to indicate some of the business which occupied the attention of the Trustees in the early years:

August 25, 1913: The superintendent was granted $15 a month toward buying feed for his horse.

Charles Peasley, beloved principal of Elm Street School, Medicine Hat, for some 40 years.

August, 25, 1913: The Superintendent was authorized to hire a woman doctor to conduct medical inspection of all school children at a salary not to exceed $1,200 a year. (The next month's minutes showed an amendment raising this salary to $1,300. At the same meeting the principal of Toronto Street School was to receive $1,450 a year.)

October 13, 1913: The janitor of Connaught School was authorized to sleep at the school until the panic locks arrived to secure the new school. (He was paid a dollar a day extra, no doubt a remuneration for sleeping on the job.)

Connaught School class, about 1920. Identified are Gerry Grant, Mac Rae, Bill Wallace, Gavin Begg, Jean Fleming, Jack Allan.

February 28, 1916: The Board requested the Provincial Government to construct the next Normal School to be built in Alberta in Medicine Hat. (However, Post secondary education in the City was delayed for 55 years until the Medicine Hat College opened in 1965.)

October 28, 1918: Montreal Street School was used as a hospital to cope with the 'flu epidemic. The school children from the area were accommodated at Toronto Street and Elm Street Schools. (Which must have prompted those who attended those schools to wonder if there was any escape from school — even by being sick!)

During the Dirty Thirties, with tax revenue reduced, the Trustees of School District Number 76 were faced with the unpleasant task of reducing expenditures; in all cases salaries of teachers and other personnel were the last items to be cut, but eventually these too felt the effects of the Depression and teachers in common with other wage earners carried on with reduced incomes. Another measure adopted by Trustees was to release all women teachers, and to avoid hiring married women teachers. The Trustees — as indicated in the minutes — had a difficult time enforcing these regulations.

As the Thirties progressed, conditions began to improve and by 1934 Trustees and administrators began to look toward improvements in the schools' programs. Commercial classes again resumed in the Alexandra High School and in 1936 "Enterprise Education" made its appearance on the educational scene. Although violently opposed by its critics, the Enter-

159

prise Program served the main purpose of focusing the attention of educators on the child and his or her interests, rather than on a standard curriculum for all pupils.

A further indication that progress was being made as the Depression receded was the appointment of P.L.F. Riches as Superintendent of Schools and principal of Alexandra High School effective May 1, 1938. Riches held these two positions until he resigned from the staff in 1943.

Group of students from Grade Ten C, Alexandra High School, 1927.

The pall of the Great Depression lifted and the economy of the Nation and the City once again resumed normal progress. Then along came the Second World War which led to a continual change of staff as men and women teachers left the classrooms for service in the Canadian forces. Wartime economy produced shortages of a wide variety of materials and school maintenance and upgrading proved to be extremely difficult.

The immediate post-war years brought with them, in the 1950s, the first "baby boom" and Medicine Hat elementary schools were flooded with a wave of children, filling all available accommodation to capacity. Additions were built on Connaught and Riverside Schools in 1950 and 1951 and then in rapid succession the following buildings were constructed: Medicine Hat High School (1953-1954); Alexandra Junior High School (addition 1955); Crescent Heights High School (1957); Central Park (1957); Herald (1958); Crescent Heights High School (addition 1958); River Heights (1960); Vincent Massey (1960), Crescent Heights High School (addition 1961); Webster Niblock (1961); Crestwood (1961); and additions to Medicine Hat High School in 1962 and 1966, to Vincent Massey in 1966 and 1967, to Herald School in 1967, to Crescent Heights High School in 1967 and to Crestwood School in 1970.

An era ended on June 30, 1960 when the first permanent school in the city, Toronto Street School, fell under the wreckers' hammers. Originally built at a cost of $3,600, it sold for $200,000 to the O.K. Economy Stores with the profit from the sale going to the School District to construct an administration office and warehouse at 601-First Avenue South West. Prior to that the headquarters of the school system had been accommodated in one remodeled classroom in the top floor of the Toronto Street School.

Alexandra High School expanded its education program to such an extent that in 1949 the name became the Alexandra Composite High School. Shop facilities were provided at an annexed building on the far east end of First Street. Household economics were available and the commercial department expanded. Technical Agriculture was instituted, using facilities at the Annex and at the former Prisoner of War camp area on Crestwood. At this time the composite school assumed responsibility for the education of high school students from Redcliff, Ralston and most of School Division Number 4. The school division also built and operated a dormitory for rural area students to encourage them to complete their high school education in the City.

By the early 1950's it was obvious that the facilities of the Alexandra Composite High School would not be able to provide for the increased number of students anticipated to enrol in the coming decade. Plans were made to construct a new high school. This building was completed in 1954. The building vacated was upgraded to accommodate all grade 7, 8 and 9 students from the City. The City now had a junior high school to provide specifically for the special needs of this age group.

The early 1960s saw the introduction of the Federal-Provincial Vocational School Building Program whose terms enabled a school district to obtain up to 90 per cent of the cost of building and equipping vocational school facilities. In 1962 the school district completed the vocational wing to the Medicine Hat High School and complete vocational services were now available to the City students.

During the latter part of the 1950s, the City expansion moved from the Southwest Hill Area to north of the river, and the Crescent Heights Area expanded so rapidly that within a decade two elementary schools, Vincent Massey and Webster Niblock were built, as well as Crescent Heights School, which was started as a six-room elementary school, expanded in 1967 to a 12-room elementary Junior High and within a few years was enlarged to accommodate all grades 7 to 12 in the Crescent Heights area.

Post-secondary education was finally recognized in the Medicine Hat area in the early 1960s with the inauguration of the Medicine Hat Junior College which until 1970 occupied premises in the Fifth Street wing of the Medicine Hat Vocational High School.

September 1972 marked the completion of the rebuilding of the original Alexandra High School. This structure, which originated in 1909, experienced a series of renovations and additions and almost climaxed its use as a school when a fire in 1970 gutted the interior of the gymnasium and adjoining area. This area was rebuilt and then in 1971 the provincial Department of Education authorized the razing of the original building and its replacement by a new structure which featured open-area construction and a variety of facilities which enabled the building to provide a flexible educational program.

It should be of interest to note the names of the teachers who served as principals of Alexandra High School to that time: C. Sansom (1910); W. Hays (1912 to 1923); D. M. Sullivan (1923 to 1929); J. T. Cuyler (1943 to 1952); N. Wait (1952 to 1955); F. R. Millican (1955 to 1971).

After a period of over 15 years without a Superintendent, the board engaged Dr. O. P. Larson to assume this position on September 1, 1960.

Toronto Street School as it looked shortly before it was demolished to make room for OK Economy Store at the corner of Third Street South East and MacLeod Trail.

As with the sale of the Toronto Street School marking the end of an era, another era was marked in June 30, 1970 with the retirement of a number of teachers and principals who had served the school system for most of their teaching careers: G. S. Grant, Fred R. Millican, H. Whitney, W. R. Morris, H. E. McBain, J. R. Johnston, E. Elford, Miss M. Carr, Miss P. Dunn, Mrs. I. Elford.

The 1970s opened with a new problem facing Trustees and administrators — too few children. A number of factors produced a problem which could only be solved through reduction of staff, a move which proved most unpopular with the principals of the schools involved. Paralleling this problem was that of inadequate school accommodation on Crestwood and the necessity of transporting classroom groups of children to Hill Area schools — a solution unfavorable with residents of Crestwood.

After almost a decade of economic stagnation the community experienced another wave of industrial expansion and population growth. Ed McKenzie, Deputy Superintendent at the time, said "with adequate school accommodation available, it seems that the educational future should be characterized by advances in the area of concern for children and the way they learn. The Worth Commission Report published in June 1972 points the way in this direction — hopefully our schools may realize their potential."

The concern must have been responded to because progress in many areas continued. The year 1972 was marked by three main incidents: with an extension of consultative services made available to the schools, an expansion of office space of the administrative building was necessary. The Bridge Street wing of Elm Street School (built in 1911) fell into disrepair because of unstable soil conditions and had to be demolished. And the 1955 wing of Alexandra Junior High School was named the F. R. Millican Wing in honor of the school's longtime teacher and principal.

The district moved into the computer age in 1973 with its Program Accounting and Budgeting. Discussions were hot and heavy on a divided school year for the system whereby the school year would be divided, using

Elm Street School, Medicine Hat, 1911. One of the early fine school buildings still being used.

the Christmas vacation as a mid-point. It never came to pass. An Education Clinic was established to provide services to students who had learning disabilities. And the district's first speech therapist — Miss Janet Osman — was hired.

Frank Riddle, Superindentent of Schools since 1968, retired on December 31, 1974. Dr. Kenneth Sauer, formerly the principal of Lethbridge Collegiate, was appointed Superintendent on January 1, 1975.

Curriculum development took on a new meaning with a great deal of emphasis on communication and computational skills. Schools in the district were reorganized into elementary (1-6), junior high (7-9) and secondary (7-12) rather than mixtures of 1-9, 1-7, 9-12, or other combinations. In 1976 Deputy Superintendent Edwin MacKenzie retired. Over the many years MacKenzie was responsible for a great number of innovations, such as the "ungraded" elementary schools.

Harold Storlien, principal of Crescent Heights High School, was appointed Deputy Superintendent. And also in 1976, a first for the system occurred when a Child Development Specialist was appointed to serve Montreal Street and Elm Street Schools.

In 1977 the development of Articulated Language Arts Program was begun for grades 1-12. Two more Child Development Specialists were appointed to serve Riverside and Vincent Massey, and Crestwood. Southview Community School, the first school to be built for 14 years (Webster Niblock was built in 1962) was opened in January, 1977. In 1978 a study of the impact of daily physical education in the district's schools was undertaken. A year later work began on a new elementary school in the Ross Glen Community area. An Education Plan Update was carried out to indicate progress made on the Education Plan approved in 1976.

The Provincial Government declared in 1976 that curriculum was to have more structure and specificity. The full impact of that statement was felt in Medicine Hat District in 1980 when Special Administrator and Central Office-Board Seminars were held to lay out a "Blueprint for the 80s". A great deal of time and effort had to be expended to develop specific objectives and learning outcomes.

Only six years after Alberta became a province, St. Louis Separate

Ed MacKenzie: "Hopefully, our schools may realize their potential."

163

School District No. 21 came into existence. From humble beginnings, the system developed until it was responsible in 1981 for the education of nearly 1,900 students under the guidance of a staff of nearly 90 persons.

The pioneer school in this system is St. Louis. Following the formation of the District on June 26, 1911 the School Board, made up of Rev. A. Dadonx, J. G. Millar, F. B. MacKinnon, L. P. O. Noel and J. B. Barreau, borrowed funds and purchased the St. Louis School site for $5,250. Construction was begun on January 3, 1913 and Sister Anna Mary and Sister Mary Veronica of the Sisters of Charity of St. Louis commenced classes. An addition of an auditorium and two classrooms in 1956, plus interior renovations completed more recently, made the venerable institution ready to serve the needs of the District for many more years.

From 1915 to March 1957, St. Theresa's Academy also served the needs of students in the city. Through cooperation of the University of Ottawa, it served as a degree-granting institution for several years. Initially, this was a private institution but in later years it became part of the Separate School System through an agreement with the Order.

Two temporary structures, the Little Flower and the Marian School, offered temporary relief following the post-war population rise. In 1952 St. Patrick's School on Riverside was constructed. This marked the beginning of a rapid period of expansion in the District.

Facilities for high school classes at St. Theresa's proved inadequate so in 1957 St. Mary's School was constructed. Initially it housed all elementary students in the Hill area — the Marian School being closed — and all junior high and senior high students in the city. In a short time it became evident that a new structure was required and on April 10, 1961 McCoy School was opened and the high school was transferred to this building. Elementary students from Crescent Heights were housed in the north wing of McCoy.

Within two years a new elementary school was completed so that McCoy became a high school in its entirety.

St. Francis Xavier was opened in 1963 and until 1966 adequately housed the elementary pupils from both North East and North West Crescent Heights. St. Thomas Aquinas School was completed in 1963, taking some of the pressure from the St. Louis School attendance area, as well as providing for the newly-developed Crestwood Area. Rapid expansion of North West Crescent Heights necessitated the building of St. Michael's School. The original building which opened in 1966 was doubled in area for the 1968 school year. Beginning in the fall of 1974, all grade 7 students residing north of the river were accommodated at St. Michael's.

In 1968 expansion of McCoy High School was completed; included were home economics and industrial arts facilities, a business education suite, a modern media centre and a staff work space. In 1969 a four classroom re-locatable school was placed on the St. Mary's school site. The complex was self-contained and the classrooms carpeted. A second re-locatable building was purchased in 1975 to accommodate expanding enrolments at St. Thomas Aquinas School. This four-roomed cluster featured ready access to the core facilities in the main building through a heated corridor.

A new Catholic Education Centre was opened by the School District on December 1, 1979 on First Avenue South West. This is an administration building with special services. Plans were made for the opening of the $1.8 million Catholic Elementary School in Ross Glen.

For many residents of Medicine Hat it was like a dream come true when Medicine Hat College opened its doors on October 3, 1971. After more than seven years of planning, designing and waiting, the modern facility of higher learning opened on a 107 acre tract of land located west of the Connaught Golf Club, overlooking Kin Coulee. The site was chosen in November 1967 on land donated by the City.

Planning began in January 1963 when Jim Newton took his idea for a regional college to the Medicine Hat School District 76 Board of Trustees' meeting. The School Board soon approved the idea, supported by the other four area school boards in planning and financing the College.

On February 26, 1964 more than 100 enthusiastic citizens attended a meeting of the Provisional Junior College Board at Medicine Hat High School to hear a discussion on the need for such a college and what programs would be offered. A report approved by Dr. O. P. Larson, Superintendent of Public Schools, was unanimously approved.

With no firm site for the College in view, a beginning was made by renting temporary quarters in the high school, two rooms in the Herald School and two in Connaught. The College authorities also rented two houses, one for faculty offices, one for music and drama departments; the houses were later purchased.

On March 25, 1964 the College received a welcome shot in the arm when the Alberta Legislature approved a bill providing 90 per cent of new building costs and a per capita grant of $635 for each fulltime student. An order-in-council passed in June 1964 made a new College the third to be established in Alberta.

This meant that students in Medicine Hat and district could attend their first two years of university near home, with expenses considerably reduced.

Dr. Neville O. Matthews, first Dean of the College, moved into his new office in Medicine Hat High School in September 1964 to prepare for the opening of the new facility in the fall of the following year. The first chairman of the Provisional Junior College Board of Trustees was Dr. H. F. McKenzie, whose duties were later taken over by Doctor Larson. The members of the board were: Mrs. E. G. F. Skinner, J. L. Levinson, Jim Newton, Dr. H. F. McKenzie and Vern Sanders, all Public School Trustees. Rod Ashburner represented the Separate School District; A. M. Pennie represented Ralston, D. N. Jenson, Redcliff and B. E. Plummer, Newell County School Boards.

The Board of Governors of the University of Alberta approved affiliation of the university with Medicine Hat Junior College for one year, later extended to several more years. Affiliation meant the College could carry out its academic program in consultation with the Calgary campus (now the University of Calgary) and offer first year courses in arts, sciences and education equivalent in content to those regularly offered at the university.

The first permanent Junior College board was established in 1965 consisting of Dr. McKenzie, Mr. Ashburner and Mr. Jensen, joined by Ted

Roll, R. E. Eastman and J. M. Pritchard, representing the participating school boards.

Fund-raising began, including one imaginative scheme by Crescent Heights students who wrote to celebrities asking them for one of their favorite ties to be auctioned off in aid of the College construction. The College coat of arms was adopted in November 1965 with the motto *Scientia mentum sustinet* — Science and knowledge supports man. The insignia identified the College with Alberta, the University of Alberta and the local district.

The inauguration ceremony for the College was held later in November with Dr. Herbert Armstrong, president of the University of Calgary, delivering the theme address.

A setback occurred in July 1967 when vandals ransacked its temporary location. About $20,000 damage was done when a fire hose was turned on, flooding the foyer, auditorium, offices and classrooms. Fortunately, books valued at $40,000 in the library were not damaged.

By the fourth year, the College was developing well. The School Board was told that the students of Medicine Hat Junior College, who had gone on to university, were progressing, with a failure rate lower than average. This confirmed an earlier report that students attending their first two years at a junior college were more likely to achieve better scholastic standing later on.

When Dr. J. H. Snedden, chairman of the College Board in 1971, read off the list of invited dignitaries to the opening of the College, it was like a Who's Who of politics and education in the province. Alberta's Lieutenant-Governor, Grant MacEwan, officiated.

The College instituted a Citizen Of The Year award to recognize area residents for their contributions to the region and to the College. First recipients were Eugene Burton, George Davison and the Honorable Bud Olson. (A complete list is included in the final chapter of this book.)

Davison, who became a major in the British Army (through the "Canloan" scheme of exchange of officers) during the Second World War, and was a longtime educationist in Medicine Hat District, said the most satisfying work he had done was his involvement with the Medicine Hat College. An Alderman, he recalled in 1981 the cold bleak day when the first sod was turned:

"The dean of the College announced if we could get 40 students for the opening day we could make a go of it. So we hired six instructors, and opening day there were 90 students. We never looked back."

In June 1980 a $10 million Provincial expansion program was announced that would increase the campus size by a third and would double student population when the facilities were completed in 1982. Trade and apprenticeship programs were expanded and housing for 250 students built. Fulltime student population in 1986 was projected to be between 1,100 and 1,300. In 1980 the fulltime students numbered 798. The Provincial Government aim was to train people to meet the massive demand for skilled workers in Alberta in the 1980s.

Local industry, which was already cooperating with the College in on-the-job training, was delighted with and fully supportive of the planned expansion.

166

13.

The Great Wars — And In Between

"Germans Invade Luxemberg" — "Officers Throughout Canada Making Offers To Raise Militia To Assist Mother Country" — "British And German Warships Have Been Seen Cruising In The North Sea; The German Ships Carry No Lights" — "Governor-General Receives An Ovation When Special Train Enroute To Ottawa Arrives Here."

These are headlines taken from the *Morning Times* "War Special", dated Sunday, August 2, 1914. Obviously, the Nation was rallying around Britain for the call to arms for the First World War. Like their counterparts elsewhere, Medicine Hat men were quick to troop to the colors, the only question being where, when and how.

Lieutenant-Colonel F. O. Sissons was not long in finding out what the situation was. He fired off a telegram to Sam Hughes, the Minister of Militia, in Ottawa. The telegram read simply: "Can raise a mounted regiment of volunteers at this point if necessary."

Medicine Hat, August 1914, in front of Cavalry Building (no longer standing), which was on First Street S.E. Photo shows first 125 men to be accepted into Tenth Canadian Mounted Rifles of Medicine Hat. Checking list is Sgt. Mgr. Jim Hallworth.

Bobby Barnes riding remounts for the Third C.M.R.'s at Medicine Hat Fairgrounds.

In a front page article the *Times* said its office was "besieged by persons seeking the latest news from Europe" and the *Times'* leased wire was run all night to receive the information available. Small wonder that the "sole topic of conversation" on the streets was the war situation and "when the news got out that Medicine Hat is offering a regiment through Colonel Sissons," the interest took on a "local form and became even more intense."

Colonel Sissons was interviewed by a *Times* reporter, telling him "Canada should not lose a moment in offering assistance to the mother country, in both men and treasure." He declared that Canada should as soon as possible offer to Great Britain a sum of money at least equal to the amount that had been proposed as naval aid during the Parliamentary Session of 1912. He thought that this was the "unanimous opinion of the Canadian people."

A call for volunteers, Sissons was sure, would meet with an overwhelming response and he believed that it would be an easy matter to raise 25,000 men in the Prairie Provinces.

Queen Victoria's cousin, Kaiser Wilhelm, made his own pitch to the Germans in a front page item just beneath Colonel Sissons' impassioned plea: "The Emperor, speaking from a window of the castle last night to the crowds beneath said, 'I thank you for the love and loyalty shown me. When I enter upon a fight, let all party strife cease. We are German brothers and nothing else. All parties have attacked me in times of peace; I forgive them with all my heart. I hope and wish that the good German sword will emerge victorious in the right.'"

In another dispatch, this one from Ottawa, it was stated that the "Department of Militia" had been inundated with offers of service from "all kinds and from all parts of the Dominion." In some cases the offers came from individuals and others from officers commanding "offering their own and the services of squadrons, regiments, for artillery brigades." The list included one aviator, H. L. Andry of Quebec City. Such was the state of readiness on August 2, 1914.

It is not the intention of the author to try to attempt a history of the Regiments that were made up primarily or in part by Medicine Hat citizens. To do so would be to ignore the part played by those who joined the other services. A book or two could be written about the experiences and individual heroisms of those men and women who took part in both Great Wars from the Medicine Hat area. Since there is not space in this history for it, an attempt will be made only to try to recreate some of the flavor of the times. However, a summary of major military units of the District is appended to this chapter.

On August 1, 1914 the Governor-General, the Duke of Connaught, arrived in the City on a special train. He was accompanied by his wife, the Duchess, and their daughter, Princess Patricia. The vice-regal couple and the Princess were on their way back east from Banff where a vacation was cut short due to the war emergency. According to the *Times* reporter the Duke, nevertheless, was "evidently taking much interest in the pretty scenery west of the station."

The Duke and his family were met by Mayor M. A. Brown and Nelson Spencer, the Member of the Legislature for Medicine Hat. The two officials were accompanied by their wives and two Spencer daughters. (Miss Myrtle

Spencer presented "a beautiful bouquet of flowers to the Duchess, while sister Verna handed one to Princess Patricia.")

The *Times* reporter speculated on rumors about the Duke gadding about the country in this time of crisis. "Many wiseacres having in mind his military training, and the important offices in the army which have been so satisfactorily filled by His Royal Highness, suggest that his counsel and services are required in England." At any rate, the Duke was only in Medicine Hat because the engine on his special train had to be changed.

"After hearty cheers for the royal party and the King, proposed by Mayor Brown, His Royal Highness said a few words about a particularly hearty demonstration and the royal train pulled out of the station to the strains of God Save The King, played by the Citizens' Band. All the way through the event was particularly pleasant and thoroughly enjoyed and appreciated by the citizens."

It is interesting to note that an unrelated item on the same page of that historic newspaper carried a Chicago dateline in which Countess Wastasis Tolstoi told of Count Leo Tolstoi's last message to the Czar of Russia. Tolstoi was a bit of a soothsayer and went into a trance in 1910, four years prior to the start of the First World War, predicting a general European war "in which a new Napoleon appears and holds Europe in his grip until 1925." At that time we would see the "end of the kingdoms, the church and the empire and the world will form a federation." His predictions may have been premature if the rise of Hitler and the forming of the League of Nations were what were meant, but at the time the scene was certainly being set for some very important alterations of the world as it was.

The men and women of Medicine Hat, as elsewhere in the Commonwealth, were getting ready to stop the Kaiser from making those alterations. Within a very short time, Colonel Sissons received word from Ottawa that the mounted regiment he was prepared to recruit was "to hold itself in readiness for overseas service" with enlisting to start right away. However, only 65 men were to be recruited immediately, the balance to be accepted within a week.

To get things ready for the tedius task of sorting out the fit from the unfit, an "engineer" came out from Ottawa "to immediately take in charge the fixing up of the fair grounds for the lodging of the men while drilling, and while waiting for orders to proceed overseas." The City had offered to supply natural gas and water to the makeshift barracks and the balance of the work expenses were to be charged to the Federal Government.

In the meantime, men had begun to filter into the City wanting to join up. There was no place for them to go, nor were all of them of military quality. Colonel Sissons sought temporary housing for them in the City because — according to the *Times* — there were "quite a number of men around who are practically destitute and he has wanted to take care of them." Forms had to be received from headquarters before Sissons could make any important decisions. To facilitate matters, he called Colonel Cruikshank to send him the forms he needed from Calgary so the men could be attended to.

In Pincher Creek, Alberta, Colonel Kemmis told Sissons he wanted to recruit a squadron from there. It was decided that if 158 officers and men

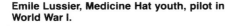

Emile Lussier, Medicine Hat youth, pilot in World War I.

170

were recruited at that point and the balance made up of Medicine Hat and area recruits, a regiment of "war strength, which means 552 all told" would be ready to go.

Sissons said the men would be given "a couple of weeks of foot drill" before they were mounted. First of all, they had to have horses. The Federal Government was to attend to the purchase of the mounts. The horses were to be sought in the immediate areas. (Incidentally, these horses were found, trained, and sent overseas; many of them served in various theatres of war, having been split up when they arrived on the battle grounds.)

The *Times* revealed that the men who were to form the first recruitment had been fed by the City at a cost of $400 a week but "with the recruiting the men will immediately be placed on government pay and will be able to pay their own way."

During this time, about 60 members of the Medicine Hat Rifle Corps turned out to drill at the roller rink, then paraded to the Armory to inspect a new gymnasium. The Corps had "quite a pleasant time trying out some of the equipment," according to an item in the newspaper.

Almost as a postscript to this call to readiness and all the excitement generated in the City by men being recruited for war in a distant front, is a tiny advertisement: "Just received, It's A Long Way To Tipperary, Edison, Amberol record 2487. Call and get yours before they are all gone. Assiniboia Music Store." The song was to become well-identified with the First World War and the volunteers who went to serve their country.

The war effort came at a time when Medicine Hat and other parts of Canada were facing high unemployment and cutbacks in public projects. At the time recruiting began the City announced that a gang of 30 men who had been employed on sewer installation in the southeastern part of the City were to be laid off. The City had been hiring small "batches" of men for three days at a time to keep the relief rolls down. The police department handed out "work tickets" to the most needy, particularly married men with families and those who had been out of work the longest.

War news was eagerly sought through radio broadcasts and daily newspapers, which were gleaned for reports from cover to cover. It wasn't long before items of local interest were being carried, including the "killed in action" reports that carried heartbreak into the community. With its high percentage of German-born residents, it is surprising that there were as few rascist incidents as there were. School children of German origin were subjected to a certain amount of abuse, but the general feeling in the community was that the residents of German origin, many of whom had come from Russia, were good Canadians and their ties with the "Old Country" were tenuous.

As equipment and horses arrived and the fairground became a military camp, men were being processed for the first contingent. Of the first 70 men to be examined by Dr. H. Orr, only six were turned down outright. Four had defective eyesight, one was too short and one had varicose veins. This turned out to be the smallest percentage of defective recruits of anywhere in the Province, according to army officials. Twelve of the men who presented themselves had teeth problems, but these individuals were attended to by being sent to the dentist where they "had their teeth fixed up or drawn" before being accepted.

171

A certain number of the men were named each day to get mounting and riding instructions. Nineteen horses had been acquired for this drill. A Sergeant Major Marshall of Calgary and Captain H. K. Oakes of Medicine Hat were instructors.

While all this activity was taking place in relative peace (some local men were training during the day and returning to their homes at night), a Victoria soldier was taken off the train and thrown into jail, wanted on a charge of rape. An officer from Victoria proceeded to pick him up and take him back to the coastal city to face the charge.

Incongruously, at a time when the country was uniting to fight a common enemy on another continent, the Dreamland Theatre was presenting "Wolfe — The Conquest of Quebec" a "marvelous production by the Kalem Co. of New York City", which had been filmed on the Plains of Abraham. The film, according to an ad in the *Times*, was "considered the greatest military photo play to date, complete in five reels."

The Medicine Hat Agricultural Society announced it would hold its annual, general meeting in the City Hall at which time reports for 1914 and the election of officers for 1915 would take place. The important piece of new business on the agenda was the granting of a lease of the fair grounds to the Dominion Government for "military purposes."

Not all of Medicine Hat's young men stuck around town waiting to get inducted into the army here. Some went to Calgary to join up, hoping to get into action even quicker. Privates F. Fisher, F. Batty, N. Campbell and J. Robertson were among those who took their training in the foothills city. They hoped to "break camp" at Christmas time. It was rumored in Great Britain that by then the conflict would be over and young men from across Canada were eager to be in on the "mopping up" operations. (In retrospect, it is seen how optimistic such a prediction was.) In letters home, the Medicine Hat soldiers in Calgary (part of "F" Company) complained of the weather being "hard" on them.

Men of Third C.M.R. stationed at Fairgrounds, 1915. Inspecting and cleaning rifles.

If the weather was hard and the training even tougher, the meals at least were edible: "The food is well-cooked and wholesome, although not always the best," one recruit wrote. Already the word was out that army cookery was ingenious, if not positively inspired. "They serve beans in many different ways," they wrote. "Beans are served with beans, with beans as a side dish." Maybe the officers fared better. D. R. Ware, formerly of the Canada Customs staff in the city, was Sergeant in charge of the officer's mess in Calgary's Currie Barracks.

Out on the Medicine Hat parade grounds the soldiers were drilling. They had no uniforms, no weapons to accompany their awkward movements. One observer said "it brings tears to the eyes to watch them". Day after day they improved under the guidance of Colonel Potts so that in September 1914 the Third Canadian Mounted Rifles were ready for battle. The men did themselves proud, although many died in battle or were seriously injured since they were among the first to be caught in the gas attacks at the beginning of the conflict.

World War I Signallers in front of Armoury, First St., 1916.

On January 19, 1916, Lieutenant-Colonel Nelson Spencer was asked by the Minister of Defence to form a battalion in Medicine Hat, a formidable task since the area had already supplied many men. Nelson had been a Commanding Officer in the Southern Alberta Regiment. W. H. Williams was Adjutant and recruiting began the very next day with Sidney J. Warner the first local man to join up. Men arrived from all over the district, from farms and ranches and industrial operations and out of high schools. They were billeted in a vacant factory where bunks had been hastily installed. On April 8 the regiment was up to 800 men and on June 6 they left for Calgary. Relatives and other citizens turned out enmasse to see them off on troop trains.

173

Third C.M.R. Parade through Medicine Hat two or three days before leaving for overseas on June 1, 1915.

Following a training period in Calgary they sailed on the *S. S. Saxonia* for England where the 175th merged with the 137th and 138th to make up what was known as the 21st Reserve. They were sent to France on November 30, 1916 where six officers and 175 other ranks were killed in action and 16 officers and 285 other ranks were seriously injured. Many medals were awarded for acts of heroism. Lt. Colonel Spencer won the Distinguished Service Order.

His colleague, Colonel F. O. Sissons, and the Third Regiment of the Canadian Mounted Rifles went into camp in tents at Schorcliffe, near Folkstone in Kent, England. The First and Second CMRs came from Manitoba and British Columbia, the Third from Medicine Hat and the Fourth, Fifth and Sixth from Eastern Canada. Training continued in England until August 1915 when the units went into battle at Mezzines, near Baillioux, France. The troops were spread too thin, so they were pulled out before Christmas and re-formed into battalions.

The First, Second and Third CMRs became a brigade under Brigadier General F. O. Sissons. Other officers in the Medicine Hat group were Majors E. G. Benwell and A. J. Mort; Captains H. K. Oakes, H. Orr and C. S. Pingle; Lieutenants J. J. Boyce, G. B. Davies, T. H. Fennel, J. J. Foster, W. McIntosh, H. A. Smith; R.Q.M. Sergeant C. A. Krauss and Staff Sergeant-Majors S. Charters and J. H. Hallworth. Transport Sergeant in charge of horses, which carried guns and supplies through the mud and death of the battlefield, was William Crockett.

The CMRs saw service in Ypres, Vimy and the Somme, Sanctuary Wood and Passchendaele. They helped drive back the Germans at Amiens in August 1918. They moved back to Arras and then forward to Mons before the war ended on November 11, 1918.

Another regiment that Medicine Hat has reason to be proud of is the South Alberta Regiment whose lineage goes back to the Rocky Mountain Rangers of 1885 when the community was little more than a trading post.

According to the *Canadian Pictorial and Illustrated War News* of June 20, 1885 the Rocky Mountain Rangers were a colorful lot. "Tanned faces almost hidden beneath the brim of huge stetsons strapped on for grim death. Around many of their necks were silk handkerchiefs which, besides being an embellishment, prevented the irritation by their coarse brown duck or 'Montana' broadcloth coats. Over pants of the same material were drawn a pair of chaps. Cross belts pregnant with cartridges, a sixshooter, sheath knife, a Winchester slung across the pommel of the saddle and a coiled larriat completed the belligerent outfit. Mounted on brochos good for 60 to 100 miles a day, they soon disappeared in the distance, a loud clanking of bits and jingling of their huge Mexican spurs now gave place to the rattling of transportation wagons."

A romantic description indeed! And the *Fort Macleod Gazette* of April 29, 1885 added to their mystique: "The corps is composed of a particularly fine body of men . . . there was but one opinion expressed regarding them and that was that they would make it extremely unhealthy for several times their numbers of rebels or half-breeds or Indians, should occasion require." These were not regular military men, the *Gazette* pointed out: "Troops for service in the West only require enough drill to be able to act in unison and any efforts to make them mere drilling machines only trammels them and detracts from their efficiency."

William Black, secretary of the South-Western Stock Association, said on July 9, 1885, "We are well aware that the country so faithfully watched over by you offered, by its exposed condition and peculiar resources, great inducements to savage marauders who wrought such havoc to the north of us and that our district was not the theatre of such scenes of pillage and murder as there prevailed is due to the alacrity with which you responded to the call of duty at the first intimation of danger."

When the First World War began there were young men ready who had been trained under a retired Colonel named Horace Jenkins. He gathered about 150 recruits from around the district, men who had no barracks or shelter and who had to forage for their own food. They had no uniforms but went through their formations in baggy pants and farm overalls and shirts of all colors. They marched down city streets and paraded on vacant lots.

According to Major G. L. Macdougall, who wrote *A History of the South Regiment,* there were no survivors of this gallant group when they went to war.

The Regiment was reorganized shortly after the First World War was over and at various times there were companies at Lethbridge, Brooks and Redcliff. In September 1939 the Regiment was not called upon for active service, but many of its members, both officers and men, joined other ranks. However, in June 1940 the Regiment was moved to Edmonton for further training and later served in various parts of Canada until it sailed for England in August 1942. They were soon at battle where they won the praise of Supreme Allied Commander Dwight D. Eisenhower. More than 200 were wounded and many made the supreme sacrifice.

During both wars, the women in Medicine Hat — those who were not in the services — were busily engaged in more than just keeping the home fires burning. They became involved in Bundles For Britain, War Workers, Liberty Bond Drives, Red Cross supply work, knitting, and the continual

First Tag Day for First World War efforts at Medicine Hat. Women's Group that sold tags pose in front of Huckvale Block, now Assiniboia Hotel, corner Third and South Railway Streets.

comforting of the anxious and the bereaved. In St. John's Presbyterian, for example, the Ladies' Aid put on dinners for the soldiers. In February 1916 Mrs. F. O. Sissons, wife of the Commanding Officer, presented a Canadian flag to the church to be hung in the Sanctuary until the end of the war. St. John's gave its best to the best: 168 to the 3rd CMRs and 124 to the 175th.

The jarring way that commercialism entered the "war effort" is exemplified in a Gillette Safety razor advertisement that appeared in the *Times* of April 22, 1916. Disguised as a recruiting ad, it ran under the banner and crest of the 175th Battalion, listing the officers to further fool the reader into thinking it was a legitimate appeal. Listed were Colonel Spencer and Adjutant Williams, Quartermaster Captain H. Baker, Paymaster Captain H. W. Ireland, and Captains G. Davies, H. W. D. Cox, James Bruce, C. W. Rideout, H. L. Flemming and J. W. McCoubrey.

When the First World War dragged to its bloody end, the survivors staggered home to try to resume a normal life in a world that even then was starting to feel the strain of burst economies. As nations around the world reeled from the cost of the conflict in terms of lives and money, the grim specter of depression gathered in the dark corners.

Socialism and strikes became the theme: "Lawlessness and disorder are rampant through the city all day and every day. Men and women are

The First World War was over — cause for celebration at Medicine Hat. Here is a view of the crowd that gathered at City Hall corner November 10, 1918 to hear speeches and take part in the celebrations. Notice the natural gas street lamps in several places.

wantonly assaulted upon the streets." That was W. Pleman in a 1919 *Toronto Star* report from Winnipeg. Approximately 30,000 workers left their jobs on May 15, 1919 in a sympathy protest supporting the metal and building trades over the issue of collective bargaining. The incident's importance was heightened by the fact that policemen, firemen and other essential service employees joined the walkout and left Winnipeg in disarray.

The strike's popularity was inspired by the workers' "triumph" following the Russian Revolution in Petrograd and by Winnipeg's high unemployment rate and the slow war demobilization process. Special police forces and the military were called in when local authorities couldn't handle the disruption. Nevertheless, the demonstration remained non-violent until June 21 when a growing crowd attacked an RCMP officer who had fallen from his horse. The special police unit responded by firing into the mob, killing two men and wounding 20 others.

Four days after that "Bloody Sunday" the strike was called off and its instigators, including J. S. Woodsworth (who later became the first socialist Member of Parliament in Canada), were charged with sedition and criminal intent. Not only was the Winnipeg Strike one of Canadian history's bloodiest chapters, but as *Maclean's Magazine* analyzed: "Its outcome contributed to the rise of a socialist sentiment in the West."

Welcome home from overseas, 31st Battalion, Medicine Hat, North Railway St., June 1st, 1919.

With its sound industrial base of ranching, farming, railroading, brick and pottery-making and greenhouse production, Medicine Hat was in a better position than many Canadian centres to weather the poor times ahead. What did add much to the hardship were the periods of drought that plagued the Prairies during the Twenties and Thirties.

Clare Crane is one of many Medicine Hat residents who remembered the time well. "There was great unemployment in the whole district," she told the author in 1980. "Glen, my husband, and I lived off the vegetables we grew and fruits such as rhubarb which I canned and put down in sealers. I walked to the edge of town to pick native fruits like chokecherries and black currants. My folks lived close to the CPR tracks and nearly every day when they were sitting down to dinner a knock would come to the door and there would be one or two unshaven, smoke-sooted railway bums, begging for something to eat before they caught the freight out. Unemployed, poor, looking for work, riding the rods."

Mrs. Rupert (Elizabeth) Cann recalled the Depression as hard times but, "With my husband working in a grocery store, we never went short." Mrs. Cann's mother was Clara Bassett, the first white girl born in Medicine Hat. "Some of the men in town were given work putting in brick sidewalks," she said. "They were paid 35 cents an hour, but it didn't go in their pockets, it went towards paying town taxes."

One Medicine Hat woman made history during that period. Winnifred Grace Baker was the nation's first woman returning officer for a general election. She served three times between 1921 and 1928.

Born Winifred Grace Hubley in 1873, Mrs. Baker was qualified as a nurse and as a teacher. But in 1904, she and her husband Angus headed west where they took up land in 1909 at Seven Persons. They farmed for 20 years and raised two children.

Five years after women won the vote in Alberta, the provincial government appointed Mrs. Baker as returning officer for the by-election in Medicine Hat on December 9, 1921. She held the position again on June 28, 1926 and on May 1, 1928. The year 1921 signified yet another first for Mrs. Baker. The Medicine Hat local of the United Farm Women of Alberta was organized and she was elected its first president. Mrs. Baker edited the United Farmers of Alberta page in the *Medicine Hat News* and served as federal secretary of the Medicine Hat UFA.

In 1932 the CPR was still the source of the largest payroll in the City and indications were that passenger and freight service were on an upward trend. The year 1932 was crucial in many respects, as it marked a turning point in the Depression. Although prices to the farmer were still very low, demand for produce and grain was strong and, with an increase in wheat prices, the farmers were able to purchase more of the merchants' products and slowly the supply and demand spiral resumed.

Winnifred Grace Baker, Canada's first woman returning officer for a general election.

Street parade of Stinson Detroiter Tractors manufactured in Medicine Hat. This view is on Main St. (now Second) in 1920. Wars come and go, but agriculture marches on.

179

The City, under its relief program, especially relating to the Public Works Department, made considerable improvements to roads, water system and street lighting. The completion of surfacing of the highways between Medicine Hat to Maple Creek and from the City to Bow Island brought money to depleted coffers.

Grain shipped from the Medicine Hat division of the CPR showed a sharp increase for the year ending July 1933, being the heaviest since the peak year of 1929, the year of The Crash. The total shipment was 32,570,000 bushels compared with 16,401,000 in 1932, meaning that almost 100 per cent more grain was shipped in 1933 than in the previous year.

Bank clearances for the city showed a healthy improvement; as a barometer of increased production and consumption, it was a good sign. Other parts of the country were not showing such progress out of the hard times and one such indication touched Medicine Hat, although in a less dramatic way than it hit Regina. It was Dominion Day in 1935 when the so-called "Battle of Regina" was waged.

In an excellent article in *Saamis Review,* L. J. Roy Wilson, Consulting Editor, wrote about the unemployed "trekkers" who stopped in Medicine Hat on their way to the confrontation with the authorities in Regina. Most of the men who took part in the protest had been assigned to relief camps throughout the country and were fed up with conditions there, a general feeling of hopelessness.

Additionally — according to Wilson — government and police officials believed that the discontent among the unhappy young men confined to these make-work camps was being stirred up by communist and socialist agitators. Others believed that it was the very existence of the camps that led to the unrest. The Prime Minister, R. B. Bennett, was hard-pressed to arrive at a solution that would keep thousands of men off the streets, out of bread lines and away from the freight trains, the common method of transportation between hoped-for jobs.

On June 3, 1935 a group of men gathered at the CPR freight yards in Vancouver and made ready to hitch a ride on the freight cars to Ottawa to protest their lot, picking up recruits along the way. At Kamloops and Golden in British Columbia, and at Calgary, men eagerly clambered aboard the freight to add their strength to the general grievance.

There was a certain amount of excitement and trepidation in the air the night before the unemployed were to arrive in Medicine Hat, their number having swelled to about 1,200 by then. A local men's association held a public meeting to discuss a number of issues, and the mass protest was certainly on the agenda. A deputation arrived in the city. The council offered them $200 if they would keep going. A circus was playing the town at the time and the City Fathers felt a distraction like 1,200 unemployed men could lead to violence. The delegation turned the offer down. They needed some place to rest and regroup and to make their pitch to the local residents. The City decided to allow the men to use the ball park to camp on and the arena for sleeping accommodation. They provided wood and bricks for fire pits. However, they refused to allow the men to hold a tag day to raise money. (The Provincial Government provided $250 to cover the cost of food they ate.)

After the main body of men arrived aboard the CPR freight train, they clambered down and formed into four-man ranks, marching off to the ball

On to Ottawa. Scene at Medicine Hat Station, June 1935.

On to Ottawa Meeting at Riverside Ballpark, Medicine Hat. These are local spectators. June 1935.

park for a meal and then to the arena for a sleep. A food depot had been set up at the Ukrainian Labor Temple where donations to the "trekkers" fund were received. In defiance of the ban, a tag day was held on the city streets and $225 realized. A rally was held at the park that night after a soccer game in which the local Canadian Legion beat the visitors by a score of five to one.

Member of the Legislature, Hector Lang, chaired the meeting, declaring his sympathy for the strikers. Lang caused a slight altercation when he objected to Matthew Shaw's "political propaganda." A former student at the University of Saskatchewan, Shaw was later one of six strike leaders arrested in Regina. The crowd, increased to 2,000 with local participants, clearly enjoyed Shaw's remarks about the relief camp system because they shouted down Lang's objections.

At 6:30 a.m. the young men climbed aboard 52 cars of the eastbound CPR train. At least one local man, Edward Silvester of Ranchville, about 50 miles south of Medicine Hat, joined them. For Medicine Hatters, that was the last they saw of them for the time being. When they reached Regina, word had come down from Ottawa that they were to be stopped. The railway would carry no more "troublemakers" beyond that point.

In Medicine Hat, 13 members of the rearguard, who stayed behind at major stopping points to assure that everyone cleared out and that there were no civic feelings left ruffled, were prevented from boarding a freight to join their brothers. The local RCMP and CPR police took this action. They were obviously acting on orders from Ottawa as well, and not on their own initiative. To thwart this attempt to impede their progress, a group of private citizens in the city collected the bus fare necessary to send the men on their way. Among the citizens were Social Creditors A. A. H. Reilly, Dr. John L. Robinson and Walter J. Harper. Liberal MLA Hector Lang was also among those who contributed to the fund to reimburse the group who paid for the bus fare. The fund was oversubscribed.

On to Ottawa Scene at Medicine Hat. Freight loaded and headed East. June 1935.

The strike leaders were grateful for this support, exhorting Lang to follow up his backing by organizing a protest action against Prime Minister Bennett's plan to interfere with the Ottawa march.

Citizens across Canada, meantime, were breathlessly awaiting news of what was happening in Regina. It was apparent that neither the strikers nor the Government were about to back down. Eight strike leaders went to Ottawa to a meeting with Bennett and members of the Cabinet while the strikers cooled their heels in the Prairie city. Waiting in Winnipeg — scene of the earlier bloody conflict — were about 1,000 other unemployed men ready to jump aboard the strike train.

Among the strike leaders in Ottawa was Art Evans, already tainted by the press as being communistic, and there were allegations that there was a wider political conspiracy involved. Evans fanned the flames of insurrection by telling 6,000 supporters in Regina that the streets would "run with blood if the police interfere."

His prediction came true, although not as dramatically as that. On June 27 the Cabinet passed a special Emergency Act designed to halt the march. The strikers revolted but were driven from the streets by police and militia. One man was killed and scores more were injured from flying bricks and police clubs. Men and women were trampled by horses' hooves.

When the dust settled, the march on Ottawa was off and the strikers worked their way back to their homes or settled where they were for the time being. But the effect of the "trek" was felt for a long time; nor is it forgotten today. Wilson editorialized in *Saamis* that the marchers were "used by everyone." The strike leaders urged them on to make their particular political statement. "The Prime Minister permitted them to move on and on

182

until his back was completely up against the wall at Regina." (Opposition members earlier took a slap at Bennett for not applying the stop order in Calgary, charging that he had not done so because the city was in his own constituency.) Wilson said the Opposition politicians and their "journalist minions" saw the trek as their "one great opportunity to embarrass the Government of the country. Altogether, the great crusade was a failure both for its friends and its enemies."

Nevertheless, there are people alive in Medicine Hat today who, as children, looked upon the stopover here as great entertainment and a break from the monotony of the Depression.

Regardless of strikes, and aided by the organization of labor and farmers' unions and associations, the economy in Medicine Hat continued to bound along until it reached a near-normal level. Then the black clouds of war again loomed and men and women again responded to the call to aid the "Mother Country." With the war machine now greased more efficiently, it was not necessary to organize regiments at the local level to the extent that

Two photos showing the manufacturing process of shell cases at Alberta Foundry and Machine Shop in Medicine Hat. The plant handled a contract for the Federal Gov't. in World War I and World War II.

183

had been done for the First World War. Recruiting offices in all major centres were flooded with applicants and the streets were soon thronging with khaki and blue-uniformed men and women, some local, many passing through in troop trains.

The city was also "invaded" by the British going to Suffield, prisoners arriving for an extended stay just outside of town (both subjects discussed in subsequent chapters) and airmen arriving to take part in the Wartime Emergency Training Program at the Dominion-Provincial War Emergency Training Centre which was located at the end of Second Street South East in the old Factory Building, adjacent to the Malcolm cannery building which burned down.

One group, known as Flight 29, was probably unique in that it was an entirely western bunch. No one came from east of Manitoba. Bert Reynolds, now a resident of Kelowna, British Columbia, told the author what it was like to be in Medicine Hat in the 1940s:

"We arrived on the noon train on October 1, 1943. Most of us had been out of high school less than a year, had enlisted in the RCAF only weeks previously, and were about to begin the first stage of our mechanic's course in a large old brick building on the bank of the South Saskatchewan River. Like most of the airmen before us, we had never visited Medicine Hat and did not know what to expect."

For the new arrivals, there were no billets and no station regulations outside the school. The men were given an Air Force living-out allowance and told to find private accommodation with the civilian population. "A Mrs. Slater took six of us at $35 a month each, fed us good sturdy meals and patiently withstood the antics of exuberant airmen who ate too much and came in at the most atrocious hours, dropping heavy issue boots that sounded like cannon in the night," Reynolds recalled.

Medicine Hat was good to the men, the townspeople treating them as their own. Two of the local movie theatres charged the servicemen a special 25 cents admission. Airmen and local girls made eyes at each other over a "black and white" at several soda fountains in the city. Recreation was no problem: four theatres, the Bowladrome, skating on city rinks or the river, as well as Friday night dances at the Wartime Emergency Training Centre, kept most airmen satisfied.

"Some people were luckier than others," Reynolds said. "I do not know why. I was among the lucky ones. I was, more or less, adopted by the Mogridge family, who had a son in the Air Force some distance from home. Mrs. Wren Mogridge was probably the best cook in town and let me join the family on Sunday for a feast I hadn't known since leaving home. Father Mogridge was usually stoically quiet in his chair at the head of the table, though I'm sure to this day he wasn't certain whether I was there to mooch a meal or to chase his pretty blue-eyed daughter, Margie. Most of the time I wasn't sure myself."

On March 1, 1944, when Flight 29 left for St. Thomas, Ontario for further training, more than a few of the airmen hated to leave. The 'Hat' had become a second home to them. "I had learned to file and fit, some carpentry, metal work and rigging from the school," Reynolds concluded. "More importantly, I had been given friendship and affection from total strangers, allowed to become part of a family.

"Those warm, light-hearted hours I spent with the Mogridges remain as special today as they were 30 odd years ago. If awards were given to civilians in Medicine Hat for special actions during World War Two, the Mogridge family would head the list."

Mr. Reynolds' remarks could just as well have been made by the hundreds of other young men who made the city their temporary home during the long years of the Second World War.

As noted, there was a distinct difference between the way recruiting was done in the First World War and the way it was carried out for the second great conflict of 1939 to 1945. The 15th Alberta Light Horse, in conjunction with other Alberta units, mobilized the 31st (Alberta) Reconnaissance Battalion on March 18, 1942. This unit was redesignated 31st (Alberta) Reconnaissance Regiment on June 8, 1942. It served in Canada with the 6th Infantry Division. It embarked on January 31, 1945 for the United Kingdom where it was disbanded on February 15, 1945. The 15th (Reserve) Alberta Light Horse served in the Reserve Army.

The South Alberta Regiment Bugle Band in May, 1942. They are (left to right): Douglas Mackie, Morton Grandie, Edgar Robinson (behind), Bob Simpson, Lawrence Huston, Jim Simpson (behind), George Westwood (with drum), Hector Smith, Harvey Williams, Roy Harris, Randolf Norris, Harry Morrice, Galvin Desharnais. Adjutant George Davison is the man on the extreme right, rear. Man in the doorway of the old Armories (corner Division Avenue and Third Street South) is Teddy Osgood. The man at the head of the formation is unidentified. (Photo courtesy of George Davison).

H.M.C.S. Medicine Hat. Sailors, officers and mascot on board minesweeper named for the City of Medicine Hat (sponsored by the Citizens of Medicine Hat during her period of service, 1941-1945). The ship's bell is preserved in City Hall as a gift from the ship, launched June 25, 1941 at Montreal.

The 22nd Field Battery, in conjunction with the 78th Field Battery, mobilized the 22nd/78th Field Battery, CASF on May 24, 1940. This unit was reorganized as two separate batteries on January 1, 1941, designated 22nd Field Battery and 78th Field Battery. The 22nd Field Battery embarked for the United Kingdom on November 1, 1941 as part of the 13th Canadian Field Regiment with which it landed in Normandy, France on June 6, 1944. The active unit was disbanded on November 14, 1945. The 22nd (Reserve) Field Battery served in the Reserve Army.

The South Alberta Regiment mobilized The South Alberta Regiment CASF on May 24, 1940. This unit was redesignated 29th Armored Regiment (The South Alberta Regiment) on January 26, 1942. It embarked on August 22, 1942 for the United Kingdom where it was redesignated 29th Armored Reconnaissance Regiment (The South Alberta Regiment) on January 1, 1943. It landed in Normandy, France on July 24, 1944 as a unit of the 4th Canadian Armored Division. Major D. V. Currie of this Regiment won the Victoria Cross in a battle between August 18 and August 20, 1944. The active unit was disbanded on February 15, 1946. A 2nd Battalion served in the Reserve Army.

(The author is indebted to W. A. B. Douglas, Director of Directorate of History with National Defence Headquarters in Ottawa, for supplying the foregoing information.)

"An impressive ceremony, one that will be stamped indelibly upon the minds of the beholders" was held on Wednesday, May 24, 1922 when Brigadier General A. H. Bell unveiled a Cenotaph to the memory of those killed in the First World War. The Militia, The Province of Alberta and the City of Medicine Hat joined in the dedication of the monument before a huge crowd of citizens. Brigadier Bell said he was proud to be asked to officiate because on the monument were the names of men from his own 31st Battalion.

Money began to be raised for the project after a meeting on October 4, 1920 of the Great War Next-Of-Kin. Names of those killed in the Second World War have been added to the Cenotaph, site of the November 11 ceremonies saluting Canada's war dead.

A landmark of the City and a reminder of the Second World War was demolished at the Airport in August 1980. It was an old airforce drill hall that was used by thousands of Allied airmen for parades and ceremonial occasions while they trained for combat missions during the war.

Built to last 20 years, the hall nearly doubled its lifespan. With five hangars, the airfield was the hub of the Royal Air Force No. 34 Service Flying Training School (SFTS). In 1981 two hangars remained in use. SFTS was the nerviest bit of derring-do since young Billy Bishop in his Nieuport fighter plane tangled with the "Red Baron", Manfred Freiherr von Richtofen, and his flying circus in the First World War. In December, 1939 the Canadian cabinet signed a contract with Great Britain, Australia and New Zealand to train fighter personnel for another go-round with the German air force. The RCAF could muster only 3,100 airmen of all ranks, 270 largely obsolete aircraft and 19 war-worthy Hurricane fighters on a handful of hand-me-down airfields. Yet Canada committed itself to mount and operate the Plan which, over the next five years, would turn out 130,553 pilots, navigators and air gunners on airstrips hacked out of bush and prairie from Nova Scotia to

Vancouver Island. That, in no small measure, was how the war in the air was won.

Number 34 Service Flying Training School was one of the flying fields established across Canada under the Commonwealth Air Training Plan. More than 3,000 airmen were trained in Medicine Hat during the three and one-half years the school operated here.

The facility was officially opened on March 14, 1941 when 450 airmen and officers arrived in the city by train. About 1,100 airmen and crews, most of them in their early 20s, trained at the base at peak periods. Bomber training was done in the twin-engined Avro Anson and the Airspeed Oxford, while fighter pilots often trained in single-engined Harvards.

Ralph Palmer, a former ground crewman and later vice-principal of Vincent Massey School, told Ken Johnstone of the *Medicine Hat News* in 1980 that the school had a very high standard. It received the coveted RAF "E" (for efficiency). The pennant now hangs in honor at St. Barnabas Anglican Church. The school's chief flying instructor, Wing Commander Colin Scragg, MBE, was later promoted Air Vice-Marshal and received a knighthood.

Number 34 SFTS closed in August, 1944 and for the next 35 years the drill hall was used by various commercial concerns and the City transit system. The buses moved out in June, 1979, when a new depot was completed.

City's new Transit Depot and garage as it appeared from the air in 1981.

At the end of the First World War and before the beginning of the Second, Medicine Hat was honored with the visit of Royalty. The Prince of Wales made a brief stopover and received a trumultuous reception in Riverside Park on October 3, 1919. When the royal train arrived in the CPR depot at 9:30 a.m., he was welcomed by an official party consisting of Mayor M. A. Brown; Colonel Nelson Spencer, MLA; Captain C. S. Pingle, MLA; and Alderman Walter Huckvale.

187

In his address the Prince congratulated Medicine Hat on the valor shown by the soldiers from this city and afterwards he presented a number of military medals. After inspecting a group of war veterans, boy scouts and nursing sisters, the Prince (later Duke of Kent) was taken on a brief tour of Medalta Pottery Limited.

On May 26, 1939 the largest crowd ever assembled in Medicine Hat swarmed into the area surrounding the CPR station to welcome King George VI and Queen Elizabeth. Thousands of visitors poured into the city

King George and Queen Elizabeth. King George VI and Queen Elizabeth visited Medicine Hat May 26, 1939. Behind and between the King and Queen is Fred Richardson, who had trained with the same R.A.F. unit as King George. The King recognized Richardson when they met in Medicine Hat, and had a chat. Behind the Queen, at right of photo, is Mayor Hector Lang.

Canadian Legion Pipe Band, Medicine Hat, in 1950.

188

from all parts of Southern Alberta, Saskatchewan and Montana. Crowds began to gather before 6 a.m. and by the time the Royal train arrived people were lining the tracks for three miles out of the city.

Prime Minister Mackenzie King presented Mayor Hector Lang and Mrs. Lang to Their Majesties and in turn the Mayor presented Member of Parliament A. H. Mitchell and Mrs. Mitchell and MLA Dr. J. L. Robinson and Mrs. Robinson to the King and Queen.

The King did not make a speech but the Royal couple mingled with the platform guests and chatted with a group of school children and veterans before returning to their train.

A festive mood prevailed in the city with a midway being set up between Armory Park and North Railway Street. The day reached a climax at 10:30 p.m. with a spectacular display of fireworks set off at Crescent Heights.

A summary of major military units of Medicine Hat & District:

Rocky Mountain Rangers	*1885*	*Active Cavalry unit raised and deployed from Fort Macleod to Medicine Hat to protect South-Eastern Alberta during The North West Rebellion 1885. Disbanded 1885.*
"I" Squadron, The Canadian Mounted Rifles	*1901-1905*	*Militia Cavalry Squadron raised and based in Medicine Hat.*
"D" Squadron, The Canadian Mounted Rifles	*1905-1908*	*Redesignation of "I" Squadron, The Canadian Mounted Rifles.*
21st Alberta Hussars	*1908-1920*	*Militia Cavalry Regiment raised by expansion and redesignation of "D" Squadron, The Canadian Mounted Rifles.*
3rd Regiment, The Canadian Mounted Rifles	*1914-1920*	*Active Cavalry/Infantry Regiment raised by 21st Alberta Hussars for overseas service during World War I. Broken up in France for reinforcements 1916. Disbanded 1920.*
31st Battalion, Canadian Expeditionary Force	*1915-1920*	*Active Infantry Battalion recruited in Southern Alberta for overseas service during World War I. Disbanded 1920.*
113th Battalion, Canadian Expeditionary Force	*1915-1920*	*Same as 31st Battalion. Broken up for reinforcements 1917. Disbanded 1920.*
175th Battalion, Canadian Expeditionary Force	*1915-1920*	*Same as 113th Battalion.*
187th Battalion, Canadian Expeditionary Force	*1916-1920*	*Same as 113th Battalion*
1st Regiment, The Alberta Mounted Rifles	*1920-1930*	*Redesignation of 21st Alberta Hussars. Transferred to Vegreville 1930. Later amalgamated with 19th Alberta Dragoons.*

1st Battalion, The Alberta Regiment	1920-1924	Militia Infantry Battalion raised and based in Medicine Hat.
"C" Company, 13th Machine Gun Battalion, CMGC	1919-1936	Militia Machine Gun Company raised and based in Medicine Hat. Amalgamated with the South Alberta Regiment 1936.
The South Alberta Regiment	1924-1954	New Militia Infantry Regiment raised by the redesignation of the 1st Battalion, The Alberta Regiment.
Headquarters, 13th Machine Gun Battalion, CMGC	1932-1936	Battalion Headquarters was transferred from Calgary and located with "C" Company, 13th Machine Gun Battalion, CMGC. Disbanded 1936.
The South Alberta Regiment, CASF	1940-1942	Active Infantry Battalion raised by The South Alberta Regiment and four other Alberta Militia, units for overseas service during World War II.
2nd (Reserve) Battalion, The South Alberta Regiment	1940-1946	Militia Infantry Battalion raised by The South Alberta Regiment during World War II.
Suffield Experimental Station	1941-1967	Canadian Army establishment created to conduct scientific and technical research. Transferred to the Defence Research Board in 1947.

Number 34 Service Flying School	*1941-1944*	*Active Royal Canadian Air Force Flying School created to train aircrew under the British Commonwealth Air Training Plan during World War II.*
29th Armoured Regiment (The South Alberta Regiment)	*1942-1943*	*Active Armoured Regiment raised by the conversion and redesignation of The South Alberta Regiment CASF.*
29th Armoured Reconnaissance Regiment (The South Alberta Regiment)	*1943-1946*	*Active Armoured Reconnaissance Regiment raised by the conversion and redesignation of 29th Armoured Regiment (The South Alberta Regiment).*
Number 132 Prisoner of War Internment Camp	*1943-1945*	*Active internment camp created to hold 10,000 non-officer personnel captured from the armed forces of the Axis powers during World War II. The camp was staffed by personnel of the Veterans Guard of Canada.*
Number 10 Surplus Equipment Holding Unit, RCAF	*1945-1946*	*Active Royal Canadian Air Force unit created to hold and dispose of surplus equipment left from World War II.*

The South Alberta Regiment	*1946-1954*	*Militia Infantry Regiment recreated by the reversion and redesignation of 29th Armoured Reconnaissance Regiment (The South Alberta Regiment) and 2nd (Reserve) Battalion, The South Alberta Regiment.*
"A" Squadron, The South Alberta Light Horse (29th Armoured Regiment)	*1954-1958*	*Squadron of a Militia Armoured Regiment created by the amalgamation, conversion and redesignation of 41st Anti-Tank Regiment (Self-Propelled), RCA, and 68th Light Anti-Aircraft Regiment, RCA of Calgary and The South Alberta Regiment.*
"A" Squadron, The South Alberta Light Horse	*1958-1960*	*Redesignation of "A" Squadron The South Alberta Light Horse (29th Armoured Regiment).*
The South Alberta Light Horse	*1960-*	*The entire Regiment was transferred from Calgary and based in Medicine Hat as a Militia Armoured Reconnaissance Regiment.*
Defence Research Establishment Suffield	*1967-*	*Redesignation of Suffield Experimental Station.*
Canadian Forces Base Suffield	*1971-*	*Regular Canadian Forces Base created at and partially amalgamated with Defence Research Establishment, Suffield to support Canadian Forces and British Army Training.*

14.

War Behind Barbed Wire: Medicine Hat's P.O.W.'s

Because of its close affiliation and fondness for the CPR, train movements within the City of Medicine Hat have always had a particular fascination for the residents. The three trains that left the city on February 10, 1946 however were of more than casual interest — they marked the end of a historical event. The trains held Nazi prisoners of war on their way home.

There were no cheering crowds, brass bands or waving flags. The only noise or clamor were the shouted instructions of armed guards as they commanded the prisoners to take their places in the coaches. Soon, two more trains from Lethbridge joined the three from Medicine Hat and they were bound for the east, where the *Mauritania*, a luxury liner converted to a troopship for wartime use, waited to receive part of Hitler's armed forces. One can speculate on the thoughts that went through the minds of those men on the trains: steamed up windows, frozen landscape; a last farewell to the city that had been their home for several years.

Bill Westgate, now a resident of Calgary, was a member of the RCMP at the time. He told the author in 1979 how he and his fellow guards stood around in heavy coats with loaded rifles while the prisoners were loaded. Westgate had already had extensive experience with the prisoners and with a tragic event in the camp.

The majority of the prisoners held in the local internment camp were captured in Normandy and North Africa. They had been here as long as four years and — according to Camp Commandant Lieutenant-Colonel B.B.W. Minard — some were anxious to get home, although many indicated they would rather stay in Medicine Hat as immigrants. Their requests were turned down.

Guards, working in six hour relays, stood in the vestibules, Sten guns cradled under their arms. Precautions were made to prevent escape at division points where the trains stopped. The prisoners sat 50 in a car, three to every double seat. They were not allowed to use the upper bunks in the coaches but had to sleep three in the lower bunks. Using their own utensils, the POWs were fed from the CPR commissary car with seven men from each coach carrying the meals to their comrades. All prisoners had been given typhus and tetanus shots.

Operation withdrawal went off smoothly and a reminder of the war effort that came to Medicine Hat soon was shunting off into the east, leaving only memories of the years that the prisoners had been here.

It was on the land where the Stampede Grounds are now located that

The Medicine Hat Prisoner of War Camp was completely fenced until the end of 1946. By the end of 1957 very little of the fence was in evidence, as this view shows.

6,000 Germans sat out the war. Toward the end of the conflict, when the Axis forces were on the run, an additional 6,000 prisoners were moved into the 320 enclosed acres. It was like having a middle-sized Prairie town moved onto the city's outskirts. In fact, the prisoner population outnumbered that of the resident population by more than 850. The camp, with its full complement of prisoners, required 800 guards. Construction commenced in the fall of 1942 and it opened on January 1, 1943. Second largest camp in Canada, it cost $2 million and was closed in July 1946.

Considering the number of prisoners and the small number of guards, the camp was amazingly peaceful. The tradition of allowing POWs to run their own affairs inside the compound was respected. The camp held a representative number of hardened Nazis which helped make life interesting for those inside and outside the barbed wire. But, aside from sex crimes which were summarily dealt with by the prisoners' own rule of law, there were no major incidents. That is until the murders.

August Plaszek was hanged from a cross beam in the recreation hall of the camp on July 22, 1943. Karl Lehmanm was taken to a classroom where he had taught some of the other inmates French and hanged in a corner of the room from a gas pipe on September 10, 1944.

These killings were minor incidents in a brutal war but the impact was felt for several years as investigations were begun to discover who had engineered the plots to kill the men, and to punish those responsible.

It was a jarring note to the people of Medicine Hat who had come to have a grudging respect for the men behind the wire. The citizens did not seem to object to the presence of the camp, or to the good treatment given to the Germans. Many had sons and fathers in POW camps in the Rhineland and it was important to them that Canadian authorities be kind to the prisoners in the hope that the Nazis would do the same Overseas.

The food was good — local beef and poultry, fresh vegetables that the prisoners grew themselves on a farm outside the camp, the best of canned goods. The best of everything, in fact, because the Geneva Convention required it. For recreation, the prisoners had playing fields behind the recreation halls. They had the use of sports equipment for soccer and volley ball. Boxing gloves and punching bags were available for the settling of disputes and for entertainment. And there were musical instruments for a marching band established by the prisoners. A beer hall in the compound supplied illegal home brew and the taps often flowed well past the curfew.

The townspeople recognized the Germans in their midst. Trusted prisoners were allowed into the city to work on outside farms and on these trips to and fro they were required to wear distinctive garb: a dark blue smock with a large red bull's eye on the back. Supposedly they could be quickly spotted if they decided to make a run for it!

Some prisoners bought radios in the city and took them back with other possessions to the camp. Inside the compound, these radios were dismantled and rebuilt into shortwave receivers capable of bringing in the news from Berlin. The Canadians in charge of the camp knew of the radios but turned a blind eye to their use. Camp Commandant Colonel Roland Osbourne Bull was an officer with a good sense of humor, a valuable commodity under the circumstances. He made it clear, however, that he expected the Germans to act like prisoners of war, even to the extent of trying to escape. But he also made it very clear that escapes made from within the compound were the only escapes that would be tolerated. He told the internees that it would be considered a serious breach of trust if anyone tried to escape while visiting the city or working outside the camp. Such attempts would result in prompt suspension of this privilege.

About 750 guards watched over the Germans. They were members of the Veteran's Guard of Canada — men who had served in the Boer and First World Wars. They were too old for combat in the Second World War, but eager to lend their efforts in whatever way they could. Their duties included manning the guard towers and patrolling the barbed wire. As mentioned, the Germans ran their own affairs inside the fence.

That something was amiss in the affairs within the compound became abundantly clear one warm summer day — July 22, 1943: Private Reginald Herbert Beck of the Veteran's Guard was on duty at his post in tower number seven, about halfway along the west side of the camp. It was 5:20 p.m. Some of the prisoners could be seen getting ready to line up for dinner in the mess halls.

Beck was alerted when he heard shouting coming from the direction of one of the residential huts. Soon a man in stocking feet came running toward the tower. A crowd of yelling men were close at his heels. The man, Christian Schulz, waved a white handkerchief, a symbol of surrender. He did not hesitate when he came to the "warning wire", a single strand rigged a few feet from the ground, some 45 feet inside the main fence. Beck had orders to shoot anyone who crossed the warning wire and he raised his rifle as the frightened Schulz approached. Something in Schulz's appearance and the pathetic waving of his white handkerchief stopped him from firing. Schulz fell panting at the back of the guard tower and Beck turned his attention to the crowd chasing him.

The dozen or so had swollen to a mob of about a thousand. They began to throw rocks at the crouching figure and shouting "traitor!" Guard Beck raised his rifle again as some of the prisoners yelled at him in English, "Send Schulz back!" The men threatened to cross the wire until Beck fired a shot over their heads and they retreated.

More guards arrived on the scene. They came weaponless, fearing that in the mêlee that might follow the rifles would end up in German hands and a full scale riot could follow. The Guards ran down the strip between the fence and the warning wire to rescue Schulz. Afraid that the POWs would grab him if they led him back out over the warning wire and through the main gate, they boosted him over the barbed wire and out of the compound.

While all this was taking place, the POWs in other parts of the camp were racing around in every direction, trying to find out what was going on. And August Plaszek was being hauled away to the recreation hall, where he was to be hanged. Like Schulz, Plaszek had served in North Africa in the 1930s as a member of the French Foreign Legion. When the Germans began to mobilize, former members of the French Foreign Legion had to attend classes held in "re-education camps" run by the Nazis. After this bit of brain-washing, they were inducted into the Nazi forces.

There were many Germans who viewed these ex-Legionaires with suspicion. They may have been German nationals, but was it possible to be a good German if one had fought in Africa for the French? The fact that they had also fought in Africa for the Germans had not convinced some of their complete loyalty to the Third Reich. They were wary of men like Plaszek and Schulz who had retained their old allegiance to the Legion and its strict traditions of honor. These prejudices against the ex-Legionaires were strengthened when the men persisted in holding what appeared to be clandestine meetings in isolated places in camp. Mumblings about a plot to take over control of the camp began to circulate. When it was picked up on radio from Germany that Hitler was asking that all traitors to the Fatherland be immediately killed, the more fervent Nazis among the Medicine Hat POWs decided to carry out his orders.

Schulz explained all this to the Canadian Guards, denying that he or any of the former Legionaires were attempting a coup. He was not enthusiastic about the job being performed by the Non-Commissioned Officers, nor had he reason to feel grateful to them. He pointed out abuses that took place, especially against him and his comrades of the Legion. He mentioned a "trial" that took place in an orderly room in one of the huts that the Germans used as an office.

Sergeant-Major Richard Elstermann, Acting Commander, sat on the bench. (The ranking Commander was ill in hospital at the time.) Schulz said he was frightened by the turn of events. The questioning did not go well. Elstermann wanted to know what the Legionaires discussed in their private talks. Why were they so secretive and selective of who shared these confidences? Were they dissatisfied with the orders given by the Non-Coms who ran the camp?

At the end of the interrogation, Elstermann told Schulz that he had contradicted himself and he would have to remain in detention until further investigation could be arranged. He ordered another non-com to take him into custody. As Schulz was being led from the room, he broke loose and bolted for the fence. If August Plaszek had jumped up and run off with him, he might have lived too.

Plaszek had been waiting outside the room while Schulz was being questioned. He sat quietly on a bench, with Staff Sergeant Ludwig Kammermeier beside him. After about 10 minutes the German guard said he was going for dinner and left Plaszek alone. Moments later the mob burst into the room. Four of them grabbed Plaszek and dragged him outside where one of them picked up a rock and hit him on the head with it. Semiconscious, he was pulled toward the recreation hall where Sergeant Werner Schwalb waited. He had a rope in his hands.

The camp became fairly quiet and life returned to near-normal after the hanging. There had been disruption of course while the Guards came in to examine the scene and call a doctor. Plaszek's body was taken to Pattison Funeral Home in the city and the RCMP arrived. Corporal Arthur Bull (no relation to the Camp Commandant), a detective from the RCMP detachment in Lethbridge, began an investigation that was to take more than two years. (Corporal Bull later became Medicine Hat Police Chief.)

Christian Schulz was transferred to another camp. Wisely, the ex-Legionaires still in the camp did not meet any more for their little exchanges and the Nazis turned their attention to another source of irritation.

The focal point was Karl Lehmann, a man who was already accused of spreading Communist propaganda. He had gained the reputation in another POW camp at Oldham in England and news of his involvement in Communism had preceded him to Canada. Lehmann, who could converse intelligently in half a dozen languages, made a habit of reading the local daily newspapers and translating them aloud to those who were interested. This became a source of suspicion to the Nazi element since there were discrepancies in the news reporting coming from Berlin over shortwave, and that read by Lehmann from the Alberta newspapers. Obviously the papers carried news that was less favorable to the Germans than what they heard on their radios. In addition to this, Lehmann was accused of believing more of what he read than of what he heard.

Soon Lehmann was being accused of plotting the overthrow of the camp government. He was reported to have told one of the ex-Legionaires: "Go over at noon today and look around. See if any persons have come along who might be useful to us." Lehmann was not a Legionaire and what he was saying might have been an innocent request to find some more people to attend his language and discussion classes. But the man who overheard this conversation was Corporal Walter Wolf (or Wolff), an aggressive infantryman from the Afrika Korps. He enjoyed a reputation as a busybody who liked to become involved in camp politics. When he was told to keep his eyes and ears open for any clues to a plot, he soon compiled a list of names, most of them Legionaires'.

On July 20, 1944, almost a year to the day that August Plascek was murdered, the secret shortwave receivers in the camp crackled with the news that there had been an attempt to assassinate Adolf Hitler. One of the men accused in the attempt was Field Marshall Ernest Rommel, a man much admired by the Legionaires. The strident voices on the radio urged all loyal Nazi soldiers, airmen and sailors to purge the German forces of traitors. Privates should consider themselves authorized to execute officers, if necessary. It was at this point that Staff Sergeant-Major Bruno Perzonowsky's interest intensified.

The war had been a big disappointment for Perzonowsky. Although he had flown 60 missions across enemy territory and had given a good account of himself as a Luftwaffe pilot (First and Second Class Iron Cross with Silver

Bar), he had ended up being shot down during the Battle of Britain and captured in Wales. He'd spent four years as a prisoner of war in England and Canada and thirsted for more action. Here was an opportunity to make a contribution to the German war effort.

In September, the camp was in an uproar again. A new rumor of takeover of the camp by the Legionaires was rife. The 18 men on Walter Wolf's list, plus another dozen of suspected cases, were rounded up. There was talk of hanging the lot of them, but saner heads intervened and nothing came of the suggestion. This disgusted Perzonowsky, a Prussian, and a devout member of the Nazi Party. When he heard that he and many of his fellow Nazis were to be moved to another camp at Neys, Ontario he was furious. He interpreted this as an attempt to separate the Nazis from the non-Nazis.

On September 10, the day before the transfer was to be made, Perzonowsky called Wolf to his room and discussed orders to "dispose of Lehmann." He was to be assisted by Wolf, Heinrich Busch and Willi Mueller (or Muller), both Non-Coms. Busch and Mueller were known as camp brawlers, Mueller having demonstrated his boxing skill in and out of the ring. They were taking no chances with Lehmann, the agitator.

As a ruse, Lehmann was told to come to his classroom that evening to sign certificates of proficiency for those of his students who were being transferred. He arrived looking wary and perplexed. Perzonowsky looked at him with distaste: "Do you know anything about the Communist activities in this camp?" he sneered. Before Lehmann could open his mouth to reply, Mueller struck him on the jaw with his fist. Perzonowsky quickly stuffed a rag in Lehmann's mouth to keep him from yelling while Mueller tied a rope around his neck.

The three men dragged Lehmann to the side of the room and hoisted him kicking and squirming up to the gas pipe. The rope broke and had to be retied. The second time it held and Lehmann was soon dead of strangulation.

In court much later Doctor W. C. Campbell would tell how he examined the body two days after the murder and RCMP Corporal Bill Westgate would testify how he had cut the rope and let the body down.

The trials for all the men charged in the two murders took place in the Medicine Hat Court House on First Street South East. The three men charged in the murder of August Plaszek on July 22, 1943 were Sergeant Werner Schwalb, Adolf Kratz and Johannes Wittinger. Separate trials were held for each man as requested by Council L. S. Turcotte and granted by Chief Justice Howson. All three men had been arrested on July 22, 1945 in the Lethbridge camp where they were being held since being transferred there earlier that year.

The first to be tried was Schwalb, on February 25, 1946. The jury was comprised of Harry Morris, Foreman, William Mulholland, A. C. McDonald, Warren Porter, all of Medicine Hat, V. C. Elliott of Whitla and Fred Tonberg of Seven Persons. Schwalb was sentenced to be hanged on June 26, 1946 at Lethbridge jail.

On March 16, 1946 Adolf Kratz came before the Chief Justice. His jurymen were W. B. Dempster, Jury Foreman, J. S. McNaught, Donald

Brenner and Thomas Nesting of Medicine Hat, and Bernard Thacker of Redcliff. A verdict was reached on Saturday, March 16, 1946. Kratz was judged guilty as charged, but with a strong recommendation for mercy. Nevertheless, he was sentenced to hang June 26, 1946 but on June 24 his sentence was commuted to life imprisonment by the Governor General in Ottawa. His sentence was altered because of ill health and Kratz eventually returned to Germany.

The third man to be tried for the murder of Karl Lehmann was Johannes Wittinger who found himself being judged by Gordon Bissett, Foreman of the Jury, Peter Bruins, G. L. Eskestrand, George Fisher, Joe P. Haverty and R. Lonson, all of Medicine Hat and District. When the fact that Eskestrand was found to be only 24 years old and jurors must be a minimum of 25, a new trial was ordered. This time, on June 17, Leonard Bell, Dudley Driscoll, Kenneth Kinvig, Bert Kinnard, Howard Millen and Stanley Ridell, all of Medicine Hat, brought in a verdict of not guilty.

Lance Corporal Wittinger was placed in custody of the authorities until his release and return to his homeland.

On April 6, 1946 Sergeants Walter Wolf, Willi Mueller, Heinrich Busch and Sergeant-Major Bruno Perzonowsky were arrested and charged with the hanging murder of Corporal Karl Lehmann, from a gas pipe in Drill Hall 132 at the Medicine Hat camp on September 10, 1944.

Perzonowsky was the first to face the judge and jury. Anthony Jacobson, John Hatley, L. G. Blanchard, Donald Lefever, Hartman Peterson and Jack Mellor, all of Medicine Hat, were chosen. Crown Council in this case was W. D. Gow, K. C. of Medicine Hat. The case lasted one week with the jury bringing in a verdict of guilty on June 30. Like Schwalb, Perzonowsky was sentenced to hang at Lethbridge jail.

Next on the docket was Walter Wolf. He faced jurymen Wilfred Dahlstrom, George Church, Gordon Sissons, Orville Lyon, Ernie Watkin, Harry Leinweber, all of Medicine Hat, on July 2, 1946. They brought in a verdict of guilty of murder and Wolf was sentenced to be hanged on December 18, 1946.

Heinrich Busch then came forth to stand trial for the murder of Lehmann with A. Pederzolli, James Sparrow, Robert Ayling, Horace Wood, Walter Charles, all of Medicine Hat, and Harry Dacre of Redcliff in the jury box. On Saturday, July 13 Busch was judged guilty and sentenced to hang at Lethbridge jail on December 18, 1946.

The fourth man charged in the Lehmann case was Willi Mueller but his case was delayed due to W. D. Gow taking ill. On Monday, July 29, 1946 William Milroy, Wilfred Worrall, Frederick Gee, Robert Howe, Wilfred Knight and Archie Marshall, all of Medicine Hat took their places on the jury benches. On August 1 they brought in their verdict of guilty.

The execution date was set but on October 3 a month reprieve was ordered and a new date set for November 13. Mr. Rice, Council for the accused, had his request for appeals dismissed in the Calgary Appeal Court and the hangings were carried out on December 18, 1946 at Lethbridge. Joining the four men of the Lehmann killing was Sergeant Werner Schwalb.

Sergeant Schwalb made headlines with his last words. The 31-year-old former Afrika Korps infantryman showed no emotion as he walked the last few steps to the gallows. As the black hood was placed over his head he said, "My Fuehrer, I follow thee."

The trials in Medicine Hat came at a delicate time. Nazi leadership was on trial in Nurenberg and the Canadian government was determined that the trials here be as free as possible of the overtones of war. Louis St. Laurent, who later became Prime Minister, was Justice Minister in the Liberal Government. He personally called L. Sherman Turcotte, a lawyer, and asked him to be defence counsel. Turcotte told reporter Doug Sagy that he "got the job because I was a Liberal." He took on the Plaszek case and turned the other over to George Rice, "the other Liberal lawyer in town."

Rice's defence consisted of two main points: the trial should have been before a military court because the men involved were soldiers; the court had no jurisdiction in the case. Chief Justice W. R. Howson of the Alberta Supreme Court took note of the fact but over-ruled the objections.

The fairness of the trial was apparent, even to the prisoners, especially to Walter Wolf, who told the judge and jury, through an interpreter: "I stand here as a soldier of a foreign power which, until recently, was at war with Canada. I could not place full confidence in this court but, through sitting and listening to everything, everything the witnesses said, and the evidence, it was shown to me and has fully convinced me that this trial was very fair."

The fact of their being soldiers came up again when the verdict was read. Perzonowsky, Meuller and Busch all complained that since they were soldiers they should die like soldiers: before a firing squad; not by a hangman's noose. The POWs also complained loudly about being hanged the same day as a sex murderer. To draw attention to their plea, two of the men attempted suicide by slashing their wrists the night before the hangings were to take place. But the doctors in the jail sewed them up enough so that they were in shape to go to the gallows along with the sex offender on December 18, 1946.

The executions constituted the second largest mass hanging in the history of the country. The largest was in 1886 when eight Indians were hanged at Battleford, Saskatchewan for taking part in the Riel Rebellion.

Perzonowsky, the Luftwaffe pilot who was vexed by his capture in Wales and subsequent incarceration for the duration of the war, signed two confessions which were read in court. He took full responsibility for the Lehmann murder. He said that the command to destroy traitors came from Hitler himself and he was bound as a soldier to carry out that order. Lehmann had a death warrant signed on him while he was still in the English camp and had only escaped it when he was transferred to Canada. It was only a matter of time until someone carried out the order.

"The others involved in carrying out the death sentence are not responsible," Perzonowsky told the court in impeccable English. "I was solely responsible. They were only following the orders given to me from higher up."

When asked if he had anything to say before he was taken away, Perzonowsky, a policeman in the city of Elbing in East Prussia, in civilian life, said in loud, clear English: "No!"

(Incidentally, the spelling of the names of Perzonowsky, Mueller and Wolf varies in newspaper accounts, official records and on the men's gravestones with documents supplied by the German War Graves Commission.)

The bodies of the POWs hanged in Lethbridge were later removed to Kitchener, Ontario for burial in Woodland Cemetery, near Kitchener, the final resting place for German prisoners of war who died in Canada in The First World War and the Second World War.

Mr. Justice Howson remarked that except for two newspaper reporters and two practising lawyers from Medicine Hat, no other persons were in attendance in the Court Room during the trials. Obviously Medicine Hat residents had had more than enough of war, and the aftermath, including the trying of Nazi criminals.

One of the men who spent the war behind barbed wire in Medicine Hat counts himself lucky that he escaped the same fate as Lehmann and Plaszek. Max Weidauer, now a Toronto business executive, was suspected by Nazis within the camp to have been a Legionnaire, although he never served in the French-operated service.

Weidauer told Frank Jones of the *Toronto Star* in March 1981 he was scooped up and interrogated by the Nazis in the camp because he had been seen translating copies of Canadian newspapers smuggled into the camp by the former Legionnaires who used to meet in a hollow beside the sports field. He was led into a room and questioned by Sergeant Major Richard Elsterman about his loyalty and remarks made regarding his country's war effort. Weidauer managed to convince them of his positive attitude toward the outcome of the war.

Although he was released, he feared for his life; he could not sleep and finally escaped from a work detail at a Medicine Hat pottery. He worked on a sheep ranch in the Aldershot district for several weeks before the RCMP found him and returned him to the camp. He continued to escape and finally Canadian authorities made a deal with him: if he would promise not to escape, he would be allowed to work on a farm.

Max Weidauer won the trust of sugar beet farmer Ben Ober of Coaldale, Alberta and "became like a member of the family." He was one of 50 German prisoners of war selected by Canadian authorities to remain in this country after the conflict ended. However, there was an outcry from veterans and other groups in Canada and all POWs were shipped back overseas. Weidauer was freed in April, 1947 in Germany and returned to Canada in 1955.

He had only one complaint to make about his incarceration in the Medicine Hat camp: "The Canadian Guards allowed us to maintain our own discipline in the camps, and that meant the Nazis were in charge. There was a Gestapo man in every hut."

So ended another chapter in the life of Medicine Hat, another chapter that drew attention from across the country. The thousands of prisoners that had been interred here were returned to Germany, some to become prominent citizens in their wartorn land. More than a few came back to Canada, and Medicine Hat area, as immigrants. They have become worthwhile additions to the fabric of our country. The fairness with which they were treated by Medicine Hat residents and the Canadian Guards, along with the strict but just verdict delivered by the judge and jury in the trials, undoubtedly had a positive effect on the men who served out the war behind barbed wire in Medicine Hat.

15.

Mayor With A Flair: The Veiner Years

Medicine Hat has had its share of distinctive politicians, but more than any other civic official Harry Veiner, through his crazy antics, backed by sound economic judgment, has brought international attention to the city. Veiner has not gone without criticism for some of his shenanigans. There were those who said his zany capers were making the city "the laughing stock of the world." Veiner shrugged off such unimaginative thinking. After all, the city had come out the winner — and so had he.

Harry Veiner was born on May 13, 1904 at Dysart, Saskatchewan, where his father homesteaded and pre-empted other land. Farming with oxen, Veiner's father made a success of the farm and encouraged his children to aspire to great things in life. As a Jewish immigrant, he had known tough times and he wanted his children to be prepared for whatever the fates dealt them.

When Harry Veiner was selected as Citizen of the Year by the Board of Medicine Hat College on May 9, 1973, Chairman George H. Davison said of him: "He is a colorful son of the Prairies, steeped in self-determination, who learned early that enterprise was to be his watchword."

It wasn't Veiner's only watchword: physical-fitness was another. From his earliest days he was athletically-inclined. There was scarcely a sport at which he did not excel. Sam Veiner, a Calgary dental surgeon, recalled that "Harry's youth was completely concentrated on competitive athletics." Track and field were his forté. "Very few athletes in Saskatchewan could beat Harry in the 100 yard dash, the 220, the 440 or the 880," his brother added.

So fast was Harry on his feet that once when he was coach of the Dysart hockey team he made a bet that he could run faster along the railway tracks than the horses and wagon carrying the players could make it along the road. This was on a cold day in January with the thermometer registering 20 below zero. Harry won. He almost always did.

The only thing that Harry could do better than run, jump and throw was to fight. "He was the greatest street fighter since Joseph Kennedy," brother Sam claimed, referring to the late Ambassador Kennedy, father of the assassinated John Kennedy, who gained a reputation for using his fists while growing up poor in Boston. "The reason Harry got in so much practice as a fighter," Sam said, "was the fact that he wouldn't allow anyone to attack a minority, particularly the Jewish minority, which was very prevalent in the Depression days."

It was Harry Veiner's zest for life and his ability to combine his natural

Harry Veiner, Mayor of Medicine Hat from 1952 to 1966 and from 1968 to 1974. Sportsman, businessman, public servant, Veiner, through his involvement in extracurricular affairs helped put Medicine Hat on the international map.

athletic ability with his business accumen that allowed him to succeed in both fields. During the 1930s, Veiner owned a store and hotel in Lemsford, a store in Prelate, and a store and hotel in Sceptre, three adjoining towns in Saskatchewan — all about 10 miles from each other. Long before jogging became a fad, Veiner would keep in shape by running the 30 miles to look after his business interests.

Veiner was only 14 years old when he lied about his age and was taken into the Canadian Army during the First World War. He served well, but never got out of Canada before the war was over. During the Second World War his contribution was more outstanding. As a Lieutenant-Colonel, Veiner was Inspector of Messing and Catering for Prisoner of War camps in Alberta from 1941 to 1942. It is on record that he saved the government millions of dollars by making sure that nothing useable was wasted. What couldn't be utilized by humans was sold to pig farmers or disposed of in other ways.

However, Harry had his detractors. On the basis that he allegedly mistreated Prisoners of War in his own backyard of Medicine Hat, he was soundly defeated by the large German population in the city when he ran for the Medicine Hat federal constituency as a Liberal in the late 1940s. However, when he ran again he lost by only 360 votes (down from 8,000) to the locally-strong Social Credit Party candidate.

In 1952, Veiner successfully ran for Mayor of Medicine Hat, a post he held from then until 1966 when he was defeated in his bid for re-election. At that time, there were those who said he was through, "washed-up." But in 1968 Veiner again entered the political fray and won the mayoralty elections of 1968 and 1971. As for the so-called anti-German bias during the war, Veiner claimed he had not one complaint from the prisoners, some of whom sent him gifts and paintings after the war. Some of this memorabilia was displayed in his home.

Mr. Veiner won the Canadian Industrial Development Award for the year 1973 in recognition of his efforts in the promotion of industry in Medicine Hat.

As Mayor, and earlier as a young man growing up in a world that did not suffer its ethnic minorities gladly, Veiner refused to accept defeat or become depressed or discouraged.

In one amazing display of competitiveness and endurance, he won almost everything in sight at the fair, including the pretty girl! It was in 1927. He entered the 12 mile "marathon" around Qu'Appelle Lake, coming in far ahead of his nearest rival. He then ran the 100 yard dash and the 220 in rapid succession. Next, he played two games of soccer with the Scotch McDonald Hill teams, of which he was captain, and danced all evening at the social event of the fair. His date lived in Regina, so he drove her 60 miles home before driving back in time to go to work.

Harry Veiner had his weak spots, of course, as the coach of the Regina Roughriders told him. It was in the early Thirties. His brother Sam recalled: "Harry wasn't the best football player in the Western world. As a matter of fact, the coach felt he was one of the worst, technically speaking. But he was also the toughest."

When he was Mayor of Medicine Hat, Harry Veiner turned his attention to beating his peers in other realms. He began to challenge mayors in other parts of Canada and Abroad to a weird assortment of duels. He challenged

Seldom separated from his Stetson, Harry Veiner is seen here with Ernie Heald at the opening of an irrigation dam.

speak. He defeated Barney Ross, the former lightweight boxing champion of the world, in a three-round match in Vancouver.

Veiner was featured in a *Time Magazine* article when he raced a horse at Brooks, Alberta over a 25-yard course — and won. He challenged the Mayor of The Pas in Manitoba to a dog sleigh race and Indian wrestling, two sports that rank high in that community's annual winter celebration. He won both events.

His skill at racing on ice vanquished many a challenger at the mayoralty level. He went to Moncton, New Brunswick to kick his heels up on the frozen surface and flattened his opponent in City Hall there. The Mayor of Moncton had invited him. Veiner came home and won a skipping contest, ate his way to the core of an apple-eating contest, won a tobaggan race at Beausejour, Manitoba and took top honors in a milking contest and twist dancing affair at Ponoka, Alberta. His opponent was the Mayor, Mrs. Debs Nelson.

In between all these jousts, Harry Veiner continued to dominate in other fields. For three years (1948 to 1950) he was the largest sheep rancher in Canada. He ran a total of about 16,000 sheep on ranches in Alberta and Saskatchewan. In England he bought a sow from Sir Winston Churchill's prize stock. He later sent a piglet from this sow to Churchill. It was shipped from Calgary in dry ice, with an apple in its mouth. It was later served at some special occasion — which the Prime Minister of Britain attended.

In his book *The Savoy*, the romance of the great hotel, by Stanley Jackson (Muller, London, publishers), Sir Winston mentions his "good friend from Medicine Hat, Alberta, Canada." (Page 226 of the book.)

Not forgetting his Jewish heritage, Veiner sent gift sheep to Israel to establish flocks, donated acreage for establishment of a hostel and in more than one instance donated funds to an Israeli bond drive, matching dollar for dollar the total donation.

Veiner did not contain his largesse to his own faith. In the Dirty Thirties he sent a carload of coal to Notre Dame College at Willcox, Saskatchewan. He and Monseigneur Athol Murray of that famed institution were longtime friends. After a trip to Israel he brought stones from Ben Gurian, the Prime Minister at the time, to be worked into the "Tower of God" at the College. He donated profits from a potato chip factory he owned at Brooks, Alberta to the same college.

There is not enough space in this history to list the major and minor accomplishments of this amazing individual. However, something must be said about his record as mayor. In 1955, three years after coming into office, he pulled off his major industrial coup — a land initiative which led to the establishment of the Northwest Nitro-Chemicals plant, mainly because of his quick action in putting together a package deal with the help of the then City Finance Director, Tom Legge. The land deal was not sanctioned by City Council but Veiner was certain the aldermen would not object because a delay would have meant no deal.

Similar unorthodox wheelings and dealings led to the Goodyear Tire and Rubber plant establishing in Medicine Hat in 1959. Goodyear was interested in building a plant in the city but as a source of water the South Saskatchewan River was too warm in the summer months. Veiner had

Mayor Harry Veiner and a city asphalting crew. Veiner liked to take the job of Mayor to the people — because he was one of them. (City of Medicine Hat Photo)

struck an underground river on his farm east of the city while drilling a well. He hit upon the idea that Goodyear could use the water supply for their needs if the stream could be located on City-owned land. City gas engineer Bob Beitz drilled an experimental well at Police Point on City property.

"A lot of people — and one alderman in particular — were very indignant and demanded to know what right I had to spend the City's money on drilling the well," Veiner told Gordon Pollard of the *Medicine Hat News* in an interview published January 9, 1973. "But the critics fell silent when the aquifer was found and the company decided to locate in Medicine Hat as a result."

Mayor Veiner helped the City get out of some thorny problems, as well as making deals that created controversy at the time. In 1970 Wittke Iron Works moved from Norwood, a residential area on the southeast hill, where motel operators threatened to take legal action against the City. At the Mayor's suggestion, the City bought the Wittke building and assisted the company in relocating at Brier Industrial Park, north of the river where industry is located. Threats of court action dissipated.

Harry Veiner said there are three major qualities that a good mayor must possess in order to be a successful servant of the people: "Honesty is the most important quality. No one can be successful as mayor unless he is scrupulously honest. Second, a mayor must be someone who knows value and has shown himself to be responsible in managing his own financial affairs. And thirdly, a mayor has to have a good understanding of people and human nature."

Veiner has proved the second point with his own success: he owns and operates the "Hat" Hardware, Medicine Hat Greenhouses, Hycroft China Factory, Golden Valley Farm (along the river a few miles from the city), various apartment buildings and a trailer camp, as well as 18 farms in Alberta and Saskatchewan and one in Ladner, British Columbia.

He derives his greatest satisfaction from the performance of Hycroft China Ltd. When he bought it from its Vancouver-based owners in 1958 it was losing about $180,000 a year. He took drastic action to turn the compa-

206

ny into a money-maker: he increased the wages of the workers at the plant and dismissed "all the high-priced managerial staff the former owners brought in from California," he said. He gave senior employees positions of authority in the plant and soon the business was doing 10 times what it was before he took it over.

Despite his own flair for the dramatic, Veiner has no time for dreamers with "grandiose development plans" with no real foundation or understanding of the territory. During his 20 year reign, he was approached by hundreds of "pie in the sky dreamers and jokers." He points to the success of Medicine Hat Brick and Tile as a company that has the two qualities required to pass his "litmus test" — a sound financial base and capable of making a profit.

"The division of IXL Industries realized the potential of a local resource," he said, "but Medicine Hat Brick and Tile might not have become one of the largest companies of its kind in Canada had it not been for the outstanding ability of the Sissons family." Veiner expressed admiration for Gordon Sissons (President of IXL). "He is without a doubt one of the most tremendous salesmen in Canada." His success with the company contrasted sharply with "some of the hare-brained development proposals that have been made to Council over the years."

"It is better to get one solid industry than 10 shaky ones," Veiner said in an interview in the *News*. He mentioned Wilson's Electric and Bick's Pickles, which established in the city but were later forced to shut down. Wilson's had hoped to do a large amount of business with the Alberta Government but the company found itself undersold by its competitors, Veiner said. As for Bick's, "it failed because it couldn't get the farmers in this area to produce enough cucumbers to supply its plant."

These two examples serve as a "sobering lesson" to Medicine Hat, Veiner said. "Fortunately, they were financially sound and were able to pay their bills before closing down their operations in Medicine Hat." Nevertheless, such failures tend to sully the City's reputation in the economic sweepstakes. "It is better," he said, "for a company to locate elsewhere than to come here and then be forced to leave."

Jack Barrie, who interviewed Harry Veiner on January 16, 1980, asked him at that time what plans, schemes and antics he had prepared for the future. He was then a spry 76. "The same thing I'm doing now," he declared. "You can't quit."

The Town Moving West - 1900

16.

Those Daring Young Men: Medicine Hat's Innovators

Hang-gliding was rapidly becoming a major sport in North America in the 1980's, but it was unheard of when Norman Bruce of Medicine Hat took to the air with his first armpits glider in 1922. The son of Major James Bruce of the famous First World War 175th Regiment, 15-year-old Norman was the mastermind behind Canada's first "hang-on" type glider.

With his arms supporting the wings, and utilizing his feet as landing gear, Norman Bruce made his historic flight. What is interesting about young Bruce's innovation is that he had never seen an airplane up close before he built his model, and he never received any professional help in the construction of the glider.

At that time there were gliders around that could be lofted by being towed by aircraft or automobile. Norman Bruce eschewed such conventional methods of joining the birds. With the aid of five other youths, he stepped into a rough cockpit in the middle of his 40 pound craft and began to run pellmell down a hill near town. With the tail bouncing behind him he ran until he felt the tail lifting. He was airborne!

The glider soared down the hill, about three feet off the ground, for a distance of about 50 feet. This was the year 1926 and this was the first recorded free flight in Canada.

After the wind smashed the glider, Bruce began to construct a more elaborate model, embodying ideas that had come from his first experience. He used boat varnish for the wings, to strengthen them. At this point an officer from the High River Air Station inspected his work and congratulated him on his imagination.

The officer also had a word with Major Bruce about the danger his son faced in flying such a fragile craft. However, he gave young Bruce a tour of the High River installation and Norman returned home, abandoning his construction on the second glider. Instead, he concentrated on building a more sophisticated third model.

The result was a glider with a wing span of 22 feet and a wicker chair for the pilot to sit in. What it lacked was a controllable rudder. Nevertheless, Bruce made three successful flights in the glider before it crashed. He was not seriously injured.

Completely bitten by the flying bug, he took a course in aeronautical engineering in the United States and when he returned in 1930 to Medicine Hat he was imbued with the gliding light. He organized the Cloud Rangers

Gliding Club to interest other young flyers and began to build his fourth glider.

During this period, brothers Lawrence and Tom became pilots. Unfortunately, Lawrence, who was also a talented musician, was killed when the glider he was flying stalled during a towed takeoff and dived straight down into the ground from 200 feet up.

It was a sad time for the Bruce family and for a while public opinion locally turned against gliding as a sport. But Norman Bruce could not be grounded for long and soon he formed a women's group, the Skylarks Gliding Club. Two Medicine Hat women, Patricia Terril and a Mrs. Ellick became two of the first Canadian women to take wing.

During the 1930's daring young men in flying machines dazzled audiences across the country with their aerobatics. The stuntmen were called barnstormers. Norman Bruce, James Fretwell and Paul Pelletier decided to try their luck with a demonstration of gliding. They formed the Canadian Gliding Boosters and with a knocked-down glider in a trailer attached to their car, set out on a tour of Prairie towns.

From May 25 to July 1, 1935 they rode the air currents over 22 towns and cities from Calgary to Winnipeg. On land they covered a distance of about 1,100 miles. Although they made more than 400 flights, many of them under adverse conditions, the audiences were reluctant to reach very deep into their Depression-ridden pockets to pay for the privilege of watching them. With only $214 profit, about 50 cents a flight, the young men decided to give it up and come home.

To add insult to financial ruin, a capricious wind sprang up one night while they were asleep in their tent and smashed the glider to matchwood. Sadly, they placed the salvageable parts in a box and drove back to Medicine Hat.

It was not the first or last time that Norman Bruce would have encounters with wind and weather — and other disasters that make flying an adventurous sport. One night the glider was left in a farmer's field for safekeeping and when the owners returned in the morning to retrieve it, something was missing. The farmer's cattle liked the taste of the fabric so much they had eaten one wing! On another occasion a student pilot crashed into a pig pen south of Calgary. Although the pilot was unharmed, the pigs were scattered and never found again.

During the Second World War Bruce was stationed in England where he worked in a factory that produced military gliders. He also trained paratroopers in glider operation. It was during this period that Bruce nearly lost his life. The glider that he was testing hit an air pocket causing it to plunge. He bounced right out of the cockpit. Luckily, he hit the wing and bounced right back in again.

"After that, I never flew without a safety harness," he said, in an interview with the *Calgary Herald* in 1969.

Prior to his death in Calgary in April 1970, Norman Bruce was honored with a Life Membership in the Soaring Association of Canada, commemorating more than half a century of personal service to the sport of gliding. Sometimes called the father of sport gliding in Western Canada, his contribution was recognized in Frank G. Ellis' book *Canadian Flying Heritage*

(University of Toronto Press), from which some of this background was drawn.

Norman Bruce's final glider was a far cry from the one he flew with its wobbly wings and kitchen chair seat: it was a modern, all-metal Schweiger sailplane equipped with blind flying instruments and two-way radio.

Norman Bruce was not the only Medicine Hat resident to have lofty thoughts. J. E. Caldwell spent three years in the city producing a full-size working model of a machine called an Ornithopter. According to Caldwell, a Montreal inventor, the Ornithopter was "a moving wing aircraft that lifts and glides with the same wing at the same time." It was a revolutionary principle, one which Caldwell predicted would "prove of much greater commercial value than atomic energy."

J. E. Caldwell's ORNITHOPTER, Flying Machine (1954 probably), at Medicine Hat Airport runway.

He described the method as the "flight formula of birds" and introduced "a new science in transportation because it utilizes air for a highway and gravity for 95 per cent of the power."

Caldwell's assistant in developing his working model in Medicine Hat was the late Hartley Shannon, an aeronautical engineer. Caldwell produced the blueprints for the machine and supervised and experimented along with Shannon during the three years of trials here. Dick Northam, a licensed pilot, worked with Caldwell and Shannon, on one occasion getting the machine 75 feet into the air. It did not seem to have the power to stay aloft and it came back to earth rather heavily, observers said.

No further flights were made in Medicine Hat and Caldwell took his model to Montreal where he tried to interest an aircraft manufacturer in testing it further. It was said that he spent a fortune in trying to get his experiment off the ground. Nothing concrete seems to have resulted from his efforts. Interestingly enough, Russia developed a similar machine, also called an Ornithopter, about two years after the failure of Caldwell's attempts to revolutionize air travel.

Mrs. Hartley Shannon was interviewed by Jack Barrie in November 1980 and the photographs shown here, along with some of the background on Caldwell, Northam and her husband, were supplied at that time.

211

How Hartley Shannon came to be involved with Caldwell is believed to have been because Caldwell was staying at the motel run by the Shannon family. And Caldwell had heard that Hartley Shannon had spent three years in Kansas City, Missouri studying aeronautical engineering. At that time Shannon was working for the City of Medicine Hat as a welder and gas inspector. Also useful to Caldwell was the small factory on the Shannon property at the foot of Dunmore Road along Seven Persons Creek.

Hartley Shannon of Medicine Hat at the helm of the Ornithopter manufactured by J. E. Caldwell and patented. Photo taken in hangar at Medicine Hat Airport.

In 1940 the three Shannon brothers, Bert, Hartley and Gordon, constructed the factory near the two-storey brick house that their father had built in 1882 and which is still in use. The factory was used for production of a Shannon invention, the "Conversion Gas Burner", which converts coal-burning stoves and heaters to natural gas-burners. Shannon used the facilities of the burner factory for the production of small parts for Caldwell's Ornithopter while assembly was carried out at a Medicine Hat Airport hanger.

Another Medicine Hat man, Richard E. Taylor, born here in 1929, took his talents a long way to utilize them in one of the most advanced techniques in the field of theoretical physics. Taylor is one of an elite world class of experimental physicists at the Stanford Linear Accelerator facility in Palo Alto, California, working on producing a supercharged electron beam that analyzes matter. More than two miles in length, it is the longest linear accelerator in the world and is also the most powerful. These accelerators produce beams made up of subatomic particles moving at tremendous speed. The impact of the particles on others is the way scientists gather data about subatomic relationships and composition.

In 1979 Taylor and the other Palo Alto scientists used the accelerator to demonstrate the relationship between electromagnetic force and nuclear force, two forces which determine the behavior of the atom. Three physicists at the facility were awarded the 1979 Nobel Prize in physics.

Prior to that, Taylor and another crew at the California laboratory were the first scientists to provide evidence of "quarks" inside nuclear matter. In electron-scattering experiments done over a 10 year period, Taylor and the others isolated data supporting evidence of the existence of the tiny particles, too small to be detected individually.

Richard Taylor is the only child of the late Mr. and Mrs. Ted Taylor of Medicine Hat. His father, who was a flour salesman in the Depression, rose to become manager of the Ogilvie Flour mill. Richard attended Kitchener Elementary, Connaught Intermediate and Alexandra High School before going to the University of Paris to study physics. While visiting the city he sees his cousins Frank Anderson, Betty Butler and Chick Taylor.

Although career-entrenched in California, Taylor told Tom Adams of *Pacific News Service* on the eve of receiving an honorary degree from the University of Paris in 1979, "Medicine Hat was a very comfortable place to grow up in. It left me with a feeling that I belong to some society and have an individual worth. Nothing ever takes that away from you."

Arnold Lesk, son of Mr. and Mrs. Benjamin Lesk, is head of Motorola Incorporated's solar energy program and has received many honors for his research in this vital field of alternative energy sources. Born in Regina, Dr. Lesk came to the city of Medicine Hat with his parents in 1931. He attended public school and Alexandra High School, graduating in 1944. He was class valedictorian. He entered the University of Alberta when he was just 16 years old. He graduated with distinction, winning the Henry Birk Gold Medal and a Fellowship at the University of Illinois where he received his doctorate at the age of 23.

After several years with General Electric, he joined Motorola in 1960 and rose to become manager of the solar energy program. He has 10 issued patents, 10 active applications, more than 22 publications and has chaired more than 20 professional committees.

Not bad for a Jewish boy from Medicine Hat who was a King Scout in the St. Barnabas Troop!

Meanwhile, another Medicine Hat man was bringing attention over solar energy to the region. Roger Breault was creating momentum for a proposed solar energy research centre in the Medicine Hat area. It was described by Economic Development Manager Dave Cormier as "an all-encompassing program that will make use of the area's impressive solar potential and should nicely round out the Community's title of the "City with Energy".

Almost every type of sport can be found in Medicine Hat. Photo courtesy City of Medicine Hat.

214

17.

Sports Of All Sorts

Sports and entertainment have been an integral part of the Medicine Hat scene right from the earliest times when horse-racing and cowboy competitions provided a harmless outlet for exuberant spirits.

Horse races were held at the old Fair Grounds (now the site of the airport) where a developed track was complemented by corrals and barns. But long before then, horses were raced on the "Flats" and at other locations — anywhere men with horses could get together to compete and bet. Observance of the Sabbath was overlooked, Sunday racing being frowned upon by church and the law, especially since the drinking of whiskey of dubious quality was considered a part of the main event.

The first real stampede or rodeo to be held in Medicine Hat was in July of 1901, on the "Flats". There were three main events: bareback riding, saddle bronc riding and wild steer roping. DaRome Allen, a popular local cowboy, managed the show, assisted by Jack Hargrave and Jim Mitchell. Others involved were Jim McLellan, Jim Fisher, A. C. Whiffen and Jim Fleming. As well as this being the first rodeo in Medicine Hat, it was also the first commercial event of its kind to be held in the Canadian West. In earlier days, work stampedes were held on the ranches throughout the district. The 1901 commercial venture continued at various suitable grounds in the city until 1910 when the bustling City of Calgary entered the stampede scene with its big outdoor show in 1912. It has always been an understandable source of pride to citizens of the 'Hat that the stampede held here is older than that held in the Foothills City.

Bronco Busting Exhibition in Medicine Hat, Athletic Park, Riverside, Christmas Day, 1912.

215

Bucking Horse contest at Medicine Hat in December 1912.

World-famous rodeo clown "Slim" Pickens seen outrunning a steer at the Medicine Hat Stampede. Pickens, who later became an actor, was here in 1949. (Courtesy City of Medicine Hat)

The history of the stampede, rodeo or Wild West Show was commercialized beyond recognition by showmen like Buffalo Bill Cody who took to the road with an entourage of trick riders, trick ropers, quick-draw artists, updated Annie Oakleys and declining Indian chiefs, whereas the authentic rodeo was a simpler affair.

Without such refinements as today's pickup riders and stopwatch judging, cowboys would get together for an annual holiday in which the contestants entered strictly for the fun of trying to outride or outrope each other. If there was any money to be made it was from bets made among the contestants and the small group of onlookers, generally comprised of friends and relatives, and neighbors from nearby ranches.

Big ranches in the district hired professional horse breakers who earned their living taming broncs for use on the ranch. Today's rodeo rider is of a different breed. He climbs onto the back of a professional bucking horse that is held inside a "chute" until a signal is given to release horse and rider for a few seconds of action before a breathless audience in the bleachers. Such a rider does not have to be a good horseman. In earlier times, to be considered a good rider of a bucking horse meant being a man who could handle, ride and "gentle" green, unbroken range horses in a manner that

216

left them with a good mouth, well-reined and generally suitable for practical ranch and range work. The rodeo rider of today needn't bother with such mundane considerations.

To launch the Medicine Hat stampede, a committee was struck to operate the annual event, which, as we shall see, was not always annual. Under the more professional management, Medicine Hat gained eminence as one of the top stops on the "B" fair exhibition circuit. It took until 1964 to achieve that high standard.

Considered the fourth largest rodeo in Canada, with more than $20,000 in prize money, the three-day stampede event in Medicine Hat in mid-July attracts top performers from throughout North America. An Exhibition, Horse Show and 4-H Exhibits start on the Monday. The event is now held on the grounds that once was home to thousands of prisoners during the Second World War.

While it had many ups and downs during its early history, the Stampede got its rebirth shortly after the Second World War was over. Mayor William MacKenzie approached Colonel Dirk Scholten and asked him to devise an attraction that would unite the citizens of the entire area. Scholten had been Overseas during the war and had settled in Medicine Hat where he became a successful businessman and City Alderman. The idea was that the right venture would enhance the community and cement good relations between all residents.

Scholten called a meeting of interested persons. Fifty turned out to invest $100 each of their own money to form the non-profit Medicine Hat Exhibition and Stampede Company Limited.

Scholten then contacted world-famous rodeo performer-turned-rancher, Herman Linder of Cardston, Alberta to obtain his advice about construction of bleachers, arena, holding pens and catch pens. A member of the American Cowboy Hall of Fame, Linder also accepted the job of arena director for the first stampede to be held under the new management.

Now that he had succeeded in getting the grounds set up, Scholten

217

Pancake breakfast, Medicine Hat downtown, Stampede Week.

Everybody loves a parade! The Exhibition
and Stampede parade is comparable to any
in medium-sized cities in North America.
Photo courtesy City of Medicine Hat.

went in search of a midway operator, aware that a popular exhibition and
stampede must also have a good selection of rides and attractions for young
and old. He contacted an Eastern man who agreed to bring his show to
Medicine Hat. Scholten was dusgusted when the troupe arrived. The
"show" consisted of a few broken-down rides and about 20 women of
various ages. They were referred to as fortune tellers, but the directors of the
Stampede had other names for them.

Scholten told the man his band of "gypsies" would not fit the bill for
family entertainment and bade them farewell. He turned to the task of
acquiring good bucking horses and other stock. Meanwhile, the "gypsies"
set up camp on the stampede grounds. No amount of cajoling or threats
would budge them.

While Scholten continued his search for a bona fide attraction for the
midway, a group of cowboys mounted up for a stampede of their own. It was
never revealed who these cowboys were or who gave them their assign-
ment, but with lassos swinging, the shouting riders swooped down on the
gypsy camp. Tents and occupants went flying in all directions. When the
dust settled, the vigilantes were gone and so were the gypsies. Nothing was
heard of the "fortune-tellers" again.

Despite its shaky beginning, the Stampede of 1947 was a rousing
success and today, with 30 directors and 70 associate directors on the
board and Ralph Murray as manager working year-round, the Medicine Hat
Exhibition and Stampede is enjoying more success than it has in years.

The Stampede received an award from the Canadian Association of
Exhibitions as Regional Fair Of The Year. It is the highest award a regional
fair can receive.

A number of events have added to its popularity: pony chuckwagon
and chariot contests and a 4-H calf sale. A mammoth parade on Thursday
kicks things off. The introduction of horse racing forced the chuckwagon and
chariot attractions off the program for one year until the board of directors
bowed to community pressure to restore them.

218

Pony Chariot Races at the Medicine Hat Stampede prove popular evening attractions. (Photo courtesy Garth McCorkle, McCorkle Studios)

One "performer" did not return after her first appearance. It seems a young woman was retained by the Board in the early 50s to remain in a cage stationed 50 feet above the ground on a pole beside City Hall. Her duty, while thus suspended, was to phone every household in the city and ask residents to attend the Stampede. She lasted two weeks at this unique employment, according to an article in the July 30, 1977 *Medicine Hat News*. Firemen attended to her daily needs by climbing up to her canvas shelter. One morning the ladder slipped and two firemen fell to the pavement, one of them breaking his heels.

Although such gimmicks have not been used for some time, the financial status and popularity of the Stampede has continued to increase. If there are complaints, they come mainly from oldtimers who object to the impersonal attitude of the latest crop of competitors. The story is the same across the continent wherever major rodeos are held. Whereas in the old days the competitors were mostly homegrown boys competing against each other — neighbors watching — for meagre rewards such as belt buckles or saddles, today's events are computerized, with strangers competing with strangers for the right to substantial prize money.

Early in 1980 a $1.2 million grandstand was completed. The 2,500 person facility included a kitchen/cafeteria complex with seating for 150. Under construction was a multi-purpose pavilion for conventions, athletic events and exhibitions. A 36 stall horse barn was also underway on the site.

While competition has always been hot in the arenas and corrals in Medicine Hat district, there never has been a shortage of action elsewhere on the sports entertainment field. By the time the North West Territories had become the provinces of Alberta and Saskatchewan in 1905, there were a number of first class hockey, baseball and lacrosse teams already in operation. Horse racing — as noted — was popular, and even some polo was being played, along with cricket and other sports imported from England.

The lacrosse club was formed as early as 1892 with W. J. Finlay as president. In 1896 a hockey team from Medicine Hat went to Calgary to win a championship. A golf club was organized in 1899 and in 1901 a contract was let for construction of a hockey rink. The rink, 150 feet by 66 feet was located opposite the hospital and had a curling rink on the east side.

219

Medicine Hat Cricket Club, North West Territories Champs in 1886.

Curling — A Medicine Hat sport since 1884, when first games were played on the frozen South Saskatchewan River. Shown here, early champions with their trophy. Left to right: Mayor Brown, W. B. (Billy) Finlay, Thomas Allan, George Pingle.

The Ed Lukowich curling team from Medicine Hat won the Canadian Brier in 1978 and represented Canada in March of that year at the Silver Broom World Curling Championship in Winnipeg. They made a creditable showing but were eliminated in the semi-finals by Norway. Other members of the team were Mike Chernoff, Dale Johnson and Ron Schindle. Curling has always been popular in the city.

Professional baseball enjoyed two periods of support, the first from 1907 to 1910 and the second from 1912 until the First World War began. The Monarchs ball club was formed with local talent but after the First World War some players were imported from the United States to compete with teams in Alberta and Saskatchewan.

Names of the players on the first professional ball club in 1907 included Hopkins, Hamilton, Tolman, Perry, Lurlage, Boyland, West, Benny, Works, Frieschel, Hollis and Fox. The calibre of play was high and some

A game of cricket being enjoyed in Medicine Hat Ball Park, Riverside, January 1, 1913.

220

Medicine Hat Athletes were active in many sports as the seasons changed. Probably because of the small population, there was an overlap in various sports. Some of this group as a Lacrosse Team from Medicine Hat in Calgary, in 1924, were also active in hockey, football, field sports and baseball, etc. (Mayor Bullivant in centre of photo in overcoat and hat.)

Jack Bellamy of Medicine Hat baseball fame.

players went on to compete for Calgary, Saskatoon, Edmonton, Regina and Winnipeg clubs. The Monarchs played as far afield as Spokane, Washington, and Winnipeg. In 1920 the Monarchs compiled a remarkable record of 30 straight wins.

Players performing with the Monarchs during that period included Al Smeaton, Milt Cory, Harlan ("Hop") Yuill, Jack Bellamy, Lloyd Bracken, J. Pennington, Norm Trimble, Bill Mulholland, "Speed" Wilson, Harry O'Neill, Frank Lewis, Jack Clark, Jack Carpenter, H. Green, Jack Rogers, "Swog" Cory, Laurie Scott, Bob Lussier and Bill Strothers.

James Fleming's name always comes up when the talk turns to professional baseball in Medicine Hat during the early days. Fleming had played professional ball in Minnesota and Illinois before marrying Hattie Auger of Maple Creek and settling in Medicine Hat in 1896. He bought the American Hotel in 1900 and operated it until prohibition arrived in 1916.

Fleming's hobbies were baseball, curling and hunting and he gave generous financial support to many community projects. He is credited, along with William Cousins, as being responsible for Medicine Hat having a team in the Western Canada Baseball League. Messers Fleming and

Medicine Hat Monarch Baseball Team, Alberta Champions, 1919-20.

Cousins were also involved in establishing the old Athletic Park on Riverside, where for many years football, baseball, field sports and bucking horse contests were held. Along with Bill Finlay, Fleming formed the first midget baseball teams in Medicine Hat.

The Rotary Club sponsored junior baseball in 1920 and intermediate ball in 1921. Governor General Byng officiated at a game and in 1925 the local team was named the Byngs in his honor. In 1924 an industrial baseball league was formed and operated on a diamond on Industrial and Allowance Avenues.

SENIOR CHAMPIONS SOUTHERN ALBERTA 1923
MEDICINE HAT
ALBERTA AMATEUR BASEBALL ASSOCIATION

Senior Baseball Champions, Medicine Hat, 1923.

The CPR club and the Royals were formed and in 1934 John Read organized a semi-pro league with the Royals competing against Calgary and Lethbridge. Prior to the Second World War some keen games were played between local teams and others from Taber, Lethbridge, Picture Butte and Saskatchewan points.

Less successful was the attempt in 1951 to transplant a California team to Medicine Hat as part of the Western Canada League. Wet weather and poor attendance at games led to its early demise. Owner-manager of these Monarchs was "Brick" Swegle.

The current membership in the Pioneer League, a Toronto Blue Jays farm operation, keeps Medicine Hat fans part of the baseball scene in Canada.

Tennis was a favorite in early Medicine Hat, and the game is still enjoyed as a major sport. There are City-owned courts in the South West

Hill area and in the Flats area. Sol Prasow was a junior player of championship calibre in the 30s, as were the Pritchard boys in the late 60s. And at one time lawn bowling was a big draw in the city. Between 30 and 40 teams belonged to the Medicine Hat Bowling Green Association which had Mayor Walter Huckvale as its Honorary President and C. S. Pingle as Honorary Vice-President. President was J. W. Wright, Vice-President H. Noble, Secretary-Treasurer W. C. Wade. On the executive were W. Morrison, W. D. Cousley, Chief Bill Hatcher, C. W. Twaites, C. Middleton and E. Jameson.

As well as bowling on the greens, golf was, and is, high on the interest list. Few communities the size of Medicine Hat boast two 18-hole golf courses. A typical tournament between the ladies from the Golf and Country Club and the Municipal Club took place in June 1932 and reports of the event were prominent in the sport pages of the *Daily News*. (Country Club defeated Municipal by 11 to 7.)

The Connaught Golf Club house renovations, which cost $542,000, were completed in 1980. The Medicine Hat Golf Clubhouse burned down and was rebuilt about the same time.

Hockey in Medicine Hat, as elsewhere in Canada, remains the sentimental favorite when it comes to sports. The first hockey began in the area on the frozen South Saskatchewan and creeks. Despite a short season, interest developed rapidly. The settlers from the east brought their love of the game with them and were not long in setting up exhibition games outdoors. It wasn't until 1901, however, that a large rink was built on Second Street opposite the old hospital.

This building remained in use for many years, and not just for hockey. During the summer it served as an assembly hall for political meetings and even when it was hockey season, community skating and band concerts were frequently held there when no games were being played.

The CPR Lawn Bowling Club. The Club was located east of the railway tracks by the Second Street Railway crossing. The members consisted of CPR employees and their wives and families. There was some afternoon bowling but usually it was in the evenings. Left to right are Mrs. Albert Worsley, Mrs. Harry Cove, Mrs. Arthur Foulston, Mrs. William Gallagher, Mrs. Thomas Samson. The ladies were in Vancouver for a tournament in August, 1938.

Medicine Hat Arena Gardens, corner Fourth St. and Fifth Avenue. Built 1923, destroyed by fire 1932 and rebuilt the same year but again destroyed by fire in 1969. The original home of the Monarch Hockey Team.

A new rink was built in 1912 but much hockey in the district was still being played outdoors. Records show that a large crowd gathered at an open rink in Redcliff one winter evening in 1913 when the temperature dropped to 48 degrees below zero.

Junior and intermediate hockey flourished before the First World War with some of the local players including J. Fallow, D. Cottery, W. Porter, L.

223

Smith, M. Cory, R. Wilson and P. Smith. Local junior hockey received a boost in professionalism in 1918 when Joseph Harlan "Hop" Yuill returned to Medicine Hat after spending three years with St. Andrews of the Ontario Junior Hockey Association. Other junior stars active in the city at that time included Wilf and Stan Knight, Barney and Bill Mason and Chuck Morris.

Many of the outstanding junior players graduated to the Medicine Hat Monarchs, another Monarchs club, not be be confused with the baseball team of the same name. This team developed into a powerful unit, capturing the championship of the Alberta-Saskatchewan Hockey League in 1925-26. Members of the championship team included W. Woodhouse, G. Bond, G. Teel, R. McKay, M. Crawford, T. Knight, W. Knight, W. Shinbein, K. Horne, J. Scott, J. Rattray and E. Holley. Management was V. W. Parrish, president, C. G. Murphy, secretary-treasurer, B. W. Bellamy, vice-president and H. Scott, manager.

Probably the best-known local hockey star of the time was Wilf Knight who was active for 21 years in leagues in Medicine Hat, starting as a

Medicine Hat Monarchs, Hockey Champions in any league.

member of the Connaught School team and winding up as star defenceman with the Monarchs.

"Stonewall" Knight finished every game he started during his career and not once was he knocked out or did he suffer a serious injury. And in those days the game was even more rugged than that played today. Players were on the ice for 50 minutes or more at a time.

Knight told a *Medicine Hat News* reporter in June 1967 that he was never considered a candidate as most popular player by the opposition team's fans. "I remember one game in Blairmore," he said, "When I handed out a crushing body check to the star centre of the Blairmore team. The police had to protect me so I could get off the ice."

Fans threw pieces of coal at him while a crowd of about 50 women waited for him outside the dressingroom. They were armed with hockey sticks and other weapons. "The only way I was able to leave the arena was to crawl out the window in the dressingroom," he said. "And I was in such a hurry I didn't even take off my skates!"

Robert Joseph Lauder is another name associated with the famous Monarch hockey team. He was the trainer for the intermediate team when they became Provincial champions in 1927-28. A professional wrestler, Lauder also took a keen interest in boxing, hockey and soccer. The Lauder family contained four families in one, so it was a lively household. When his first wife died, Robert was left with four children and when his brother Henry was killed in the First World War he adopted three orphans from that family. Robert then married Agnes Lauder, widow of his brother Jim, who had two daughters. Robert and Agnes had three children of their own.

The Lauder home was filled with trophies, signifying a sports-active family. Billy Lauder, brother of Robert Joseph, was lightweight boxing champion of Canada for six years. Billy started a sign-posting business in Medicine Hat and for many years operated a gym where he taught boxing in his spare time.

Another of the stars of the Monarch team was "Peewee" Lyons who later advanced to the National Hockey League where he played for the Boston Bruins.

During the 1930s a City League was formed with teams representing Alexandra High School, the CPR, the Canadian Legion and the Argos. Junior hockey continued to be played through the years with Bill Hunter and Fred Gibbs investing considerable effort in promoting the Medicine Hat Tigers before that club ran into financial difficulties and had to disband.

The original Medicine Hat Junior Tigers hockey team was made up entirely of local boys. They learned their hockey on school teams and on outdoor rinks such as Gray's. They played most of their competition games in the early 1930s in the old Arena on the corner of Fifth Avenue and Fourth Street. Ted Gray, Joe Smythe, Don Emery, Albert McDougall, George Appleton, Bill Gray, Clint Larder, Jack Moody, Norm Bannan, Roland Cook and Frank Bennett made up the Tigers team. They were the Southern Alberta champions and Provincial finalists in 1936-37. Chris Jeffries, local restaurant owner who helped them financially many times, was president of the club. Coach was Ross McKay of the early Monarch hockey team.

In later years the Medicine Hat Tigers became a farm team for the

Chris Jeffries, who came from Greece in 1912 and finished his schooling here. In 1926 he opened a fruit and confectionery business and promoted local sports.

225

Chris Jeffries, Chas. W. Pattison, Nick
Chacaleas. Jack McDougal, Fred Lait, Ed.
Holley, Ross McKay, Howard Teel. Kenny
Gray, Tommy Charles, Norman Wood, Karl
Kettler.

Medicine Hat Callies Football Club, 1927-28.

majors and very few local men were involved. In 1972-73 the Tigers were owned by three local promoters, Joe Fisher (a local boy who made the pros, playing for Detroit Red Wings), Rod Carry and George Maser. Their home ice is the large new Arena built on the Flats close to the river a few years ago. The Tigers were Western Canadian Champions in 1972-73 as members of the Western Hockey League. The represented Western Canada in the Memorial Cup finals in Toronto.

The Medicine Hat Cantalinis were active in intermediate hockey in the city for over a decade and captured the Intermediate A championship in the 1956-57 season. Members of the championship team included Vic Link, Jim Baird, Lloyd Pudwell, Alvin Besplug, Phil Stach, Bud Kornelson, Lorne Baumback, Don Smith, Lou Ramstead, Jim Crawford, Bill McCully, Grant Hall, Ron Craven, Bill Chicalias, Ron Mach, Jack Irving and Don Vogan.

The Carson Creek Rats, the Pucksters and the Gray and Foulston rinks never caused a great deal of excitement outside of Medicine Hat but they take their place in the affections of members of the community.

Mrs. E. M. Helgeson recounted for the author the effort the Carson Creek Rats (or the Carson Grocers) put forth for Canada's national game and its preservation as a community sport.

From 1933 to 1939 the Rats made use of Seven Persons Creek, which runs through the valley of Medicine Hat on its way to the South Saskatchewan River. The determined young men dammed the creek west of Shannon Bridge using shovels, wheelbarrows and muscle. Each year the dam was washed away with the spring runoff. In the fall the boys would be back working like beavers rebuilding the dam so they could have a skating rink.

At first they flooded the ice by utilizing a bucket brigade. They dug a hole in the ice above the rink, filled buckets and barrels with water, placed them on hand-drawn sleighs and dragged the sleighs down to the rink where the water was dumped. For some time Shannon Brothers, who operate a motel 100 yards from the creek rink site, loaned the boys a manual pump until they were able to obtain water from Dederer's Mill, located across the tracks.

The boys borrowed garden hoses to transport water across the tracks and on more than one occasion a hose was cut in sections by passing trains. The term of usefulness of the hoses was considerably extended after the Rats took to passing them under the tracks.

A shack was built in which to keep warm and put on hockey gear. It was built on the south side of the creek from railway ties and slabs. Edward Gargett donated a large pot-bellied stove which kept the boys occupied hauling scrap wood and coal to feed it.

Money was scarce during the Depression but the boys scraped up enough to buy one ton of coal and also collected more by hauling it from the old Ajax coal mine (located about six miles from the city. It was originally the Swan or Swanny Mine, and prior to that the Ansley Coal Company mine). The shack was lit with a coal oil lamp until Benny McLean obtained enough signatures on a petition to convince the City to supply the rink with three electric lights.

To pay expenses, some of the boys swept out boxcars at the flour mills and sold the wheat and chaff to neighbors who had cows, chickens, geese,

Not to be outdone, young women were on the sports scene. The Hub softball team, with a little help from their (male) friends are: B. Holmes, H. Leitert, B. Cooper, J. Foulston, J. Blair, E. Foulston, Y. Everett, H. Townsend, N. Phillips, B. Scott, G. Hutchison. Sue Banning supplied this 1940 photograph.

227

George Carson, with wife and son, as they appeared in a Christmas card photo. Carson was the sponsor of the "Creek Rats."

pigeons, rabbits and pigs. Charles Peasley and Ross McKay, then teachers at Elm Street School, gave cash donations, as did a Mr. Eck from Alberta Clay Products.

The boys' first goal pads were homemade and stuffed with straw. The goal nets were constructed of pipe and gunnysacks. Shin pads were magazines held in place by rubber bands cut from discarded inner tubes. Pieces of old tires were used for shoulder and knee pads. Chris Jeffries loaned the boys sweaters that once belonged to the Tigers so the Rats could look reasonably professional when they played other teams. Then George Carson entered the picture. The general store owner sponsored the team, bought the boys sweaters of their own and from then on the Creek Rats were known as either Carson Creek Rats or Carson's Grocers. The Rats played against Maple Creek, Ogilvie Grahams and Gray's Bombers. They won the Commercial League championship five years straight.

The Carsons also played baseball in the City League which was made up of seven teams: Carsons, Heralds, Assiniboias, The Hub, Medaltas, Five Roses and CPR.

The shack on the creek remained home base and the boys maintained strict rules: a member had to be at least 16 years old and pay dues of 10 cents a week; skating parties were held at a cost of 25 cents each with sisters, mothers and girlfriends supplying cake and cookies. Mixed skating took place on the rink on Sunday afternoons and when no games were being played. Young and old frequented the ice the boys had created. They came from the Flats, Dunmore Hill and Riverside to skate and watch the fun.

Working on the dam. (Left to Right) Phil Gendron, Ed Plotsky, J. Gargett, Alf Smith, Bob McCulley.

Winter was fun elsewhere too. Mrs. Helgeson recalls a winter carnival "of sorts" was held at the Arena. Mary McCulley, in a Carsons' sweater, entered a speed race of four laps around the Arena. She won a pair of silk stockings. Jack Leitert, also in Carson colors, entered two races: a speed race of 11 laps and an obstacle race. He won both and became the proud possessor of a leather belt, *and* suspenders.

When they held a skating party, Mrs. McCulley made the coffee and boiled water for the hotdogs. Mrs. Gargett baked dozens of tarts. "Sometimes they had a wind-up gramaphone on the ice playing records," Mrs.

Helgeson said. "One night it was 50 below and the oil in the gramaphone got so stiff the music stopped. The shack was bursting at the seams that night because nobody could skate around the rink more than twice without coming in to get warm."

While the Creek Rats were busy in their area of the city there was another outdoor arena being taken care of during the winter by a family named Gray. William Gray and his wife had seven sons and one daughter and they built a skating and hockey ice surface adjacent to their home at number eight Aberdeen Street in the South East hill area. The outdoor rink was 190 feet long and 96 feet wide, was enclosed by a four foot high wooden fence and lit by 25 light bulbs so activities could continue every evening, seven days a week.

On the rink. *Back Row*: (Left to Right) Johnny Nittel, Frank Stewart, Jack Leitert, Oliver Nikiel, Alf Mew, Walt Gargett. *Front Row*: (Left to Right) Sam Weiss, Rasty Rudolph, John Gargett, Arch Naismith, George Deans.

Creek Rats. *Back Row*: (Left to Right) Walt Gargett, Oliver Nikiel, Johnny Nittel, Alf Mew, Jack Leitert, George Deans. *Front Row*: (Left to Right) Sam Weiss, John Gargett, Arch Naismith. 1938 was the year.

The lots used for the rink (except 25 feet of their own lot) were leased from the city. Grays provided heated change houses and operated every winter from 1929 to 1940. The ice surface was used for hockey games, hockey practice and skating. Sunday and weekday skating was popular, with loudspeaker music provided by Mrs. Gray from her livingroom.

Midget and Juvenile hockey was catered to and the players on the original Tigers of 1936 were all boys who started and improved their hockey experience at Gray's rink. The Gray boys were good players; father Gray was a great promoter of amateur hockey. The whole rink was operated on a "donation at the gate" basis; it is doubtful that any profit was made, but the Grays provided a wonderful service to that area of the city.

The Gray boys, Kenny, Dick and Bill became players on senior teams. Kenny was killed in the Second World War. Dick Gray, as manager, trainer and coach of the Lethbridge Maple Leafs, took his team Overseas where they won the World's Amateur Hockey Championships in the 1951-52 season.

The Rats and Gray's rinks weren't the only places in town where there was action. In the 1930s the Foulston skating rink at the corner of Braemar Street and Allowance Avenue was a postage stamp in comparison to the arenas of today. However, what it lacked in size (30 feet by 40 feet) it made up for in the enjoyment and entertainment it provided.

The Foulston Rink, with shack in background, as it appeared in 1937. Eager for the winter scene are an unidentified group of youngsters.

The rink was built by young men of the district who were in their late teens or early twenties: Jim and Ray Foulston, Mike Luten, Stan and Larry Townsend, Ray Laing, Eric Harvey, Don and Bev Bray, and others. Building the rink consisted of banking the edges and flooding the area by hand, the latter a tedious job that had to be done all winter — as did the removal of snow.

The rink was patronized by kids of all ages who lived on the "Flats" — from First Street to Elm Street. Alderman Ernie Warham, who lived on Braemar Street, arranged to have the city install a light in the back lane just for the rink. A building at the back of the lot was fixed up with an old wood stove and some benches and was used for putting on skates, and on the colder nights, some feet were warmed before it. In February 1981 Sue Banning told the author that the "girls tried — and sometimes succeeded — in getting the boys to rub their cold feet. Some nights there would be spontaneous entertainment in the shack. Mouth organs were very popular and most of the boys had at least one. One of the boys was good at playing the saw. As with any gathering of a number of young people, there was many a squabble, many a romance, some of which ended in marriage, and some in heartache. But there was always a lot of fun."

The "Pucksters" in the 1936-37 season. Some of the players are identified: Ray Laing, Ray Foulston, Stan Townsend, Larry Townsend, Mike Luten, Jim Foulston.

A team was finally formed from among the skaters. Someone donated sweaters with the letter P, so the boys called themselves the Pucksters. The rink was so small they went down to the creek to practice for games.

"New Year's Eve was a special night at the rink," Sue Banning recalled. "Anything that would make noise was used at midnight, old washtubs, bells, whistles. There would be singing and laughing, saw playing, mouth organs. The great moment would arrive and the New Year would be brought in with a bang!"

"Those were simpler, happier times," Mrs. Helgeson agreed. "Looking back one can see how very dull our lives would have been during the hard times but for the energy and drive of those young men and women. Without alcohol or drugs of any kind, they gave us all something to do and something wonderful to remember.

"And, the boys always tightened the girls' skates. In those days, women must have been a little special."

Outdoor skating rink at night in "simpler, happier times." Rink for the "Rats" in 1938. Photo supplied by Mrs. E. M. Helgeson.

The Medicine Hat General Hospital and
Lady Aberdeen Nurses' Home as they appeared in the days when Alberta was part of
the North West Territories.

18.
"A Trifling But Grateful Tribute" The Hospital & Nurses' Home

Sir Thomas Browne, who lived between 1605-1682, admitted he was not so much afraid of death as he was ashamed of it. "'Tis the very disgrace and ignominy of our natures that in a moment can so disfigure us that our nearest friends, wife and children stand afraid and stare at us," he wrote. It is small wonder that Sir Thomas counted the hospital "not as an inn and a place to live in, but a place to die in."

Poet Elizabeth Barrett Browning, who was born 200 years later than Sir Thomas, had a more charitable view of the healing wards: "How many desolate creatures on the earth have learnt the simple dues of fellowship and social comfort in a hospital."

For the pioneers flocking to the North West Territories in 1883 there was no hospital west of Winnipeg in which to either die or seek fellowship. It wasn't until 1889 when the Medicine Hat General Hospital opened that there was such an institution between Winnipeg and Vancouver. At that time there were about 250 people living in the city and only a few settlers in the

Stained glass window originally above ward doors in Medicine Hat General Hospital, 1889. When building was demolished, this window was saved and is now on display at Medicine Hat Museum. The CPR generously supported the hospital. Note the large letters CPR in background and names of CPR executives who supported the ward.

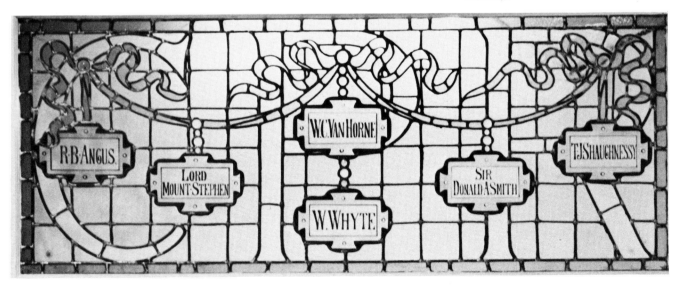

C.R. HOSMER MONTREAL.

W. SEWARD WEBB. M.D. NEW YORK.

C.H. CVMMINGS BOSTON.

Stained glass window originally above ward doors in Medicine Hat General Hospital, 1889. When building was demolished, this window was saved and is now on display in Medicine Hat Museum.

surrounding area. The cost of building a hospital, even one that had only 25 beds, was considerable.

Medicine Hatters, so original in other ways, used a unique method to raise some of the funds for their first hospital. As noted in a previous chapter, "Nancy" the bear was exhibited near the CPR station and those who came to watch her in her paddock had to throw a few coins into a receptacle for hospital-building purposes.

But that was still in the future. In 1888 an application was made to the Legislative Assembly of the North West Territories to incorporate the hospital and the following were named directors: J. M. Niblock, J. Horner, Rev. G. Lyon, M. Leonard, R. McCraig, S. Hayward, W. T. Finlay, William Cousins, Thomas Tweed, G. Noble, Rev. J. Herald, Rev. D. Garton, Sir John Lister-Kaye, L. Dobin and R. E. Starks.

Niblock, who was the superintendent of the CPR in Medicine Hat, was a major force behind the building of the hospital, served as president of the board for seven years and spent much time and effort raising money for construction and furnishings. The Medical Officer for the North West Mounted Police, a Dr. Bullock, also served as the first Medical Superintendent. He was succeeded by a Dr. Ballender and later by a Dr. Oliver.

When Dr. Oliver died of typhoid in 1901, Dr. J. G. Calder succeeded him as Medical Superintendent, having come to Medicine Hat in 1890 as surgeon for the CPR. Calder became well-known throughout the district. His was a familiar figure seen driving horse and buggy along the muddy streets and roads to his patients' homes. Many operations were performed by this frontier medic while his wife acted as anesthetist.

The city lays claim to many colorful doctors, not the least of which was Dr. C. F. Smith, another CPR medical man, who was the owner of the first automobile in town. A Maxwell touring model, red in color, it rattled along the town's rutted streets scaring horses and riders. As mentioned in a previous chapter, Dr. Smith also adapted an automobile to travel on CPR rails so he could cover his widespread practice.

First auto in Medicine Hat, 1905. A Maxwell, red in color. Owned by Dr. C. F. Smith. Dr. and Mrs. Smith and son and daughter. Note patched tire. Probably no spare tires available at this early date.

In the days when medicare was unknown, CPR employees were reasonably well cared for, especially when compared with what was available to the general populace. When Dr. Smith died in 1914 and Dr. F. W. Gershaw took over the CPR practice, workers received $1.25 a month for themselves and their families for medical costs, plus free drugs. The hospital charged $1.25 a day for a bed in the general ward. A fee of $15 was set for maternity cases.

The Canadian Pacific Railway was from the very first a great supporter of the Medicine Hat General Hospital. Wards were built from funds supplied by Sir William Van Horne, Sir Donald Smith, Lord Mount Stephen, W. Whyte, and T. J. Shaughnessy (all CPR executive officers). Acknowledgement was made by attaching a leaded glass panel over the ward doors on which the aforementioned names were worked in color over a background of the letters, C.P.R.

Another panel has the names C. R. Hosmer, Montreal, W. Seward Webb. M.D., New York, C. H. Cummings, Boston. These two panels were rescued from the building when it was dismantled and are now preserved in the Medicine Hat Museum with other artifacts from the old hospital.

But more about Nancy the bear. On September 5, 1893 a special meeting of the Hospital Board was held in Niblock's office to discuss the bear, which had been brought from Banff by some Indians who turned it over to James Hargrave. The plan was to exhibit the bear and appeal for funds for hospital construction. Messrs. Leonard, Jessel, Adsit, Crawford, Robertson, Cousins and Spencer were present. After the virtues and vices of the bear had been fully discussed it was decided to make a suitable cage for her which would be so arranged that no one could see her without paying a small fee.

Waxing poetic, the writer of the September 11, 1893 minutes described what transpired later: "The bear's life was in jeopardy for some time, owing to the anxiety for some for target practice, the gastronomic proclivities for others, the desire for warm clothing for others. Human councils finally prevailed and it was decided to build her a cage."

The bear, as noted earlier in the book, was known to have a quick temper and to be protective of her territory. She once escaped and on several occasions got in her licks at tormentors. She came to a sad end; she took ill and had to be "put to sleep."

Nancy's temper roughly matched that of one of the nursing staff. This is a quotation from the September 4, 1891 minutes of the Hospital Board after a complaint was made about the good woman's sharp tongue: "Allusion was made to the peculiar temper of one of the members of the nursing staff whose occasional displays were more human than angelic. As her strongmindedness serves as a powerful preventive against soft-hearted swains making love during convalescence and as no instance was cited when one of these displays of temper had disturbed the equilibrium of the nervous system of any patient, the matter was not deemed of sufficient importance for anything but a few mild comments."

View of the Medicine Hat General Hospital as it appeared in 1925 after alterations and additions were made to the original building, which was built in 1889. The building was torn down and replaced by a modern new hospital on the hill, overlooking the city. The old hospital site is now the location of Medicine Hat Police Office.

Good nurses were hard to come by in those days and training them on the job was deemed not only wise but cheaper than hiring a fully-trained graduate from "down East." The training school for nurses began in 1894 in Medicine Hat and has continued since that time. The first director of nursing was Grace Louise Reynolds who later married Dr. J. G. Calder. Miss Reynolds resigned her post in December 1891. One of her aides was Miss Mary Eleanor Birtles who wrote in May 1939 what life was like in the hospital in those times:

"There was no domestic help and Miss Reynolds and I managed the work between us; she prepared the meals and did the downstairs work while I attended to the furnace and did the upstairs work, sweeping, dusting, etc., besides attending to the patients. When any surgical work was to be done, we had to arrange the work accordingly. Miss Reynolds gave the anesthetic and I looked after the instruments and waited on the doctors. There was no sterilizer so we had to resort to boiling the instruments in a large saucepan with a steamer on it for towels and dressings." The two women were on call every hour, day and night.

In 1904 a nurses' home was built; a neat, comfortable, two-storey brick building with stone facings, it cost $6,813. Named for Queen Victoria, the first graduates from the school were Miss Jean Miller and Miss Gertrude Halls. The decision to name the nurses' home after Queen Victoria came after a report by board president W. T. Finlay in 1900.

Finlay said "that name which we often sang so sincerely that the King of Kings might truly bless, and whom we not only loved as a Sovereign, but looked up to as everything that was beautiful in womanhood . . . might we not, away in this western portion of Canada, pay a trifling but grateful tribute to so great and good a name by calling our nurses' home the Victoria Nurses' Home?"

Training in the school and living in residence meant living by the book of rules and regulations laid down by the board of directors, Medical Superintendent J. B. Peters and Lady Superintendent Miss A. C. Millar. There were three different sets of rules that had to be adhered to: First Division: a printed form of rules that came with the employment application and to which the nurse had to agree by her signature to conform; Second Division: "for the assistance and direction of the nurses in some of the routine duties in the wards; Third Division: which "related more generally to domestic arrangements and the good order and discipline of the school."

Postcard of the early days in Medicine Hat medical history shows (top) the General Hospital, (left) the Maternity Hospital and the Nurses' Home.

Any applicant between the ages of 25 and 35 would be considered, although a younger woman would be given a chance if she possessed "some special qualification." The applicant had to have a letter from a clergyman or "other responsible person" testifying to her good moral character, and another from a physician stating that she was in good health. "Women of superior education and cultivation, when equally qualified for nursing" would be preferred to those who "do not possess these advantages."

During the month of probation nurses were boarded at the expense of the hospital, but received no other compensation. They were given $10 a month the first year, $12 a month for the second year and third year, and those who completed the full course and passed the final exam "shall be entitled to receive $25 with their certificates."

A nurse was expected to perform her duties at the hospital and "when sent to private cases among the rich or poor in any part of the Territories" was not to receive any extra remuneration. If any was offered to her it had to be sanctioned by the Lady Superintendent because "their education is considered a full equivalent to remuneration."

Working hours for nurses was from seven in the morning till seven in the evening and for night nurses from seven in the evening to seven in the morning. Each nurse on day duty was allowed one hour in the afternoon for rest, besides meal times, plus an afternoon off each week and one-half of Sunday "except in emergencies." Two weeks' holidays were given at "such time as the Lady Superintendent in view of the requirements of the hospital may arrange." It was expected that nurses would attend the church of their choice every Sunday.

As well as looking after her spiritual life, the nurse had to stay healthy. She was to spend at least 15 minutes in the open air every day, to be punctual for meals and in her room at 10 o'clock, with lights out at 10:30. It was advised that every nurse get at least seven hours sleep a night and she was warned not to leave the hospital or the nurses' home before four o'clock without special permission. Any time lost at work, except through illness, had to be made up or it would be deducted from wages.

The nurse was instructed to cultivate a character of "steadiness, thoughtfulnes, modesty and tact which will justify confidence in those who may employ them . . . and reflect credit on them and the school."

Decorum maintained while on the wards was extended to the nurse's room as well: "Combings, refuse, eatables, match-ends, wastepaper, refuse of all kinds must be thrown into the waste basket and never into the slop jar." Closets and drawers were to be kept clean and old clothing ("such as old shoes, corsets, etc.") were to be discarded.

Aware that all work and no play makes for a dull nurse, the rules on socializing nevertheless had to be approved by the Lady Superintendent. Gentlemen were never allowed in the nurses' parlor without special permission. Lady visitors could enter the sitting room and the nurse's private quarters if her roommates approved.

The staff of the General Hospital. Front: C. E. Smyth, nurse Hales, nurse Andrews, nurse Miller, Medical Superintendent C. F. Smith. Back: H. McWhirter, nurse McCall, Lady Superintendent Miss A. C. Miller, nurse Poet, President J. Niblock.

238

Alfred E. Whiffin, who came to Medicine Hat from Manitoba in 1896, was on the Board of Trade and an active booster of the General Hospital. He was the instigator behind raising the funds to build the original nurses' home next to the hospital.

In 1895 a separate cottage hospital called the Lady Aberdeen Women's Hospital was constructed on hospital property for the special care of maternity cases. It was formally opened on August 11 of that year by Lieutenant Governor Mackintosh. The corner stone for the building was dedicated at a ceremony on October 11, 1894 by Lady Aberdeen, wife of the Governor General of Canada.

Hospital records show 408 patients were treated in 1900, while the number increased to 815 by 1907. During the year the City was incorporated a total of 94 babies, 52 girls and 42 boys, were born in the Lady Aberdeen. There were 31 deaths in the general hospital, five of whom died within 48 hours of admission: one was an "incurable"; one committed suicide and others were suffering from "incurable diseases on admittance."

The year 1907 was so active that a large tent had to be used to accommodate "appropriate cases." Doctors and nurses were called upon to treat a wide variety of illnesses, ranging from abscess of nasal septum to boils, cirrhosis of the liver, fractures and frost bite. Also "la grippe" and ingrown toenails. Two men recovered from gunshot wounds and there were patients who were given medical attention for ulcers of leg, lip, arm, shoulder, foot, neck, cornea and tongue. Two patients with "vomiting of pregnancy" recovered.

The patients suffering from anaemia (simple and pernicious), appendicitis (acute catarrhal or acute gangrenous), carbuncles, dysentery or beri beri were well cared for. So much so that in his report in 1907, J. K. Drinnan, president of the Hospital Board, proudly announced that during that whole year not a single complaint either from the public or patients had reached the Board.

To help keep the hospital in the black, donations "in kind" were accepted. The Cypress Club could always be counted upon for magazines of every description while dozens of fresh eggs came in from farmers for the use of the nursing staff. "A friend" in 1909 donated four dozen oranges and four pounds of biscuits for the women of the wards while the Women's Christian Temperance Union provided fresh cut flowers for the patients.

Mrs. Thomas Tweed gave six boxes of strawberries to the nurses while Mr. W. Martin donated two dozen beer. It was not mentioned whether these also went to the nurses or were for the patients. Mrs. R. Becker donated cucumbers for the nurses, Mrs. M. Leonard brought in pickles and ketchup and Mrs. R. Hardy a box of oranges for "the old men." Messers Endersby and Hamilton donated port wine while "Santa Claus" shared two boxes of oranges, one box of apples, figs and raisins and five pounds of chocolates. Mrs. E. M. Cawker gave a box of cigars and one of the Lodges gave three pipes and a shawl for the "incurables." The donor obviously did not specify what the patients were "incurable" of — perhaps pipe-smoking may have been one addiction.

By 1929 Medicine Hat had grown to become a community of 9,000 and still the only medical centre between Bow Island, Alberta and Piapot,

Saskatchewan. Hospital rates were two dollars a day and ranchers and farmers continued to pay their bills with produce whenever they could.

Pneumonia, known as the children's enemy and the old man's friend, was the chief cause of death in hospital with tuberculosis, polio and the traditional children's diseases close behind. Immunization against disease was not available, antibiotics did not appear until the Second World War and penicillin was not yet discovered. Patients with cancer or heart ailments quickly made arrangements with the undertaker.

Harry Yuill Sr. family home on First Street, Medicine Hat, next to Court House. An example of the many fine homes built in the early days. When vacated by the Yuill family it was used as offices for the Medicine Hat Health Unit. Eventually it was torn down.

Nurses were earning $40 a month (bed and board included), plaster was made in the hospital for casts and blood transfusions were a major operation with tubing connecting two patients if a donor could be found at the same time the patient needed the blood.

General anesthetic required ether. Mothers often died during childbirth at home. There was widespread use of midwives, although doctors still made house calls and were expected to do so. One of those who did, Dr. Wilfred C. Campbell, said the farthest he travelled for a house call was to a farm 29 kilometers south of Maple Creek. A woman had been reported to be in labor and when he arrived the baby was already born.

Another doctor reported that he drove his horse and buggy 20 miles to attend a rancher who had suffered from a fall. When he drove into the yard he saw the rancher back up on the barn roof resuming his shingling job. The farmers and ranchers joked that the reason they didn't get ill much was because they couldn't afford to and the doctors countered with stories about how they had successfully operated on many kitchen tables. "And," one said, a twinkle in his eye, "I've never lost a kitchen table yet."

In June of 1929 Wilfred Campbell arrived in the city hoping to "stay a while, make some money and leave to continue my studies." Within the year the stock market had crashed, the Great Depression had begun and Campbell found himself entrenched. Some 51 years later he was still here, a respected surgeon and community worker.

More than 200 people gathered at Medicine Hat College to honor Campbell, 75, as the city's 1979 Citizen of the Year. Dr. Campbell told the audience that having a good sense of humor had helped him through many

240

The medical staff at Medicine Hat General Hospital as of January 8, 1948. *Back*, (Left to Right): F. W. Gershaw, W. C. Campbell, J. S. Macleod, G. G. Elder, L. Lewis, D. S. Pattison, M. Davis, D. N. MacCharles. *Front* (Left to Right): E. D. MacCharles, B. C. Armstrong, H. C. Dixon, S. F. McEwen.

a bad time. He praised the Depression: "It had to be good to some people because it forced me to stay in Medicine Hat."

President of the Medical Arts Clinic at his retirement and originator of the Medicine Hat Red Cross blood donor clinics, Dr. Campbell was president of the Alberta College of Physicians and Surgeons in 1957, president of the Alberta Medical Association in 1960 and a president of the Medicine Hat Medical Society. Honored with Senior Membership in the Canadian Medical Association in 1970, Dr. Campbell said that doctors in the city have always been of the highest calibre.

Dr. Campbell was one of the early supporters of the Medical Arts Clinic. Also involved were doctors D. N. MacCharles, F. W. Gershaw, G. W. Elder and S. F. McEwen. The first clinic was located at 826 Second Street but later moved to 50 Sixth Street South East in 1958.

The previous year, on Wednesday, November 27, the Medicine Hat Municipal Hospital and Nurses' Residence perpetuated 68 years of hospital service in the city when Hospital District No. 69 celebrated the opening of a 260 bed hospital and a 100 bed nurses' residence. Ownership and management of the General Hospital was taken over by the City in 1948 from the public corporation that had operated it since its inception in 1888. In 1953 the Municipal Hospital District was formed, the old hospital condemned, and plans made for construction of new buildings. Actual construction began in 1955 with the foundation stone being laid by the Honorable J. J. Bowlen, Lieut-Governor, in September. Construction began on the new Nurses' Residence in 1956; a year later the old premises were abandoned.

Riverheights with the new Medicine Hat General Hospital in the top centre as it appeared from the air in 1981. Photograph was taken by Tom Willock.

At the opening ceremonies the Hospital Board was represented by Chairman J. Weldon Douglas and Directors Donald S. Hawthorne, Edward Sept and John A. Bell, City Alderman. David R. Broadfoot, Vice-Chairman, represented the Town of Redcliff, Emil Schneider the Town of Irvine, William Widdop the Municipal District of Forty-Mile No. 2 and Edwin Hermann, Improvement Districts No. 11 and 22.

At the time of opening, Miss Noreen Flanagan was Secretary-Administrator of the hospital and Miss Elizabeth Bietsch was Director of Nursing. Miss Marilyn Binns, President of the Student Nurses' Association, cut the ribbon to officially open the Nurses' Residence. Rev. D. J. Crawford dedicated the hospital building. Greetings were brought from the Provincial Government by MLAs Mrs. E. G. Robinson and Harry Strom and from the City by Mayor Harry Veiner.

At the time of the opening of the new hospital and nurses' residence it was thought that Medicine Hat was well provided with facilities for some time. However, in 1980 a $25 million plan for extended hospital facilities was well underway with work progressing on a $1,037,000 two-level parkade on hospital grounds. A new wing, plus ambulance adminstration and mechanical facilities were to be built.

In addition to modern hospital facilities and clinics, the City of Medicine Hat is blessed with nursing homes. In 1947 the Northern Conference of the Baptist Church in Canada established Haven of Rest in a building that originally accommodated flying students during the First World War. A new building is now home for more than 90 people.

The provincial government paid for the construction of the Cypress View Lodge which was opened October 1, 1960 by the Minister of Public Health. A good view of the city, the railway and the distant Cypress Hills is available from the lodge which has many lawns and flower beds for the enjoyment of residents and visitors.

On May 30, 1956, Bishop F. P. Carroll gave his blessing to St. Joseph's Home For The Aged on Riverside. Impressive as this building is, it is the building behind it that has the interesting history and which has a major significance in regard to the site upon which St. Joseph's stands. The house in question was a wedding gift from James Hargrave to his son Dr. Campbell Sissons Hargrave and his bride, the former Mary Jane Porter.

The newly-weds' residence was built adjacent to James Hargrave's own house which was demolished when the property was bought by the Presbyterian Church, first for a training school, then for the present Riverside Presbyterian Church.

Incidentally, James Hargrave donated a park and land up the Crescent Heights hill so the City could build a road.

SS City of Medicine Hat near the north shore of the South Saskatchewan River, 1907. The two houses that may be seen are the homes of James Hargrave, Sr. and his son, Dr. Jack Hargrave.

Doctor Hargrave's home was built of brick from the Brier Brick Plant, also on Riverside, but about three miles further west on Leonard Flats, along the river. The brick was of a very light red color, made from clay mined beside the plant in the cliffs below Redcliff.

It was this brick home and approximately one and one-quarter acres that was sold in 1951 by Dr. Hargrave's widow to the Carmelite Sisters who have lived in the house approximately from that date. The three-storey modern brick structure known as St. Joseph's Home was built in front of the house, completely hiding it from view from the front. The Sisters however still resided in the old Dr. Hargrave house but operated St. Joseph's Home and attended to their guests by entering the building from the home at the rear of St. Joseph's.

With its spacious grounds and proud towering trees, the setting is ideal for a home for the beloved aged of the City.

The Medicine Hat Museum displays the city's exciting heritage through exhibitions and artifacts of a proud past. The Art Gallery is a "Class A" gallery featuring exceptional touring exhibitions from around the world and also highlighting the efforts of talented artists at the local and provincial level. (Photos courtesy City of Medicine Hat)

19.

Welcome To The Club
A Short History of the
Arts and Organizations

Thomas Hobbes said it: "In a state of nature, no arts, no letters, no society. And, which is worst of all, continual fear and danger of violent death, and the life of man solitary, poor, nasty, brutish and short."

Almost from the start, Medicine Hat has been a community of diverse interests. For a settlement so far from so-called civilization, it soon established many clubs, organizations and societies devoted to music, the arts, charitable works and good fellowship. There was little reason for the life of man to be solitary, poor, nasty, brutish and short.

At least four major organizations were founded in Medicine Hat before the turn of the century: the Mason's Medicine Hat Lodge No. 2, the Loyal Orange Frontier Lodge 1549, Independent Order of Odd Fellows Lodge No. 3 and the Ladies' Aid to the Medicine Hat Hospital. Others followed shortly

J. L. Peacock was one of the first of the large-scale livestock dealers from the United States to invade Western Canada. He remained to farm and ranch in the Medicine Hat district and make hundreds of friends. The view shows his friends honoring him at a farewell reception at the Cypress Club, 1912.

after 1900, including the famous Cypress Club, Medicine Hat Rotary and the Women's Literary Society.

Dispensation for the Masonic Lodge was granted on June 16, 1885 when Medicine Hat was barely out of rompers. The first meeting to be held in the community of shacks and tents was in a hall located on the present site of the new Assiniboia Hotel, which was originally the Huckvale Block on the corner of Third and South Railway Streets, remodelled into a hotel. It was designated as Medicine Hat Lodge No. 31 in the District of Assiniboia, North West Territories, under the Grand Lodge of Manitoba. Original officers were Thomas McPherson, Silas Barry Yuill, Thomas Tweed and James Peter Mitchell.

In 1889 the Lodge was moved to a new hall on South Railway Street and was moved several more times before being installed in a building erected on Fourth Street in 1909. This building has since been demolished to make way for a highrise apartment block. The Lodge now occupy a building near the airport. In 1905, when Alberta became a Province, the Grand Lodge of Alberta was formed and the Medicine Hat chapter became Lodge No. 2.

Early entertainment consisted of "smokers" and formal dances or balls. The Lodge has continued to prosper and grow through the years.

A charter for the Loyal Orange Lodge was issued on June 24, 1885. Early officers of the Loyal Orange Institutions, which is an Irish society begun in the province of Ulster in 1795 to maintain Protestant ascendancy and named for William III of England, were W. B. Dempster, Roy Woollven and George Bainbridge.

The Independent Order of Odd Fellows was begun on June 5, 1889 with the first meeting being held in Colter's Hall on Third Street. In 1912 the IOOF hall was built where the Granada Apartments now stand. Later a hall was built in 1929 at the corner of Third Street and Fourth Avenue. This hall was demolished in 1979 and they now have a new hall on Crescent Heights.

The first officers in the IOOF were W. Crawford, E. S. White, A. McWayne, J. J. Reynolds, J. C. Colter, J. C. Clark, G. Seaton, T. C. Blatchford, M. Muir, J. Niblock, J. Young, G. Nicholson, J. K. Drinnan, S. S. Lloyd and W. Cousins. The Medicine Hat Lodge furnished a four-bed ward in the old General Hospital with its lodge emblem over the door. Members were admitted for $10 a week including board, medical attendance and nursing care. Other good deeds from the IOOF included a donation of chairs to the public library and funding for an eye bank.

Aram Encampment No. 5, a branch of the Odd Fellows started in 1919, has as its chief function assistance for crippled children. The IOOF also established lodges at Winnifred (1910), Redcliff (1912), Cypress (1913) and Hilda (1913).

When the original hospital was built in Medicine Hat in 1889 with a capacity of 25 beds, the Ladies' Aid was already formed and had been actively engaged in fund-raising for four years. Meetings were held in the city council chambers to discuss means to raise money for purchases such as hospital linen. A sewing committee within the Ladies' Aid kept the linen in a good state of repair.

The group disbanded during the 1930s but a similar association

246

became active during the Second World War years and in 1949 the Women's Auxiliary to the Medicine Hat General Hospital was formed. The original membership consisted of 97 women from various church organizations and service clubs, along with other interested volunteers. As the provincial government assumed more responsibility for maintenance of hospitals, the Auxiliary turned its efforts to volunteer services to the patients and additional recreational facilities for their benefit.

Mrs. W. Williamson, who came to Medicine Hat in 1895, is credited with founding the Women's Literary Society. The first meeting was held on November 26, 1906 after Mrs. Williamson attended a literary club meeting in a town near Boston. She was so impressed, she rushed home to try the idea out here. Other charter members were Waldock, Desbrisay, Morrow, Carbert, Hamilton, Hooper, McBean, Walker, Hawthorne, Sissons and Ransom. First names were not provided in the early minute books.

Unfortunately, the minute books for the period from 1906 to 1911 have been lost but it was in 1911 that members set to work to introduce a local library for the community and area. Here is an excerpt from the minute book of that day, March 19, 1911:

"Mr. W. C. Hay, superintendent of schools, was a speaker at our club and gave us a short talk on the advisability of procuring a public library in our city — not necessarily a building, but a reading room; also asked the club to appoint a member to draw up a committee which will be formed. The following resolution was drawn up at the home of Mrs. Fewings by Miss Fraser: 'We, the members of the Women's Literary feel that a public library would be a great benefit to the city and as a society we have felt the lack of a reference library in connection with our work.'

"The resolution was moved by Mrs. A. K. Miller and seconded by Mrs. R. C. Black. Mrs. Tweed was appointed to represent the club on the central committee."

The pioneers who took these three steps to establish a library in the city were not forgotten. On October 3, 1964 a beautiful new library, rivalling any similar facility in Western Canada, was opened at 414 First Street South East. The Dedication read: "Even as they laid the steel and broke the sod and brought civilization to the great plains, they kept alive a love of good books, an interest in good music and art, and a delight in good dialogue, all of which have become part of our cultural heritage. This building is dedicated in their honor."

Chairman of the Library Board of Trustees was George Davison while Barbara Whyte was Vice-Chairman on this momentous occasion. Also on the Board were Alderman Helen Beny Gibson, Edgar Elford, Lyle Flynn, and Fred McGuinness. Mayor Harry Veiner and Chief Librarian Phyllis Lapworth were in attendance when the official ribbon was cut and the plaque unveiled by Thomas Tweed.

This historic event reminded some guests of 1912 when a Mr. Hazard became the first man in charge of the library, which had been established in the Huckvale Block. From 1919 to 1929, under the guidance of H. Warner, the library was moved four times, all within a one block radius, finally coming to rest at 302 South Railway Street (the old Bank of Montreal building) where it remained until 1964. H. Burbidge was Chief Librarian from 1934 to 1948 when Robert Block assumed control. Land was purchased for the site of the present modern building in 1960. The building opened with a collection of 55,000 books which has since been expanded to well over 100,000. When Phyllis Lapworth left the post of Chief Librarian, Robert Block returned to Medicine Hat to take up those duties again.

During its long history the Literary Club supported many other clubs and women's causes, including the Women's Christian Temperance Union's campaign for prohibition. After 38 years it withdrew affiliation with the local Council of Women and decided not to have connections with outside organizations.

At the Society's 70th anniversary in 1976, Chief Librarian Bob Block praised the women of the Literary Club for their efforts in helping establish a library in the city. Special guest was Minister of Culture Horst Schmid who commended the members for carrying on the traditions laid down by their predecessors.

In May 1980 Ida Scanlan was honored for her 12 years as children's librarian and the Library Board announced the establishment of a scholarship in her name to be awarded to a Medicine Hat resident wanting to study library science anywhere in Canada.

For many years Ida Scanlan read children's stories on CHAT's Story Time on Sunday mornings. She also organized the Reading Club as another way to attract readers. Another Story Time was held in the library which grew so popular the Monarch Theatre had to be used to contain the audience.

The Cypress Club was chartered in 1903 as a social club with meetings held in a house acquired on Second Street across from the present City Hall. It was not until July 1907 that the contract to build the present Cypress Club was let to Oakes & Evered Contractors. The building probably was not completed until 1908.

Rooms were provided where ranchers could gather while in town for supplies. Another objective was to have a place where men from the country could meet men from the town to exchange ideas and to form economic bonds.

Charter members were F. L. Crawford, William Cousins, O. W. Kealey, F. O. Sissons, F. G. Forster, E. M. Cawker, C. R. Mitchell, A. C. Hawthorne, C. S. Pingle, D. G. White, D. Milne, E. J. Fewings, Thomas Tweed, James Fleming, F. F. Fatt, Dr. Holt and Dr. C. E. Smyth.

During the years 1925-26, 20 members of the Club were forced to resign. They did not at that time have the $30 for their annual dues.

Cypress Club members were active during the Depression, however, gathering funds to purchase clothing for the needy in the City who were on relief.

The Cypress Club is historically the oldest private club in Alberta and is still doing a flourishing business serving meals to members and guests and in continuing its original function of bringing together men from town and country. During the war years it was turned over to armed service personnel for their use.

The Medicine Hat Rotary Club held its first meeting in the old Assiniboia Hotel on April 2, 1918. The charter of affiliation with the International organization was dated June 1, 1918. First Rotary president was W. W. McNeely and the other first officers were L. McTavish, C. W. Rainbow and James Kellas.

On May 6, 1976 Dr. Leo Lewis published a short history of the Rotary Club of Medicine Hat in the local newspaper. As Lewis noted, the first president's tenure was short. McNeely died of influenza during the epidemic that began after the First World War was over. McNeely was succeeded by J. E. Davies.

The Rotary's first major accomplishment in community service was to assist in the establishment of a swimming hole in Seven Persons Creek known as Beaver Dam. An unfortunate event occurred when a youth was drowned and the need for a supervised pool was highlighted. A site was found at the corner of Fifth Avenue and Aberdeen Street where the concrete basement of a proposed vocational school was halted by the outbreak of the 1914 war. The basement became the nucleus of the first Rotary Club swimming pool.

In 1921 the local Rotary raised about $2,000 toward the purchase and installation of an elevator for the old general hospital. The two-storey structure also had a basement and patients frequently had to be carried in stretchers up and down flights of stairs.

(Richard Cecil Becker, who arrived in Medicine Hat shortly after he was born, was the principal sponsor behind the first elevator in the General Hospital. He served several terms as an alderman and as a director on the hospital board. Becker owned the AT Ranch on Ross Creek and built one of the early business blocks in the city.)

The annual Rotary Carnival was first held in 1921 in what was then the

Rotary Club Past Presidents, Medicine Hat. *Back Row*, (Left to Right): Fred Millican, Syd McEwen, George Davison, Gerald Grant, Art Finch, Bert Dempster, Willard Lutes, Rod Ray, Dick Dickson. *Front Row*, (Left to Right): Bert Marshall, Maurice Stone, W. A. Church, Jack Dempster, Nort Dowson, Roy Keating, Harry Hutchings.

Swimming in the South Saskatchewan River at Medicine Hat on south side of river, c. 1920. Swimming pools, indoor or outdoor, were not to appear in Medicine Hat for a few years yet. Cooling off in the river in the hot dry summers was the thing to do.

curling rink, a long low building that once stood on what is now the Health Unit parking lot. From the Carnival, and the Carnival Queen Contest which preceeded it, sufficient funds were raised to build the first modern swimming pool in the city, in Rotary Park, across the railroad tracks. Built in 1930, the pool was in use for many years until repairs became too costly. (Another 1930 event was the first boys' hobby show which was replaced 45 years later by the science fair at the College.)

In 1937 the Rotary Club contributed to a new pool two blocks from the original pool which was abandoned. The new site was Robertson Park, named for James Peter Robertson, the city's only Victoria Cross winner.

During the Depression, many active members had to withdraw because of declining fortunes but the club continued with a reduced membership, providing recreational facilities and helping to lighten the load for economically depressed residents of the community. In 1939 the club marked its 21st anniversary with the revelation that during its years of service it had raised about $100,000 for community work. In 1940 the club was given the No. 2 International Award for community service.

To commemorate their 50th Anniversary the Club provided the Sun Clock, designed and engineered by the Erickson Memorial Company of Denver, Colorado.

250

The dial, measuring six feet, nine inches long, six feet, three inches wide, six inches thick and weighing 3,450 pounds, is made of solid granite, carefully ground so that upper and lower surfaces are parallel. To follow the seasonal changes in the position of the sun, the upper side is carved to indicate "Sun Time" in spring and summer and the lower side to show "Sun Time" in fall and winter.

The Sun Clock was located on the lawn in front of the Medicine Hat Museum and the National Exhibition Centre on Bomford Crescent. At the time this book was written there was speculation that it may be moved to the area of the new City Hall and Cultural Centre which was then being planned. The Sun Clock has drawn attention from all over North America. In addition to many other services, Rotary has given scholarships, paid the expenses of a young citizen to visit Ottawa, furnished wards in the new municipal hospital, donated money to the Redcliff Recreation Centre and sponsored the Red Cross Water Safety Program.

Although not as old as the Rotary Club in Medicine Hat, the Kiwanis Clubs here have been involved in community service since the first club, now called the "Downtown Kiwanis", received its charter in 1924. The Charter president was Dr. W. H. MacDonald. The Gas City Kiwanis club received its charter in 1961 with Jim McCorkle as Charter President. A third club in the city, the Medalta Kiwanis Club, was chartered in 1978 with Dr. Larry Anderson as Charter President.

All three clubs are business and professional men's clubs dedicated to extending community service to everyone. The name "Kiwanis" comes from "Nun Keewanis", an Indian word which has been shortened and means "self-expression".

Services provided by the three clubs consist of rendering service to children with learning disabilities; providing medical, dental and optical care for under-privileged children; promoting amateur sports; presenting awards and scrolls, as well as financial assistance to District 4-H Clubs, scholarships to high school and college students; sponsoring of Key Clubs in the high schools; promoting Kiwanis Best Kept Block contests to encourage city beautification; providing entertainment for hospital shut-ins, the Handicapped Association, Senior Citizens and many others, by the Kiwanis Band.

The Kiwanis also provide improvements to Kiwanis Central Park and Kiwanis River Park and a facility to train pre-school children on street safety.

Funds are raised through an apple sale campaign, Stampede branding parties, auction sales of donated articles, casino operations and concession booths at air shows.

The Robertson Memorial Branch of the Canadian Legion has roots that go back to May 12, 1917 when the Sons Of England Lodge loaned its rooms to 15 men who had returned from service in the First World War. They formed the Great War Veterans' Association. Provisional officers were honorary president C. S. Pingle, president Mr. Harrop, secretary-treasurer Mr. Batty.

The purpose of the organization was to help returned men in every way possible and to provide a meeting place where war veterans and visitors could be entertained and enjoy companionship. In 1926 the Association

251

became the Medicine Hat branch of the British Empire Service League which eventually became the Royal Canadian Legion. In 1956 the Medicine Hat branch named its organization after James Peter Robertson, VC.

According to the May 1980 issue of *Legion*, the action that won Robertson the Victoria Cross took place on November 6, 1917 during the attack of Passchendaele, Belgium. The official report described Robertson's bravery: "For most conspicuous bravery and outstanding devotion in attack." The magazine said when Private Robertson's platoon was held up by barbed wire and machine gun fire, Robertson dashed to an opening in the flank, rushed the machine gun and, after "a desperate struggle with the crew", killed four of them. He then carried the captured machine gun, firing it at the fleeing enemy and "his gallant work enabled the platoon to advance."

According to the citation for the VC, Robertson's "courage and coolness cheered his comrades and inspired them to their finest efforts." But Robertson did not rest on his laurels. Later, when two Canadian snipers were lying badly wounded in front of his trench, Robertson crawled out and dragged the men to safety, one at a time. He was under severe fire continually. He was killed just as he returned with the second man.

Robertson was born in Pictou, Nova Scotia and moved to Medicine Hat as a child with his parents in 1899. He worked for the CPR as an engineer until early in 1915 when he joined the 13th Canadian Mounted Rifles in Lethbridge. He later transferred to the 27th Canadian Infantry Battalion while in Britain.

In a guest editorial in the *Royal Canadian Legion Bulletin*, Jack Oldham paid tribute to some of the men and women who helped make the local branch one of the most vital in the country. For service during the formative years, Oldham cited Jim Hallworth, District Commander and Vice-President, Jack Wright, first Secretary, and Teddy Jordan, one of the first Executive members. Each of these men had their names on the original charter of the branch.

He said Tom Samson, Ken Allen, Charles Richardson, Ernie Middleton and George Herman, First World War veterans, all played a vital role in the building of the organization.

Oldham pointed out that the branch's Ladies Auxiliary was the first in the Province of Alberta to be chartered and continued to be one of the most active. He praised the work of Mrs. Craven, Mrs. Carlisle and Mrs. Simpson.

The members of the War Veterans' Association first met above the old Foodland Store across from the CPR station but moved to its own club house in 1921. The building had been used as the Court House and was purchased from the Province for one dollar. The property on which the present building stands was purchased from the Government of Canada for $3,000. Frank Cooney was president at the time of the purchase. Part of the parking lot was originally occupied by the old Ronnenberg Blacksmith Shop. The buildings moved from the property to make room for the present buildings were from Police Point. They had been the guard house, stable and harness room for the Royal Northwest Mounted Police prior to the Legion purchasing the property.

Ranchers who donated beef and pork for distribution by the Legion to needy citizens during the Depression were — among others — Jack Halliwell, Jack Watkins, Dick Webster and Ernie Heald. Shortly after the First

World War the branch took on sponsorship of the Medicine Hat Pipe Band which had been formed with such members as Police Chief Joseph Mc-Queen, George McIntosh, Billy Williamson, Harry Mathews and Alex Hosie, as Pipe Major. In later years Hector Smith, Donald McGreggor, Peter Simpson and Sonny Collins, all artists in their own right, formed part of the Band.

Oldham saluted the local Legion for its services to the community through its Poppy Campaigns, Polio Campaigns and Poppy Services. Especially praised were former Presidents Jim Briggs, Art Carlisle, Walter Rooker, Fred Cutts, Ernie Hawes and Carman Jackson. "We have a reputation as the friendliest branch in Canada, and I feel rightly so," Oldham said.

Clubs and organizations, like the Great War Veterans' Association, come and go and, in many instances, change costumes after a few acts. How many Medicine Hatters recall the Medicine Hat Juvenile Operatic Society? Under the auspices of the Women's Hospital Aid Society the Operatic group staged "The Golden Whistle" in February of 1925, one of many such offerings to the public.

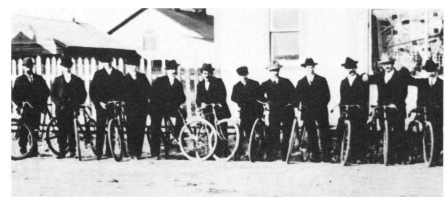

The young men of Medicine Hat (in about 1905, as near as can be determined) decided to ride their bicycles to Dunmore, a distance of about 7 miles, on New Year's day. Here they are photographed at Dunmore. Bicycles in those days had wooden rims but balloon tires they did not have.

The cast numbered more than 50, plus a backstage complement of managers, directors, costumers and musicians. "The Golden Whistle" was one of numerous semi-professional and professional entertainments produced in Medicine Hat in the heyday of light opera, musicals and drama in all forms.

A good-sized directory could be filled with the names of early thespians, men and women like John and Roderick Ashburner, Loraine Tweed, Katherine Spencer, Helen Spencer and Honor Currie. Another large cast presented "Two Crooks and a Lady" in the Empress Theatre on Friday, November 8, 1935. The same evening saw two more local efforts staged: "As The Tumbrils Pass" and "Good Medicine". These plays were produced by the Little Theatre Association of Medicine Hat.

As can be expected, people who took active roles in one association may have been involved with other groups as well. Actors in Medicine Hat were and are renowned for their adaptability.

Ron Miller has been an actor, director and playwright for nearly 40 years, starting at 14 years old when he played the butler in "Rebecca", by Daphne DeMaurier. He was 28 when he played James Dunbar, a prisoner of war in the play "Stalag 17" which became a Broadway and film hit. The Medicine Hat play was an entry in the Dominion Drama Festival.

Like many other Medicine Hat thespians, Miller played roles backstage as well as on stage. Winner of Best Supporting Actor Award in the Medicine Hat Drama Festival one year, he told reporter Sarah Jones in 1980 that "this city is doing more than others much larger in the area of amateur theatre, musical theatre, the touring company, Firehall, Lunchbox and the spring production of a dinner theatre."

Small wonder that theatre people in the city felt snubbed in 1960 when Calgary and Edmonton decided to ignore the Provincial Drama Festival which was held in Medicine Hat. Medicine Hat Civic Theatre had won the right to represent the province in the Dominion Drama Festival the previous year. Bruce Hogle, a former Medicine Hat reporter who became news director at CFRN-TV in Edmonton, deplored the attitude taken by the two large Alberta cities.

"The real reason was probably that Edmonton and Calgary have gone high hat," he editorialized. "As the Medicine Hat News suggests, it is due to affluence engendered as a result of having provincial auditoriums of such striking proportions."

Such a snub and the lack of Jubilee-style auditorium did not deter Medicine Hat from putting its best foot forward. The Medicine Hat Musical Theatre launched its first production in 1961 on money it had to borrow. "Oklahoma" hit the boards under the presidency of Henry Allergoth. The production was such a success that the theatre group was on good financial footing from then on. President John Dunlop announced a scholarship program to aid and promote advancement of young talent in the area with the recipients to attend Banff School of Fine Arts (now Banff Centre), drama workshops at Drumheller and Olds and scholarships at the annual Rotary Music Festival.

Richard Mells directed the Theatre's first three productions and after that Dorothy Jones, Adele Armstrong, John Komanchuk and others lent their talents to bring Medicine Hat audiences the best in professional musicals.

A native-born Medicine Hatter, Adele Armstrong has long been a mainstay of the arts in the city and the province. A graduate of Alexandra High School, Mrs. Armstrong was active in school music and drama programs with mentor J. R. Vallis and Henry Allergoth. She studied voice from Robert Bullen and Velva Brough and piano and organ with Isabel Novak.

Daughter of Reginald and Elizabeth (Owen) Havard, Mrs. Armstrong has to her credit many festival wins both locally and provincially and in one year captured top honors in all three division of the festival: vocal, piano and speech arts. She was church organist at Westminster United Church and for 20 years organist then organist and choir director at Fifth Avenue United Church. She formed the intermediate girls choir, the Teen Tones (described later).

Mrs. Armstrong performed on the famous Rococo Organ in the Oliwa Cathedral in Gdansk, Poland before more than 2,000 people. She formed the Saamis Singers, junior counterpart of the Teen Tones and the Adele Armstrong Singers, a senior community choir. All three choirs are local and Provincial winners at festivals.

A graduate of the Masters course in Kodaly from Wellesley College,

Boston with Distinction/Honors, Mrs. Armstrong is an executive member of the Alberta Choral Directors Association and has been Citizen of the Year (1974). She has also received the Queen's Commemorative Medal (1975), Alberta Achievement Award for Music (1979) and Quota Club Lady of Merit (1980).

Like the Medicine Hat Musical Theatre, Ralston Experimental Players also remained independent. The group of about 30 members staged two productions a year with every member involved somewhere. For example, president Mary Green said when Elsie Park Gowan's "Airman's Forty-Eight" was being produced, "we felt like a large family learning about the theatre together."

Versatile was the word used to describe the people who staged the various musical and dramatic events on and off stage in Medicine Hat. The same word can be applied to the programs. The Medicine Hat Little Symphony, as a typical example, had something for everyone. Consider the annual concert held at the Towne Theatre on Sunday, March 1961:

Conductor Robert Thompson put his musicians through their paces with the "Coronation March" by Meyerbeer, ballet music from "Rosamunde" by Schubert, "The Typewriter Song" by Leroy Anderson and the "Wee MacGreegor" or Highland Patrol, which signalled intermission. Included in the second half of the program were the Spanish Suite "Andalucia" by Ernesto Lecuona while guest artist Judy Armstrong ended the concert with a medley of Scottish and Irish folksongs.

One of the oldest and busiest performers in the Little Symphony was McLaren Ewart who played bassoon in that 1961 concert. Retired from a career with the CPR in 1954, Ewart moved back to Medicine Hat from Moose Jaw. He took up the violin in the orchestra. "This was in the days before the symphony was founded and received money from the government, so it didn't matter that I wasn't very good" he said modestly.

The City of Medicine Hat Band, c. 1910. Identified: Milt Cory, second left, top row. Bob Shaw, fourth left, top row. "Sing" Cope, first left, front row. "Tip" Volway, second left, front row. A. Scudder, third left, front row. J. Snider, Bandmaster, fifth left, front row.

McLaren Ewart

"We rehearsed in church basements, in the radio station and in the library. We used to give concerts quite regularly and we played some pretty demanding stuff." Ewart switched to bassoon at the conductor's request. "I went out and picked one up and taught myself to play. I quit the orchestra when it became the Medicine Hat Symphony because they had a good bassoon player available and there wasn't room for someone who wasn't as capable."

Ewart was also a member of the Elks Club Band and played bassoon for them until 1975 when he switched to clarinet. On his 91st birthday in 1980, McLaren Ewart said, "we don't stand on much ceremony in the Elks band, but we do have a good time."

Another veteran on the muscial scene is Joe Levinson who made major contributions to both the business and artistic communities since his arrival in the city in 1930. When he settled here he got involved with the CPR Tennis Club where he met his wife.

(Beatrice Levinson recalls having tea at the Tennis Club every Saturday where white clothing was de rigeur on the courts. The club operated until the Second World War after which the courts were turned into parking lots.)

With two other men, Joe Levinson founded the Rangers Athletic Club which ran for several years, supplying activities for men up to the age of 20. Membership reached 120 with lacrosse, hockey, soccer and baseball all being played. "One year we cleaned up at the Alberta Track and Field meet," Levinson recalled. "Another time, two of our boxers went to the Dominion finals in Winnipeg."

After marrying in 1937, Joe and Beatrice became involved in almost all facets of the arts in the city, including the Little Theatre.

"We used to run plays in the old Empress Theatre," he told Sarah Jones in August 1980. "When that was sold we moved into the auditorium of the library on the corner of Third Street and South Railway."

Levinson, a founder of the city's Allied Arts Council, eventually sold his fur business and turned his talent fulltime to running a music store. He ordered music for the Adele Armstrong Singers and the Medicine Hat Little Symphony. He sold the store on South Railway Street in 1975.

When that first production of "Oklahoma" was produced by the Musical Theatre, Levinsons were taking tickets at the front of the house. Still active in community affairs, Joe Levinson said at 72 years old, "this has been a great town to live in and we have never had a dull moment."

Membership in the Little Symphony Orchestra rose to around 25 in the mid-Fifties and regular performances were well-received. Toward the end of the Sixties interest waned and the orchestra disbanded. Then interest in classical music was renewed with the opening of the Medicine Hat College. It was decided that the city was large enough and musical tastes mature enough to support a full scale symphony orchestra. In 1972, under the leadership of Alex Shand, membership in a revived orchestra reached about 46. A Citizen Of The Year, Shand was recognized for his contribution to music in the community. In 1975 Larry Krantz assumed responsibility for conducting the orchestra in a regular season of five concerts featuring local and international guest artists. In 1981 Zdenek Kriz was conducting.

To satisfy music lovers' tastes for more exotic and international music fare, Overture Concerts have been featured for more than 20 years. The first such concert was held on April 28, 1959 and Overture official Noreen Flanagan recalled earlier days when the Celebrity Concerts were held here.

"The Celebrity Series began about 1946," she said. "We used to hold shows in the old Empress and then have receptions and parties afterwards. We had singers, musicians, dancers, all kinds of entertainment. It was lovely, now that I look back on it."

The series was run by the Beta Sigma Phi sorority and other service clubs in town. Miss Flanagan said when the concert schedule was being made up today it was different from when things were quieter in Medicine Hat. "Now we have to look out for hockey games, musical theatre and music festivals. There's so much going on in the city it's hard to fit it all in."

The same can be said for the art world in Medicine Hat. But it was as recent as 1945 when the first stirrings of an organized art club was felt. Helen Beny Gibson and Rev. L. T. H. Pearson, rector of St. Barnabas Anglican Church, attended the Banff School of Fine Arts that summer. They came home enthusiastic about the idea of forming an art club in Medicine Hat.

Arranged through Senator Donald Cameron at Banff School, an instructor was sent to Medicine Hat early in October that year to assist the 40 students who had enrolled in the 21 week course for a cost of eight dollars each.

As Mrs. Patricia Gordon wrote in her booklet commemorating the club's 20th anniversary in 1965, the students were fortunate to get H. G. Glyde, ARCA, as their first instructor and advisor. After being on the staff of the Institute of Technology in Calgary for many years Glyde had been appointed Professor of Art and head of the newly-formed Department of Fine Arts at the University of Alberta in Edmonton. Launched in the fall of 1945 in the city hall council chambers, Miss Marion Newman (later Mrs. Dan Jensen) took up her duties as Glyde's part-time instructor.

The first exhibition of work was held in the city hall on March 16, 1946; it consisted chiefly of paintings by the members as well as a small number of Mr. Glyde's own work. Over 300 people came to see this first exhibition.

Reverend Pearson was the Medicine Hat Community Art Association's first president. Mayor Hector Lang and Mrs. Lang consented to be patrons. Other members of the first executive were Mrs. Helen Beny Gibson, J. R. Vallis, Jack J. Barrie, J. M. Naismith, Mrs. D. S. Hawthorne and Mrs. Monica Bain. Assistant instructors who took over when Professor Glyde was not present were Mrs. Bain, Mrs. W. R. Clark, Miss Newman and Jack Barrie.

Over the years the Art Club has contributed to the cultural life in Medicine Hat in many ways: individual members have judged poster contests, painted stage sets, donated paintings for raffles and to public institutions, judged parade entries and Christmas decorations and helped to generate an enthusiasm and awareness of the importance of art to the community at large.

At present the "Hat Art Club" is actively carrying out their activities in an old downtown building provided by the City under the name "Arts Centre".

Besides painting and drawing the Arts Centre is providing working area and instruction in weaving, batik, silk screen, egg decorating and other expressions of art. The instructors included Donna MacLean, Nancy Ruth Sissons, Barbara Whyte, Isabel Sharp, Anne Shepherd, Anita Schmidt, Evelyn Kleis, Diana Campbell, Jack Barrie and many others who helped out from time to time.

The Club in 1981 was looking forward to construction of the City's new Cultural Centre which was expected to provide facilities of a modern nature.

Scouting as a recreational and spiritual pursuit for young men in Medicine Hat had its beginning as a boys' club sponsored by St. John's Church in 1910 under the leadership of J. Jessop Nott. Nott, a local undertaker, held the first meeting in his business establishment. Then, through the generosity of H. C. Yuill, the new club was provided with larger quarters at the rear of his residence, then opposite St. John's Church. The club house was completely furnished by Yuill for use by the boys.

Group of King Scouts of Medicine Hat just before leaving for Boy Scout Jamboree in England, date 1929. Identified (Left to Right): Fred Fisher, Stan Morris, John Woznow, Frank Driscoll, Pat MacCharles, Rod Ashburner.

Meantime, the Boy Scout movement was in full swing throughout a large part of the English-speaking world, having been founded by Lord Baden-Powell in England. Early in 1911 the St. John's Boys' Club was officially recognized as a Boy Scout Troop with a Royal Warrant of Appointment being presented to Mr. Nott. He was also appointed the first Scoutmaster.

Nott soon found himself deluged with applications from boys of other denominations to join the St. John's Scout Troop. Sixty-one young men provided strength to the group:

Clare Becker, Norman Rossiter, John Yuill, Harlan Yuill, Frank Millican, Edward Purcy, Gordon Anderson, Sydney Holt, Ivan Rossiter, Alex Agnew, Laurie Rossiter, Harold Ferguson, James Burns, James Cain, Raymond Limbert, Donald Limbert, George Crockford, Harry Mathews, William Muir, David Milne, William Cockerill, Wes Becker, Graham Becker, Frank Crissal, Darcy Smith, Smyth Fleming, Walter Brotherton, Jay Watson, Ralph Smyth, Alvin Smeaton, Wilfred McKay, Earl Bell, Ralph Foster,

Horace Whiffen, Archie Hawthorne, Maynard Patterson, Norman Evans, William White, M. Mahood, George Gardner, Edgar Cooper, Earl Cooper, John McCarger, Albert Cameron, John Shields, James Galloway, Keith Muir, Willard Yuill, James Robinson, Harry Freeman, Bruce Morris, Stuart McRae, Gerald Rankin, Gus Widden, Edward Morris, Eric Lyall and E. Matthews.

In May 1938 J. Jessop Nott was honored for his many years in scouting in Medicine Hat. He was presented with a specially designed silver tray. In November 1980, Jack Sissons was presented with the Silver Acorn Award, the second highest award in scouting, for his exceptional service to the movement.

Sissons started his scouting activities in 1932 when he became a wolf cub when meetings were being held in St. John's Church. He was a King Scout, patrol leader, assistant Scout Master, troop Scouter, counsellor, member of the group committee, president of the district and treasurer of the region. Sissons headed the drive for construction of a new district Scout hall.

Jessop Nott, the originator of the Scout movement in Medicine Hat.

At the same presentation, Doreen Byam was presented with a Medal of Merit for good service to scouting, service which spanned 22 years. A wing in the Scout Centre in Redcliff has been named for her.

Jim Hogg was also given the Medal of Merit for helping organize activities in Medicine Hat for the Scouts' centennial year in 1967. He served as president and vice-president of the district. Emily Aldred received a Medal of Good Service and a 15 year adult service medal for her long involvement in the movement.

The First Medicine Hat Troop celebrated its 70th birthday in 1980. A cheque for $1,000 was presented to the organization by Ken Aldred on behalf of the Fraternal Order of Eagles, an active service club in the city.

The Young Mens' Christian Association in Medicine Hat had humble origins. A decision was made in 1912 to establish a hostel and recreation centre in the city for use by young Christian men. The original purpose of the "Y" was to improve conditions and opportunities for young men, after it was founded in London in 1844. A United States movement began in 1851 and in Canada shortly afterwards. Housing facilities, summer camps and recreational programs are provided. Bible study was emphasized.

A prime mover to get a Y established was Edward D. Bennett who had come to Medicine Hat about 1908 as a land locator. He had been born on a poor farm in Nebraska and after living in Winnipeg and Calgary, came to the city where he became wealthy. He was well-known for his honesty and generosity to his adopted home and in 1912 made the Y possible with a generous donation to the organization's building fund. Bennett also donated the land to the city on which Central Park is located in the South East Hill area.

In 1913 a YWCA was formed in Medicine Hat to provide room and board and convalescence rooms for girls and women in the city. The first YWCA was in the old private residence and hospital operated by Dr. J. G. Calder at Fourth Avenue and Sixth Street South East. It was almost in ruins but served the purpose. Between then and 1924 the YW operated from many different locations. In 1924 a large white house at 409 First Street S.E.

was purchased. In 1955 a gymnasium was added on the back of the house and the Y began health and physical education programs under a joint YM and YW association.

In 1959, with the aid of the Rotary Club, a renewed YMCA was formed to serve boys and men in the community and shortly afterwards the YWCA and the YMCA amalgamated to form the YM-YWCA. From 1969 to 1971 a fund raising drive was held to raise money for a new building which opened at 150 Ash Avenue South East in October 1972.

In 1980 another campaign began to raise funds for an addition to the building. About $450,000 was expected to be raised privately with support promised from various levels of government.

Since the opening of the new building in 1972, membership grew from 300 to more than 1,500 and average monthly attendance in programs exceeded 15,000. In 1979 a total of 20 per cent of all children in grades 1 to 8 were members of the Y and another 10 per cent were enrolled in programs.

Muriel McLaren Roberts, a former reporter for the *Medicine Hat News*, said women in the early days held many fund-raising teas for a multitude of organizations. The tinkle of teacups provided background music for the serious job of collecting money for community endeavors. As well as working for establishment of the YWCA, Mrs. Roberts was a member of the local Council of Women. "We badgered the Provincial Government for many a reform," she said. One resolution was that all illegitimate children born in the province be registered in their father's name. "That was heady stuff in those days," Mrs. Roberts said. "One member sat in silence while this was going on and when she was asked if she favored the resolution said, 'No. I don't want to find little McDuffy's every place I go!'"

Mrs. Roberts, whose father was the Reverend A. E. McLaren, told a story about her mother who belonged to the Women's Liberal Club in Medicine Hat. "William Lyon Mackenzie King addressed them one day at a luncheon," she said. "Mr. King thanked my mother at the close of the meeting for all the kind things she had done for him and hoped he could do something in return." 'You can, Mr. King,' she said. 'I have three unmarried daughters.'"

One organization which deserves proper mention in this chapter is the Medicine Hat and District Historical Society which was formed in 1948 to preserve artifacts and history of the area and its peoples. Through the Society the Historical Museum became a reality. Eva Davison, a member of the Society and of the Retired Teachers' Association in the city said: "We had to save a lot of relics that people were throwing out and set up a museum — all with no money. There were never more than 20 of us at a time, so it was a great community effort."

The first meeting of those interested in forming a Historical Society was attended by Mr. and Mrs. Hector Lang, Mr. and Mrs. Thomas Murray, Mr. and Mrs. Thomas Hargrave, Mrs. Manly Miller, Tom Bassett, A. McColman and Mrs. Hope Michael. The first executive included chairman Mayor Hector Lang, vice-chairman Thomas Murray, secretary, Mrs. Hope Michael, treasurer Mort Fulton and provincial representative Mrs. Thomas Murray.

As the members of the Society began to interview oldtimers to collect historical records many relics of pioneer days were offered. It became apparent that a building would be necessary to house them in. Under the

leadership of Mrs. Lorne Laidlaw plans were made to build a log cabin. The site was at the east side of Riverside Park.

To help finance the building, pioneer families donated $25 each and in return their names, with date of arrival, were branded on the logs. The logs were donated by the Provincial Government and cut in the Cypress Hills. The Museum was officially opened with a ceremony on July 4, 1951, the key being turned over by Mrs. Manley Miller.

Group of "Originals" of the Medicine Hat Historical Society. Photo taken in front of the original log cabin museum building. (Left to Right) Tom Hargrave, Roy Keating, Billy Burton, Hope Michael, Art Grant, Eva Davison, Lisa Sissons, Jimmy Williamson, Mrs. Bomford, Morton Fulton, John Fisher (Mr. Canada), Mae Laidlaw, Mac Higdon. (Mr. and Mrs. Tom Murray — not present.)

View of the original Medicine Hat Museum — small log cabin structure in Riverside Park.

Mrs. Laidlaw was the guiding light in the Museum endeavor in the years it was housed in the small log cabin structure on the highway. Her tower of strength during this period was Stewart Wallace, who spent all his spare time working in the building, restoring and creating displays.

After the First Street subway was built in 1956 it became necessary to move the log structure to a new location. The City of Medicine Hat offered a site on Bomford Crescent at the cloverleaf by the Trans-Canada Highway. Still using logs, an addition to the Museum reopened there in July 1957. The addition was financed by funds from the Alberta Jubilee Committee. It was now three times its original size.

As the Museum collection continued to grow the Historical Society decided in 1964 to apply for Centennial funds to build a large, modern building on the Bomford location. The brick and tile building — with the tiny original log cabin set up inside — was opened in June 1967 in time for Canada's 100th Birthday. The City was without a Museum for one year when the log building was torn down and the collection put in storage.

Official opening at the Medicine Hat Museum new building, June 19, 1967.

Funding for the new building was taken care of by the three Centennial sources: Federal, Provincial and Municipal. The City of Medicine Hat assumed the responsibility of providing personnel and money to operate the Museum. Jack J. Barrie was installed as its first Curator.

During the 11 years that Barrie served as Curator and later as Director, he organized two important additions to the building. One doubled the size of the Museum display area, the second provided the City with the first National Exhibition Centre building in Alberta. The NEC building included a modern humidity controlled Art Gallery which made it possible to bring to the City touring art shows of national stature.

Upon Barrie's resignation in 1978, Tom Willock was engaged as Museum Curator and Nancy Townshend was hired as Art Curator of the NEC building.

As noted earlier, mention would be made of the Medicine Hat Teen Tones. Under the leadership of Adele Armstrong, the girls' chorus took top honors in the Alberta Provincial Festival, received the Pepsi-Cola Canada Award and was saluted by the Dominion Music Festial for its outstanding performances.

In July 1972 the Teen Tones participated in the International Eisteddfod at Llongollen, Wales, and at the Bournemouth Annual Festival in England captured top honors as well. The chorus has recorded three popular albums through cooperation of CHAT radio and television. Mrs. Armstrong's brother, Lorne Havard, baritone, is heard in several selections. Havard is a well-known local TV interviewer and broadcaster.

Lieutenant Governor of Alberta, Grant McEwen and Stewart Wallace plant a flowering crab at the opening ceremony, Medicine Hat Museum, 1967.

263

It goes without saying that a community progresses or fails on the basis of its citizens' efforts. "No arts, no letters: no society." The people of Medicine Hat care. Some of them wear many hats and so their caring reaches many. Gordon A. Simmons is a good example, as is Ida L. Hamel.

Simmons' father, George E. Simmons, came to Medicine Hat before the turn of the century. In his early years the younger Simmons became interested in sports, playing on teams that represented the city in provincial playoffs in hockey and lacrosse. After five years overseas, during World War Two, he became involved in community life. He was president of the Royal Canadian Legion, director of the Kinsmen Club, a member of the Rotary Club who organized the Winnipeg Flood Relief Fund, a president of the Medicine Hat Shrine Club, Chairman of several committees of the Medicine Hat Exhibition and Stampede Company, Chairman of the Alberta Motor Association, first president of the Regimental Association to the South Alberta Light Horse and president of the Citizen's Committee of the same organization. He managed the Corps of Commissionaires and formed Services Unlimited, which employed veterans and older, reliable men for industrial security work, the first independent security organization in Alberta.

Mrs. Hamel is president of the Christ the King Catholic Women's League, secretary of the Navy League, Social Services chairperson of the Women of the Moose and on the phoning committee of the Brownies.

With the dedication exemplified just by such individuals, there was no worry that in centennial year of 1983 or beyond that Medicine Hat citizens would lead lives that were "solitary, poor, nasty, brutish, and short."

Scoutmaster Jim Castle — Troop No. 1. Winners of MacCharles Trophy — St. John Ambulance: Colin Jackson, Claud Deihl, Jim Strachan, Leslie Deihl, Jack Jackson, Jimmy McLeod.

20.

Where Do We Go From Here?

The City of Medicine Hat Crest consists of a steam locomotive, a factory, a stooked wheat field and gas well derricks. The locomotive denotes the importance of the railway which was constructed to the area in 1883. The factory depicts Medicine Hat's many industries. The stooked field recognizes the agricultural area around the city and the derricks represent Medicine Hat's famous gas fields.

The Shield is flanked by maple leaves and has a beaver above, showing Medicine Hat's Canadian ties. The Crest is topped with Medicine Hat's motto: "Enterprise".

The City Seal, used for official purposes, consists of a woman holding a shield with a background of sun, trees and grain. In 1906 a contest was held in the local schools for the design of a shield. It was won by Miss Jessie Cousins. The Latin motto means: "With spirit and faith".

With Enterprise, Spirit and Faith, Medicine Hat boldly faced the future.

In a *Development Review and Forecast,* David Cormier, Manager of Economic Development for Medicine Hat, said the city was well prepared for the dramatic increase in economic activity it shares with the Province of Alberta: good location, excellent transportation facilities, stable population, self-sufficiency in energy and business-minded government. These are some of the plusses, Cormier said, that securely anchor the city's future in the 1980s.

While the importance of one of the major factors in the city's development, the railway, had declined, the other industries symbolized in the Crest had become increasingly important, and would continue to be so.

Just as in the beginning, the city's gas reserves led to a number of industrial expansions — some of which were short-lived. However, the proximity of the resource continues to enhance the city's economic climate. And the increase in oil and gas activity prompted many service companies to build larger facilities.

On February 4th, 1982 the City purchased 3 additional gas fields for the sum of $46,000,000 which will ensure an adequate supply of natural gas well into the 21st Century.

Oil is expected to make an impact over the next several decades thanks to an announcement in 1980 that medium grade crude oil had been discovered about 40 miles west of the city. The find stretches from Brooks, Alberta southward in a series of pools to the American border. As the major

The City of Medicine Hat downtown looking west, as it appeared from the air in 1981. "Good location, excellent transportation facilities, stable population, self-sufficiency in energy and a business-minded government." Photo by Tom Willock for the City's Department of Economic Development.

Heavy crude was also the subject of excitement because of a $9 million pilot project being built at the Suffield Military Reserve 30 kilometers from the city. Four hundred million barrels of heavy oil are known to exist in the northwest portion of the military reserve, along with significant deposits elsewhere in and around the reserve. The heavy oil development is expected to have a marked effect on all facets of the Medicine Hat economy.

Coal was another resource that was heating up the conversations as residents looked forward to the rest of the 1980s, and beyond. A $200,000 coal gasification study indicated the process will be economic in the 1990s.

266

The area's 250 million ton Seven Persons coal seam was being studied as a site for an $85 million gasification plant which would have important ramifications for the petrochemical industries already in operation in Medicine Hat. It is expected that the industry could undergo a 25 year development period in Medicine Hat before becoming a "mature" industry. Dave Cormier said "the future looks good for a sustained growth in this industry as derivative plants and other offshoot industries located over the long term."

Dowell of Canada and Halliburton Services Limited built shops and other facilities on five and six acre parcels in the city's newest industrial subdivision in the Brier Park Industrial area. The increase in gas and oil activity around the city prompted the need for larger, consolidated facilities for both companies. Many other firms in the well-servicing, trucking, tool supply and rental business have grown and expanded their premises. The city also made room for a unique new industry: Early Bird Distributors, producers of earthworm castings for use as potting soil.

Western Cooperative Fertilizers Limited, a longtime corporate citizen of the city, was in the process of spending about $20 million to replace its aging sulphuric acid plant. Overall, WCFL was expected to spend $60 million over the next 10 years, Dr. Ken Neilson of WCFL predicted. A joint project was planned involving the Medicine Hat firm and Earth Sciences Incorporated of Colorado to remove "yellowcake" from Western Co-op's phosphate stream for use as fuel rods in nuclear reactors. Cost was $8 million.

IXL Industries, one of the city's first industries, doubled its facilities at Redcliff Pressed Brick through a $1 million expansion which would raise output of bricks from 14 million per annum to 40 million annually. Construction was completed by the end of 1980.

A longtime corporate citizen, IXL Industries massive development.

Alberta Gas Chemicals moved into a new era of production with its new $130 million methanol unit. The new unit doubled capacity of the company's first plant. Construction was expected to continue past the initial four years predicted for completion since AGCL had plans for derivative plants producing acetic acid, vinyl acetate monomer and other products.

As Medicine Hat looked into the future, it was from a clear and stable base. Its increasing industrial output remained at a constant three per cent per year, while percentage growth from many other Alberta cities declined. George Mitchell, writing in the December 1980 issue of *Trade & Commerce Magazine,* described Medicine Hat as "the leading industrial centre in Western Canada, on a per capita basis."

The commercial sector of the city was pleased to learn that the British Army renewed a 10 year lease on the Suffield Experimental Range about 24 miles north of the city where an average of 7,000 troops trained annually. It was estimated that the troops and army capital programs would add $13 million a year to the Medicine Hat economy.

In the period prior to the publication of this history there was a flurry of activity on the commercial scene in Medicine Hat: a $20 million shopping mall was built, a new air terminal was constructed, a new $5.4 million bridge was opened to take traffic across the South Saskatchewan River. A $20 million addition was made to the General Hospital, a similar amount was spent on an addition to the City's own electrical power plant and an exciting redevelopment scheme was unveiled for the downtown core.

One project was the new City Hall to be located on the site where the Medicine Hat News office sat for so many years. It was slated for completion in 1983, in time for the City's centennial.

An aerial view of Goodyear Tire and Rubber which located in the city when a source of water could be found.

At the outset, a Community Cultural Centre was to be built on City-owned land on the North side of First Street between Sixth Avenue and the existing Federal Courthouse, adjacent to the new City Hall. The theme was "City Hall in the Park", using the main elements of the river, river parkland and the downtown core to good effect. However, only the City Hall went ahead.

In a last moment switch in plans, Council agreed to participate in the financing of a cultural centre on the grounds of the Medicine Hat College since the City would save all the operational costs. Eileen Sissons, President of the Allied Arts Council, said many people were disappointed with the decision but urged everyone to have faith in the Council to make a joint-use agreement — intended to protect the interests of cultural and art groups — work effectively.

On Thursday, July 16, 1981 the $2.5 million Cypress Centre was officially opened, giving the city a pavilion at the Stampede grounds large enough to hold 326 animals, with room for 1,200 persons for banquets and dances. Robert Porter, past President of the Medicine Hat Exhibition and Stampede, dedicated the new building to Lorne Thompson, one of the founders of the Stampede and a prominent district rancher. MLA Jim Horsman conducted the official opening, which was funded through Alberta Agriculture.

In his dedication speech Porter said Lorne Thompson was one of the most important individuals on the building committee and greatly responsible for the new complex. Thompson was Stampede President in 1971 and 1972 and had worked with the event from the time it was organized after the Second World War. The Thompson brand was burned onto a piece of cowhide and placed on a display panel. Russell and Needham were the architects and D & H Construction, also of Medicine Hat, was the contractor.

On Thursday, January 18, 1980, Orv Kope, President of the Medicine Hat Exhibition and Stampede Company, took delivery of a $1.3 million cheque from Horsman as part of the $3.6 million grant that Alberta Agriculture paid toward the construction of a new grandstand on the exhibition grounds.

As part of the Centennial events in 1983 — and indicating the growing interest in the sport of curling — Tink Kreutizig, Vice-Chairman of the International Curling Federation, announced on July 22, 1981 that the city had been chosen as the site for the Uniroyal World Junior Curling Championship. Lyle Flynn and wife Simonne headed the organizing committee that won the bid for the championship staged March 13 to 19 as part of the city's 100th birthday celebration.

Ten countries participated: Canada, USA, Scotland, Sweden, Switzerland, Denmark, Norway, Germany, Italy and France. Alderman Pete Simpson said, "I think it is one of the finest things to happen to the city." Simpson was speaking as Chairman of the Community Services Committee.

On the commercial scene, a new $1 million Canadian Tire Store, the first in southeastern Alberta, was built in 1980, while Revelstoke Companies Ltd. built an $850,000 home service centre nearby. A new $10 million 246-room hotel was planned for Dunmore Road in that area.

Ltd. built an $850,000 home service centre nearby. A new $10 million 246-room hotel was planned for Dunmore Road in that area.

On the agricultural side, the Provincial Government had a project aimed at southern Alberta which was expected to have a significant influence on and benefits for Medicine Hat. At a cost of $334 million, a 10 kilometer long man-made lake southwest of the city would relieve irrigation restraints and put between 30,000 and 50,000 additional acres of land under irrigation between Medicine Hat and Bow Island, a community 30 miles to the southwest. The project would lead to the development of recreation on the lake, such as fishing and boating.

In keeping with its policy to provide a land bank for upcoming industrial projects, the City purchased one-half section of land on the northwest city limits. This brought to a total of seven the number of quarter sections the City could offer to large industry, in addition to 200 acres of smaller industrial lots for light industry. A new 40 acre light industrial addition was put on sale in the southwest light industrial area and another 40 acres were being readied adjacent to it for future expansion.

With expansion of the city in mind, a parcel of property located west of the city, was purchased for $1.8 million. The 1,197 acres of land, west of the city limits, bordering on the South Saskatchewan River south of Redcliff, included the Running Bar X Ranch.

A bird's eye view of Alberta Gas Chemicals expansion as it appeared in 1981.

The property included 140 acres of flat river valley land and 400 acres of cliffs and hills along the river. Mayor Ted Grim said on Thursday, March 12, 1981 that the "Council's position is that we will maintain an aggressive role in land development." The City bought the property from Manalta Holdings Ltd., a company described as one of the "Bow Valley group", an oil consortium.

The land, which was to be leased to farmers, is to remain agricultural for many years. Land bank reserve funds were used to purchase the property.

Commercial land for development was available primarily in the western portion of the city and around the new mall in southeast Medicine Hat. Hat Development Ltd., a private developer, and the City itself were the main commercial land developers.

While the City was looking out for its industrial and commercial interests, it was not ignoring the needs for recreation and cultural activity. A Flats Neighborhood Community Centre was provided to make a meeting and recreational facility available for residents of the Flats. As mentioned elsewhere in this book, a $1.2 million grandstand was completed on the grounds of the Medicine Hat Exhibition and Stampede Company. The 2,500 person facility included a kitchen/cafeteria with seating for 150. A multi-purpose pavilion costing about $2.5 million was built available for conventions, athletic events and equestrian shows.

Two popular recreation areas southeast of the city, Cavan Lake and Golden Sheaf Park, were on the list for development by Alberta Parks and Recreation. Raquetime, a $725,000 raquetball facility, opened its premises for this fast-growing sport with 16 courts, while a 16-lane bowling alley next to the Connaught Golf Course opened in southeast Medicine Hat.

In 1980 the City received the A. V. Pettrigew Award for the quality of recreational facilities in the Community. The excellence and variation as well as emphasis on family recreation were deciding factors in giving Medicine Hat the award.

The Culture and Recreation Department of the City publishes a "Community Organization File" The Brimming Hat which lists animal clubs and clinics, church organizations, clubs for the promotion of regional and national cultures, entertainment (dancing, music and theatre), handicapped organizations, hobby clubs, professional clubs, recreational centres (which feature everything from archery to boxing, from skydiving to water polo), senior citizens' clubs, service clubs and youth organizations. There is hardly an activity anywhere that is not represented in Medicine Hat, whether it be pigeon racing or membership in the South Alberta Pipe Band.

As an indication of how far culture had come in a short time, Chief Librarian Bob Block made the following comment to the author in 1981: "When I first arrived here about 10 years ago I asked a man on the street where the library was. He didn't know. And with something akin to pride in his eyes he told me he had never read a book. I couldn't believe it. Now, we have a library with more than 150,000 books and a society catering to every conceivable interest. I met the same man recently and he knew not only where the library was, but all about what was happening there. We've come a long way."

271

Getting the message about how far Medicine Hat has come since its "birth" 100 years ago has become a prime concern for those interested in attracting tourists to the area. With its Stampede a big drawing event and a bi-annual Air Show to attract outsiders, the future of tourism looked bright for the future. A $1 million giant water slide, the first of its kind in Alberta, was built by Riverside Amusements, a group of local and out-of-province investors. The attraction features six slides, splash-down pool and concessions. The promoters were confident that this would be the first of several tourist-oriented activities in the area. The City planned 60 to 80 acres of land adjacent to the water slide for further tourist commercial developments to go with the slide, amusement park, riverboat ride and trailer park already planned.

The Trans-Canada Highway bridges "twinning" was completed in 1980, although when this photo was taken, the approaches were not yet completed.

In order to get tourists to the area, it was necessary to upgrade transportation facilities. Time Air, the scheduled airline in the city, ordered the very latest in equipment and applied to the Canada Transport Commission for permission to operate a Medicine Hat-Vancouver service. This would add a new dimension to the already excellent air service in Medicine Hat.

The Trans-Canada Highway from the city to Calgary was to be the object of much attention as it was to be upgraded to four lanes in the next five to 10 years. Cost of the project was estimated at $1.8 billion but would vastly improve capacity and safety on this vital link. Highway Number 3 through the Crowsnest Pass was also to receive attention in a promotional effort to increase awareness of the highway as a tourist route. Hundreds of thousands of tourists pass through Medicine Hat each year on both highways. With all the recreational projects mentioned, and more to come, the 1980s appeared to be a growth decade for the tourist industry in Medicine Hat.

On the subject of growth, in 10 short years the city's population leaped from 26,000 to almost 38,000, a 3.7 per cent increase in one year — from 1979 to 1980. From 1980 to 1981 the increase was a whopping 5.9 per cent, making the population well over 40,000 at the time of this writing. The biggest area increases came in the Norwood, South Ridge and Ross Glen areas, all in the southern part of the city. The population was projected at 44,000 for 1985 and 51,000 for 1990.

Having firmly established itself in the petrochemical industry, agriculture and ceramics, and with energy-related industries and tourist developments popping up around the city, Medicine Hat moves confidently into the future.

Mayor Ted Grimm.

Photo montages by Rory Mahoney, Tom Willock, Michael Keeling and James Marshall. Appreciation expressed to Grassroots Studio, Medicine Hat, and Dept. of Economic Development.

Seated, from the left: Lorne Thompson, Public Works Director; Frank O'Connell, City Solicitor; Mayor Ted Grimm; Larry Godin, City Clerk; Robert Ardiel, Finance Director. Standing, from the left: Al Hagan, Community Services Director; Ald. Bill Keith; Ald. Jim Hirsch; Ald. Harry Yuill; Ald. Pete Simpson; Ald. Ken Sauer; Ald. Lee Anderson; Ald. George Davison; Ald. Sam Stone; Winston Kerr, Utilities Director.

274

21.

The Last Word: A Who's Who

For any community to prosper as Medicine Hat has, it is necessary to have a core of hard-working individuals on various boards and councils. To complete this history of the city, we have compiled lists of the names of some of these selfless persons. Not all the lists are complete, due to the fact that complete records are not available in some cases.

Members Of The Municipal Council and the City Clerk Of The Town And City Of Medicine Hat From 1899 to 1981:

1899
Marshall, W. B.	Mayor	Spencer, J. H.	Councillor
Yuill, H. C.	Councillor	Noble, G.	Councillor
Blatchford, T. C.	Councillor	Penhale, T.	Councillor
Hawthorne, A. C.	Councillor	Adsit, W. N.	Sec.-Treas.

1900
Finlay, W. T.	Mayor	Penhale, T.	Councillor
Mitchell, C. R.	Councillor	Yuill, H. C.	Councillor
Ross, H. H.	Councillor	Spencer, J. H.	Councillor
Luno, G. A.	Councillor	Adsit, W. N.	Sec.-Treas.

1901
Finlay, W. T.	Mayor	Hutchinson, T.	Councillor
Luno, G. A.	Councillor	Penhale, T.	Councillor
Ross, H. H.	Councillor	Yuill, H. C.	Councillor
Forster, F. G.	Councillor	Adsit, W. N.	Sec.-Treas.

1902
Finlay, W. T.	Mayor	Hutchinson, T.	Councillor
Forster, F. G.	Councillor	Penhale, T.	Councillor
Cook, Jas.	Councillor	McKay, T.	Councillor
Milne, D.	Councillor	Adsit, W. N.	Sec.-Treas.

1903
Hawthorne, A. C.	Mayor	Milne, D.	Councillor
Forster, F. G.	Councillor	Nelson, Robt.	Councillor
McKay, T.	Councillor	Cook, Jas.	Councillor
Smith, C. F.	Councillor	Adsit, W. N.	Sec.-Treas.

1904
Hutchinson, T.	Mayor	Penhale, T.	Councillor
Drinnan, J. K.	Councillor	Smith, C. F.	Councillor
Stewart, H.	Councillor	Nelson, Robt.	Councillor
Forster, F. G.	Councillor	Adsit, W. N.	Sec.-Treas.

1905
Forster, F. G.	Mayor	Smyth, C. E.	Councillor
Penhale, T.	Councillor	Sissons, F. W.	Councillor
Drinnan, J. K.	Councillor	DesBrisay, A.	Councillor
Stewart, H.	Councillor	Adsit, W. N.	Sec.-Treas.

1906

Forster, F. G.	Mayor	Hunt, E. J.	Councillor
Penhale, T.	Councillor	Smyth, C. F.	Councillor
Stewart, H.	Councillor	Sissons, F. O.	Councillor
DesBrisay, A.	Councillor	Adsit, W. N.	Sec.-Treas.

1907

Cousins, W.	Mayor	Drinnan, J. K.	Alderman
Penhale, T.	Alderman	(Part term)	
Hunt, E. J.	Alderman	Tweed, H. L.	Alderman
McKay, T.	Alderman	(Part term)	
Hutchinson, T.	Alderman	Adsit, W. N.	Sec.-Treas.
Baker, H. A.	Alderman		

1908

Cousins, W.	Mayor	Penhale, T.	Alderman
Baker, H. A.	Alderman	Forster, F. G.	Alderman
McKay, T.	Alderman	Huckvale, W.	Alderman
Tweed, H. L.	Alderman	Spencer, Nelson	Alderman
Morrow, H.	Alderman	Roberts, E.	City Clerk

1909

Milne, D.	Mayor	Collier, J. H.	Alderman
Morrow, H.	Alderman	(Part term)	
Spencer, Nelson	Alderman	Adsit, W. N.	Alderman
Penhale, T.	Alderman	(Part term)	
Huckvale, W.	Alderman	Fatt, F. F.	
Howson, J. E.	Alderman	(Part term)	Alderman
Robertson, P.	Alderman	Perry, A. T.	Alderman
McKay, T.	Alderman	(Part term)	

1910

Milne, D.	Mayor	Bridgman, W. H.	Alderman
Spencer, Nelson	Alderman	Forster, F. G.	Alderman
Adsit, W. N.	Alderman	Fawcett, S. T.	Alderman
Robertson, P.	Alderman	Howson, J. E.	Alderman
McKay, T.	Alderman	Perry, A. R.	Sec.-Treas.

1911

Milne, D.	Mayor	Robertson, P.	Alderman
Forster, F. G.	Alderman	Pingle, C. S.	Alderman
Howson, J. E.	Alderman	McKay, T.	Alderman
Fawcett, S. T.	Alderman	Brown, M. A.	Alderman
Bridgman, W. H.	Alderman	Perry, A. R.	Sec.-Treas.

1912

Spencer, Nelson	Mayor	Johnston, W. G.	Alderman
Brown, M. A.	Alderman	Howson, J. E.	Alderman
Robertson, P.	Alderman	(part term)	Alderman
Ansley, W.	Alderman	McClellan, S. E.	Alderman
Doty, W. H.	Alderman	(part term)	Alderman
Pratt, Chas	Alderman	Baker, H.	City Clerk
Evans, Geo.	Alderman		

1913

Spencer, Nelson	Mayor	Pratt, Chas	Alderman
Brown, M. A.	Alderman	Evans, Geo.	Alderman
Robertson, P.	Alderman	Johnston, W. G.	Alderman
Ansley, W.	Alderman	McClelland, S. E.	Alderman
Doty, W. H.	Alderman	Baker, H.	City Clerk

1914

Brown, M. A.	Mayor	Niblock, W. G.	Alderman
Boyd, O.	Alderman	Penland, W. R.	Alderman
Collier, R.	Alderman	Robertson, Peter	Alderman
McLean, W.	Alderman	Pratt, C.	Alderman
Morrow, H.	Alderman	Baker H.	City Clerk

1915

Hawthorne, A. C.	Mayor	Morrow, H.	Alderman
Boyd, O.	Alderman	Penhale, T.	Alderman
Collier, R.	Alderman	Penland, W. R.	Alderman
Cruikshank, S.	Alderman	Spencer, J. H.	Alderman
Ireland, H. S.	Alderman	Baker, H.	City Clerk

1916

Hawthorne, A. C.	Mayor	Leveque, L.	Alderman
Berry, J. T.	Alderman	Penland, A.	Alderman
Cruikshank, S.	Alderman	Spencer, J. H.	Alderman
Hamilton, W. C.	Alderman	Worthy, G.	Alderman
Ireland, H. S.	Alderman	Blackburn, F.	City Clerk

1917

Cruikshank, S.	Mayor	Hamilton, W. C.	Alderman
Berry, J. T.	Alderman	Leveque, L.	Alderman
Bell, E. A.	Alderman	Marshall, J.	Alderman
Burns, A. P.	Alderman	Worthy, G.	Alderman
Bennett, E. D.	Alderman	Becker, R. C. (part term)	Alderman

1918

Brown, M. A.	Mayor	Hotson, G.	Alderman
Bell, E. A.	Alderman	Lang, H.	Alderman
Bennett, E. D.	Alderman	Leveque, L.	Alderman
Burns, A. P.	Alderman	Marshall, J.	Alderman
Finlay, W.	Alderman		

1919

Brown, M. A.	Mayor	Huckvale, W.	Alderman
Bell, E. A.	Alderman	Leveque, L.	Alderman
Burns, A. P.	Alderman	McLarty, N. A.	Alderman
Finlay, W.	Alderman	Marshall, J.	Alderman
Hotson, G.	Alderman		

1920

Brown, M. A.	Mayor	Hole, J.	Alderman
Bell, E. A.	Alderman	Huckvale, W.	Alderman
Bellamy, B.	Alderman	McLarty, N. A.	Alderman
Boyd, O.	Alderman	Montgomery, T.	Alderman
Burns, A. P.	Alderman		

1921

Huckvale, W.	Mayor	Delf, J.	Alderman
Bellamy, B.	Alderman	Fawcett, S. T.	Alderman
Boyd, O.	Alderman	King, J. A.	Alderman
Bullivant, I.	Alderman	Montgomerie, T.	Alderman
Davidson, J. R.	Alderman		

1922

Huckvale, W.	Mayor	Delf, J.	Alderman
Bellamy, B.	Alderman	Fawcett, S. T.	Alderman
Bannan, W. T.	Alderman	King, J. A.	Alderman
Bell, T.	Alderman	Montgomerie, T.	Alderman
Cunliffe, J.	Alderman		

1923

Huckvale, W.	Mayor	Browne, C. B.	Alderman
Bannan, W. T.	Alderman	Boyd, O.	Alderman
Bellamy, B.	Alderman	Davidson, R. B.	Alderman
Bell, T.	Alderman	Simpson, P.	Alderman
Baker, H.	Alderman		

1924

Huckvale, W.	Mayor	Browne, C. B.	Alderman
Baker, H.	Alderman	Davidson, R. B.	Alderman
Bannan, W. T.	Alderman	Hole, J.	Alderman
Bell, T.	Alderman	Simpson, P.	Alderman
Boyd, O.	Alderman		

1925

Huckvale, W.	Mayor	King, J. A.	Alderman
Bannan, W. T.	Alderman	Mitchell, B.	Alderman
Bell, T.	Alderman	Morrison, J.	Alderman
Boyd, O.	Alderman	Simpson, P.	Alderman
Hole, J.	Alderman		

1926

Bullivant, I.	Mayor	King, J. A.	Alderman
Boyd, O.	Alderman	Marsh, J. P.	Alderman
Davidson, J. R.	Alderman	Morrison, J.	Alderman
Duggan, H. O.	Alderman	Simpson, P.	Alderman
Hole, J.	Alderman	Blackburn, F.	Alderman

1927

Bullivant, I.	Mayor	King, J. A.	Alderman
Boyd, O.	Alderman	Marsh, J. P.	Alderman
Davidson, R. B.	Alderman	McCombs, J.	Alderman
Currie, J.	Alderman	Simpson, P.	Alderman
Hole, J.	Alderman		

1928

Bullivant, I.	Mayor	Hole, J.	Alderman
Andrews, A.	Alderman	King, J. A.	Alderman
Bannan, W. T.	Alderman	McCombs, J.	Alderman
Currie, J.	Alderman	Simpson, P.	Alderman
Forster, H. T. W.	Alderman		

1929

Bullivant, I.	Mayor	Hole, J.	Alderman
Andrews, A.	Alderman	King, J. A.	Alderman
Bannan, W. T.	Alderman	McCombs, J.	Alderman
Currie, J.	Alderman	Simpson, P.	Alderman
Forster, H. T. W.	Alderman		

1930

Bullivant, I.	Mayor	Currie, J.	Alderman
Forster, H. T. W.	Alderman	McCombs, J.	Alderman
Hole, J.	Alderman	Rae, J. M.	Alderman
Ireland, H. S.	Alderman	Simpson, P.	Alderman
Watson, W. D.	Alderman		

1931

Bullivant, I.	Mayor	Ireland, H. S.	Alderman
Black, R. C.	Alderman	McCombs, J.	Alderman
Boyd, R. S.	Alderman	Rae, J. M.	Alderman
Currie, J.	Alderman	Simpson, P.	Alderman
Hole, J.	Alderman		

1932

Bullivant, I.	Mayor	McCombs, J.	Alderman
Black, R. C.	Alderman	Parrish, V. W.	Alderman
Boyd, R. S.	Alderman	Simpson, P.	Alderman
Currie, J.	Alderman	Warham, E.	Alderman
Morrow, H.	Alderman		

1933

Bullivant, I.	Mayor	Parrish, V. W.	Alderman
Baker, H.	Alderman	Patterson, J. R.	Alderman
Black, R. C.	Alderman	Simpson, P.	Alderman
Boyd, R. S.	Alderman	Warham, E.	Alderman
King, J. A.	Alderman		

1934

Bullivant, I.	Mayor	King, J. A.	Alderman
Baker, H.	Alderman	Patterson, J. R.	Alderman
Black, R. C.	Alderman	Pratt, R. B.	Alderman
Boyd, R. S.	Alderman	Warham, E.	Alderman
Calder, R.	Alderman		

1935

Bullivant, I.	Mayor	Hole, J.	Alderman
Baker, H.	Alderman	Patterson, J. R.	Alderman
Black, R. C.	Alderman	Pratt, R. B.	Alderman
Boyd, R. S.	Alderman	Warham, E.	Alderman
Calder, R.	Alderman		

1936

Bullivant, I.	Mayor	Marshall, E. A.	Alderman
Black, R. C.	Alderman	Patterson, J. R.	Alderman
Boyd, R. S.	Alderman	Pratt, F. B.	Alderman
Calder, R.	Alderman	Warham, E.	Alderman
Hole, J.	Alderman		

1937

Bullivant, I.	Mayor	Marshall, A. E.	Alderman
Black, R. C.	Alderman	Patterson, J. R.	Alderman
Boyd, R. S.	Alderman	Pratt, R. B.	Alderman
Calder, R.	Alderman	Warham, E.	Alderman
Hole, J.	Alderman		

1938

Bullivant, I.	Mayor	Marshall, A. E.	Alderman
Black, R. C.	Alderman	Patterson, J. R.	Alderman
Boyd, R. S.	Alderman	Pratt, R. B.	Alderman
Calder, R.	Alderman	Warham, E.	Alderman
Hole, J.	Alderman		

1939

Lang, H.	Mayor	Marshall, A. E.	Alderman
Bell, J. A.	Alderman	Patterson, J. R.	Alderman
Black, R. C.	Alderman	Pratt, R. B.	Alderman
Boyd, R. S.	Alderman	Warham, E.	Alderman
Calder, R.	Alderman		

1940

Lang, H.	Mayor	Marshall, A. E.	Alderman
Bell, J. A.	Alderman	Patterson, J. R.	Alderman
Black, R. C.	Alderman	Pratt, R. B.	Alderman
Boyd, R. S.	Alderman	Warham, E.	Alderman
Calder, R.	Alderman		

1941

Lang, H.	Mayor	Marshall, A. E.	Alderman
Bell, J. A.	Alderman	Patterson, J. R.	Alderman
Black, R. C.	Alderman	Pratt, R. B.	Alderman
Boyd, R. S.	Alderman	Warham, E.	Alderman
Calder, R.	Alderman		

1942

Lang, H.	Mayor	Marshall, A. E.	Alderman
Bell, J. A.	Alderman	Patterson, J. R.	Alderman
Black, R. C.	Alderman	Pratt, R. B.	Alderman
Boyd, R. S.	Alderman	Warham, E.	Alderman
Calder, R.	Alderman		

1943

Lang, H.	Mayor	Marshall, A. E.	Alderman
Bell, J. A.	Alderman	Patterson, J. R.	Alderman
Black, R. C.	Alderman	Pratt, R. B.	Alderman
Boyd, R. S.	Alderman	Warham, E.	Alderman
Calder, R.	Alderman		

1944

Lang, H.	Mayor	Horne, E. W.	Alderman
Black, R. C.	Alderman	Leinweber, H. C.	Alderman
Bell, J. A.	Alderman	Patterson, J. R.	Alderman
Boyd, R. S.	Alderman	Scott, S. F.	Alderman
Hawthorne, D. S.	Alderman		

1945

Lang, H.	Mayor	Leinweber, H. C.	Alderman
Black, R. C.	Alderman	Oliver, W. W.	Alderman
Hawthorne, D. S.	Alderman	Rae, W. M.	Alderman
Horne, E. W.		Scott, S. F.	Alderman
Keating, R. E.	Alderman	Blackburn, F.	City Clerk

1946

Lang, H.	Mayor	Keating, R. E.	Alderman
Black, R. C.	Alderman	Oliver, W. W.	Alderman
Hawthorne, D. S.	Alderman	Rae, W. M.	Alderman
Armstrong, B. C.	Alderman	Scott, S. F.	Alderman
Horne, E. W.	Alderman	McQueen, Peter	City Clerk

1947

Rae, W. M.	Mayor	Oliver, W. W.	Alderman
Armstrong, B. C.	Alderman	Riley, W.	Alderman
Hawthorne, D. S.	Alderman	Scott, S. F.	Alderman
Horne, E. W.	Alderman	Smith, E. W.	Alderman
Leinweber, H. C.	Alderman	McQueen, Peter	City Clerk

1948

Rae, W. M.	Mayor	Riley, W.	Alderman
Armstrong, B. C.	Alderman	Scholten, D. A.	Alderman
Douglas, J. Weldon	Alderman	Scott, S. F.	Alderman
Hawthorne, D. S.	Alderman	Smith, E. W.	Alderman
Leinweber, H. C.	Alderman	McQueen, Peter	City Clerk
		Keith, W. A. (1st May)	City Clerk

1949

Lang, Hector	Mayor	Riley W.	Alderman
Armstrong, B.C.	Alderman	Scholten, D. A.	Alderman
Douglas, J. W.	Alderman	Scott, S. F.	Alderman
Hawthorne, D. S.	Alderman	Smith, E. W.	Alderman
Leinweber, H. C.	Alderman	Keith, W. A.	City Clerk

Dec. /49 to Dec. /50

Lang, Hector	Mayor	Riley, W.	Alderman
Douglas, J. W.	Alderman	Scholten, D. A.	Alderman
Gardner, R. C.	Alderman	Scott, S. F.	Alderman
Leinweber, H. C.	Alderman	Smith, E. W.	Alderman
McCombs, W. E.	Alderman	Keith, W. A.	City Clerk

Dec. /50 to Dec. /51

Riley, Wilson	Mayor	Scholten, D. A.	Alderman
Cocks, J. H.	Alderman	Scott, S. F.	Alderman
Douglas, J. W.	Alderman	Smith, E. W	Alderman
Gardner, R. C.	Alderman	Walker, L. A.	Alderman
Gust, Mrs. L. E.	Alderman	Keith, W. A.	City Clerk

Dec. /51 to Oct. 1952 — until mid-October (New City Act)

Riley, Wilson	Mayor	Scholten, D. A.	Alderman
Cocks, J. H.	Alderman	Scott, S. F.	Alderman
Douglas, J. W.	Alderman	Smith, E. W.	Alderman
Gardner, R. C.	Alderman	Walker, L. A.	Alderman
Gust, Mrs. L. E.	Alderman	Keith, W. A.	City Clerk

October, 1952 to Oct. 1953

Veiner, Harry	Mayor	McCombs, W. E.	Alderman
Douglas, J. W.	Alderman	Scott, S. F.	Alderman
Gust, Mrs. L. E.	Alderman	Smith, E. W.	Alderman
Heckbert, E. E.	Alderman	Walker, L. A.	Alderman
Gardner, R. C.	Alderman	Keith, W. A.	City Clerk

Oct. 1953 to Oct. 1954

Veiner, Harry	Mayor	McCombs, W. E.	Alderman
Douglas, J. W.	Alderman	Scott, S. F.	Alderman
Gust, Mrs. L. E.	Alderman	Smith, E. W.	Alderman
Heald, E.	Alderman	Walker, L. A.	Alderman
Heckbert, E. E.	Alderman	Keith, W. A.	City Clerk

Oct. 1954 to Oct. 1955

Veiner, Harry	Mayor	Heckbert, E. E.	Alderman
Craig, L. G.	Alderman	McCombs, W. E.	Alderman
Douglas, J. W.	Alderman	Scott, S. F.	Alderman
Gust, Mrs. L. E.	Alderman	Walker, L. A.	Alderman
Heald, E.	Alderman	Keith, W. A.	City Clerk.

October, 1955 to October, 1956

Veiner, Harry	Mayor	Heckbert, E. E.	Alderman
Craig, L. G.	Alderman	McCombs, W. E.	Alderman
Douglas, J. W.	Alderman	Scott, S. F.	Alderman
Gust, Mrs. L. E.	Alderman	Walker, L. A.	Alderman
Heald, E.	Alderman	Keith, W. A.	City Clerk

October, 1956 to October, 1957

Veiner, Harry	Mayor	McCombs, W. E.	Alderman
Craig, L. G.	Alderman	Scott, S. F.	Alderman
Douglas, J. W.	Alderman	Staritt, J. O.	Alderman
Gust, Mrs. L. E.	Alderman	Thompson, L.	Alderman
Heckbert, E. E.	Alderman	Keith, W. A.	City Clerk

Oct. 1957 to Oct. 1958

Veiner, Harry	Mayor	Scott, S. F.	Ald.
Carry, P. K.	Ald.	Starritt, J. O.	Ald.
Cockrill, W. J.	Ald.	Thompson, L.	Ald.
Douglas, J. W.	Ald.	Keith, W. A. (Jan.-June)	City Clerk
Gibson, Mrs. Helen Beny	Ald.	Broderick, D. G.	
Heckbert, E. E.	Ald.	(June-Dec.)	City Clerk

In Office or Elected Oct. 15, 1958 — Oct. 1957 to Oct. 1958

Veiner, Harry	Mayor	Gibson, Mrs. Helen	Ald.
Adam, Clifford E.	Ald.	Osborne, T. Roy	Ald.
Carry, P. K.	Ald.	Scott, S. F.	Ald.
Cockrill, W. J.	Ald.	Smith, Earl W.	Ald.
Edwards, Dr. J. L.	Ald.	Broderick, D. G.	City Clerk

In Office or Elected Oct. 14, 1959 to Oct. 1960

Veiner, Harry	Mayor	Scott, Simon F.	Ald.
Adam, Clifford E.	Ald.	Sissons, Gordon H.	Ald.
Edwards, Dr. J. L.	Ald.	Smith, Earl W.	Ald.
Gibson, Mrs. Helen	Ald.	Broderick, D. G. (Oct.-June)	City Clerk
Miller, James C.	Ald.	Shepherd, Miss A. (July)	A/City Clerk
Osborne, T. Roy	Ald.	Keith, W. A. (Aug.-Oct.)	City Clerk

In Office or Elected Oct., 1960

Veiner, Harry	Mayor	Osborne, T. Roy	Ald.
Adam, Clifford E.	Ald.	Scott, Simon F.	Ald.
Edwards, Dr. J. L.	Ald.	Sissons, Gordon H.	Ald.
Gibson, Mrs. Helen	Ald.	Smith, Earl W.	Ald.
Miller, James C.	Ald.	Keith, W. A.	City Clerk

In Office or Elected Oct., 1961

Veiner, Harry	Mayor	Miller, James C.	Ald.
Adam, Clifford E.	Ald.	Osborne, T. Roy	Ald.
Edwards, Dr. J. L.	Ald.	Sissons, Gordon H.	Ald.
Gibson, Mrs. Helen	Ald.	Smith, Earl W.	Ald.
Lutes, W. D.	Ald.	Keith, W. A.	City Clerk

1962

Veiner, Harry	Mayor	Miller, James C.	Ald.
Adam, Clifford E.	Ald.	Osborne, T. Roy	Ald.
Edwards, Dr. J. L.	Ald.	Sissons, Gordon H.	Ald.
Gibson, Mrs. Helen	Ald.	Smith, Earl W.	Ald.
Lutes, W. D.	Ald.	Keith, W. A.	City Clerk

1963

Veiner, Harry	Mayor	Osborne, T. Roy	Ald.
Adam, Clifford E.	Ald.	Simpson, Peter M.	Ald.
Edwards, Dr. J. L.	Ald.	Sissons, Gordon H.	Ald.
Gibson, Mrs. Helen	Ald.	Smith, Earl W.	Ald.
Lutes, Willard D.	Ald.	Keith, W. A.	City Clerk

1964

Veiner, Harry	Mayor		
Adam, Clifford E.	Ald.	Simpson, Peter M.	Ald.
Edwards, Dr. J. L.	Ald.	Sissons, Gordon H.	Ald.
Gibson, Mrs. Helen	Ald.	Smith, Earl W.	Ald.
Lutes, Willard D.	Ald.	Keith, W. A.	City Clerk
Osborne, T. Roy	Ald.		

In office or elected October 1965-October 1966

Veiner, Harry	Mayor	Osborne, T. Roy	Ald.
Adam, Clifford E.	Ald.	Sissons, Gordon H.	Ald.
Edwards, Dr. J. L.	Ald.	Smith, Earl W.	Ald.
Gibson, Mrs. Helen	Ald.	Wiedemann, R. J.	Ald.
Lutes, W. A.	Ald.	Keith, W. A.	City Clerk

October 1966-October 1967

C. J. Meagher	Mayor	Sissons, G. H.	Ald.
Gibson, Mrs. H. B.	Ald.	Smith, E. W.	Ald.
Lutes, W. D.	Ald.	Wiedemann, R. J.	Ald.
Renner, G. W.	Ald.	Edwards, J. L.	Ald.
Simpson, P. M.	Ald.	Keith, W. A.	City Clerk

October 1967-October 1968

C. J. Meagher	Mayor	Renner, G. W.	Ald.
Belsher, H. E.	Ald.	Simpson, P. M.	Ald.
Craven, R. M.	Ald.	Smith, E. W.	Ald.
Edwards, J. L.	Ald.	Wiedemann, R. J.	Ald.
Gibson, Mrs. H. B.	Ald.	Keith, W. A.	City Clerk

(For 3-yr. terms) October 1968-October 1969

H. Veiner	Mayor	Grimm, T. J.	Ald.
Belsher, H. E.	Ald.	Reinhardt, M. J.	Ald.
Craven, R. M.	Ald.	Renner, G. W.	Ald.
Davison, G. H.	Ald.	Wiedemann, R. J.	Ald.
Gibson, Mrs. H. B.	Ald.	Keith, W. A.	City Clerk

(For 2-yr. terms) October 1969-October 1971

H. Veiner	Mayor	Renner, G. W.	Ald.
Davison, G. H.	Ald.	Simpson, P. M.	Ald.
Gibson, Mrs. H. B.	Ald.	Tagg, M. S.	Ald.
Grimm, T. J.	Ald.	Wiedemann, R. J.	Ald.
Reinhardt, M. J.	Ald.	Keith, W. A.	City Clerk

October 1971-October 1974

H. Veiner	Mayor	Reinhardt, M. J.	Ald.
Belscher, H. E.	Ald.	Simpson, P. M.	Ald.
Davison, G. H.	Ald.	Sissons, T. A.	Ald.
Grimm, T. J.	Ald.	Yuill, H. H.	Ald.
Moyer, Mrs. Lucille	Ald.	Keith, W. A.	City Clerk

October 1974-October 1977

T. J. Grimm	Mayor	Moyer, Mrs. Lucille	Ald.
Belscher, H. E	Ald.	Simpson, P.M.	Ald.
Clement, R. W.	Ald.	Sissons, T. A.	Ald.
Davison, G. H.	Ald.	Stone, S.	Ald.
Gibson, Mrs. H. B.	Ald.	Keith, W. A.	City Clerk

Medicine Hat School District No. 76
List of Trustees

1886-

L. B. Cochran
E. Walton, Chairman

James Hargrave
G. W. McCaig, Secretary

1887-

L. B. Cochran
E. Walton, Chairman

James Hargrave, Secretary

1888-

J. Norquay
E. Walton — Chairman

J. Ewart, Secretary

1889-

Wm. Cousins — Chairman
G. W. McCaig

E. B. Coons
J. Ewart, Secretary

1890-

Wm. Cousins

1891-

Wm. Cousins, Chairman
J. W. Spencer

J. E. Ewart, Secretary-Treas.
Reverend McLeod

1892-

Wm. Cousins, Chairman
J. H. Spencer

F. F. Fatt, Secretary-Treas.
J. G. Waldock

1893-

J. H. Spencer, Chairman
J. G. Waldock

F. F. Fatt, Secretary-Treas.
N. N. Adsit

1894-

J. H. Spencer, Chairman
J. G. Waldock

F. F. Fatt, Secretary-Treas.
N. N. Adsit

1895-

N. N. Adsit, Chairman
J. H. Spencer

F. F. Fatt, Secretary-Treas.
J. F. Fisher

1896-

J. F. Fisher, Chairman
J. H. Spencer

F. F. Fatt, Secretary-Treas.
T. J. Fleager

1897-

J. F. Fisher, Chairman
T. J. Fleager
J. H. Cunliffe

F. F. Fatt, Secretary-Treas.
J. H. Spencer

1898-

T. J. Fleager, Chairman
J. H. Cunliffe
McCutcheon

F. F. Fatt, Secretary-Treas.
Wm. Cousins
J. F. Fisher

283

1899-

T. J. Fleager, Chairman
F. G. Forster
J. H. Cunliffe

F. F. Fatt, Secretary-Treas.
J. R. Clark
Wm. Cousins

1900-

T. J. Fleager, Chairman
F. G. Forster
W. M. Williamson

F. F. Fatt, Secretary-Treas.
J. R. Clark
G. H. Bailey

1901-

Wm. Cousins, Chairman
W. M. Williamson
Reverend Wm. Nicolls

F. F. Fatt, Secretary-Treas.
G. H. Bailey
J. G. Waldock

1902-

Wm. Cousins, Chairman
Reverend W. Nicolls
R. F. Collins

F. F. Fatt, Secretary-Treas.
J. G. Waldock
R. C. Porter

1903-

T. J. Fleager, Chairman
Reverend W. Nicolls
R. F. Collins

F. F. Fatt, Secretary-Treas.
W. J. Brotherton
R. C. Porter

1904-

W. J. Brotherton, Chairman
T. J. Fleager
Reverend W. Nicolls

T. H. Rhodes, Secretary-Treas.
W. G. Niblock
J. Kennedy

1905-

W. J. Brotherton, Chairman
Reverend W. Nicolls
W. G. Niblock

T. H. Rhodes, Secretary-Treas.
J. Kennedy
D. Milne

1906-

W. J. Brotherton, Chairman
Reverend W. Nicolls
W. G. Niblock

T. H. Rhodes, Secretary-Treas.
J. Kennedy
D. Milne

1907-

W. J. Brotherton, Chairman
J. C. Colter
D. Milne

E. Roberts, Secretary-Treas.
W. G. Niblock
J. Kennedy

1908-

W. J. Brotherton, Chairman
D. Milne
J. C. Colter

E. Roberts, Secretary-Treas.
J. Kennedy
W. G. Niblock

1909-

W. J. Brotherton, Chairman
A. C. Hawthorne
D. G. White

E. J. Fewings, Secretary-Treas.
J. Kennedy
F. F. Fatt

1910-

D. G. White, Chairman
A. C. Hawthorne
J. Wilson

E. J. Fewings, Secretary-Treas.
J. E. Miers
S. T. Hopper

1911-

James Wilson, Chairman
S. T. Hopper
H. Morrow

E. J. Fewings, Secretary-Treas.
W. H. Turpin
J. L. Jamieson

1912-

J. Wilson, Chairman
Dr. C. E. Smythe
H. Morrow

R. M. Napier, Secretary-Treas.
W. H. Turpin
J. L. Jamieson

1913-

Walter Huckvale, Chairman
W. N. McNeely
J. W. Hamilton

R. M. Napier, Secretary-Treas.
J. Wilson
Dr. C. E. Smythe

284

1914-

W. Huckvale, Chairman
J. Wilson
Dr. C. E. Smythe

J. L. MacCallum, Sect'y-Treas.
W. N. McNeely
J. W. Hamilton

1915-

Dr. C. E. Smythe, Chairman
R. C. Black
H. Lang

J. L. MacCallum, Sect'y-Treas.
B. F. Souch
Dr. F. W. Gershaw

1916-

H. Lang, Chairman
Dr. F. W. Gershaw
R. C. Black

J. L. MacCallum, Sect'y-Treas.
B. W. Bellamy
Mrs. Jean Williamson

1917-

Dr. F. W. Gershaw, Chairman
B. W. Bellamy
R. C. Black

J. L. MacCallum, Sect'y-Treas.
Mrs. Jean Williamson
H. S. Ireland

1918-

R. C. Black, Chairman
B. W. Bellamy
Dr. F. W. Gershaw

J. L. MacCallum, Sect'y-Treas.
Thomas B. Bell
H. S. Ireland

1919-

B. W. Bellamy, Chairman
R. C. Black
T. B. Bell

J. L. MacCallum, Sect'y-Treas.
H. S. Ireland
Dr. F. W. Gershaw

1920-

H. S. Ireland, Chairman
R. C. Black
Dr. F. W. Gershaw

J. L. MacCallum, Sect'y-Treas.
T. Bell, Vice Chairman
B. F. Souch

1921-

T. Bell, Chairman
Dr. O. Boyd
Dr. F. W. Gershaw

J. L. MacCallum, Sect'y-Treas.
B. F. Souch, Vice Chairman
R. C. Black

1922-

B. F. Souch, Chairman
H. Lang
Dr. F. W. Gershaw

J. L. MacCallum, Sect'y-Treas.
Dr. O. Boyd, Vice Chairman
R. C. Black

1923-

Dr. F. W. Gershaw, Chairman
B. F. Souch
Thos. Murray

J. L. MacCallum, Sect'y-Treas.
H. Lang, Vice Chairman
R. C. Black

1924-

R. C. Black, Chairman
T. Murray
B. F. Souch

J. L. MacCallum, Sect'y-Treas.
H. Lang, Vice Chairman
Dr. F. W. Gershaw

1925-

H. Lang, Chairman
T. Murray
R. C. Black, Vice Chairman

J. L. MacCallum, Sect'y-Treas.
B. F. Souch
Dr. F. W. Gershaw

1926-

T. Murray, Chairman
H. Lang
R. C. Black

J. L. MacCallum, Sect'y-Treas.
B. F. Souch, Vice Chairman
Dr. F. W. Gershaw

1927-

B. F. Souch, Chairman
T. Murray
R. C. Black

J. L. MacCallum, Sect'y-Treas.
Dr. M. L. Moore, Vice Chairman
H. Lang

1928-

R. C. Black, Chairman
Dr. M. L. Moore
B. F. Souch

J. L. MacCallum, Sect'y-Treas.
T. Murray, Vice Chairman
H. Lang

285

1929-

Dr. M. L. Moore, Chairman
H. Lang
T. Murray

J. L. MacCallum, Sect'y-Treas.
B. F. Souch
R. C. Black

1930-

T. Murray, Chairman
Dr. M. L. Moore
Alex McGregor

J. L. MacCallum, Sect'y-Treas.
R. C. Black, Vice Chairman
B. F. Souch

1931-

B. F. Souch, Chairman
J. P. Marsh
Dr. M. L. Moore

J. L. MacCallum, Sect'y-Treas.
A. McGregor, Vice Chairman
Dr. O. Boyd

1932-

A. McGregor, Chairman
B. F. Souch
Dr. O. Boyd

J. L. MacCallum, Sect'y-Treas.
Reverend W. H. Ellis
J. P. Marsh, Vice Chairman

1933-

Dr. O. Boyd, Chairman
W. A. Church
Dr. H. C. Dixon

J. L. MacCallum, Sect'y-Treas.
B. F. Souch, Vice Chairman
A. McGregor

1934-

W. A. Church, Chairman
A. McGregor
E. A. Bell

J. L. MacCallum, Sect'y-Treas.
Dr. H. C. Dixon, Vice Chairman
Mrs. C. W. Richardson

1935-

H. C. Dixon, Chairman
A. McGregor
W. A. Church

J. L. MacCallum, Sect'y-Treas.
Mrs. C. W. Richardson, Vice Chair.
E. A. Bell

1936-

W. A. Church, Chairman
Mrs. C. W. Richardson
C. W. Niblock

J. L. MacCallum, Sect'y-Treas.
E. A. Bell, Vice Chairman
Dr. H. C. Dixon

1937-

C. W. Niblock, Chairman
W. A. Church
Mrs. C. W. Richardson

J. L. MacCallum, Sect'y-Treas.
Dr. H. C. Dixon, Vice Chairman
E. A. Bell

1938-

Dr. H. C. Dixon, Chairman
W. A. Church
W. W. Oliver

J. L. MacCallum, Sect'y-Treas.
E. A. Bell, Vice Chairman
C. W. Niblock

1939-

W. A. Church, Chairman
T. Graham
W. W. Oliver

J. L. MacCallum, Sect'y-Treas.
C. W. Niblock, Vice Chairman
Dr. H. C. Dixon

1940-

C. W. Niblock, Chairman
W. A. Church
Dr. H. C. Dixon

J. L. MacCallum, Sect'y-Treas.
W. W. Oliver, Vice Chairman
T. Graham

1941-

W. W. Oliver, Chairman
Dr. H. C. Dixon
W. A. Church

J. L. MacCallum, Sect'y-Treas.
T. Graham, Vice Chairman
C. W. Niblock

1942-

Dr. H. C. Dixon, Chairman
C. W. Niblock
W. A. Church

J. L. MacCallum, Sect'y-Treas.
T. Graham, Vice Chairman
J. D. Fairless

1943-

T. Graham, Chairman
W. W. Oliver
Dr. H. C. Dixon

J. L. MacCallum, Sect'y-Treas.
J. D. Fairless, Vice Chairman
C. W. Niblock

1944-
C. W. Niblock, Chairman
W. A. Church
Dr. H. C. Dixon
J. L. MacCallum, Sect'y-Treas.
W. W. Oliver, Vice Chairman
T. Graham

1945-
W. A. Church, Chairman
J. Boylan
T. A. Burwash
J. L. MacCallum, Sect'y-Treas.
T. Graham, Vice Chairman
C. W. Niblock

1946-
W. A. Church, Chairman
C. W. Niblock
T. Graham
G. H. Davison, Sect'y-Treas.
T. A. Burwash, Vice Chairman
J. H. Boylan

1947-
W. A. Church, Chairman
C. W. Niblock
T. Graham
G. H. Davison, Sect'y-Treas.
J. H. Boylan, Vice Chairman
J. L. Wyatt

1948-
J. H. Boylan, Chairman
W. A. Church
T. Graham
G. H. Davison, Sect'y-Treas.
J. L. Wyatt, Vice Chairman
C. W. Niblock

1949-
J. L. Wyatt, Chairman
J. H. Boylan
T. Graham
G. H. Davison, Sect'y-Treas.
W. A. Church, Vice Chairman
C. W. Niblock

1950-
J. L. Wyatt, Chairman
J. H. Boylan
T. Graham (replaced by
Mrs. McAffer later)
G. H. Davison, Sect'y-Treas.
W. A. Church, Vice Chairman
C. W. Niblock

1951-
W. A. Church, Chairman
H. Grant
Mrs. R. McAffer
G. H. Davison, Sect'y-Treas.
C. W. Niblock, Vice Chairman
J. L. Wyatt

1952-
Mrs. R. McAffer, Chairman
J. L. Levinson
A. E. Stanley
G. H. Davison, Sect'y-Treas.
W. A. Church, Vice Chairman
C. W. Niblock

1953-
C. W. Niblock, Chairman
J. E. Newton
Mrs. R. McAffer
G. H. Davison, Sect'y-Treas.
J. L. Levinson, Vice Chairman
A. E. Stanley

1954-
C. W. Niblock, Chairman
Mrs. R. McAffer
J. E. Newton
G. H. Davison, Sect'y-Treas.
J. L. Levinson, Vice Chairman
A. E. Stanley

1955-
C. W. Niblock, Chairman
Mrs. R. McAffer
J. E. Newton
G. H. Davison, Sect'y-Treas.
J. L. Levinson, Vice Chairman
A. E. Stanley

1956-
J. L. Levinson, Chairman
Mrs. R. McAffer
C. W. Niblock
G. H. Davison, Sect'y-Treas.
A. E. Stanley, Vice Chairman
J. E. Newton

1957-
Mrs. R. McAffer, Chairman
J. L. Levinson
J. C. Miller
G. H. Davison, Sect'y-Treas.
J. E. Newton, Vice-Chairman
C. W. Niblock

287

1958-
J. C. Miller, Chairman
Mrs. M. E. McAffer
Mrs. E. Skinner

G. H. Davison, Sect'y-Treas.
J. L. Levinson, Vice-Chairman
C. W. Niblock

1959-
J. L. Levinson, Chairman
J. E. Newton
C. W. Niblock

G. H. Davison, Sect'y-Treas.
Mrs. E. Skinner, Vice-Chairman
Dr. H. F. McKenzie

1960-
C. W. Niblock, Chairman
J. L. Levinson
J. E. Newton

G. H. Davison, Sect'y-Treas.
Mrs. E. Skinner, Vice-Chairman
Dr. H. F. McKenzie
Dr. O. P. Larson, Superintendent of Schools

1961-
C. W. Niblock, Chairman
J. L. Levinson
J. E. Newton

G. H. Davison, Sect'y-Treas.
Mrs. E. Skinner, Vice-Chairman
Dr. H. F. McKenzie
Dr. O. P. Larson, Superintendent of Schools

1962-
C. W. Niblock, Chairman
J. L. Levinson
J. E. Newton

G. H. Davison, Secretary-Treasurer
Mrs. E. Skinner, Vice-Chairman
Dr. H. F. McKenzie
Dr. O. P. Larson, Superintendent of Schools

1963-
C. W. Niblock, Chairman
J. L. Levinson
J. E. Newton

G. H. Davison, Secretary-Treasurer
Mrs. E. Skinner, Vice-Chairman
Dr. H. F. McKenzie
Dr. O. P. Larson, Superintendent of Schools

1964-
Mrs. Edna Skinner, Chairman
J. L. Levinson
V. Q. Sanders

G. H. Davison, Secretary-Treasurer
J. E. Newton, Vice-Chairman
Dr. H. F. McKenzie
Dr. O. P. Larson, Superintendent of Schools

1965-
J. E. Newton, Chairman
J. L. Levinson, Vice-Chairman
J. Clarke Moon (1st December) 1964
Dr. R. A. Gray (1st February)

G. H. Davison, Secretary-Treasurer
Mrs. E. Skinner
V. Q. Sanders
Dr. O. P. Larson, Superintendent of Schools

1966-
J. E. Newton, Chairman
J. L. Levinson, Vice-Chairman
Dr. R. A. Gray

V. Q. Sanders
Dr. V. Ivan Reed
G. H. Davison, Secretary-Treasurer
Dr. O. P. Larson, Superintendent of Schools

1966-67
J. E. Newton, Chairman
J. L. Levinson, V. C.
Dr. R. A. Gray

V. Q. Sanders
J. Anderson
G. H. Davison, Secretary-Treasurer
Dr. O. P. Larson, Superintendent of Schools

1967-68
J. E. Newton, Chairman
J. L. Levinson, V. C.
Dr. R. A. Gray

V. Q. Sanders
J. Anderson
G. H. Davison, Secretary-Treasurer
Dr. O. P. Larson, Superintendent of Schools

288

1968-69
J. E. Newton, Chairman
Dr. R. A. Gray, V. C.
J. Anderson
F. M. Riddle, Superintendent of Schools

Dr. F. W. Findlay
H. K. Hannah
G. H. Davison, Secretary-Treasurer
E. Murray, Deputy Secretary-Treasurer

1969-70
Dr. R. A. Gray, Chairman
J. G. Anderson, Vice-Chairman
K. R. Biddell
Dr. G. W. Findlay
J. E. Newton

G. H. Davison, Secretary-Treasurer
E. Murray, Deputy Secretary-Treasurer
F. M. Riddle, Superintendent of Schools

1970-71
Dr. R. A. Gray, Chairman
J. G. Anderson, Vice-Chairman
K. R. Biddell
Dr. G. W. Findlay
J. E. Newton

E. Murray, Secretary-Treasurer
F. M. Riddle, Superintendent of Schools

1971-72
J. G. Anderson, Chairman
Dr. R. A. Gray, Vice-Chairman
K. R. Biddell
F. R. Millican

Mrs. E. H. Wright
F. Riddle, Superintendent of Schools
E. Murray, Secretary-Treasurer

1972-73
J. G. Anderson, Chairman
K. R. Biddell, Vice-Chairman

Dr. R. A. Gray
B. G. Laidlaw

F. R. Millican
F. M. Riddle, Superintendent of Schools
E. Murray, Secretary-Treasurer

1973-74
J. G. Anderson, Chairman
F. R. Millican, Vice-Chairman
K. R. Biddell
Dr. R. A. Gray

B. G. Laidlaw
F. M. Riddle, Superintendent of Schools
E. Murray, Secretary-Treasurer

1974-75
F. R. Millican, Chairman
J. G. Anderson
K. R. Biddell
Dr. R. A. Gray
Vice-Chairman on rotation basis

B. G. Laidlaw
F. M. Riddle, Sup. of Schools
(Sept.-Dec. 74)
Dr. K. C. Sauer, Sup. of Schools
(Jan.-Sept. 75)
E. Murray, Assoc. Sup. and Sec.-Treasurer

1975-76
F. R. Millican, Chairman
J. G. Anderson
K. R. Biddell
Dr. R. A. Gray
Vice-Chairman on rotation basis

B. G. Laidlaw
Dr. K. C. Sauer, Superintendent of Schools
E. Murray, Associate Superintendent and Secretary-Treasurer

1976-77
F. R. Millican, Chairman
J. G. Anderon
K. R. Biddell
Dr. R. A. Gray
Vice-Chairman on rotation basis

B. G. Laidlaw
Dr. K. C. Sauer, Superintendent of Schools
E. Murray, Associate Superintendent and Secretary-Treasurer

1977-78
J. G. Anderson, Chairman
Dr. R. A. Gray
B. G. Laidlaw
F. R. Millican

Vice-Chairman on rotation basis

E. W. N. Macdonald
Dr. K. C. Sauer, Superintendent of Schools
E. Murray, Assist. Superintendent-Business
Administration & Secretary-Treasurer

289

1978-79
B. G. Laidlaw, Chairman
J. G. Anderson
Dr. R. A. Gray
E. W. N. Macdonald

Vice-Chairman on rotation basis

F. R. Millican
Dr. K. C. Sauer, Superintendent of Schools
E. Murray, Assist. Superintendent-Business
Administration & Secretary-Treasurer

1979-80
B. G. Laidlaw, Chairman
J. G. Anderson
Dr. R. A. Gray
E. W. N. Macdonald
Vice-Chairman on rotation basis

F. R. Millican (February 1980)
Dr. L. J. Roy Wilson (April 1980-October 1980)
Dr. K. C. Sauer, Superintendent of Schools
E. Murray, Assist. Superintendent-Business
Administration & Secretary-Treasurer

1980-1983 Term of Office
1980-81
B. G. Laidlaw, Chairman
R. M. Block

E. W. N. Macdonald
Mrs. L. Shaw

Dr. L. J. (Roy) Wilson
Dr. K. C. Sauer, Superintendent of Schools
E. Murray, Assist. Superintendent-Business Administration & Secretary-Treasurer

Separate School Board Trustees:

1911-1912
Rev. A. Cadoux
J. G. Millar
F. B. McKinnon
L.P.O. Noel
J. B. Barreau

1912-1913
Rev. A. Cadoux
J. J. Quail
J. Choiniere
J. G. Millar
F. B. McKinnon

1913-1914
Not listed

1914-1915
Rev. A. Cadoux
R. J. Quinlan
M. E. Lynch
F. B. McKinnon
J. G. Millar

1915-1916
Not listed

1916-1917
Fr. Saunier
Barrio
J. MacDonald
J. A. Landry

1917-1918
J. MacCourt
J. Barreau
J. MacDonald
J. A. Landry

1918-1919
Fr. M. F. Fitzpatrick
J. Barreau
J. MacDonald
J. A. Landry
Dr. L. C. Clancy

1919-1920
Fr. M. F. Fitzpatrick
J. Barreau
J. MacDonald
J. Choiniere
Murphy

1920-1921
Fr. M. F. Fitzpatrick
J. A. MacDonald
J. Choiniere
J. B. Barreau

1921-1922
F. H. Kelly
J. A. MacDonald
Fr. M. R. Fitzpatrick
Murphy

1922-1923
J. A. MacDonald
J. Choiniere
F. H. Kelly
Murphy
Fr. M. F. Fitzpatrick

1923-1924
Murphy
J. Choiniere
C. T. Flynn
D. L. McKenzie

1924-1925
Murphy
D. L. McKenzie
C. T. Flynn
Fr. M. F. Fitzpatrick
M. E. Lynch

1925-1926
Fr. M. F. Fitzpatrick
Murphy
M. E. Lynch
C. T. Flynn
D. L. McKenzie

1926-1927
Fr. M. F. Fitzpatrick
Murphy
D. L. McKenzie
M. E. Lynch

1927-1928
C. T. Flynn
M. E. Lynch
Murphy
M. O'Malley
P. A. Gospador

1928-1929
C. T. Flynn
Murphy
P. A. Gospador
Driscoll

1929-1930
Not listed

290

1930-1931
W. F. Weiler
M. O'Malley
Cook
C. T. Flynn

1931-1932
W. F. Weiler
M. O'Malley
Cooney
H. E. DesHarnais

1932-1933
W. F. Weiler
M. O'Malley
Driscoll
H. E. DesHarnais

1933-1934
W. F. Weiler
M. O'Malley
Driscoll
Cooney

1934-1935
H. E. DesHarnais
M. O'Malley
Driscoll
McElgunn

1935-1936
H. E. DesHarnais
Driscoll
McElgunn
Cooney
M. O'Malley

1936-1937
Not listed

1937-1938
H. E. DesHarnais
M. O'Malley
Driscoll
H. LeFort
O. Beauregard

1938-1939
H. E. DesHarnais
M. O'Malley
P. KilKenny
O. Beauregard
H. LeFort

1939-1940
C. T. Flynn
H. E. DesHarnais
M. O'Malley
T. A. Botter
H. LeFort
F. G. Dillon

1940-1941
C. T. Flynn
H. E. DesHarnais
M. O'Malley
H. LeFort

1941-1942
C. T. Flynn
W. F. Weiler
F. G. Dillon
H. LeFort

1942-1943
C. T. Flynn
W. F. Weiler
H. LeFort
H. E. DesHarnais

1943-1944
W. F. Weiler
H. LeFort
H. E. DesHarnais
F. G. Dillon

1944-1945
C. T. Flynn
W. F. Weiler
L. O'Connor
H. LeFort

1945-1946
C. T. Flynn
H. LeFort
W. F. Weiler
H. E. DesHarnais
L. O'Connors

1946-1947
C. T. Flynn
H. LeFort
H. E. DesHarnais
L. O'Connors

1947-1948
W. F. Weiler
L. O'Connors
H. LeFort
J. Ouellette

1948-1949
W. F. Weiler
A. Beaudry
H. E. DesHarnais
J. E. Nugent
H. LeFort
J. Ouellette

1949-1950
W. F. Weiler
J. E. Nugent
H. R. Hutchings
J. Sharp
T. Booth

1950-1951
W. F. Weiler
H. R. Hutchings
T. Booth
J. Sharp
T. Cote

1951-1952
H. R. Hutchings
T. Booth
J. Sharp
T. Cote
W. F. Weiler

1952
C. R. Kyle
H. R. Hutchings
H. J. LeFort
D. R. Gray
T. Booth

1952-1953
J. J. Muza
C. R. Kyle
D. R. Gray
H. J. LeFort
L. Grabowski

1953-1954
J. J. Muza
Mrs. H. Gibson
C. R. Kyle
T. A. Botter
H. J. LeFort

1954-1955
Mrs. H. B. Gibson
T. A. Botter
H. J. LeFort
A. Ziebart

1955-1956
M. J. Anton
H. J. LeFort
A. Ziebart
T. A. Botter
S. Fabbi

1956-1957
M. J. Anton
T. A. Botter
S. Fabbi
C. T. Flynn

1957-1958
T. A. Botter
M. J. Anton
Mrs. N. DeMan
G. H. DesHarnais

1958-1959
G. H. DesHarnais
T. A. Botter
M. J. Anton
Mrs. N. DeMan
Dr. H. J. Brooks

1959-1960
G. H. DesHarnais
T. A. Botter
J. C. MacPhail
C. Oxenbury
Dr. H. J. Brooks

291

1960-1961
J. C. MacPhail
C. Oxenbury
T. A. Botter
M. J. Anton
R. F. Cote

1961-1962
M. J. Anton
R. F. Cote
J. C. MacPhail
Mrs. L. Moyer
R. E. Schlinker

1962-1963
J. C. MacPhail
R. E. Schlinker
Mrs. L. Moyer
R. F. Cote
C. P. Potter

1963-1964
J. C. MacPhail
C. P. Potter
R. F. Cote
R. E. Schlinker
Mrs. L. Moyer

1964-1965
J. C. MacPhail
C. P. Potter
R. F. Cote
R. E. Schlinker
Mrs. L. Moyer

1965-1966
J. Kinahan
J. C. MacPhail
J. Weisbeck
Mrs. L. Moyer
J. Bokstein

1966-1967
J. Kinahan
J. C. Rea
J. C. MacPhail
Mrs. L. Moyer
J. Bokstein

1967-1968
S. J. Lerner

J. Kinahan
V. Schafer
J. C. Rea
J. C. MacPhail

1968-1969
J. C. MacPhail
S. J. Lerner
V. Schafer
C. P. Potter
J. C. Rea

1969-1970
D. J. MacLean
C. P. Potter
J. T. Bulanda
J. C. Rea
S. J. Lerner

1970-1971
D. J. MacLean
J. H. Schmidt
C. P. Potter
J. T. Bulanda
S. J. Lerner

1971-1972
J. T. Bulanda
Mrs. V. Swan
P. R. Barth
C. P. Potter
S. J. Lerner

1972-1973
S. J. Lerner
Mrs. V. Swan
P. R. Barth
J. T. Bulanda
C. P. Potter

1973-1974
S. J. Lerner
Mrs. V. Swan
P. R. Barth
J. T. Bulanda
C. P. Potter

1974-1975
P. R. Barth
Dr. D. Habijanac
J. T. Bulanda
Mrs. V. Swan
C. P. Potter

1975-1976
C. P. Potter
Mrs. V. Swan
P. R. Barth
Dr. D. Habijanac
J. T. Bulanda

1976-1977
C. P. Potter
Mrs. V. Swan
P. R. Barth
Dr. D. Habijanac
J. T. Bulanda

1977-1978
B. T. Stein
P. R. Barth
Mrs. L. Lanigan
C. P. Potter
J. T. Bulanda

1978-1979
J. T. Bulanda
C. P. Potter
Mrs. L. Lanigan
E. Ellingson
P. R. Barth

1979-1980
J. T. Bulanda
Mrs. L. Lanigan
C. P. Potter
*E. Ellingson to Feb. 1980
P. R. Barth
*R. McKee — Mar. 1980 to Oct. 1980.

1980-1981
J. T. Bulanda
C. P. Potter
P. R. Barth
Mrs. V. Swan
P. M. Vaessen
The Superintendent of Schools was Frederick B. Allore. Secretary-Treasurer, A. J. Giesinger.

Board Members — Medicine Hat Hospital

1889-1933
Sir J. L. Kaye
Mr. S. Hayward
Mr. J. Niblock
Mr. R. C. Starks
Mrs. T. P. Mitchell
Mr. R. L. W. Dobbin
Mr. Wm. Cousins
Mr. J. Horner
Rev. Mr. Herald
Mr. J. Hargrave

Mr. Wm. Walker
Mr. J. Fisher
Mr. R. Rice
Mr. P. Robertson
Mr. Thos. Tweed
Mrs. H. S. Scatcherd
Mr. Geo. McCuaig
Mr. C. D. Kevin
Mr. M. Leonard
Mr. A. Small
Mr. W. R. Wessel

Mr. Finlay
Mr. Lyon
Mr. Graton
Mr. G. Noble
Mr. Starko
Mr. Robertson
Mr. Fowler
Mr. Stone
Rev. Dobie
Mr. Cochran
Mr. Spencer

292

Library Board Trustees

293

1925
Mayor Walter Huckvale
Alderman Bannan
F. M. Oliver
B. W. Bellamy — Chairman
T. Woods

1926
Mayor Isaac Bullivant
Alderman Hector Duggan
F. M. Oliver
B. W. Bellamy — Chairman
T. Woods

1927
Mayor Isaac Bullivant
Alderman John A. King — Deputy
Chairman
Mrs. I. F. Terry
Rev. W. C. Western — Chairman

1928
Rev. Cannon W. C. Western —
Chairman
Mrs. I. F. Terry
Mayor Isaac Bullivant
Alderman J. A. King
James Bell — Deputy Chairman

1929
Alderman J. A. King
Rev. E. T. Scragg — Deputy
Chairman
James Bell — Chairman
Mayor Isaac Bullivant
T. E. Mills

1930
Rev. E. T. Scragg — Chairman
Mayor Bullivant
Ald. H. S. Ireland
S. T. Fawcett — Deputy Chairman
T. E. Mills

1931
Rev. E. T. Scragg — Chairman
Mayor Bullivant
Ald. H. S. Ireland
S. T. Fawcett — Deputy Chairman
P. L. F. Riches

1932
Rev. E. T. Scragg — Chairman
Mayor Bullivant
S. T. Fawcett
Ald. H. Morrow
Mr. P. L. F. Riches — Deputy
Chairman
Ald. H. Baker

1933
Mayor Bullivant
Ald. H. Baker
Rev. M. S. Blackburn — Deputy
Chairman
Mr. S. T. Fawcett — Chairman
Mr. P. L. F. Riches

1934
Rev. M. S. Blackburn — Chairman
Mayor Bullivant
Mr. S. T. Fawcett
Mr. P. L. F. Riches
Ald. H. Baker — Deputy Chairman

1935
Rev. M. S. Blackburn — Chairman
Mayor Bullivant
Mr. S. T. Fawcett — Deputy
Chairman
Mr. McDougall
Ald. Baker

1936
Rev. M. S. Blackburn — Chairman
Mayor Bullivant
Ald. R. S. Boyd
Mr. S. T. Fawcett
Mr. McDougall — Deputy Chairman

1937
Rev. M. S. Blackburn — Chairman
Mayor Bullivant
Mr. S. T. Fawcett — Deputy
Chairman
Mrs. L. N. Laidlaw
Ald. R. S. Boyd

1938
Mayor Bullivant
Ald. Boyd
Mr. S. T. Fawcett — Chairman
Mrs. L. N. Laidlaw
Rev. Jesse F. Butcher — Deputy
Chairman
Mayor Hector Lang (from Feb. 1938)

1939
S. T. Fawcett
Robert S. Boyd (Ald.)
L. N. Laidlaw (Mrs.)
Mayor Hector Lang

1940
Mayor Hector Lang
S. T. Fawcett — Chairman
Mrs. L. N. Laidlaw — Deputy
Chairman
Ald. Boyd
Rev. J. T. Butcher

1941
Mayor Hector Lang
Ald. R. S. Boyd
S. T. Fawcett — Chairman
Mrs. L. N. Laidlaw — Deputy
Chairman
Rev. J. T. Butcher — (Canon)

1942
Mayor Hector Lang
Ald. R. S. Boyd
Canon Butcher
Mrs. L. N. Laidlaw — Chairman
S. T. Fawcett — Deputy Chairman

294

1943
Mayor Hector Lang
Ald. R. S. Boyd
Canon Butcher
S. T. Fawcett — Chairman
Mrs. L. N. Laidlaw — Deputy
Chairman

1944
Mayor Hector Lang
Ald. R. S. Boyd
Canon Butcher
Mrs. L. N. Laidlaw — Vice-Chairman
S. T. Fawcett — Chairman

1945
Mayor Lang
Rev. R. B. Layton
S. T. Fawcett
R. W. Harrison — Chairman
W. W. Oliver

1946
Mayor Lang
R. W. Harrison — Chairman
Mrs. Colin Fraser
Ald. W. W. Oliver
Rev. R. B. Layton

1947
R. W. Harrison — Chairman
Mayor W. M. Rae — Chairman
(Oct./47 - Dec. '47)
Mrs. Mary M. Fraser
Rev. H. M. Horricks
Ald. W. W. Oliver
Mr. Calhoun — Librarian

1948
Mayor W. M. Rae
Rev. V. Hall — Deputy Chairman
Mrs. Mary M. Fraser
R. W. Harrison — Chairman
C. Jackson
Robert M. Block — Librarian

May, 1948
C. Jackson — Chairman
Mrs. Mary M. Fraser
Dr. B. C. Armstrong
R. O. Bond
R. M. Block — (Librarian-Secretary)
L. A. Walker — Chairman — Sept.
1948
Mrs. B. L. Stone — (From Nov. 1948)

1949
L. A. Walker — Chairman
Mayor H. Lang
Dr. B. C. Armstrong
R. O. Bond
Mrs. B. L. Stone
R. M. Block — Librarian

1950
L. A. Walker — Chairman
Mrs. B. L. Stone
Dr. B. C. Armstrong
R. O. Bond
R. M. Block — Librarian, Sec.-Treas.

1951
Ald. L. A. Walker — Chairman
Mrs. B. L. Stone
Miss E. Cobb
R. O. Bond
Stanley Heppell
Dr. B. C. Armstrong
R. M. Block — (Librarian, Sec.-
Treas.)

1952
Ald. L. A. Walker — Chairman
Mrs. B. L. Stone
Miss E. Cobb
Dr. B. C. Armstrong
R. O. Bond
S. Heppell
R. M. Block — Librarian, Sec.-Treas.

1953
Ald. L. A. Walker — Chairman
Mrs. B. L. Stone
Miss E. Cobb
Dr. B. C. Armstrong
R. O. Bond
S. Heppell
R. M. Block — Librarian

1954
S. Heppell — Chairman
Mrs. E. G. F. Skinner — Vice-
Chairman
Ald. E. W. Smith
S. Daniel
E. Elford
Miss E. Cobb
R. M. Block — Librarian

1955
E. V. Elford — Chairman
Mrs. E. G. F. Skinner — Vice-
Chairman
Mrs. C. Flaig
Alderman Mrs. L. E. Gust
G. H. Davison
T. W. Daniel
Mayor H. Veiner (ex-officio)

1956
E. V. Elford — Chairman
E. G. F. Skinner — Vice-Chairman
G. H. Davison
Mrs. C. Flaig
Ald. Mrs. L. E. Gust
A. Staysko
Mayor H. Veiner — (ex-officio)

1957
Mrs. E. V. Elford — Chairman
Mrs. E. G. F. Skinner — Vice-
Chairman
G. H. Davison
Mrs. C. Flaig
Ald. Mrs. L. E. Gust
Rev. T. T. Gibson
Mayor H. Veiner — (ex-officio)

1958
Mrs. E. G. F. Skinner — Chairman
G. H. Davison — Vice-Chairman
Mr. E. V. Elford
Miss C. Baillie
F. McGuinness
P. J. Sereni — January-August
Ald. Roy Osborne — September-
December
Mayor H. Veiner — (ex-officio)

1959
Mrs. E. G. F. Skinner — Chairman
G. H. Davison — Vice-Chairman
Fred McGuinness
E. V. Elford
T. R. Osborne
H. J. Gordon

1960
Mrs. E. G. F. Skinner — Chairman
E. V. Elford — Vice-Chairman
George H. Davison
Mrs. H. B. Gibson
Mrs. H. J. Gordon
Miss P. Lapworth — Librarian

1961
E. V. Elford — Chairman
Mrs. H. J. Gordon — Vice-Chairman
L. G. Flynn
G. H. Davison
F. G. McGuinness
Mrs. H. B. Gibson

1962
E. V. Elford — Chairman
Mrs. B. C. Whyte — Vice-Chairman
G. H. Davison
F. McGuinness
L. Flynn
Ald. Mrs. H. B. Gibson

1963
G. H. Davison — Chairman
Mrs. B. C. Whyte — Vice-Chairman
E. V. Elford
Lyle Flynn
F. G. McGuinness
Ald. Mrs. H. B. Gibson
Miss P. Lapworth — Children's
Librarian

1964
G. H. Davison — Chairman
Mrs. B. C. Whyte — Vice-Chairman
E. V. Elford
Lyle Flynne
F. G. McGuinness
Ald. Mrs. H. B. Gibson

1965
G. H. Davison — Chairman
Mrs. B. C. Whyte — Vice-Chairman
E. V.Elford
L. G. Flynn
Ald. Mrs. H. B. Gibson
F. G. McGuinness

1966
Ald. Mrs. Helen B. Gibson
L. Flynn — Vice-Chairman
Mrs. B. C. Whyte — Chairman
Don Grant
Mrs. Leo Lewis
Mrs. Doug Bell

1967
Mrs. Barbara Whyte — Chairman
Doug Bell — Vice-Chairman
Ald. Mrs. H. B. Gibson
Don Grant
Mrs. Bee Lewis
Mrs. Hazel McKenzie

1968
Mrs. Bee Lewis — Chairman
Lewis Toole — Vice-Chairman
Mrs. Hazel McKenzie
Dr. A. Soklofske
Mrs. Clare Prasow
Rod Ashburner

1969
Mrs. Bee Lewis — Chairman
Lewis Toole — Vice-Chairman
Mrs. Hazel McKenzie
Clare Prasow
Dr. A. Soklofske
Rod Ashburner
Ald. Mrs. H. Gibson

1970
Mrs. Bee Lewis — Chairman
H. McKenzie
Mrs. C. Prasow
Mrs. S. O'Donnell
A. Soklofske
R. Ashburner
F. Millican
A. Ziegler
L. Toole
Jos. E. Carver — Librarian

1971
Mrs. Bee Lewis — Chairman
Mrs. H. McKenzie
Mrs. C. Prasow
Mrs. S. O'Donnell
Mrs. H. Beny Gibson
A. Soklofske
F. Millican
A. Ziegler
R. Ashburner
Jos. E. Carver — Librarian

1972
Mrs. B. Lewis — Chairman
Mrs. H. B. Gibson
Mrs. H. McKenzie
F. Millican
Mrs. S. O'Donnell
Mrs. C. Prasow
Mrs. K. Pratt
A. Soklofske
A. Ziegler
R. W. E. Leigh — Librarian

1973
F. R. Millican — Chairman
Mrs. H. B. Gibson
Mrs. B. Lewis
J. W. B. McCallum
Mrs. C. Prasow
Mrs. K. Pratt
W. A. Schieman
A. Ziegler
Ald. T. Sissons
R. W. E. Leigh — Librarian

1974
W. A. Schieman — Chairman
Mrs. S. Flower (replaced Mrs. Prasow Oct./74)
Mrs. B. Lewis
J. W. B. McCallum
F. R. Millican
W. Palmer (replaced Mrs. H. Gibson Oct./74)
Mrs. K. Pratt
Dr. A. W. Soklofske
Alderman G. H. Davison (replaced Mr. T. Sissons Oct./74)
R. W. E. Leigh — Chief Librarian

1975
W. A. Schieman — Chairman
Mrs. S. Flower
Mrs. B. Lewis
J. W. B. McCallum
F. R. Millican
W. Palmer
Mrs. K. Pratt
Dr. A. W. Soklofske
Ald. G. H. Davison

1976
W. A. Schieman — Chairman
Dr. A. Soklofske
Mrs. Diane Durda
R. Clement
R. Sommerfeld
R. M. Block — Librarian
P. Huckle
W. Palmer
F. Millican
A. Sheldon

1977
A. Sheldon — Chairman
H. Cyster
Mrs. D. Durda
P. Huckle
Mrs. D. MacLean
Mrs. J. Titcher

R. M. Block — Librarian
Miss Erin Doyle — Children's Librarian
Miss E. Stockburger
F. Millican
Ald. Mrs. L. Moyer
P. Parish

1978
P. Huckle — Chairman
A. Sheldon
Ald. Mrs. L. Moyer
F. Millican — Until Oct./78
Mrs. D. Durda — Until Oct./78
H. Cyster
P. Parish
Mrs. J. Titcher
Mrs. D. MacLean
J. Russell
W. Thorsteinson
R. M. Block — Librarian

1979
Palmer Huckle — Chairman
Allan Sheldon
Jack Russell
Phil Parish
Ald. Lucille Moyer
John Weatherhead
Donna MacLean
Harry Cyster
Wilton Thorsteinson
R. M. Block — Librarian

1980
Palmer Huckle — Chairman
Harry Cyster
Donna MacLean
Phil Parish
Allan Sheldon
John Weatherhead
Jack Russell
Lucille Moyer
Wilton Thorsteinson
Lee Anderson
R. M. Block — Librarian

1981
Palmer Huckle — Chairman
Harry Cyster
Donna MacLean
Beth Milne
Phil Parish
Allan Sheldon
Wilton Thorsteinson
John Weatherhead
Lee Anderson
R. M. Block — Librarian

Medicine Hat College Board Presidents:
Dr. N. O. Matthews, July 1964 — August 1971
Dr. E. E. Chase, Nov. 1971 — February 1976
R. E. Sackley, Feb. 1976 — June 1979
C. J. Meagher, June 1979 —

297

Chairmen of the Board of Governors:

Dr. H. F. McKenzie	July 1965 — Jan. 1966
D. N. Jensen	Jan. 1966 — Sept. 1966
R. E. Ashburner	Sept. 1966 — Jan. 1969
Dr. J. H. Snedden	Feb. 1969 — June 1972
G. H. Davison	July 1972 — June 1973
Hon. J. D. Horsman	July 1973 — Jan. 1975
Mrs. Lorna Shaw	Jan. 1975 — June 1977
C. J. Meagher	July 1977 — Jan. 1979
J. Driscoll	Jan. 1979 — June 1979
K. W. Lutes	Aug. 1979 —

Citizen of the Year Award Recipients

First Anniversary	George H. Davison	December 7, 1966
Second Anniversary	Eugene Burton	November 22, 1967
Third Anniversary	H. A. (Bud) Olson	November 26, 1968
Fourth Anniversary	Harry Edwin Strom	November 26, 1969
Fifth Anniversary	Miss Noreen Flanagan	January 18, 1971
Sixth Anniversary	Dr. Neville O. Matthews	October 3, 1971
Seventh Anniversary	Mayor Harry Veiner	May 9, 1973
Eighth Anniversary	Mrs. Adele Armstrong	October 7, 1974
Ninth Anniversary	Des O'Coffey	November 24, 1975
Tenth Anniversary	Miss Elizabeth A. Beitsch	January 13, 1977
Eleventh Anniversary	Robert N. Reidy	November 15, 1977
Twelfth Anniversary	Alex Shand	April 23, 1979
Thirteenth Anniversary	Dr. W. C. Campbell	April 17, 1980
Fourteenth Anniversary	Gordon A. Simmons	April 3, 1981

Medicine Hat Chamber of Commerce
Presidents

1900 — E. J. Fewings	1928 — R. C. Black	1956 — R. G. Buss
1901 — E. J. Fewings	1929 — C. Pratt	1957 — J. C. Miller
1902 — E. J. Fewings	1930 — W. A. Church	1958 — J. C. Miller
1903 — T. Tweed	1931 — H. N. Davis	1959 — R. S. McBride
1904 — D. Milne	1932 — A. P. Burns	1960 — F. C. McGuinness
1905 — W. Cousins	1933 — C. J. F. Beny	1961 — W. J. Sellhorne
1906 — F. L. Crawford	1934 — G. A. Hoover	1962 — G. H. Sissons
1907 — C. S. Pingle	1935 — R. G. Butchart	1963 — W. H. Hayne
1908 — C. S. Pingle	1936 — G.M. Blackstock	1964 — J. H. Cocks
1909 — H. Stewart	1937 — F. W. Gershaw	1965 — J. M. Pritchard
1910 — H. L. Tweed	1938 — R. S. Boyd	1966 — A. H. Wiggins
1911 — H. L. Tweed	1939 — J. Mitchell	1967 — O. F. Weiss
1912 — D. Milne	1940 — D. W. Hays	1968 — T. Dutton
1913 — L. Y. Birnie	1941 — J. H. Yuill	1969 — R. Reidy
1914 — L. N. Laidlaw	1942 — J. Galbraith	1970 — R. E. Ashburner
1915 — R. P. Stewart	1943 — A. Atkins	1971 — T. A. Sissons
1916 — W. Rutherford	1944 — R. H. A. Lacey	1972 — J. D. Horsman
1917 — H. L. Tweed	1945 — R. H. A. Lacey	1973 — O. Kope
1918 — H. L. Tweed	1946 — R. C. Tennant	1974 — R. Skidmore
1919 — E. L. Chudleigh	1947 — R. A. Burwash	1975 — C. A. Taylor
1920 — E. L. Chudleigh	1948 — T. R. Osborne	1976 — L. H. Baisley
1921 — E. L. Chudleigh	1949 — T. R. Osborne	1977 — R. Lehr
1922 — E. L. Chudleigh	1950 — J. H. Boylan	1978 — J. Warsimaga
1923 — A. F. Andrews	1951 — D. S. Hawthorne	1979 — D. Weiss
1924 — F. W. Gershaw	1952 — H. R. Hutchings	1980 — J. L. Edwards
1925 — F. W. Gershaw	1953 — R. C. Gardner	1981 — G. W. Adams
1926 — N. M. Waldo	1954 — R. E. Keating	— resigned
1927 — N. M. Waldo	1955 — W. D. Lutes	1981 — E. Eaton

Medicine Hat & District Labor Council
List of Presidents
From 1956-1980

Bert Lomas	1956	Jim Driscoll	1965-1973
Harold Lozo	1957-1958	Ted Adel	1974
Larry Messmer	1958	R. Zral	1975
Allan Bist	1959-1960	Diwen Miller	1976
Keith Freeman	1961	R. Hoffman	1977
Bev. Monkman	1962-1963	B. Crittenden	1978-1979
Harvey Ronnenberg	1963-1964	G. MacPherson	1980
Bob Porter	1965	G. MacPherson	1981

medicine hat
1883 1983